Commerce and Capitalism in Chinese Societies

The Chinese economy today is the world's fastest-growing economy and, according to the World Bank, is on a course to overtake the U.S. economy within the next two decades. *Commerce and Capitalism in Chinese Societies* looks at what gives China's economy such dynamism, focusing its study on Chinese firms and economic organization in contemporary and historical China, and within the neighbouring countries of Hong Kong, Taiwan, and Southeast Asia. Incorporating empirical data collated from interviews in several Asian societies and from historical Chinese sources, this renowned author analyses, discusses and applies an organizational approach, derived from the writings of Max Weber, to explore the various aspects of Chinese economic practice and how these contrast to those found in Japan and the West.

The book's eleven chapters provide historical, comparative and theoretically informed perspectives on the spread of Chinese capitalism, with emphasis on the difference between Western and Chinese forms of capitalism. Including sections on China's pre-industrial economy as well as the growth of modern Chinese capitalism, this collection will be a valuable resource for students of Asian and Chinese studies as well as those concerned with the economics of Chinese societies.

Gary G. Hamilton is a Professor of Sociology and of International Studies at the University of Washington. He has written numerous articles and books, including most recently *Emergent Economies, Divergent Paths: Economic Organization and International Trade in South Korea and Taiwan* (with Robert Feenstra) (Cambridge University Press 2006).

Commerce and Capitalism in Chinese Societies

Gary G. Hamilton

Routledge
Taylor & Francis Group

LONDON AND NEW YORK

First published 2006
by Routledge
2 Park Square, Milton Park, Abingdon, Oxon OX14 4RN

Simultaneously published in the USA and Canada
by Routledge
270 Madison Avenue, New York, NY 10016

Routledge is an imprint of the Taylor & Francis Group, an informa business

© 2006 Gary G. Hamilton

Typeset in Times New Roman by
Taylor & Francis Books
Printed and bound in Great Britain by
Antony Rowe Ltd, Chippenham, Wiltshire

British Library Cataloguing in Publication Data
A catalogue record for this book is available from the British Library

Library of Congress Cataloging-in-Publication Data
Hamilton, Gary G.
  Commerce and capitalism in Chinese societies / by Gary G.
Hamilton.
    p. cm.
  Includes bibliographical references and index.
  ISBN 0-415-15704-8 (hardback : alk. paper) -- ISBN 0-415-15705-6
(pbk. : alk. paper) 1. Capitalism--China. 2. Capitalism--China--
History. 3. China--Commerce. 4. China--Commerce--History. 5.
China--Economic conditions. 6. China--Foreign economic relations. 7.
Comparative economics. I. Title.
  HC427.H26 2006
  330.951--dc22

                                    2005028808

ISBN10 0–415–15704–8 ISBN13 9–780–415–15704–9 (hbk)
ISBN10 0–415–15705–6 ISBN13 9–780–415–15705–6 (pbk)

**For my parents,
Glen and Ethel Hamilton**

Contents

List of Illustrations

Tables

Figures

Acknowledgements

Each chapter in this book is organized around one or another sociological thesis about Chinese society that I convey to the reader through a comparative analysis. For me, comparisons embody a methodological approach, perhaps better described as a rhetorical strategy, that enhances the development of sociological theory. Although there has been a lot of work on Chinese economic activity since the earliest of these chapters appeared in published form, I have not rewritten them, because to do so would undermine the comparative framework that is at the core of most chapters. Instead, I have elected to let the articles remain largely in the form of their original publication.

In developing the ideas that inform these articles, I have incurred many debts. Many of the following chapters contain a list of acknowledgments. I will not duplicate those acknowledgments here. Still, some individuals need to be singled out again, because they deserve special recognition, and other individuals need to be added to the list of those previously acknowledged.

The idea for this book originally came from three former students, now friends and colleagues in Taiwan, Chang Wei-an, Jai Ben-ray, and Chen Chieh-hsuan. In 1990, they collected, translated into Chinese, and published a set of my essays, and recommended that I do the same in English. I began this task in 1995, with the encouragement of Victoria Smith, who was then the Asian Studies editor at Routledge. Unfortunately, my close colleague and friend, Marco Orrù, died shortly afterward, which prompted Nicole Biggart and me to publish a collection of articles representing the project that Marco, Nicole and I had worked on for a number of years, under the title *The Economic Organization of East Asian Capitalism* (1997). Several of the articles intended for the current volume went into that book.

Very different than the one originally conceived, this book represents work done before and after that collaboration. The earliest two essays (Chapters 2 and 3) came out of research done for my dissertation. This work was deeply influenced by Pierre van den Berghe and especially by Guenther Roth. It was from working with Guenther Roth that I learned about Max Weber and was able to develop a Weberian approach for my own work. Long after the dissertation was done, both continued to serve as sources of inspiration and advice.

Except for these two chapters, all the other chapters have been written after I first conceived of collecting and publishing a set of essays.

I have been particularly fortunate throughout my career to have a number of close colleagues and friends with whom I have shared research and writing. For this occasion, I especially want to single out Nicole Woolsey Biggart, Kwang-Ching Liu, Robert C. Feenstra, and Kao Cheng-shu.

Although none of our joint publications appear in this volume, Nicole Biggart and I have been co-authors many times. Her critical comments and her unflagging delight at intellectual work have helped me immeasurably for many years.

I want also to thank Kwang-Ching Liu, the eminent historian of Imperial China, and a longtime colleague of mine at the University of California, Davis. Without K. C. Liu's encouragement, support, and insight into Chinese society, I am sure that my enthusiasm for studying China would have waned, or at least would have taken me in a very different direction than I have followed.

Rob Feenstra is an economist, also at the University of California, Davis. Although collaborations between economists and sociologists are rather rare, I must say that the decade-long collaboration with Rob has been one of the highpoints of my career. My work with Rob has allowed me to rethink economic sociology and to take my sociological work along a new path. The major product of our collaboration is a recently published book, *Emergent Economies, Divergent Path: Economic Organization and International Trade in South Korea and Taiwan* (Feenstra and Hamilton 2006). I am deeply grateful to him for his open-mindedness, for his intellectual curiosity, and for his genuine regard for empirical explanations.

Kao Cheng-shu has taught me more about Chinese society than I care to admit. Kao Cheng-shu directed the Graduate Institute and chaired the Department of Sociology during the 1984–85 academic year when I was a Fulbright Fellow at Tunghai University in Taiwan. As the year progressed, Cheng-shu and I recognized our common orientation to sociology and became good friends and then collaborators in what has turned out to be a continuing project on the industrialization of East Asia. That year in Taiwan sealed my fate, for since that time I have never thought seriously about studying anything else except that which would further my understanding of East Asia. Our collaboration has recently taken a new form. Drawing on twenty years of joint research, we are now working on a book manuscript entitled "Making Money: How the Global Economy Works from an Asian Point of View".

I want to acknowledge a number of other people whose assistance I have received so generously over the years and who have made significant contributions to the chapters in this book. Drawing on earlier work done collaboratively, Chang Wei-an and Chi-Kong Lai helped me in developing the thesis presented in Chapter 4. A brilliant theorist, Misha Petrovic has done the same in Chapter 6. This chapter is the first of a number of collaborative products on which Misha and I are currently working. I also want to thank a number of colleagues and friends whose work I continually draw on for insight and inspiration: Howard S. Becker, Anthony D'Costa, Don Fels, Gary Gereffi, John R. Hall, Eun Mee Kim, Katharyne Mitchell, Benjamin Orlove, Matthew Sparke, Tong Chee-Kiong, and Wong Siu-lun. In addition, I thank Wai-Keung Chung and Jeremiah Kerr, who helped me assemble this book for publication, and a series of editors at Routledge, most recently Helen Baker, whose patience knows no end.

Finally, I want to thank my wife, Eleanor, who keeps me sane and focused in the world, and my parents, Glen and Ethel, whose love and support never wavers and to whom I dedicate this book.

I gratefully acknowledge the permission to reprint the following:

'Civilizations and the Organization of Economies' (1994). Pp. 183–205 in *The Handbook of Economic Sociology*, edited by Neil J. Smelser and Richard Swedberg. Princeton: Princeton University Press.
'Why No Capitalism in China: Negative Questions in Comparative Historical Sociology' (1985). *Journal of Developing Societies* 2: 187–211.
'Chinese Consumption of Foreign Commodities' (1977). *American Sociological Review* 42 (December): 877–91.
'The Importance of Commerce in the Organization of China's Late-Imperial Economy' (2003), (with Chang Wei-an and Lai Chi-kong). Pp. 173–213 in *The Resurgence of East Asia*, edited by Giovanni Arrighi, Takeshi Hamashita, and Mark Selden. London: Routledge.
'Hong Kong and the Rise of Capitalism in Asia' (1999). Pp. 14–34, in *Cosmopolitan Capitalists: Hong Kong and the Chinese Diaspora at the end of the 20th Century*, edited by Gary G. Hamilton. Seattle: University of Washington Press.
'Reflexive Manufacturing: Taiwan's Integration in the Global Economy' (2000), (with Cheng-shu Kao). *International Studies Review* 3,1 (June): 1–19.
'Asian Business Networks in Transition, or What Alan Greenspan Does Not Know about the Asian Financial Crisis' (1999). Pp. 45–61 in *The Politics of the Asian Economic Crisis*, edited by T.J. Pempel. Ithaca, N.Y.: Cornell University Press.
'Reciprocity and Control: The Organization of Chinese Family-owned Conglomerates' (2000). Pp. 55–74 in *Globalization of Chinese Business Firms*, edited by Henry Wai-chung Yeung and Kris Olds. New York: St Martins Press.
'Competition and Organizaiton: A Reexamination of Chinese Business Practices' (1996). *Journal of Asian Business* 12, 1: 7–20
'Ethnicity and Capitalist Development: The Changing Role of the Chinese in Thailand' (1997), (with Tony Waters). Pp. 258–84 in *Essential Outsiders: Chinese and Jews in the Modern Transformation of Southeast Asia and Central Europe*, edited by Daniel Chirot and Anthony Reid. Seattle: University of Washington Press.

Introduction

Rethinking the economic sociology of East Asian capitalism

The first sociology course I ever took, in my junior year at the University of Kansas in 1964, was a course comparing China and Japan. The instructor of that course, Norman Jacobs, had received his doctorate from Harvard University, was a student of Talcott Parsons, and entitled his first book *The Origin of Modern Capitalism and Eastern Asia* (1958). The course to some extent followed the book, and the book to a very great extent flowed from the man. To my eyes at the time, his view embodied a grand vision that offered a solution to a complex historical puzzle. As Fernand Braudel (1982: 586, his emphasis) would later commend, "In making his comparison (in this book), Jacobs (did) not hesitate to set side by side the *entire* history of China and Japan", in order to show how "the preconditions of capitalism" came out of a "very long-term evolution over many centuries". To Jacobs, this grandiose dissection of history, laying bare the functional prerequisites of capitalism, in the end yielded the answer to the puzzle explaining, in the year 1958, why Japan and not China had developed into the only capitalist country in Asia. I can say, without exaggeration, that Norman Jacobs and his first book brought me, simultaneously, into Sociology and Asian Studies, and there I have been ever since.

Despite my continuing affinity for big visions of human history, I never found evolutionary, functionalist explanations of Asian capitalism very satisfying. In 1958, when Japan had the only capitalist economy on the Asian horizon, some theory explaining Japan's exceptionalism seemed reasonable. But less than fifty years later, when most Asian economies have become significantly capitalist, an explanation distinguishing Japan from all other countries in Asia does not ring true.

When I say that most of Asia has become capitalist, I mean that throughout the region, with a few full and partial exceptions (for example, North Korea and Vietnam), national economies consist largely of privately owned firms and publicly traded companies, whose owners and managers have the authority to control and dispose of property and make individual investment decisions in more or less open market conditions where prices, production, and distribution are determined by competition; in other words, the very definition of capitalism. Even with this definition, many would continue to distinguish Japan, a *developed* country, from China, a *developing* country. The classification, however, begs the question: what is the dividing line between developed and developing? Is it per capita income? Japan wins. Is it the absolute amount of manufactured products or the diversity of manufactured goods produced or a ratio between industrial output and total gross national product? China wins on all scores. Is it some level of infrastructure, such as the tallest buildings, the largest ports, or the newest and biggest cities? China wins again.

Such dividing lines are elusive and ultimately arbitrary, but whatever classificatory measures best distinguish levels of development, one thing is certain: a capitalist orientation is not one of them. Making money and spending money are common themes nearly everywhere in Asia today. In the four decades that have passed since my introduction to Asian sociology, Asia has been transformed in nearly every respect. Therefore, those explanations that trace Asian capitalism to hoary origins, making it seem that the capitalist potential was in the cards from the beginning for one place but for not others, now seem inappropriate to a region where capitalist development is the rule and not the exception.

How, then, can this extraordinary capitalist transformation in Asia be explained? This question has been an enduring concern of mine for many years, and the chapters in this book represent different aspects of the answers that I have developed. The book is divided into two parts. The first part addresses China's economy during the late imperial period, roughly from the seventeenth to the early twentieth centuries. Chapter 1 places this topic into a comparative perspective, with particular reference to the explanations that have been offered for the development of capitalism in Europe. The remaining three chapters in Part 1 examine the different facets of the imperial economy (for example, merchant organization, patterns of consumption, and the effects of commerce on the organization of the imperial economy in general), especially as these facets relate to the spread of Western capitalism to China during the nineteenth century. I explicitly use a comparative framework to explore each of these topics.

Part 2 focuses directly on the development of Asian capitalism after World War Two. In Chapter 5, I show that post-World War Two economic growth is a continuation of patterns of capitalist diffusion established in the nineteenth and early twentieth centuries. I also argue in this chapter that two distinct trajectories of economic development began before and then rapidly expanded after World War Two – one a Chinese, and the other a Japanese, pattern of development – and that the rapid expansion after the War resulted from the connections of Japanese and Chinese businesses to Western buyers. This explanation for the post-World War Two boom is developed more fully in Chapter 6. Drawn from very recent work (Feenstra and Hamilton 2006), this chapter demonstrates that the so-called "Asian Miracle" is directly connected to the "retail revolution" that began in the United States during the 1960s and

1970s. This demand-side explanation for Asia's capitalist transformation is an alternative to the supply-side market and strong state explanations offered, respectively, by most economists and by most political scientists and some sociologists. Chapter 7 details this demand-side explanation from the point of view of Taiwanese manufacturers and shows that Taiwanese businesspeople developed a reflexive system of production that allowed them to be "demand-responsive". Using the Asian financial crisis of 1997 as a decisive moment to analyse Asian capitalism, Chapter 8 suggests that shifts in demand-responsive production beginning after the Plaza Accord in 1985 were primary background factors leading to the financial crisis. The beneficiaries of the shift were, and continue to be, Chinese manufacturers from a variety of countries, who gained greater share of the global market in consumer goods at the expense of Japanese and Korean enterprises.

In the last three chapters, I concentrate on some key organizational aspects of capitalism in Chinese-dominated economies. All the chapters in this book take an organizational perspective, which essentially means a focus on the organization rather than on the institutions of the economy. Later in this introduction, I explain more fully what this perspective means and how it differs from the more commonly used institutional perspective. In Chapter 9, I analyse the two primary organizational dimensions of Chinese family-owned conglomerates: patriarchy within, and relational networks among, independently owned businesses. In Chapter 10, I describe how relational networks among Chinese firms have been used to gain positions of economic power in relation to competing firms, and I suggest that the future of non-Chinese businesses in China will be determined by their ability to avoid direct competition with Chinese production networks. Finally, in Chapter 11, using the case of the Chinese in Thailand, I show that Chinese networks are not static features of Chinese economies, but rather represent organizational resources that Chinese entrepreneurs have been able to adapt to their economic needs, as these needs are defined within different institutional and economic settings.

Although the chapters in this book cover nearly thirty years of research, and represent work on many different topics, there is also considerable consistency in the theoretical stance and empirical focus that I have taken over the years. Throughout this period, I have been a thoroughgoing Weberian: I have adapted Weber's organizational approach for the analysis of Asian economies, have always been concerned with the past and present spread of capitalism in Asia, and, from the very first days in graduate school, have been interested in commerce and consumption. Because these theoretical and empirical interests show up in nearly every chapter of this book, and because these interests provide a point of contrast between my work and that of many other interpreters of Asian economies, they deserve to be singled out and described more fully in this introduction.

Weberian approaches

Although cloaked in Parsonian terminology, Norman Jacobs's explanation for capitalism in Japan and the absence of capitalism in imperial China derives from a creative misreading of Max Weber, and in that he shares a lot of company. Strange it is that most explanations of capitalism in Asia, or the lack thereof, should turn on some concept or some analysis attributed to Weber. Max Weber died in 1921 at the age of 56. During his lifetime, Weber was a well-known German economic and legal historian who avowed sociology only in the last decade of his life and whose works published in his lifetime included a still-controversial book on the origins of Western capitalism, *The Protestant Ethic and the Spirit of Capitalism* ([1904–5] 1958), as well as the beginnings of a series of books and articles comparing different world civilizations and religions with Western civilization and Christianity. After his death, Weber became an iconic figure in the discipline of sociology, a so-called "founding father".[1] In the years after his death, his standing among sociologists was greatly elevated by Talcott Parsons's translation of *The Protestant Ethic and the Spirit of Capitalism* which first appeared in 1930 (Weber [1904–5] 1958), by Parsons's influential book *The Structure of Social Action* (1949), which featured Weber as one of a handful of pathbreaking European thinkers in the late nineteenth and early twentieth centuries, and by Hans Gerth and C. Wright Mills's publication of the ever-popular and still widely-read *From Max Weber* (Weber 1946). By the time Weber's posthumously published *magnum opus*, *Economy and Society* (Weber 1978), appeared in English, Weber had become a sociologist *par excellence*, a much revered liberal intellectual whose work in the Cold War era kept Marxism at bay. By 1968, his identity as one of the leading German economists of his day had been largely forgotten.[2]

To understand Weber's writing on China, it is important to keep in mind that Weber was, foremost, a sociologically inclined economist trying to understand Western capitalism. The economist part of Weber's work is important to emphasize, because it is Weber's odd fate that his importance in post-World War Two sociology was to stand in opposition to a resurgent Marxian sociology, where Weberian sociology came to represent the study of "non-economic" and "non-rational" aspects of society. In fact, throughout all of his work, Weber was trying to decipher how organized economies worked in economic terms, and, most of all, how capitalism worked economically. His great insight was to understand that societal institutions – laws, religions, politics, and above all structures of authority – influenced the economics of economic activity. This significant insight is too little understood even today.

Weber was not, and did not pretend to be, a Sinologist. Although Weber mentioned China occasionally in his later writings, he only wrote one extended piece about China, *The Religion of China: Confucianism and Taoism* ([1920] 1951). In this book, Weber contrasts Confucianism and

Taoism with Christianity, particularly Puritanism, and examines the linkages between religious worldviews and political, social, and economic institutions. Weber concluded that the religions of China did not have the potential, which Puritanism did in Europe, to transform the institutional environment, especially the patterns of authority, so that capitalism could *independently* emerge in China. Weber's theory about the origins of Western capitalism and his "test" of that theory in Asia have formed the backdrop for many subsequent discussions about capitalism in Asia.

In the following chapters, I, too, call on Weber frequently and use a Weberian approach. It is, therefore, important from the outset to distinguish my use of Weberian concepts and methodology from that of many others. In the next chapter, I outline my own reading of Weber's explanation for the rise of Western capitalism, and so there is no need to repeat that here. But it is worthwhile to remind readers that Weber saw his sociological framework as a guide to developing historical explanations, as a practical way to disentangle the causative structure of complex historical trends. Weber was forever the historian. Weber's goal was never to fashion general sociological theories, was never to seek a level of reality beyond the world of human affairs and human interaction. The historical trends that he worked on for most of his life were uniformly those arising out of Western civilization, especially the formation of market capitalism and the rise of Western rationality, and he used his comparative analyses of world religions to triangulate the uniqueness of Western civilization.

Throughout the chapters in this book I remain mindful of Weber's approach. I, too, think that social science should explain historical trends and that social science concepts should not be ends in themselves, but rather should serve as guideposts to historical analysis. As I explain in several of the following chapters and elsewhere (Hamilton 1984b, 1990), being mindful of Weber's approach does not mean that his concepts and historical conclusions about Europe are uniformly valid for Asian societies. Indeed, they are not. The very logic of Weber's ideal-typical methodology makes his concepts and conclusions more appropriate for the analysis of Europe than for that of Asia.[3] To follow Weber's methodological approach in analysing Asia is to develop ideal-typical concepts that have particular relevance for Asian societies and to draw conclusions about Asian development from an analysis using those concepts. That has always been my approach.

Many writers, however, apply Weberian concepts and conclusions directly to their analysis of Asia without assessing whether they introduce a Eurocentric bias. The typical approach is like this: Japan (or more recently East Asia) has industrialized. Or conversely, imperial China failed to industrialize. The causes of these conditions are necessarily endogenous to each country or region. Applying the logic of Weber's analysis of Europe, the observer of Asia looks for and discovers (or fails to discover) in Asia conditions similar to, or at least the functional equivalents of, what Weber said happened in Western Europe.

For the successful Japanese case, most analysts look for similarities with the West, similarities that are typically found in the distant past.[4] A contemporary of Norman Jacobs and also a student of Talcott Parsons, Robert Bellah (1957) offered the best-known example of this kind of analysis in a book entitled *Tokugawa Religion.*[5] The ethic of the samurai class, *bushido*, a unique combination of Buddhism and Confucianism, served as the Japanese equivalent of the Protestant ethic. According to Bellah (1957: 2), the samurai ethic explains the reason that "Japan alone of the non-Western nations was able to take over very rapidly what it needed of Western culture in order to transform itself into a modern industrial nation." More recently, another Weberian, Randall Collins (1997), located the origins of Japan's extraordinary patterns of growth in religious changes occurring in Heian Japan (700–1185 AD).

For the successful post-World War Two cases of East Asian industrialization, a number of writers reject Weber's conclusion about Confucianism's lack of a transformative potential, even as they reaffirm the validity of applying Weber's Protestant ethic thesis in Asia. For instance, noted Weberian, Peter Berger (Berger and Hsiao 1988: 7), wrote "quite simply, that Weber was wrong . . . [H]is theories about Asian culture have been empirically falsified" by the fact that East Asia industrialized. Berger then asks, what are "the cultural roots, especially religio-ethical roots, of modern Asian capitalism? Weber's questions were eminently important, even if some of his answers have to be discarded." In his provocatively titled book, *The Spirit of Chinese Capitalism* (1990), Gordon Redding carries Berger's thesis forward, arguing that, contrary to Weber's conclusion, "the role of Confucianism as the bedrock set of beliefs" strongly shaped the development of a distinctive form of capitalism among the overseas Chinese (e.g., Chinese in Hong Kong, Taiwan, and parts of Southeast Asia). In these and other works, religion and social ethics shape the necessary institutional foundation for capitalist development in Asia, just as, according to these writers' interpretation of Weber's works, they did in Europe.

Those writers more concerned with politics than with religion and culture have embraced another of Weber's insights (1978: 224) about Western capitalism, namely that "capitalism in its modern stages of development requires bureaucracy". By analogy, they argue that the primary reason that East Asian economies were able to industrialize so quickly was due to their states' efficient bureaucracies. These bureaucracies supposedly promulgated and implemented rational economic policies, spurring local entrepreneurship, controlling markets, and creating capitalism. The best-known advocate of this position is Peter Evans (1995; Evans and Rauch 1999), who makes "Weber's bureaucracy hypothesis" the cornerstone of his strong-state explanation of East Asian industrialization. South Korea and Taiwan serve as the exemplars of his theory.

Writers not only explain the successful, but also the unsuccessful, cases of Asian capitalist development by selectively analogizing Weber's conclusions about Europe. As I discuss in several of the following chapters, many writers have tried to explain the absence of capitalism in pre-modern China by turning China into a negative case, into a mirror image, of what occurred in the West. Imperial China lacked certain features of Western society and, therefore, so the argument goes, failed to develop capitalism.

In all of the above examples, Western Europe implicitly serves as the rule against which Asian societies are measured. The ideal-types that Weber developed to disentangle the initial causes of capitalism in Europe become the contemporary concepts used to explain, case by case, the diffusion of capitalism throughout the rest of the world. When using this approach to analyse Asia, one assumes, as Weber did not,[6] that the causes for the diffusion of capitalism are similar to, or the same as, the causes for the initiation of capitalism in the first place. Viewed in this way, the historical development of capitalism is not treated as a one-time-only historical event, but rather is re-enacted again and again, society by society. Capitalism becomes a fundamental, irreducible economic configuration. Each society has the potential to develop this configuration internally, and thereby itself to become capitalist. But some societies succeed in making this capitalist transition, whereas others do not. Therefore, according to this logic, the proper approach to analyse capitalism, Asian or otherwise, is to conceptualize economies endogenously, as a product of forces within individual societies. Each society becomes a case of successful or unsuccessful capitalist development, and each successful case should, in positivist theory, have the same or functionally similar causes, although the resulting structures of capitalism may be quite different from each other. Analysts generalize these causes, making them variables so that differences among societies can, in principle, be measured and correlated with known outcomes.

Institutional versus organizational perspectives

This approach, similar to what Peter Evans (Evans and Stephens 1988) identifies as "comparative political economy" and to what Fligstein (2001) calls a "political–cultural approach", slants the analysis of capitalism in one direction: toward the state and toward the society constituted by state boundaries. The approach assumes that states are the main unit of analysis, that all economies are national economies, and that an aggregation of national economies makes up the global economy. By focusing on those institutions that supposedly frame and constrain economic actions, this approach adopts an institutional perspective when applied to the analysis of capitalism. Because from this viewpoint the state is the most comprehensive institution, which in turn affects all other institutions, the state and society bounded by the state become the defining locus of the economy.

The inevitable outcome of this institutional perspective is the conclusion that there are "varieties of capitalism", that the state and society conspire, so to speak, to become a distinctive whole, with functionally intertwined sets of institutions that stamp a brand on the type of capitalism that emerges within. The result of this approach is to posit nearly as many types of capitalism as there are successful cases. Among those offered as distinctive types are French, German, Japanese, Chinese, Korean, British, and American varieties. Some even add Polish, Czech, and Hungarian ones. The theoretical conclusion of this literature is that societal institutions define the organization of capitalism, or, using the vocabulary of Mark Granovetter's 1985 article, the organization of capitalism is "embedded" in an institutional environment, from which it takes its characteristics. In short, with the institutional perspective, explaining the institutional foundation explains the nature and organization of that variety of capitalism.

It is fair to say that I have contributed to this literature (for instance, Hamilton and Biggart 1988; Orrù, Biggart, and Hamilton 1997). That said, however, I have always been more preoccupied with the organizational aspects of economic activity, including consumption, than with the social institutional backdrop that shapes this activity from society to society. Institutional and organizational perspectives appear to be very close to each other, especially since the early 1990s when the "new institutionalism" began to dominate the sociological studies of complex organizations (Meyer and Rowan 1977; DiMaggio and Powell 1983; Powell and DiMaggio 1991). These two perspectives, however, are not as close as they seem, especially in economic sociology. A number of the chapters in this book, as well as a number of recent works (Hamilton *et al.* 2000, Feenstra and Hamilton 2006), explicitly address this distinction, and show that an organizational perspective is necessary in order to analyse capitalist economies. A short statement here would help clarify this position from the outset.

Richard Swedberg's assessment goes right to the heart of the matter:

> Today's economic sociologists have often taken capitalism for granted and have failed to develop a sociology of capitalism. On the whole, they have preferred to deal with middle-range phenomena, such as firms and networks of various kinds. . . . When it comes to the discussion of capitalism among contemporary sociologists . . . the desire to show that social relations and institutions matter is often so strong that the key mechanism in capitalism – the generation of profit and its reinvestment in production – is hardly ever mentioned, and rarely theorized. This leads to a flawed view of capitalism, and a failure to understand its dynamics as well as its capacity to mobilize people and resources for its purposes.
>
> (Swedberg 2003: 63–5)

Swedberg's insight is crucial. Merely showing that social relations and institutions somehow influence economic activities does not, at the same time, inform us how capitalist economies (or any type of economy for that matter) actually work. Many economic sociologists have assumed that institutional environments in which economies operate shape the actual organization of economic activities in those environments. Indeed, this assumption is merely a restatement of DiMaggio and Powell's dictum (1983; Powell and DiMaggio 1991) that exterior processes of institutional isomorphism shape the internal structure of organizations. Moreover, the institutional argument is easy to make because, clearly, governments do have the capacity to define and control aspects of economic activity within their borders and, through those actions, to influence economic activity even beyond their borders. Equally, it can also easily be shown that social institutions, such as the family, shape the organization of firms and of inter-firm networks.

Therefore, it is not surprising to find that many analysts see a one-to-one causal link between institutional frameworks and organizational outcomes. For example, developmental state theorists argue that state economic policy causes the formation and organization of business groups. As I discuss at length in Chapter 8, economists make a similar linkage between institution and organization, only they suggest that the lack of "proper" economic institutions causes market failures that result in such organizational "distortions" as large business groups. Robert Feenstra and I (2006) have shown in detail, however, that this causal attribution between institution and economic organization is inaccurate and that economic organization is better conceptualized as an emergent outcome of competition in and across capitalist markets.[7] In other words, the way economies become organized results directly from capitalist economic activities, and only indirectly from institutions that in various ways frame these activities.

The equation of state/society with capitalist economy misses most of what Weber himself thought was crucial about capitalism.[8] As Swedberg suggests, the equation misrepresents the ways that economic players actually orient and organize their activities in the world today. As described more fully in Part 2 of this book, a more accurate way to conceptualize capitalism is to add three organizational dimensions to the definition of capitalism given above (see page 129). First, capitalism should not be thought of in terms of countries, but rather in terms of people (e.g., entrepreneurs, workers, managers), firms, money, products, markets, industries, and the interrelationships among all of these. Second, capitalism should be conceptualized as ever-changing movements of these things in time and space, as having historical and geographical characteristics. Third, this movement in time and space should be conceptualized as complex economic activities that people constantly try to control in some fashion. Entrepreneurs try to organize these activities, often in competition with each other; workers want to limit them so they don't dominate their lives too much; government officials try to regulate and tax them, usually in opposition to somebody; bankers try to channel them, always to their own advantage. The idea is that capitalism represents contested economic movements in time and space that are always organized and struggled over to a considerable degree.[9]

When conceptualized in this way, capitalism is not a stable and readily identifiable configuration that, like a flower, suddenly bursts forth in bloom. Instead, it is a term that covers an extremely wide range of diverse economic activities organized in the context of often difficult and contentious competition among participants, who themselves have the right and obligation to control and dispose of properties, quite apart from the desires of any state planners. In such a context, participants do not make sequential decisions; they do not queue and take turns in planning their next move. Instead, they make simultaneous decisions, each calculating what others will do as a way to decide a course of action.

Institutions frame such decisions rather than determine their outcome. Participants live in a taken-for-granted world, a mix of different institutional spheres. These lived-in spheres of life (e.g., politics and government, family and kinship) provide possible resources for the contested economic activities in which participants are themselves engaged. However, it is not these institutional spheres that drive capitalist participation, at least not directly. Rather it is the processes and possibilities of making money and of the rational calculation that is integral to making money that drives the organization of capitalist economies.

The activity of making money creates a world of meaning that is linked to, but still separate from, political, social, and even economic institutions. If capitalism involves rational calculation, cost accounting, profit-making, risk assessment, and some level of visibility and predictability into the future, then capitalism also involves a high level of inter-subjectivity. Within some range of accuracy, in order to make informed decisions, participants need to be able to objectify their own positions relative to the positions of those with whom they are economically involved. This necessity for making informed decisions pulls participants into common frames of reference, which are sometimes referred to as markets (e.g., capital, labor, property, and product markets), but are also more extensive than markets. The important point is that these common frames of reference are not benign. They are historical; they are actively and conjointly constructed by participants who seek their own advantage, but not always according to their own dictates.

It is the knowing and active participation in these inter-subjective worlds of capitalist acquisitiveness that links economic actors, who are grounded in the institutions of their local society, to the organization of global capitalism. To analyse the development and spread of capitalism in Asia involves more than just understanding how social relations and institutions become tools in the pursuit of capitalist wealth and social honor. It also involves understanding the capitalist dynamics of Asian economies and how these dynamics are linked to and integrated in the world economy. The chapters in this book address all three levels: the collective use of social institutions as a means to achieve economic goals, the broader organizational dynamics of Chinese economies, and the link between these dynamics and the organization of global capitalism.

The diffusion of capitalism in Asia

The origins of capitalism in Europe and its causes should not be confused with the global diffusion of capitalism and its causes. The debates about the origins of capitalism have been long and lively and are still unsettled.[10] Although scholars disagree about the time, causes, and precise location, nearly everyone agrees that capitalism began in Europe. The issue in this book, however, is not about the exact circumstances surrounding the origins of capitalism, but rather about how capitalism has spread in Asia since its initial development.

It is certain that the diffusion of capitalism throughout Asia and the rest of the world is highly varied, with many differences between places and across time. In his book on medieval technology, Lynn White Jr. (1964) shows that even the diffusion of such a simple device as the stirrup in the first millennium A.D. led to widely divergent outcomes from location to location. Capitalism is certainly no less so. Most interpretations, however, make the transition to capitalism such a transformative departure from a pre-capitalist past that there is no continuity between pre-capitalist and capitalist eras. As I explain in Chapter 1, this emphasis on the transformative qualities of capitalism is a legacy from nineteenth- and early twentieth-century theorists whose primary object of interest was to explain the new capitalist order in Europe and the radical departure from the past. There was no room in their analysis for continuity of any kind. In the four chapters that follow this introduction, I discuss the shortcomings of such an approach and show that there is in fact considerable continuity between eras. The fact that there is continuity, however, does not lessen the transformative nature of capitalism, but rather gives it substance and direction.

Capitalism spreads by the diffusion of economic practices. Carried by all manner of agents, from gunboats to merchants to missionaries, capitalist practices enter into economies that are already fully occupied with participants and well-established sets of economic activities. The practices may be introduced for any number of reasons, and the organizational changes that accompany these practices are often, at least initially, quite limited and subtle and not always very successful. But, as new markets become better integrated and as market participants become more attuned to making money in those markets, then organizational changes may magnify over time

An example will help to explain this process. Throughout the Qing dynasty, which ended in 1911, economic activities were institutionally framed by regional associations (*huiguan*), which had linkages into rural areas and which, along with the state, were the organizing medium for much of the economy. Virtually all firms represented in these associations were independently owned, either by a single family or by partners. The strong egalitarian rules within these associations gave predictability to collective economic activities that were otherwise unregulated, and, therefore, these rules were often strongly enforced (see Chapters 2 and 4).

By the end of the nineteenth century, however, Chinese entrepreneurs working along the China coast came into direct competition with Western firms. Small firms embedded in a framework of regional associations could not compete with Western firms in such areas as banking, insurance, mass-distribution department stores, and manufacturing plants. Chinese entrepreneurs needed larger and more highly capitalized firms to compete in the same sectors as Western firms. Hong Kong and Shanghai were the principal locations where this competition occurred. As Wai-keung Chung (2004) has described, Chinese entrepreneurs began to experiment with corporate forms borrowed from the West, especially the limited liability company. Although only a few entrepreneurs found this practice useful at first, by the late 1930s nearly all the largest Chinese firms in both Hong Kong and Shanghai had adopted this corporate form and had raised considerable amounts of money from shareholders, who acted as silent partners to the owners and managers of the companies.

Initially, limited liability companies remained "embedded" in regional networks. The legal framework within which corporations operated in Europe and the United States was virtually nonexistent in China and was relatively unimportant. The organizational format was used primarily to raise money through interpersonal connections, mostly from people from the same hometown region as the entrepreneur. Adopting this corporate form, however, had the effect of removing Chinese firms from the regionalized institutional framework that merchant associations provided in the late imperial period. The new firms, instead, revolved around the personal networks of entrepreneurs, who increasingly operated within a legal framework provided by colonial governments in Hong Kong, Southeast Asia, and even Taiwan. In the post-World War Two period, when these off-shore Chinese economies industrialized, this corporate form predominated, allowing the emergence of large Chinese-run businesses throughout the region.

The modern Chinese firms that I describe in Chapter 9 are the direct descendants of those adopting the Western corporate format. These now quintessentially Chinese firms, however, are not imitations of Western firms, but rather, to paraphrase Eleanor Westney's superb analysis of modernization in Japan (1987), are Chinese reinventions of their own way of life. The diffusion of capitalism involves these reinventions, these innovations that result from borrowing the ideal and material artifacts of another society and adapting them and inserting them into one's own already full way of life.

The spread of capitalism involves many similar reinventions, some small and some large, some successful and many unsuccessful. The important point is that capitalism involves practices and processes that lead to new ways of organizing existing ways of life. The institutions may remain the same, or nearly so, but, if successful, the modes of organizing may take on lives of their own.

Commerce, consumption, and the demand factors in the organization of economies

What drives economic activities? Most studies of modern capitalist economies are analyses of production. Chandler (1977, 1990), Piore and Sabel (1984), Williamson (1975, 1985), Hollingsworth and Boyer (1997), Whitley (1999), Fligstein (1990; 2001), Burawoy (1985), White (2002), and Saxenian (1994) – in these and many other works, and in a wide variety of ways, scholars emphasize systems of business and institutions relating to the manufacture of goods. Marxist and world systems perspectives also have a decided bias toward manufacturing as the core activity of capitalist economies. Despite clashing differences among these interpretations, these studies share the view that the institutions relating to production, as well as the actual organization of producing firms, form the decisive factors in the development of capitalism. It is, therefore, very unusual for any of these studies to examine commerce, distribution, and consumption in the same light as production, if these activities are mentioned at all.[11]

Largely absent in the analysis of capitalism, commerce and merchants are, however, the stuff of traditional economies. Even in the work on pre-capitalist economies, however, merchants are often portrayed as passive agents in national and global markets. Their primary role is merely to truck goods from where they are abundant to where they are scarce. In this conception, the markets pre-exist the actions of merchants and operate in a lineal way, with production, distribution, and consumption all lined up in chronological order. Chronological ordering, however, implies neither causation, nor an accurate depiction of how economic activities are organized, or for that matter who controls the activities. In Chapter 4 I argue that, in late imperial China, regional merchant associations controlled the marketing of most goods. Merchant power was great enough that their actions had direct "backward" effects on the organization of production. These merchant associations can be thought of as wholesale clearing houses that directly influenced both supplier markets for the goods, on one side, and consumer markets for the same goods, on the other. Merchants were the market makers.

Merchant associations are the pre-capitalist counterparts of modern retailers, the intermediaries that make markets. Unlike merchants, however, modern retailers are almost entirely ignored in the literature about contemporary capitalism. Factories and manufacturing get all the attention, and retailers are merely assumed to be impersonal conduits between manufacturers and consumers.

Considering the lack of work on commerce and retailing in general, it is, therefore, not surprising that studies of capitalist development in Asia also have a supply-side bias.[12] Beginning in the 1970s and continuing through today, a huge literature has emerged analysing and attempting to locate the causes for Asia's post-war industrial transformation. Even after the Asian financial crisis, the debate about the East Asian Miracle continues (Stiglitz and Yusuf 2001; Woo-Cumings (Woo 2001); Amsden 2001; Woo, Sachs, and Schwab 2000). In such books as Stiglitz and Yusuf's *Rethinking the East Asian Miracle* (2001) and Woo-Cumings's *The Developmental State* (1999), theorists rework the same three sets of causes that first appeared in the late 1970s and 1980s: (1) the macro-economic environment (i.e., market fundamentalism); (2) the developmental state; and (3) the importance of non-state institutions, such as the family and authority systems, and related cultural factors. Moreover, the critiques of this literature that have appeared in recent years and that gained prominence during the Asian business crisis (e.g., Young 1992, 1993, 1995; Krugman 1994) also disparaged one or more of these sets of causes without introducing new factors.

Throughout this debate there is an unexamined assumption that the causes for Asian economic growth (or the lack thereof), as well as the causes for continuing changes in the Asian economies, are to be found solely in Asia, and that the story of Asian industrialization is strictly a "supply-side narrative". Nearly all participants in the debate share the underlying assumption that the Asian Miracle is a country-centered Asian product. In each interpretation, the presumed set of causes (e.g., market failure, macroeconomic management, state policy, institutional environment) forms an institutionalized structure of constraints, incentives, and "organizing logics" (Biggart and Guillén 1999). This institutionalized structure is external and temporally prior to economic activity and, in turn, produces a specific set of organizational and performance outcomes within the economy. Although the interpretations are usually couched in causal terms, the actual connections are rarely examined and explained. In addition, although many of these standard explanations acknowledge the importance of what is ambiguously described as "globalization" or "global capitalism" or the "world economy", very few theorists of whatever bent incorporate globally significant economic or organizational factors in their causal explanations of local and national economic development.

The extraordinary thing about all of these interpretative accounts is how rarely any of them ever mention the demand-side of Asia's export orientation. To be sure, theorists frequently cite export trade as "the engine of growth in East Asia" and emphasize the bilateral trade with the United States as being particularly significant for Asian economic growth (e.g., Chow and Kellman 1993). But then, when they give causal explanations for these observations, they examine the producers of goods and, more frequently, the circumstances of production, rather than the buyers of goods and the circumstances relating to consumption. Even those strong-state theorists, such as Amsden (1989, 2001), Wade (1990), and Evans (1995, 1997), who are most critical of market explanations, simply assume that market processes prevail at the demand end. Somehow, all those manufactured and exported products find overseas buyers.

The only concerted effort to analyse pull factors has been the global commodity chain approach, first developed by Gary Gereffi (1994b, Gereffi and Korzeniewicz 1994) and elaborated by others (Appelbaum and Smith 2001, Bonacich *et al.* 1994). This approach, however, has been used primarily to examine specific industrial sectors, such as garments and footwear, and has not been incorporated into explanations of larger economic phenomena, including Asian industrialization. Put more precisely, the global commodity chain approach misses both ends of the phenomena in question: it examines neither changes in the organization of demand nor the consequences of global commodity chains on the organization of production. It is focused on industries rather than economies.

The core theoretical issue concerning local- and national-level economic development in the contemporary world is not whether a supply-side or a demand-side perspective leads to a more accurate explanation. Instead, it is that producer-driven, supply-side narratives cannot account for the emergence and operation of global markets. These narratives remain rooted in the local and national economic, political, and social institutions, with each economy being conceptually isolated from every other economy as well as from global capitalism.

By contrast, introducing a demand-side perspective not only makes markets a core topic needing explanation, but also allows one to hypothesize that "market-making" processes, including those undertaken by merchants and retailers, play causative roles in the constitution of Asian economies, past and present.

Notes

1 Almost all books recounting the history of sociology place Weber among the originators of the discipline. However, nothing could be further from the truth. Sociology was a well-established academic discipline in the United States, with graduate programs, lively theoretical debates, and active disciplinary journals, before Weber took up the mantle of sociology in the decade after 1910. Weber was "discovered", converted from an economist to a sociologist, and then canonized in the decades after his death by sociologists who used Weber's profound insights into Western society to construct the theoretical foundations for the discipline in Europe and the United States after World War Two.

2 The best treatment of Weber's economic sociology is Swedberg (1998). Also see Hamilton (1996b).

3 The best explanation of Weber's ideal-typical methodology is contained in Ringer (1997). In Hamilton (1984b, 1990), I explain the logic of using ideal-typical concepts from China to assist in the analysis of China, and show that Weber's use of patrimonialism to analyse Europe does not hold for China, where very different principles of domination emerged. Also see Chapter 1 of this book.

4 Besides Bellah and Collins, discussed above, I should also add S. N. Eisenstadt, who argues in his book, *Japanese Civilization: A Comparative View* (1996), that Japanese exceptionalism resulted from the absence of a transformative religious breakthrough such as those occurring in China, India, and the West. The resulting religious continuity in Japan allowed the Japanese to seal themselves off from, or to "Japanize", foreign influences. Paradoxically, Eisenstadt maintains, this insularity bestowed a self-confidence allowing the Japanese to adopt Western

practices without destroying the cohesiveness of their society. Although at odds with some aspects of Weber's analysis, he is very much in tune with the style of argument made by Jacobs and Bellah.

5 Another Parsons student, Marion Levy (1953/54), also offered a well-known comparison between China and Japan in which he argues that Japan's social structure allowed development, whereas China's did not.

6 Weber is very clear on this point. In the penultimate paragraph on his essay on China, he makes a prediction about the diffusion of capitalism in East Asia, as well as an assessment about the absence of an independently developed capitalism in China:

> The Chinese in all probability would be quite capable, probably more capable than the Japanese, of assimilating capitalism which has technically and economically been fully developed in the modern culture area. It is obviously not a question of deeming the Chinese "naturally ungifted" for the demands of capitalism. But compared to the occident, the varied conditions which externally favored the origins of capitalism in China did not suffice to create it.
>
> (Weber 1951: 248)

7 Economic organization in this context means the broader organization of economies.

8 This point is further emphasized by the fact that Weber discussed not one type, but rather many types of capitalism (e.g., pariah capitalism, adventure capitalism, political capitalism, rational capitalism). He identified each type of capitalism by how and by whom economic activity is organized. Weber's historical explanations of Western capitalism focused on the type of capitalism that appeared in full bloom in his lifetime, what he called rational capitalism or market capitalism, and so for him it was important to distinguish other and earlier forms of economic organization from this one. But he did not conceptualize rational capitalism as anything other than an ideal type that was useful to analyse the economic organization of his day.

9 This paragraph is also found in Chapter 5. It is worth noting that these organizational dimensions are also found in *Economy and Society*, where Weber (1978: 108) describes money in capitalist economies as "primarily as a weapon" in the competitive struggle of "man against man".

10 One of the most recent entries in this debate is by Kenneth Pomeranz (2000), who broadly contrasts China and Europe in an effort to locate the causes of capitalism in Europe and the absence of capitalist development in China. I discuss this book and other recent entries in the China end of the debate in Chapter 4.

11 There is, however, a small, three-pronged, but largely disconnected literature that has examined distribution and retail more directly. The first branch is from economics and consists of research on intermediaries and intermediation. Drawing on the terminology used by economists Spulber (1996, 1998) and Rauch (1999, 2001a, 2001b), intermediaries are firms that engage in intermediate activities – such as marketing, merchandising, and retailing – in value-chains. The second branch of research comes from industry studies. Of these, the most insightful study of intermediation and its impact on manufacturing is done by Abernathy and colleagues (1999), *A Stitch in Time: Lean Retailing and the Transformation of Manufacturing: Lessons from the Apparel and Textile Industries*. This study demonstrates that advances in intermediation processes, in the book identified as "lean retailing", have changed the manufacturing industries for apparel and textiles. A third group of scholars, featuring a number of sociologists, (e.g., Porter 1990; Gereffi 1994a, 1999; Appelbaum and Smith 2001; Dicken 1998; Reardon *et al.* 2003) recognizes that retailing is an important

activity organizationally linked to manufacturing. Despite this recognition, most of these writers remain focused on understanding production, and on conceptualizing production in terms of commodity chains, value chains, and globalized networks. Moreover, except for key studies on apparel manufacturing and food production (Abernathy *et al.* 1999; Reardon *et al.* 2003), the connections between retail and manufacturing have not been extensively examined and linked to the industrialization of developing countries.

12 The paragraphs following this note draw from the thesis developed in Feenstra and Hamilton 2006.

Part I

China's pre-industrial economy in comparative perspective

1 Civilizations and the organization of economies

In the Vatican, in a large vaulted room once designed to be the private library of the pope, called the Stanze della Segnatura, is Raphael's majestic fresco, *Disputa*, or *Disputation over the Sacrament*. Nested under the vault and filling one of the dome-shaped sides of the wall, the fresco is one of the finest representations of authority in Western civilization. Immersed in the neo-Platonic intellectualism of his time, which glorified art as a "new instrument of an investigation of reality in all its complexity", Raphael self-consciously used his painting as a way to transcend the images of his composition (Becherucci 1969: 90). In this, his most brilliant creation, he drew what is certainly the finest line-and-block chart ever drawn.

Clearly laying out the command structure of Western Christendom, the fresco describes three levels of power. At the uppermost part of the dome is God, depicted as a man wrapped in upward-seeking energy emanating from the surrounding heavenly host. His body, centered at the top, is steady and his gaze fixed outward and downward, as if he is looking directly at the observers of the fresco. One shoulder juts forward slightly with a hand raised and fingers extended in a gesture of complete wisdom. His other hand holds a globe, signifying, in the year 1509, the roundness of the earth and God's complete and knowing control.

The second level, occupying the entire middle portion of the fresco, portrays Jesus sitting, slightly elevated, at the head of a neatly arranged semicircle of seated figures floating on a layer of clouds borne by angels. His head framed by a large halo, Jesus is in the middle of the semicircle, directly below God. The Virgin Mary is to his right, John the Baptist to his left, and they are flanked on either side by the disciples from the New Testament and the patriarchs from the Old. Jesus alone, like God above, looks out and down at the observers of the fresco. He has both hands raised, palms out, as if blessing those below.

The third level, the ground level, depicts those who are in charge on the shop floor, so to speak. These are the earthly rulers, the theologians empowered with duties and responsibilities among the living and who, in this portrayal, are arguing about the meaning of the sacraments. In contrast with the tranquility of the second level, the earth-bound figures are caught in motion – standing, stooping, reading, gesturing, and debating with all the vehemence that earthy power demands. Locked in disputation, these figures do not look out from the fresco. Nevertheless, no observer of this Raphael masterpiece could doubt that, whatever vagaries exist in its exercise, earthly authority has layers upon layers of transcendental legitimation.

This fresco is a picture of Western civilization. The term "civilization" itself, even when modified with "Western", is an ambiguous term,[1] but Raphael's depiction of the earthly right to rule is unequivocal, for it captures a quintessential element of rulership and domination common to all societies that claim Western origins. The powers that be in these societies legitimate their authority over earthly jurisdictions, including the economy, by invoking abstract, transcendental justifications, whether God or natural law or a generalized will of the people. Raphael's fresco convincingly portrays the logic of Western power: legitimate authority comes from the top down, an arrangement that represents a *fundamental* ordering of the world.

There are many representations of this same motif in Western art and architecture – in the sculptures on the facade of the north transept of London's Westminster Abbey, in a sculptured frieze on the ancient gate of Paris, in the ornamentation on innumerable medieval tombs, and in many court and religious paintings – but none of these representations is so superbly crafted and so minutely detailed as the Raphael fresco. Whether well crafted or not, the depictions of this motif should not be seen simply as artistic embellishments, but rather as symbolic enactments of real worlds of power and privilege. In Western states, these symbolic enactments belong, more properly, to a world of discourse, to a broad vocabulary of legitimation, in which the phrase "one nation, under God" has literal as well as figurative meanings. In a literal sense, while the substance of earthly judgments may be open to question, the invoked abstract right to make those judgments is indisputable. The institutionalized structures of legitimate command in the West are always configured from the top down, as if they had been certified by God or by some other combination of forces that are beyond the actual circumstances of domination.

Imagine, for a moment, a civilization that was not historically shaped by Christianity or by any other form of monotheism and that, in addition, did not, as matter of course, conceptualize a meaningful level of human action and causation beyond the world of human experience. As will be outlined in the final section of this chapter, the Confucian regions of East Asia, stretching from Korea and Japan in the north to China and Vietnam in the south, fit this definition. In such a location, then, further imagine how political orders are legitimized and institutionalized so that rulers and subjects alike articulate and justify, in their own distinct vocabulary of legitimation, the prevailing patterns of authority. Given this context, would power be legitimized in the same top-down fashion as it is in the West?

For most Westerners, this is a difficult mental experiment. While it may be easy for many Westerners nowadays to imagine a world without Christianity, it is nearly impossible for most to envision a world without the institutions that Christianity and other forms of transcendentalism have shaped historically. These very institutions now constitute the reality in which Westerners live themselves, but the patterning of these institutions is so taken for granted that it is difficult to imagine a world put together in any other way.

Such a mental experiment, however, is useful to try. An integrated world economy has become a reality only in the most recent times. If we are to comprehend this world economy, it is important to understand the influence of civilizational forces on economic activity. To oversimplify this point, one can think about these influences by posing two diametrically opposed lines of argument. On the one hand, one could argue, as many have, that Western capitalism and Western ways of life more generally have swept away the great non-Western world civilizations – the Chinas and the Indias – and have created the conditions for the formation of a single worldwide civilization: global capitalism.

On the other hand, one could argue, as some have, that such a characterization of modernity is so crude as to miss all the subtleties of civilizational forces. What we witness with the development of a global economy is not increasing uniformity, in the form of a universalization of Western culture, but rather the continuation of civilizational diversity through the active reinvention and reincorporation of non-Western civilizational patterns. This line of argument leads to the conclusion that Japanese, Chinese, and Indian styles of capitalism build on and revitalize their own distinct institutional patterns. Though these societies assimilate diffused economic practices from the West, they have incorporated these practices into consistently understood ways of life that are very different to those found in Western societies. As Eleanor Westney (1987) put it in her study of the nineteenth-century Japanese incorporation of European organizational forms, the very act of imitation involves innovation. In copying others, people re-create themselves, by fashioning new versions of their own way of life.

Both lines of reasoning represent alternative ways to interpret the spread and trajectories of globalized economic activity. Although it is important to evaluate these alternatives, because they point to very different conclusions about the direction of the world economy, such an evaluation is rarely attempted. Most analysts simply assume the universalization of Western civilization. To do otherwise would require a civilizational analysis, and that is difficult to do well, since it must include an examination of the taken-for-granted aspects of a lived-in world. These aspects are particularly elusive. They span both historical time and political boundaries. They are pervasive, and therefore very difficult to pin down empirically. For this reason, when people examine how economies actually work, a civilizational level of analysis is rarely considered, even in passing, by anyone – by sociologists, historians, not to mention economists. To most students of the economy, whatever their discipline, a world in which the Eucharist is an important topic of dispute seems as far removed from markets as Raphael does from

Adam Smith, and yet it is the integration of these levels that a civilizational analysis must attempt.

This chapter aims at such an integration. It begins by summarizing the works of the major scholars who have examined the interaction between civilization and economic life. These works can be divided into two varieties of interpretation that correspond roughly to the two lines of argument outlined above, one for the global spread of Western civilization and the other for a continuation of civilizational diversity. The second of these two lines of interpretation will be stressed here, particularly in describing the sociology of Max Weber. A variety of Weberian theories will then be used to outline the relation between Western civilization and the rise of the Western capitalism. Finally, a sociological sketch will be given of the civilizational context and organizational structure of modern capitalism in East Asia. It will be argued that, although capitalism has become nearly a universal way of life, a more adequate interpretation of global capitalism grows out of the second line of reasoning; civilizational factors continue to be significant, because they distinctively frame and structure the actual organization of economies.

Civilizations and the analysis of Western modernity

What is the role of civilization in patterning economic activity? Very few theorists have asked this question directly, because to do so one needs to construct a conceptual framework that allows for a *continuity of causation* – for a production and reproduction of similar forms – across time and space. Most social theorists have been relatively uninterested in understanding historical and spatial continuities. They have wanted, instead, to explain the collapse of tradition and feudalism and the formation of what they call "modernity" in all its positive and negative forms. Therefore, when theorists have analysed the relation between civilizations and economies, they have usually done so in the course of explaining the break from the past in connection with the rise of a modern way of life.

In describing the formation of modernity, theorists normally account for civilizations, in the form of trans-societal patterns, in one of two ways. The most common way is for them to explain the causes of the transformation in Western Europe by showing that one or two key institutional spheres led the way for a break with the past. Using their historical analysis as the basis for a general theory, they then go on to argue that the same or similar sets of factors have been responsible for the globalization of patterns that originated in the West. Scholars do not agree on which spheres were historically the most crucial, but most of them narrow their argument to whether states or markets have casual priority. The substantial literature making this kind of an inference, it will be suggested, has only limited utility in understanding how civilizations structure economies.

The non-Weberian debate over the historical causes of Western modernity centers on which institutional sphere has causal priority: politics or economics. Proponents of each point of view have developed theories of economic organization that align with their distinctive slant on the rise of the West. In each case, the search for the causes of modernity focuses on explaining discontinuities – the revolutions, disruptions, and transformations that occurred in Western Europe from the 16th century onwards.

States and political economy

In the debate over what caused the rise of the West, many scholars have argued that the key institutional arena creating the break with the past was establishment of a new type of political order, the nation-state. As many have described from various points of view (Anderson 1974a; 1974b; Bendix 1964, 1978; Eisenstadt 1963; Foucault 1979; Huntington 1968; Poggi 1978; Tilly 1992; Wallerstein 1974), the nation-state rose gradually but decisively in the sixteenth century in Western Europe. The reasons for its formation are many and diverse. The legal foundations of feudalism changed to favor the kings' courts over other possible assemblies (Strayer 1970); with the diffusion of gunpowder, the technology of warfare altered the pursuit of political power (McNeil 1982); taxation and administration created organized regimes that turned kingdoms into centralized regimes (Mann 1986; Tilly 1975, 1992); and overseas territorial and economic expansion led to new sources of revenue, creating more interstate competition that fueled and even accelerated the cycle of nation building (Wallerstein 1974). Whatever the historical and sociological causes for the nation-states, many theorists (Eisenstadt 1963; Bendix 1978; Tilly 1992) interpret the rise of the nation-state as the decisive turning point in modern world history and of particular importance to modern economic development.

Theorists who argue for the causal priority of political over economic institutions advocate theories of economic organization that can be identified as political economy, that is, theories arguing that the economy is decisively shaped by political forces. Despite a general agreement on the importance of politics over other institutions, political economists have, over the years, differed somewhat on how to conceptualize the state and how to explain its influence on the economy. On the one hand, there are those who view the state as an *organized regime* and, on the other hand, those who view the state as an *organized political community*.

The first group of political economists, the strong state theorists, conceptualizes the state as simply an organization for holding and exercising power (e.g., Evans, Rueschemeyer, and Skocpol 1985). States create internal jurisdictions, mark boundaries, and control the means of coercion. States, however, differ among themselves in terms of their autonomy from internal class forces and their administrative capacity to accomplish goals. Authoritatively claiming territory, controlling people, and organizing activity, states are, therefore, the basic actors in world-historical changes. Moreover, with the rise of the nation-state in Western Europe, a new type of

state came into existence, a state with a bureaucratic administrative organization that was capable of exercising vastly more power than states had been
able to exercise before (Tilly 1975, 1992). The new organizational power of
the state was directed inward to control its subjects and their livelihood and
outward to compete with other states.

This view of the state as an organized apparatus implies that the state, as
a condition of its power, must organize its economic base and encourage
economic growth as an ongoing source of revenue. This need for revenue,
therefore, from this perspective, is the invisible motor of economic development. In recent times, this general line of reasoning has become what some
writers have called "a new paradigm", "an intellectual sea change" (Evans,
Rueschemeyer, and Skocpol 1985: 347; Evans and Stephens 1988). Following
Alexander Gerschenkron (1962), many students of Third World development are now arguing that the late-developing states, if sufficiently strong
(i.e., authoritarian), will be able to industrialize successfully (Amsden 1989;
Evans and Stephens 1988; Woo 1990). Among development economists,
notes Gordon White (1984: 97), the strong state perspective has become
orthodoxy: "The modern notion of 'development,' and not least the discipline of 'development economics,' rests on a more or less explicit concept of
the state as crucial stimulant and organizer of socio-economic progress."
Similar theories, most closely associated with the work of Theda Skocpol
(1979, 1985), Fred Block (1987), and Peter Evans (1979, 1985; Evans and
Stephens 1988), also dominate the investigation of the newly industrializing
societies.

The second group of political economists, the pluralists, conceptualizes
the state as being constituted by a political community, with the economy
being one of several sources of power within that community.[2] Having its
origins in eighteenth- and early nineteenth-century European liberalism, this
interpretation maintains that states develop from natural historical collectivi-
ties, the people; the people establish the governments; and the governments,
in turn, create a climate conducive to the livelihood and interests of their citizens. In this characterization, the nation embodies the state; pluralism and
diversity of interests prevail, and therefore government is an essential means
by which individual interests are reconciled for the common good. From the
state flow the guarantees for individual rights, social order, and economic
prosperity. The state represents its people and, therefore, ought to be, in
some measure, representative or democratic; and the economy that grows
from this pluralist base rests on the free interactions of people whose individual economic interests lead them to pursue a course of political stability.
Here, the economy is a spontaneous creation of the community that constitutes the state, which in turn represents them.

From this point of view, economies are, by definition, essential parts of
nations. An economy emerges from the natural resources owned publicly and
privately and from the labor and entrepreneurial talents of its citizens. From
the eighteenth century on, the view that all economies are really "domestic"

national economies emerged as the dominant perspective, and one that strong state theorists have readily accepted. Theorists of political pluralism, however, typically argue that creating a sound democratic state is a necessary step toward establishing a genuine progressive national economy. Without democracy, believed many such theorists (e.g., Almond and Coleman 1960; Almond 1966; Apter 1965), there is a limit to capitalistic development.

In both the strong-state and pluralist versions of political economy, the state or nation is the essential actor. Both sets of theorists argue that the creation of the nation-state, with sovereignty vested first in the absolute monarch and later in a nation's citizens, created the conditions for the transformation from a feudal past to a modern world. From its European origins, according to these theorists, the nation-state, as a model of both political order and belligerence (Tilly 1992), spread around the world, creating a nearly universal concern with human rights, citizenship, and democracy. Becoming a global form of political institutions, each nation-state constructs its own economy, and, hence, the world economy represents an aggregation of national economies.

A civilizational level of analysis has very little room to operate within a political economy perspective. The state so dominates every interpretation that a perspective transcending the state, as does a civilizational approach, makes little sense. Therefore, when state-centered theories are used to analyse trans-societal phenomena, the state continues to be the unit of analysis.[3]

Economies and capitalism

In opposition to state-centered theories of modernity, another equally diverse group of scholars argues that the economy and not the state created the conditions for the modern transformation. Unlike the state-centered approaches, however, economy-centered approaches assume a trans-societal focus, and accordingly scholars writing from this perspective have been concerned with a civilizational level of explanation.

An economy-centered perspective first took shape in Adam Smith's *The Wealth of Nations* ([1776] 1991). Like other Enlightenment thinkers, Smith took a statist view of the economy, but to this view he added a new way to see God's design for mankind. Neither the state nor the political community was responsible for creating the livelihood and wellbeing of a nation and its individual citizens. Rather, nations rested on their economies, and economies worked according to natural laws. These God-given natural laws operated, said Smith, through self-equilibrating markets. The state could either enhance the natural workings of these markets or would suffer the consequences in creating the conditions for its own downfall. In Smith's view, the economy created the conditions for national survival.

Karl Marx, of course, added his own interpretation to the "bourgeois" economics of Adam Smith. He wrote in the preface to *Capital: A Critique of*

Political Economy ([1876] 1967: 13), that the economy formed the natural base of human life and that it worked "with iron necessity towards inevitable results", but the model for natural law that Marx drew on was not heavenly mechanics, but rather Darwin's evolutionary biology. Economies naturally changed, evolving in historical stages by means of the self-aggrandizing struggle between contending classes of economic actors. Class conflict eventually propelled economic orders into revolutionary transformations. Marx called each economic stage a mode of production. A slave mode of production, a feudal mode of production, a capitalist mode of production – history was seen as a succession of modes. With Marx, historical time varied among geographical locations. The more advanced locations, all centered in Western Europe and led by England, had entered modernity in the form of capitalism, while the less advanced locations remained lodged in feudal and slave modes, or worse. Asia was the worst, a system of domination, said Marx (1968), that contained no revolutionary economic contradictions, only timeless barbarism.

The Smithian and Marxian portrayals of economics as institutional foundation of modernity – both constituting theories of modernity as capitalism – continue today with undiminished vigor. The Smithian version, in spirit if not in substance, dominates the economists' view of modernity. The transition into the modern world occurred when efficient capitalist markets developed and could function freely. Many economists take this point of view for granted, as needing no further elaboration. A few economic historians have, however, supplied the details in rather masterful ways. Eric Jones, in *The European Miracle* (1981) and *Growth Recurring* (1988), attempts to lay out the many conditions for the "very long-term" economic growth in Europe and for the lack of those conditions elsewhere. Economic growth is the variable to be explained. Characteristics of economies and of economic growth are conceptually uniform across cases, and other factors, such as the state, are brought in as needed to explain the trajectory of development. The Smithian thesis is also the basic message of Douglass North and Robert Thomas, whose book, *The Rise of the Western World* (1973), is in fact an account of the rise of institutions, principally property rights, that allowed for sustained growth in European capitalist economies. States are a part of this growth, but they are secondary and play a supporting role to the formation of efficient price-setting markets. North and Thomas see the rise of the Western world as the formation of a global market economy that functions in uniform ways by the same economic rules.[4]

Others besides economists and card-carrying economic historians are equally enthusiastic in emphasizing the essential significance of economies in explaining modernity. None has done so in a more grandiose, yet theoretical, manner than Immanuel Wallerstein. The pre-modern world, the world before the sixteenth century according to Wallerstein, was dominated by empires and imperial redistributive economies. Wallerstein (1984: 164) calls these empires "civilizations", because, as imperial systems, they sought "ideological legitimations" to justify their "spectacular and encompassing" domination. In the sixteenth century, however, Western European states, through their competition with each other, created a world economy, essentially a single all-encompassing market, that became a self-sustaining, functionally integrated system. This system existed apart from any political order, but came to dominate all of them. With the triumph of the world economic system, the old empires vanished, which spelt an end to civilizations in the old sense (Wallerstein 1984: 166–7). The character of states now was determined by their location in the world system. The world economic system, argues Wallerstein (1974, 1984, 1991b), is causally prior to and, hence, is more essential than any other feature of modern world history. Today, he says that "capitalistic civilization" prevails, and in the wake of its total hegemony, people, united by "modern nationalisms", articulate the cultural anachronisms of the old civilizational ideologies in order to resist the totality of Western ideology (1984: 165; 1991b: 236). To Wallerstein, civilization refers to a legitimating system, and in modern times the only such system in existence is the "world-economy", a self-sustaining global market.

Wallerstein's theory, which Robert Brenner (1977) criticised as "Neo-Smithian Marxian", has roots in the work of two other scholars, Karl Polanyi and Fernand Braudel, whose sweeping and often global analyses are less formulaic, but are still deeply influenced by the centrality of economic institutions in modern life. In his early work, *The Great Transformation* (1957 [1944]), Polanyi argues with particular forcefulness that the transformation was the development of a market society and a free-market ideology that aspired to commodify and rearrange all human institutions to serve market principles. Polanyi maintained that economies and markets exist in all societies and that, wherever they occur, they are "embedded and enmeshed in institutions, economic and non-economic" (Polanyi, Arensberg, and Pearson 1957: 250). In pre-modern times, however, the economies of empires arose from the social fabric of the people and from the redistributional needs of the empire. But with capitalism, society and politics increasingly and irrationally become embedded in economic institutions.

Polanyi's thesis is an early schematic version of the one that Wallerstein later historicized. To assist his efforts to write the historical narrative of the rise of the global self-sustaining market, Wallerstein drew heavily on the work of a second scholar, Fernand Braudel. Braudel himself provides an equally ambitious attempt to link Western civilization to world capitalism. In two gigantic studies, *The Mediterranean and the Mediterranean World in the Age of Philip II* ([1966] 1976) and *Civilization and Capitalism: 15th and 18th Century* ([1979] 1984), Braudel addresses the historical causes of the capitalist transformation in Western Europe. Deeply descriptive and lacking an explicit formulaic analysis, Braudel's studies chronicle the slow, steady rise of a capitalist economy. He wrote that his study was "about the world" ([1979] 1984: 25), but the narrative line of his story is only about the rise of Western capitalism. Capitalism, he says, was one of a number of long-term trends occurring in Europe, including the growth of the nation-state. Constrained and channeled by the structure of European geography and environment, capitalism grew from a material base consisting of routine ways to satisfy the normal requirements for human life. Material life, coupled, hand in glove, with higher and more complex social and political patterns, grew and finally expanded through international commerce to become a capitalist world-economy.[5] At one point, Braudel contrasts world-economies with "world-civilizations". "[Civilizations] are ways of ordering space just as economies are." But he notes that they are not the same. "While they may coincide with the latter (particularly since a world-economy *taken as a whole, tends* to share the same culture, or at least elements of the same culture, as opposed to neighboring world-economies) they may also be distinguished from them: the cultural map and the economic map cannot simply be superimposed without anomaly" ([1979] 1984: 65; emphasis in original). Braudel equates civilizations with cultures, and believes that they are ancient. He equates economies with the material basis of life and commercial patterns needed to maintain it. Representing civilizational tradi-tions, large empires spawned far-flung market economies, which he calls world-economies. But, to Braudel, the capitalist world-economy is distinctive and transformative. Although civilization and the early world-economies interact even in the ancient times, they only come together in the modern age, with the rise of capitalism.

Wallerstein, Polanyi, and Braudel offer different accounts of the growth of modernity, but all of them base their accounts on the centrality of a modern global market economy. And in this sense, if in no other, they write in the spirit of Adam Smith. Other analysts, however, write in the spirit of Karl Marx.

Although far removed from the determinism of the original, the recent Marxian writings still convey Marx's initial concern with the relations of production. Such writers as Barrington Moore, Jr. (1966), E. P. Thompson (1963), Perry Anderson (1974a; 1974b), and Robert Brenner (1976; 1977) argue, in different ways, that the particular alignments of classes determine the character of the state, as well as the trajectories of economic growth. Moore's account (1966) is among the first and is probably the most influen-tial. He argues that those classes most directly controlling economic activity are those most capable of mobilizing political movements. Depending on the social location of the most economically engaged class, the outcomes of political struggles varied. In England and the United States, the middle classes, the bourgeois, were the most active participants, and in the course of modernizing political struggles, the middle class was able to tip the balance to create political democracy. In Japan and Russia, the upper class was the one most in control and in the face of modernizing change, brought on largely by the requirement to industrialize, this class created an authoritarian state. In Russia and China, where the upper classes were leisured and the middle classes were small in number, urban, and uninvolved in the rural base of the economy, the peasants were economically the most engaged, and at the moment of political upheaval they were able to turn events toward socialist outcomes.

Other recent neo-Marxist writings develop similar themes. Among the most important for the interpretation of the economy is Fernando Cardoso and Enzo Faletto's book, *Dependency and Development in Latin America* (1979). Cardoso and Faletto argue that Western economic imperialism did not impinge upon Latin American countries in a uniform manner. Instead, at the time of their writing, they observed many different economic trajectories. They explained that the various trajectories resulted from different alignments of classes at the time of the revolutionary separation from the Spanish and Portuguese colonizers. Distinctive class alignments created distinctive political orders, each of which plotted its own economic trajectory in conjunction with the interests of both the victorious class segment and the European imperialist powers. Elements of this thesis, deeply influenced by Moore and more distantly by Marx, were later incorporated into strong state theory by Evans (1979) and world systems theory by Frank (1967) and Wallerstein (1974).

This brief summary of the modern theorists writing from Smithian and Marxian points of view has only touched upon what is a vast literature. Although quite diverse, the literature is none the less centered on an analysis equating the essential characteristics of modernity with capitalism. The main thrust of this literature is to uncover the historical causes of economic growth and transformation and to generalize these causes as an important source of a modern way of life. The implicit conclusion is that in pre-modern times civilizational and economic diversity centered on the old imperial traditions, but with the coming of capitalism, Western civilization, now equated with Western capitalism, triumphed as the other world civilizations waned or marginally survived in the ideological protests of dominated people.

In summary, state- and market-centered approaches provide different foundations from which to build comprehensive perspectives explaining historical changes in Western Europe. Although it is certainly the case that political and economic institutions greatly influence the organization of economies, the search for explanations for the Western transformation invariably downplays continuities of all kinds and emphasizes disruptions. Accordingly, this overriding concern for explaining revolutions – industrial as well as political – has had a pernicious effect on our understanding of civilizational phenomena. The perniciousness arises because our understanding of how societies and economies are organized becomes trapped in Eurocentric explanations for historical change.

A more fruitful paradigm, primarily associated with Max Weber and those aligned with his approach, maintains that organizational patterns are institutionally anchored in worldviews shared by a common civilization. Modernity in the form of rationalism, Weber wrote, was originally a

Western and distinctly historical occurrence that cut across all institutional spheres in Western Europe. As it diffused to other civilizational areas, however, modern rationalism would not be an identical phenomenon and would not have the same impact in different societies as it had in the West.

The Weberian alternative and the organization of economies

What is the relation between civilization and economic activity? From a political economy point of view, the expansion of the Western nation-states generated a universal form of political structure, which in turn organizes economies and economic activity. From Marxian and Smithian points of view, capitalism created an all-encompassing way of life that became a universalized world order. From both points of view, Western modernity provides the model for world civilization and Western economic patterns become the model for economies worldwide.

The Weberian alternative goes in a very different direction. Max Weber was as interested in Western modernity as any theorist.[6] He concentrated his life-work on explaining, historically and sociologically, the transformation of Western Europe. As it changed through the course of his scholarly life, Weber's approach, however, turned out to be quite different from those arguing for the priority of one position over another. He maintained, instead, that both positions were important – and many others besides. Among them all, he believed, there was an internal resonance, an affinity of nation with market, of certain religious beliefs with the pursuit of profits. The best explanation was not whether one element was more basic than another. Rather it was the configurational resonance among all the elements that needed to be explained, and that explanation required a civilizational approach. Weber used this approach to ask, in contrast with other world civilizations, how and why was the West unique? "Only in the West", Weber would say again and again.[7]

Weber's civilizational approach grew from two basic elements of his sociology: ideal-type methodology and an institutional analysis. Weber developed the first quite early in his work and the second much later. As is well known, Weber's ideal-type methodology allowed analysts to fashion analytic constructs from experience and from historical analysis that appear useful in interpreting historical change (Burger 1987; Oakes 1988).[8] To create ideal types, these analytic abstractions are systematized, are made logically coherent so that structural and normative regularities can be derived from the concepts. So developed, ideal types are separated from any claims of historical truth or necessary historical effects. Instead, they are logical constructs whose value can only be assessed by their usefulness in disentangling real-world complexity. "In order to penetrate to the real causal interrelationships", said Weber, *"we construct unreal ones"* ([1905] 1949: 185–6; emphasis in original).

Using a battery of ideal types in his early study of Protestantism ([1904–5] 1958) and in his study of the ancient civilizations in the Mediterranean Basin

([1909] 1988), Weber concluded that Western history did not unfold from some core of central premises or a set of first causes, or even a key institutional sphere. "Nothing could be more misleading", he wrote (*ibid.*: 45), "than to describe the economic institutions of Antiquity in modern terms. Whoever does this underrates – as often happens – the basic changes effected during the Middle Ages in the legal institutions governing capital, though the mediaeval economy was itself none the less different from ours." Western history was developmental and not evolutionary, and the developmental changes could be tracked, analytically, through changes in institutions. For Weber, ideal types were the tools to trace, rather than to predict, these historical changes.

The second foundation of Weber's civilizational approach was his focus on institutions.[9] What gave Western societies such dynamism? Politics, religions, economics, even art and music – every institutional sphere in the West became transformed. Why? Weber asked. By developing typologies to analyse each institutional sphere, Weber began to theorize the nature of civilization, as well as to conceptualize the great world religions as embodiments of civilizational principles. Institutions served as the fulcrum of Weber's analysis. It was through institutions that worldviews became linked to practical activity. Worldviews were anchored in institutions, not as abstract ideas but as embedded orientations toward life, taken for granted and simply assumed to be valid representations of existence. Although worldviews were embodied in institutions and provided an organizational paradigm for them, institutions were simultaneously patterned routines of life that people, in different roles and from different strata of society, addressed, systematized, and tried to align with their material and ideal interests.

Weber's understanding of institutions as brokers between civilizational worldviews and practical activity allowed him to develop a comparative framework by which to clarify the uniqueness of Western civilization.[10] Weber's goal was to trace typologically the shifting organizational architecture of Western society in order to explain the origins of Western rationalism. He accomplished this task by constructing civilizational contrasts to serve as the institutional coordinates for his sociological map tracing the trajectories of Western development.

In the case, first of China, and then later of the other civilizations, Weber showed specific linkages between civilizational worldviews and the primary institutional spheres of life, including the economy. In pre-modern times, traditionalism in the form of patriarchalism and patrimonialism prevailed in all civilizational locations, including those in the ancient Mediterranean basin. In each location, the specific religious orientation (e.g., Confucianism, Buddhism, Hinduism, and Judaism) specified patriarchal and patrimonial modes of domination, turning them into historically distinct forms. These distinct forms penetrated not only the organizational structure of empires, but also the organization of the economy and of society. While the task requirements differed from one institutional sphere to another, the same understanding of fundamental order resonated through all institutional spheres.

The institutional embeddedness of economic activity

Weber maintained that, at a general level, economic activity, like all activity, was organized through institutions, and institutions were themselves anchored in civilizational worldviews. As with his analysis of other institutions, Weber developed his insights on the economy both typologically and substantively. His *Economy and Society* ([1922] 1978) is largely an exposition of typological frameworks that were, according to Schluchter (1989: 432), meant "to supplement and interpret" Weber's substantive work on civilizations that he compiled under the title "The Economic Ethics of the World Religions". *Economy and Society* has a long second chapter outlining the "sociological categories of economic action", in which Weber analytically isolates types of economic action and economic organization in the absence of "all questions of dynamic process" ([1922] 1978: 63). He follows this chapter with an equally conceptual discussion of the "types of legitimate domination". In the essays on the major world religions, Weber used the typologies as overlays, allowing the major civilizations each to be interpreted sociologically and to be contrasted as negative cases with the historical development of capitalism in Western Europe (Hamilton 1984b, 1990).

Even though Weber conceptually conceived of economic calculation apart from institutions, Weber's substantive analyses clearly show that, in the real world, economic activity is always rooted in institutional environments. The civilizational components of these institutions shape economic organization – the medium of economic activity – which in turn shapes economic calculation. In most historical settings, political institutions directly structured the environment in which economic activity was routinely conducted, but did so in many diverse ways. For example, the patrimonial structure of state capitalism in the Roman Empire and in the Chinese Tang Dynasty, while typologically similar, were historically quite different, with the first being absorbed into a structure of Western feudalism and the second being progressively compartmentalized by Chinese officialdom (Weber [1915] 1951). In this example, as in many other examples that Weber gave, similar institutional configurations led to very different historical results, in part because civilizations, each with a distinctive worldview, tend to work out problems in characteristic ways.[11]

Weber's very general theoretical formulation of the relation between economy and society has been reworked by a number of sociologists.[12] Typically, sociologists have followed two different lines of analysis, one toward a more general theoretical elaboration, and the other toward a specification of Weber's historical sociology. Those moving toward general theory, most notably, Talcott Parsons (1977), Parsons and Smelser (1956), Smelser (1959, 1963) and S. N. Eisenstadt (1963), maintain that societies, as they develop greater complexity, go through a process of functional differentiation by which the economic sphere becomes increasingly independent from other institutional spheres, including the religious and cultural spheres. With their focus on the development of general theories of modern society, these writers initially paid very little attention to a civilizational level of analysis.[13]

Those attempting to specify Weber's historical sociology were increasingly drawn into discussions about the uniqueness of Western civilization. Several efforts at specification are particularly relevant for the clarification of the process of Western rationalization, as well as a civilizational level of analysis, especially Elias's books on *The Civilizing Process* (1978; also see Mennell 1989); Nelson's attempts (1949, 1974, 1975) to develop a "differential sociology of sociocultural processes and patterns"; Schluchter's works on Western rationalism (1981, 1989); Eisenstadt's more recent works on axial age religions (1981, 1982, 1987); and especially (but perhaps ironically, because he rarely mentioned Weber) Michel Foucault's (1979) work on the formation of the "modern soul". These works are the basis of the following outline of Weber's developmental history of rational capitalism.

Christianity and capitalistic economic organization

At this point we should again turn our attention to Raphael's *Disputa*, because this fresco, painted in the first years of the sixteenth century, provides a starting point to outline Weber's account of Western rationalism. As Randall Collins explains, Weber's account of Western uniqueness is not a theory at all. Weber is essentially a "historicist, in the sense of seeing history as a concatenation of unique events and unrepeatable complexities" (Collins 1980). Although history to Weber is certainly a concatenation of events, it is very important to see that in Weber's sociology the developmental sequencing of historical change represents neither random outcomes, as if produced by probabilistic game theory, nor an unstructured conjuncture of events. Weber was a historicist, to be sure, but only to a limited degree.

For Weber, civilizational worldviews produce powerful normative orientations that orient action by giving action an institutional location, subjective meaning, normative directions, but not, in the end, predetermined destinations. The analogy that Weber used was that of a railway switchman: worldviews give direction to actions that are independently propelled, like trains on a track, by material and ideal interests.[14]

Weber repeatedly wrote that Christianity shaped Western institutions. Christian theology reverberated through all institutional spheres, providing normative direction and intensity that they otherwise would not have had without Christianity. Weber felt this conclusion was sociologically justifiable because of his contrasts with other world religions. Among the myriad ways that Christianity shaped Western institutions, it suffices to mention two: the configuration and dynamics of authority, and the rise of the rationalism, both of which underpinned the development of industrial capitalism.

The Raphael fresco shows so clearly that, beyond the earth, beyond this empirical, mundane realm, lies a greater reality – immovable, permanent, and absolute. This realm of greater reality was not seen to be an amorphous great beyond, as existed in Buddhism, but rather was a highly focused and anthropomorphized location. By the late Middle Ages, the transcendentalism already present in classical Greek philosophy and in Roman law (by virtue of its incorporation of the universalism present in Stoicism) had become thoroughly worked into the doctrines of the Catholic Church; this transcendentalism was so apparent and its implication so well understood that church intellectuals had written widely of the clarity and perfect knowledge that existed in God's realm. By the twelfth and thirteenth centuries, such thinkers as Grosseteste, Roger Bacon, and Bonaventura were writing about the "Book of Nature" and the "Book of Conscience", among other "Books". These intellectuals, observed Benjamin Nelson (1975: 365–6), believed that "Everything in the world was . . . the work of God's hand. Everything in the world was seen as a 'book.' . . . Everything in the world (not evidently the work of a human hand) was somehow aided by the creative spirit. As the work of God's hand, it was directly revealed as incarnate Nature. It conveyed its own image directly." Moreover, these intellectuals knew, as did Raphael, that Heaven's perfect world differed dramatically from the man-made world of sin, confusion, and disputation. In this earthly world, even the most blessed could only debate about perfect knowledge; in the end they could not know it. This is "the absolute paradox" wrote Weber ([1922] 1978: 553), "of a perfect god's creation of a permanently imperfect world".

This worldview's fundamental structuring of reality, believed Weber, had a huge impact, not only on the nature of knowledge and how one seeks it (Nelson 1975), but also on the very structure of domination. Indeed, even from Raphael's painting it is clear that, though locked in disputation, earthly authorities have a heavenly right to rule, and in turn rule through divine guidance. For Weber, one of the key aspects of Western legitimation, as opposed to that in other world civilizations, is the direct and personal nature of the bond between the transcendental realm, usually personified by God or Jesus, and the legitimated holder of authority.[15]

Weber believed that a civilizational stance existing at any one point in time is not created out of a void, but rather is built on pre-existing cultural patterns and affinities. Let me illustrate this point by outlining how Christianity built on its Roman heritage. The power holder's personal linkage with the gods, and thereby his right to rule over a prescribed set of subjects (normally within an *oikos* or a household economy), had already appeared as a characteristic feature of patriarchal legitimation throughout the Mediterranean basin during antiquity. Weber saw patriarchalism as a form of legitimation in all civilizational areas, but believed that monotheism, which "arose in Asia Minor and was imposed upon the Occident" ([1922] 1978: 552), created a strong tension in patriarchalism and patrimonial forms of domination. Within all forms of patriarchalism, Weber ([1922] 1978: 227) said, there is a "double sphere", which consists of an ever-present tension between "action which is bound to specific traditions", on the one hand, and "action that is free of specific rules", on the other hand. Sociologically speaking, Western monotheism decisively shifted the balance toward the "master's discretion" and his ability to change the rules of conduct based solely on his personal relationship with the one god, without regard to specific traditions.

By Roman times, the enlargement of the master's discretion had moved in two institutional directions. In state building, rulers rather than priests predominated, with the consequence that state-building strategies had progressively moved political institutions toward what Weber ([1922] 1978: 1160) called "caesaropapism", "a secular ... ruler who exercises supreme authority in ecclesiastic matters by virtue of his autonomous legitimacy". The movement toward more centralized state institutions also led, in the other direction, toward the routinization and depersonalization of the prerogatives of the heads of the great households (the patriarchs). This occurred in Roman law through the codification of *patrias potestas*, the customary authority claimed by the heads of Roman patrilineages (Hamilton 1984b).

The expansion of the state and the delimitation of lesser powers in Roman law provided the basis for a strictly jurisdictional configuration of authority that was rooted in legal institutions. The characteristics of both types of authority (in households and in states) were: (1) a command structure having a precise, legalistic delineation of who or what falls within the jurisdiction of command (either as a set of people who are subjects or as a defined territory within which commands can be given); (2) ultimate justifications for the right of command coming, at times through a chain of command, from a transcendental source.

All this was in place before Christianity swept through the Roman Empire. Christianity, however, greatly enlarged and altered this traditional pattern of domination by adding to it strong elements of charismatic domination (Schluchter 1989: 392–408). In the first instance, Christianity revitalized the transcendental nature of legitimation by systematizing, theologically, the nature of the absolute and by institutionalizing the theology through the creation of a universal church, itself an elaboration of Roman political institutions.[16] In the second place, as it took shape in the Middle Ages, Christian theology greatly intensified the personal nature of the linkage between power holders and the heavenly order. Raphael clearly shows that this heavenly order consisted of an anthropomorphized hierarchy: Jesus, the son of God, and a surrounding host of heavenly notables serving as direct and personal connections to God on high. By the Middle Ages, the right to exercise of power, like salvation itself, needed to be based upon direct and personal connections with God.

The personalization of legitimacy subtly but decisively transformed the two main configurations of authority, the state and the household. The basis of state institutions, including the papacy, moved from secular caesaropapist rulers to hierocracies; that is, to rulers who were either "legitimated by priests, either as an incarnation or in the name of God" or were themselves "a high priest" (Weber [1922] 1978: 1159).[17] By the Middle Ages, the Catholic Church, itself a theocracy, and the pope, one of the best historical examples of routinized charismatic succession, became officially the source of legitimation for secular power. Capitalizing on his own privileged personal relation with God, the pope used the rites of ordination and excommunication to declare whether secular rulers had a basis in heaven for their earthly commands. Weber saw that the position of both kings and pope in the West was intimately shaped by what he called their "office charisma" ([1922] 1978: 1139–41).

A second source of personalized authority proved equally important. In the Middle Ages, the Roman laws of *patria potestas* themselves became revitalized and reinterpreted under the influence of Christianity. In Roman law, the patriarchs exercised their authority by virtue of their being heads of households, as determined by rules of kinship. By the early Middle Ages, however, these patriarchal principles had become transformed through the routinization of charisma. The jurisdictional and legal premises of the head of household's right to rule within the household became intensified, in Western feudalism, by the charismatic qualities of the holders of the position. In the earliest period, the charismatic claims rested on military prowess, and the right to rule over territory went with "charismatic heroism" (Weber [1922] 1978: 1141), but this form of charisma quickly became routinized by the development of what Weber calls "lineage charisma". With lineage charisma, charismatic qualities become a feature of blood lines. According to Weber ([1922] 1978: 1136), "household and lineage groups are considered magically blessed, so that they alone can provide the bearers of charisma. . . . Because of its supernatural endowment a house is elevated above all others; in fact, the belief in such a qualification, which is unattainable by natural means and hence charismatic, has everywhere been the basis for the development of royal and aristocratic power." Christianity further intensified this development, innately by bringing fief holders under the control of the Church and encouraging, even forcing, conversion as a condition of rule. Increasingly, however, members of the emerging elite began to distance themselves from the Church's direct control by finding independent sources of legitimation for their lineage charisma. Philippe Desan (1984), for instance, documents a substantial literature arising in fourteenth- and fifteenth-century France tracing aristocratic pedigrees to mythical origins, often to one of the tribes of Israel. In fact, these symbolic portrayals of office and lineage charisma, when put on stone or into books, are where the trileveled motif dramatizing the earthly right to rule that Raphael used in his fresco originally came from.

The charismatic infusion that Christianity provided strongly personalized all institutions of domination. At the state level, kings were able to relocate themselves, symbolically as well as institutionally, by moving from being members of one among many privileged lineages to become, as individuals, God's personally selected leaders on earth. As Ernst Kantorowicz (1957) shows, by the sixteenth century a public sphere, the "corporate" state, was theologically and legally conceptualized as one of the "king's two bodies", the other one being his physical body. Foucault (1979), in *Discipline and Punish*, shows the effects of this conceptualization on the legal institutions that grew with absolutism. The effects were no less apparent on the economy. Mercantilistic economic policy, as well as various forms of public enterprise including the state corporations such as the British East India Company, were justified precisely in terms of the "body politic".

Christianity also shaped the patterns of domination throughout society. Among free men, the notion of ownership and control was conceptualized legally in terms of property and property rights, accruing initially to elite heads of households. The centralizing state was a driving force behind this codification, but the personalization of property spread to all groups and had the long-term effect of reconceptualizing property as an aspect of one's personal jurisdiction – as something that was individually created or owned, unambiguously defined, and freely bought or sold, instead of being something embedded in a household (*oikos*) economy dedicated to the satisfaction of want.[18] Personalization of property, including the personalization of one's own labor, conceptually made property divisible from family assets and increased the financial accountability of businesses; both developments, according to Weber ([1922] 1978: 375–80), form two of the most important cornerstones in the formation of modern capitalism.[19]

The rise of Western rationalism and economic organization

By time that Raphael's *Disputa* had been completed in 1509, less than ten years before Luther would nail his Ninety-five Theses to the door of Castle Church in Wittenberg, a Christian worldview had thoroughly reoriented the institutional structure of Western Europe, both at the level of the state and in everyday life. But the biggest transformation was yet to come, the institutional shift of huge proportions that Weber called the "rise of Western rationalism".

Rationalism, believed Weber, was a part of the development of new configurations of domination that had only begun to take shape by the beginning of the sixteenth century. Weber ([1922] 1978: 954) subsumed these configurations under a single type of domination, legal–rational domination, which is based on the belief that "the 'validity' of a power of command" rests on a "system of consciously made *rational* rules. . . . In that case every single bearer of powers of command is legitimated by that system of rational norms, and his power is legitimate insofar as it corresponds with the norm" (emphasis in original). Weber did not explain the rise of rationalism in a detailed historical chronology. He did, however, explain it sociologically.

With "charismatic patrimonialiom", higher authorities, blessed by God, symbolically embodied the community of subjects over whom they maintained the power of legitimate command. It is no accident that only religious notables appear on the ground floor in Raphael's fresco. No one else, least of all the people seeking salvation, really mattered in the world of religious authority. But beginning with the Protestant Reformation, when all believers individually became responsible to God for their own salvation, the majesty of patrimonial justifications began to erode. In principle, people could seek religious truths on their own; no longer were there intermediaries who had inherently greater access to religious truth than they did.

With the Copernican Revolution, the same logic spread gradually to everyday truths about the secular world. One of the earliest and greatest works of the era, Descartes's *Discourse on Method*, provided a reasoned, technique-driven, step-by-step procedure to discover the truth. External authorities – kings, popes, and judges – had no greater inherent access to the truth than any person.[20] In practical terms, in fact, they had less access, because they lacked the necessary scientific expertise. Rather suddenly (at least in historical time), the charisma that had attached so firmly to the offices of religious and secular rulers became generalized to all believers and all thinkers, so that each person had a self to save and a mind to reason.

This shift was a charismatic transformation of the first order. It was as if Raphael suddenly enlarged the ground floor of his fresco to accommodate every believer, every person engaging in disputation about the truths of their own soul and of the world. Weber recognized the importance of this transformation. It broke the "fetters of the sib" (Weber [1915] 1951: 237), undermining the legitimacy of all forms of patriarchal authority from the state to the family. But breaking the fetters of patriarchal domination did not free individuals from constraint, but rather bound them, more tightly than ever, to a new sacred condition of duty and responsibility to God on high. Weber ([1904–5] 1958: 95–154) recognized that the initial formulations in the Protestant Reformation of how individuals would be bound to God and to the world – Lutheranism, Calvinism, Pietism, Methodism, and the Baptists sects – were extremely important in channeling and institutionalizing the charismatic potential that was suddenly attached to each individual believer. Wrote Weber ([1922] 1978: 556): "only in the Protestant ethic of vocation does the world, despite all its creaturely imperfections, possess unique and religious significance as the object through which one fulfills his duties by rational behavior according to the will of an absolutely transcendental god". This was the condition of "innerworldly asceticism" that Weber saw arising out of the Protestant Reformation and that ideologically propelled the rise of rationalism.

At least in the early period of this transition, the transcendental absolute was still anthropomorphized. God was still in his heaven. But as time went on, that, too, began to change. By the time of the Enlightenment and Adam Smith, God had been subtly replaced by Nature and natural laws.

Philosophers debated whether there was a deistic god or not, a god that put the world in motion and then left it there, but they did not debate about the existence of a transcendental plane of reality. A belief in science and a cosmology rooted in scientism eased God and all his companions out of the picture while at the same time retaining the entire transcendental plane of absolute truth intact. The rapid progress in science and its technical applications in a capitalist world only provided more proof that the transcendental existed.

But Weber clearly saw the paradox in the triumph of science. Western science grew out of a belief in Christian transcendentalism, out of an attempt to discover God's perfect truth. As Gallieo (cited by Nelson 1975: 371) put it, science tells us not "how to go to heaven", but rather "how heaven goes". Bent upon knowing the unknowable through the application of rational technique, science, in the absence of Christian cosmology, drained much of the institutionalized charisma out of Western civilization. For Weber, science was the driving force behind the "disenchantment" that was an inherent part of Western modernity. "For the last stage of this culture development," Weber wrote ([1904–5] 1958: 182), "it might well be truly said: Specialists without spirit, sensualists without heart; this nullity imagines that it has attained a level of civilization never before achieved."

Scientism and objective calculation created a new language of legitimation. The charismatic core of the West shifted from kings and popes to the individual. The authority that had been personalized by Christian theology now became individualized through Protestantism and depersonalized through science. With Protestantism, religiously directed self control, which is what Weber called asceticism, was either necessary for salvation or served as a sign of election. People logically became the subjects of their own personalized jurisdictions; they became responsible for their own conduct. Scientism pushed this logic forward to create a technology of control that made people the autonomous object of their own domination and, hence, of their own rational calculation.

Better than anyone, including Weber, Michel Foucault has precisely and sociologically described the logic and the rise of this mode of calculation (also see O'Neil 1986). In *Discipline and Punish* (1979), he described the shift in thinking that occurred. Leaders and thinkers actively worked to create a new language in which to describe the human condition and to invent new techniques of domination. In so doing, they created a cultural space for the reconceptualization of the individual as an autonomous, self-reflexive, thinking, decision-making individual whose chief responsibility was self-control. Foucault identified this individual as a "docile body" (1979: 135–70), a conception that nicely matches Weber's ([1904–5] 1958: 181–2) concern with innerworldly asceticism.

What is this new form of domination? Weber saw it as the application of calculable rules and standards to all spheres of life, with pervasive bureaucratization as the result. Focusing on the role of the individual, Foucault called the new form of domination "discipline". Discipline, he wrote (1979: 215), "may be identified neither with an institution nor with an apparatus; it is a type of power, a modality for its exercise, comprising a whole set of instruments, techniques, procedures, levels of application, targets; it is a 'physics' or an 'anatomy' of power, a technology." Whatever the terminology, Weber and Foucault agree completely that this new form of domination is the paradigm out of which modern organizations emerge.

According to both writers, modern society has been restructured comprehensively and paradigmatically – so that no sphere of Western human life is left untouched by this form of control. The same technology is applied to all organized settings: schools, hospitals, factories, prisons. The new organizational paradigm differs from all older forms of domination in a very fundamental way. Before the modern transformation, groups were organized jurisdictions constituted by those in positions of command: the Church by the pope, the nation by the king, the family by the patriarch. People were subjects, were physically and symbolically incorporated as a part of that whole. The rise of the rationalist organizational paradigm produced a subtle shift in logic: groups, still as organized jurisdictions, became reconceptualized in terms of the activity in which the participants, as individuals, were engaged. The individual served as both the fundamental unit of activity and the fundamental the unit of control. The legitimate power holder becomes recast as a manager of the activity, a trainer of people, and a follower of organizational rules.

The new organizational paradigm, with its logic of normalizing activity and then normalizing people to fit into the frame of that activity, was quickly incorporated in existing forms of Western business activities and transformed them. The economy, like every other sphere of activity, was subject to this new way of thinking. Enterprise should be reconceptualized and restructured, not as a way families earn their livelihood or as a place where the master's wishes prevail, but rather as a way to systematize manufacturing activities.

This conceptualization is exactly what Adam Smith provided in *The Wealth of Nations*. Smith did not only provide the laws of markets, but also the logic of business organization. Firms should be factories, should be laid out with the goals of efficient production and marketing of commodities in mind. Like states and armies, factories should be organized and managed, and whole economies should be run on the presumption of the existence of efficient factories and efficient exchange in the marketplace. Out of this reconceptualization, carried by several generations of entrepreneurs, politicians, and economic specialists, arose the modern economic institutions that we know today: the corporations, banks, stock markets, insurance companies, and regulatory agencies of every kind.[21] All of these fixtures of modern capitalism grew on a foundation provided by the new rationalist worldview – normalized activity performed by normalized people (Biggart and Hamilton 1992). The economy and the economic institutions through which the economy is organized are consequences, rather than causes, of developmental changes in Western civilization.

Weber and Foucault clearly saw that the new organizational paradigm is a way of reconceptualizing the world in terms of activity, by rationalizing that activity sequentially in time and space. Adam Smith's description of the needle factory was among the first conceptualizations of making products as an activity requiring an organized perspective. This reconceptualization, however, came to business activities quite late, long after most other spheres had already been rethought and reorganized. One of the first, and certainly among the most precocious, spheres of activity to reflect this new way of looking at the world was painting. Two centuries before Adam Smith, painting had been transformed in the Italian Renaissance. In the struggle to capture reality and truth in painting, the Renaissance painters began to look at the world geometrically, from the perspective of the observer, with time and space organized on a flat surface. One of the greatest of the Renaissance painters, Raphael was also among the first to discover in the observer's gaze the managerial power to rearrange the world. Though not by a direct route or an inevitable sequence, Raphael most assuredly led to Adam Smith, who was another architect of space and time.

Conclusion: Western civilization and the rise of Asian capitalism

What are the effects of civilization on economies? Weber showed that the effects are as complex and as comprehensive as could be imagined. He drew this conclusion essentially by examining the West, with background contrasts with other civilizations. One of the answers that we need to know today, however, is a question that Weber did not directly address: what are the effects of modern Western civilizations, characterized by rationalism and capitalism, on the rest of the world? Although he did not answer the question directly, his analysis of civilizations shows a way to think about the question, and recent research on East Asian capitalism allows a tentative answer in line with the Weberian approach.

Civilizational logics are embedded in institutional spheres of activity where they provide orientations to action. Such logics are not static, but they are not highly changeable either. Change at the civilizational level represents developmental change, with each shift building on and altering previous orientations. If this is an accurate reading of Weber's "rule of experience" about civilizations (cf. Roth 1978: xxxvi), then one would not predict that non-Western civilizations would need to relinquish their cultural orientation in the face of rationalism and capitalism. The organizational structure of rationalism and capitalism is deeply embedded in Western life. Their diffusion to another civilizational arena, even by force, is not to transmit the whole, but only the effects of that life, the artifacts, so to speak. Rationalism, as a mode of scientific thinking, and capitalism, as a way of doing business, enter other civilizations as inventions, albeit very important ones. They enter as alien fragments into a complete way of life that has no holes, no institutional niches left unoccupied. For this reason, one might expect such civilizational encounters to result in changes, but not in a complete change. Like Christianity coming to Rome, the transformations may be great indeed, but a complete replacement of one worldview by another is impossible.

This theoretical proposition is nicely illustrated by the historical lessons we learn from the study of the rise of East Asian capitalism. For Weber, in his comparisons of all the major world civilizations, Chinese civilization was, typologically, the furthermost removed from the West (Schluchter 1989: 85–116). Chinese cosmology was not only without monotheism, but was also without a transcendental level at all. There was no great beyond where reality was permanent and unchanging. There was, instead, a cosmological ordering of this world, represented by the harmonious hierarchical interrelations of heavens, earth, and mankind. The cosmological picture of this ordering of things cannot be easily juxtaposed with Raphael's fresco, because each worldview works on its own principles, and not as two ends of a continuum. Joseph Needham (1956: 582) explains it as follows: "The Chinese notion of Order positively excluded the [Western] notion of Law. . . . The Chinese world-view depended upon a totally different line of thought [from the law-based worldview developed in the West]. The harmonious cooperation of all beings arose, not from the orders of a superior authority external to them-selves, but from the fact that [the Chinese] were all parts in a hierarchy of wholes forming a cosmic pattern, and what they obeyed were the internal dictates of their own natures."

For human power holders in China, there is no God in his Heaven, no set of God-given laws, and no transcendental level that they, as earthly leaders, could use to justify their claims to power (Bellah 1970: 76 – 99; Hamilton 1984b, 1990). A completely different vocabulary of legitimation developed, a vocabulary in which justifications for power were based on the requirements for natural harmonies in this world. Power over another was justified in terms of one's obedience to one's own position in a universal relational order. There is a natural hierarchy of relationships in this order. In the human world, for instance, a son should act like a son in relation to his parents. Obedience (*xiao*) is required as a part of that role. If the son, however, fails to act like a son, the parents have the obligation as parents to align their son's actions with the role of a son.

As I have explained in considerable detail elsewhere (Hamilton 1984b, 1989, 1990), it is useful to characterize the difference between Chinese and Western forms of patriarchalism by means of Weber's double sphere of traditional domination. Whereas Christianity in the West resolved the balance decisively in favor of the ultimate supremacy of persons, the Confucian orientation in East Asia resolved the tension just as decisively in the opposite direction in favor of the ultimate supremacy of roles. The reso-lution results in a difference that is one not of degree but of kind. Asian states and societies operate on radically different organizational principles than those found in the West (Fei 1992; Hamilton 1989, 1990). Weber ([1915]

1951; also see Schluchter 1989) clearly saw this himself, when he identified Western civilization as one that emphasized the "mastery of the world", whereas Chinese civilization emphasized "adjustment to the world".

For East Asia, organizational principles rest on the development, differentiation, and systematization of normative relationships (Fei 1992; Hamilton 1984b; 1990). Whereas in the West laws regulate the actions of people, norms in Asia order the relations among roles. The Chinese emphasis on a hierarchy of ordered relationships and on harmony among those relationships formed a powerful worldview for creating social, political, and economic institutions (Schram 1985; Hamilton 1989; 1991b). The Chinese imperial economy had always been embedded in institutions of order. The crucial issue in the Chinese setting is not the Western question of who had jurisdictional control over the economy or over economic institutions. Instead, the crucial issue for China was how should the world, including the economy, be harmoniously arranged, and how could people's livelihood be guaranteed. For the Chinese, in principle, everyone always had a part to play in creating and maintaining economic harmony.

A full discussion of the Chinese worldview at this point is impossible. The key issues here, however, are the linkages between worldviews and institutionalized economic activity. In the West, Christianity combined with pre-existing institutions to produce clear jurisdictional lines of top-down personalized authority. In the economic sphere, this led to legal definitions of property and ownership. But Chinese institutions rest on relationships and not jurisdictions, on obedience to one's own roles and not on bureaucratic command structures. Chinese institutions had, in principle, no charismatic content and no institutionalized top-down system of authority. Society was arranged as a status hierarchy, with every status position having the duty to maintain its own integrity. Each village had its council, each family its rules, and each merchant association its codes. Officialdom had the most complex of all sets of regulations to proscribe its members. All had the obligation to maintain the uprightness of people in their status group.

As Fei Xiaotong (1992) explains, Chinese society as it institutionally developed does not consist of organizations. Organizations are jurisdictional and the individual is, conceptually, the main unit of activity and control. But both jurisdictional principles and the autonomous individual are historically absent in the Chinese worldview, and thus were not incorporated in Chinese institutions. Instead, Chinese society consists of networks of people whose actions are oriented by normative social relationships. Network building, says Ambrose King (1991: 79), is the "cultural strategy" used to create society.

Much of Confucian East Asia is capitalistic and in most places scientific rationalism prevails. The effects of capitalism and rationalism in East Asia have been momentous, but they have not moved Asian societies from a civilizational trajectory of development. To use Weber's metaphor, Asians have used capitalism and rationalism to propel, like trains on a track, their ideal and material interests, but the civilizational orientation to the track is still very much in place. Weber himself made this prediction (Hamilton and Kao 1987). After having demonstrated that Chinese civilization would not have produced an independent origin for capitalism, he argued ([1915] 1951: 248) that "The Chinese in all probability would be quite capable . . . of assimilating capitalism which has technically and economically been fully developed in the modern culture area. It is obviously not a question of deeming the Chinese 'naturally ungifted' for the demands of capitalism."

As researchers have shown, Asians are "civilizationally gifted" for the demands of modern capitalism. Although industrial structure varies among societies in East Asia (Whitley 1992; Orrù, Biggart, and Hamilton 1991), East Asian capitalism has none the less organizational characteristics that distinguish the entire region from Western capitalistic economies. Looking at the corporate organizational structure of Western capitalism, one can typologically call it a firm-based economy. Western corporations have clearly-delineated boundaries, institutionalized through highly developed accounting and personnel systems that Weber thought was so characteristic of Western capitalism. By contrast, the structure of Asian economies is network-based (Biggart and Hamilton 1992; Hamilton, Zeile, and Kim 1990; Redding 1991). Students of the Japanese economy (e.g., Gerlach 1992; Aoki 1990; Okumura 1982; Dore 1983, 1987; Orrù 1991; Orrù, Hamilton, and Suzuki 1989; Imai 1988; and Clark 1979) have shown conclusively that the business group networks in Japanese are both extensively and intensively organized, far surpassing the more ephemeral structures found in the United States and even Europe. The South Korean economy is no less network-based, although the networks are institutionalized quite differently (Amsden 1989; Biggart 1990; Hamilton and Biggart 1988; Kim 1991). The same is true for the Taiwan economy (Numazaki 1991b; Hamilton and Kao 1990; Greenhalgh 1988; Hamilton and Biggart 1988). Although the economy in the People's Republic of China has until recently been a socialist economy based on state ownership, its recent, very rapid development in the private sector appears to be equally network-based.

Although these networks throughout the region certainly have economic characteristics and give Asian businesses comparative advantages in the marketplace, their organizational foundations are, to use Granovetter's (1985) term, "embedded" in networks of normative social relationships. Asian enterprises do not have clearly delineated boundaries, so much so that Redding (1991) describes them as weak firms in strong networks. Scholars, of course, vary in how to explain the pervasiveness and tenacity of these networks, and Western businessmen have been so stunned by competition from them that they have tried, with mixed success, to imitate their organizational structure and business practices. The only adequate explanation for their structure and character, however, must be derived from organizational logics that have been developed and institutionalized historically by East Asian societies (Hamilton and Biggart 1988). This is merely to restate, for the case of Asian economies, Weber's conclusion about the development of capitalism in the West.

Has Western capitalism become the model of global civilization? Or are the world's civilizations giving rise to their own versions of capitalism, each with their patterns of development and their own trajectories? The Weberian answer developed in this chapter must be seen as highly tentative, but a fully developed answer is an extremely important goal, not only for economic sociology, but also for a practical understanding of the continuing transformation in the world economy and of our role in it.

Notes

1   The term refers loosely to an advanced state of human society. According to the compact edition of the *Oxford English Dictionary*, the first use of the term with this meaning occurred in Boswell's biography of Samuel Johnson: "On Monday, March 23, I found him (Johnson) busy, preparing a fourth edition of his folio Dictionary. He would not admit *civilization*, but only *civility*. With great deference to him, I thought *civilization*, from *to civilize*, better in the sense opposed to *barbarity,* than *civility*." The term refers now, more typically, to an area delineated by a common, highly developed *system of societies*. A civilization, like Western, Hindu, or Chinese civilization, may contain many societies and many states, and these societies and states may have changed many times over many centuries, but despite all the differences across time and space there remains a common integrating system of institutions and meaning patterns. In the most general sense, then, a civilization represents a *legitimate* ordering of the world, an articulated arrangement of appropriate powers at both the institutional levels of action and the symbolic levels of meaning.

2   This tradition today is relatively small when compared with the strong-state literature. For the liberal interpretation, see Hartz (1955) and Weinstein (1968). For some very recent interpretations following this line of reasoning, with an added international twist, see Michael Porter (1990) and Robert Reich (1992).

3   For a very interesting example of such an approach see John Meyer's world system state-centered approach (Meyer and Hannan 1979; Thomas *et al.* 1987; Scott and Meyer 1994).

4   North (1990) has somewhat changed his position in his most recent book, where he attempts to develop a more complex economic theory of institutions and institutional change.

5   Braudel's account of the rise of capitalism is compatible with a Weberian interpretation, but, unlike Weber, Braudel does not systematically go beyond the material base and daily routine to link economies to larger institutional environments. For a fine comparison of Weber's and Braudel's approaches to explaining the rise of capitalism, see Roth and Schluchter 1979: 166–93.

6   For additional works summarizing Weber's life and works, especially on civilizational topics, see particularly Bendix (1977), Roth and Schluchter (1979), Turner (1981), Schluchter (1989) and Whimster and Lash (1987).

7   This phrase and a synopsis of his conclusions concerning Western uniqueness are found in the "Author's Introduction" (Weber 1958 [1904–5]: 14–15) written for "The Economic Ethics of the World Religions" but published as an introduction to Talcott Parsons's translation of *The Protestant Ethic and the Spirit of Capitalism*.

8   By the beginning of the twentieth century, Weber had altered his epistemological position in a way that allowed him to distinguish between the natural and the human sciences (Oakes 1988). Weber maintained that, for the human sciences, including economics, reality could never be captured adequately in a set of law-like propositions, such as those used in the natural sciences. Instead, the human

sciences should aim, not at discovering general laws, but rather at explaining the complexity of historical changes. Science in this context should strive to achieve an objective understanding of and historically adequate explanations for the complexity of human life and culture. Any human science that tried to isolate the truth in its concepts, Weber felt (1949 [1905]: 103), was wrong-headed. Scientisms eluded practitioners by moving their focus from the accurate study of what really is to a vision of what theories say life ought to be. The aim of the human sciences, therefore, should be objectivity, and the goal of objectivity should be to disentangle analytically the complexity that exists as an irreducible part of reality. Accordingly, concepts appropriate to the study of society could not be "valid" representations of historical reality, but rather only one-sided tools by which the real world could be understood. This epistemological position served the basis for Weber's conception of ideal types.

9 Weber's key insights into the nature of institutions occurred shortly after he published his study on ancient civilizations, and constituted what Wolfgang Schluchter (1989: 3–52) calls Weber's "second breakthrough", an advance equivalent to his first breakthrough with his development of ideal-type methodology. The insights appear to have crystallized first in his study on *The Rational and Social Foundations of Music* (1958 [1921]). Unpublished in Weber's lifetime, this short study allowed Weber to explore how to describe the notion of scientific rationalism in more analytic terms. Weber proposes a technical typology of music, which included such concepts as pentatonicism, tonality, solmization, and polyvocality. Weber's analysis sought the distinctive qualities of Western music and the forces that led to its systematic development. The study was broadly comparative, with contrasts to every musical system throughout the world on which Weber could find detailed information. Weber asked why and how Western music, despite so many similarities with other musical systems, became the only system of music that generated such dynamic changes in musical techniques, in harmony, in instrumentation, in composition, and in the very production of music itself. Weber's answer in this study centered on the fact that Western music became an institutionalized sphere of activity, an area of routine experience peopled with roles and relationships and governed by calculable rules. From this study emerged Weber's concept of rationalism. Shortly afterward, using the same methodology, Weber applied these theoretical insights almost simultaneously to political domination as an arena of institutionalized activity, and to a comparative analysis of China. At this point, Weber's civilizational approach comes into clear focus. As in his analysis of music, Weber's emphasis in both studies remained on explaining the uniqueness of the West.

10 Starting around 1914, Weber began making civilizational comparisons in developed case studies of the world religions, first in an essay on Confucianism and Taoism, and then over the next five years or so in additional essays on Hinduism, Buddhism, and Ancient Judaism, all of which were eventually published under the title "Die Wirtschaftsethik Der Weltreligionen" (The economic ethics of the world religions). "The object of study", he wrote, "is in every case the treatment of the question: What is the economic and social singularity of the Occident based upon, how did it arise, and, especially, how is it connected to the development of the religious ethos?" (cited by Schluchter 1989: 471).

11 Weber was also very clear about this point in his essay on "The Social Psychology of the World Religions". He wrote (1946: 267–8) that "externally similar forms of economic organization may agree with very different economic ethics and, according to the unique character of their economic ethics, how such forms of economic organization may produce very different historical results. An economic ethic is not a simple 'function' of a form of economic organization; and just as little does the reverse hold, namely, that economic ethics unambiguously stamp the form of the economic organization."

12 When many sociologists apply Weber's understanding of the West, they prefer to use only a small portion of Weber's institutional analysis in their own work. Organization specialists, for instance, use Weber's formulation of bureaucracy as an ideal type in their descriptions of the organization of modern businesses. Roth (Roth and Schluchter 1979) has called this use of Weber "creative misinterpretation".

13 See Hamilton (1984) for an analysis of S. N. Eisenstadt's historical comparative methodology, in which the theoretical positions of Parson, Weber, and Eisenstadt are compared.

14 The exact quotation from "The Social Psychology of World Religions" (Weber 1946: 280) is as follows: "Not ideas, but material and ideal interests, directly govern men's conduct. Yet very frequently the 'world images' that have been created by 'ideas' have, like switchmen, determined the tracks along which action has been pushed by the dynamics of interest."

15 "The occidental church", Weber wrote (1978 [1922]: 555), "is headed not only by a personal transcendental god, but also by a terrestrial ruler of enormous power, who actively controls the lives of his subjects. Such a figure is lacking in the religions of Eastern Asia."

16 "The occidental church", said Weber (1978 [1922]: 555), "is a uniformly rational organization with a monarchical head and a centralized control of piety."

17 Weber (1978 [1922]: 1159–63) calls the later type of rule a theocracy.

18 Weber explicitly contrasted the disintegration of the household from the *oikos* (1978 [1922]: 370–84).

19 In discussing the individuation process that undermined the household in the late Middle Ages, Weber wrote (ibid.: 379):

> What is crucial is the separation of household and business for accounting and legal purpose, and the development of a suitable body of laws, such as the commercial register, elimination of dependence of the association and the firm upon the family, separate property of the private firm or limited partnership, and appropriate laws on bankruptcy. This fundamentally important development is the characteristic feature of the Occident, and it is worthy of note that the legal forms of our present commercial law were almost all developed as early as the Middle Ages – whereas they were almost entirely foreign to the law of Antiquity with its capitalism that was quantitatively sometimes much more developed.

20 In fact, with the coming of the scientific revolution, the church official had considerably less knowledge about the world than others. "Philosophy", Galileo wrote, "is written in this grand book, the universe, which stands continually open to our gaze. But the book cannot be understood unless one first learns to comprehend the language and read the letters in which it is composed. It is written in the language of mathematics, and its characters are triangles, circles, and other geometric figures without which it is humanly impossible to understand a single word of it; without these, one wander about in a dark labyrinth" (*The Assayer* [1623], quoted by Nelson 1975: 370–1).

21 To be sure, the history of each market institution can be pushed back into earlier eras. Banks certainly existed by the nineteenth century, as did corporations and insurance companies. However, much as music had been transformed in the seventeenth and eighteenth centuries, economic institutions in the nineteenth century became integrated under a common logic and became subject to comprehensive rationalization processes, which as thoroughly transformed them from their pre-nineteenth-century forms.

2 Why no capitalism in China?

Negative questions in historical, comparative research[1]

Why no capitalism in China? Negative historical questions are always difficult to answer convincingly, but that has not prevented this particular
question from being among the most frequently asked in comparative
historical research.

Max Weber's (1951) answering of the question is perhaps the best-known
example from sociology, but he is neither the first nor the last Westerner to
ask why China is not more like Europe. In fact, to use China as a standard
against which to measure the stature of the West is a recurring tactic in
Western historiography. Even if one excludes travel books and missionary
accounts, genres that date from the time of Marco Polo, the practice of
using China to examine Europe is still old. It begins in the sixteenth century,
becomes an accepted style of argument during the Enlightenment, and is
used then by such illuminates as Leibniz, Montesquieu, Smith, Berkeley,
Goldsmith, and Voltaire.[2] China and India are Hegel's examples of despotism, societies "outside the World's history". The same two also provide
Marx with examples of the Asiatic mode of production, a form of economy
without contradictions, an economy that produced a "permanent immo-
bility" in society, that was "enslav[ed] beneath traditional rules". It was
common for missionaries, merchants, and scholars to write disparagingly of
China, as did E. H. Parker, a late-nineteenth-century sinologist and an
authority Weber used in his essay on China. "With Chinese law", wrote
Parker, "we are carried back to a position whence we can survey, so to
speak, a living past, and converse with fossil men" (Jamieson 1921: 6).

When nineteenth-century writers asked why China was so backward, they
were offering not an assessment of China, but rather an interpretation of
the West. They found the sources of Western superiority in racial composition, in Christian beliefs, in minimal government and free markets, and in
the contradictions of Western society, and they found the sources of Chinese
backwardness in the lack of these.

Negative questions in comparative historical research today often reveal
the same logic, if not always the same conclusions. To trace the causes of a
unique event or pattern in one society or a small group of societies, it is
often useful to test one's interpretation in a society or societies where the

event did not occur. For instance, de Tocqueville (1955) shows that a look at the absence of revolution in England and Prussia helps to pinpoint the causes and consequences of the French Revolution. In this instance, the method of asking negative questions is sound, and is an important technique of good historical research, because it is a test for uniqueness, perhaps the only such test available to historians. And, after all, uniqueness is a comparative claim, as well as a presumption underlying much historical research.

But what does the answer to a negative question reveal about the societies in which the unique event does not occur? For example, what does one learn about England and Prussia from de Tocqueville's interpretation of France in *The Old Regime and the French Revolution*? Undoubtedly one learns many interesting facts, but the integration of those facts into a comprehensive theory only occurs for France; one does not learn what is unique to England or to Prussia. The causal unity of elements is preserved for the positive case, but destroyed for the negative cases. The analytic elements of a negative case become examples of categories of cases (e.g., of societies with serfdom intact or of countries without central cities) and not the critical features of a unique society in its own right. Therefore, what one learns about a society presented as a negative case should always be viewed cautiously, with the knowledge that what makes England England and Prussia Prussia cannot be discovered fully in a theory about France.

Similarly, what makes China China cannot be learned from a theory about Europe. Yet a large part of the conventional sociological knowledge about China, and by implication about other non-Western societies as well, has precisely this source, stemming from its use as an example of a society without capitalism, as a stereotype set against the distinctiveness of the West.

In this chapter I want to analyse the organization of late-imperial Chinese commerce, not as a negative case, but rather as something to be explained in its own terms. As a part of this explanation, I will critically examine the answers that sociologists and historians have given to the question, "Why no capitalism in China?" As a first step I will summarize the theories of Western capitalism used to identify the critical factors blocking economic development in China. I will then evaluate these factors in the course of outlining the institutional framework of late imperial Chinese commerce. I will conclude by arguing that negative questions – in this case, "Why no capitalism in China?" – provide misleading answers and should not be used when one is attempting to develop theories of non-Western societies.

Theories of no capitalism

Since Weber, many scholars with different historical interests and theoretical persuasions have sought the reasons for the absence of capitalism in China, including interpreters of Western history (e.g. Moore 1966; Wallerstein

1974; Braudel 1982; Wolf 1982), interpreters of Asian economic development (e.g. Levy 1949; Jacobs 1958; Wittfogel 1957), and interpreters of Chinese civilization (Feuerwerker 1958; Balazs 1964; Needham 1969a; Elvin 1973; Murphey 1974; Myers 1980; Roxman 1981). The answers they offer are many and varied and often excellent. I will not try to present the complexity of their answers here, because their works are very different, as different as the magnificent scholarship of Braudel and Needham. Rather my aim is to summarize what these authors see as the key factors blocking the development of capitalism in China. Although it simplifies their arguments, the best way to accomplish this is to outline the three theories of Western capitalistic development that most scholars use to locate China's deficiencies. These are the class, market, and "Protestant ethic" theories of capitalism. Despite their varying interpretations, most scholars use one or more theories of Western capitalism to explain, in Rhoads Murphey's words (1970), "what went wrong" in the development of China.

Class theories of no capitalism

The theory most frequently used to explain the absence of capitalism in China draws on the least sophisticated theory of European development. This is the simplified Marxian theory that the bourgeoisie constituted the fundamental force for capitalist development in feudal Europe. Out of the tensions generated within feudal society, the bourgeoisie created the material conditions that eventually led to the development of capitalism. This theory emphasizes the class components of the bourgeoisie – merchants, artisans, and agricultural capitalists – and centers on factors of production, commercial techniques, and relations with other groups. It has long been held that the autonomy of merchant groups from political authorities, a right gained early on with city charters, was an important factor in Europe's development of capitalism.

Using this explanation of capitalism, many writers find one of China's shortcomings in the weakness of its merchant class. They disagree somewhat on the source of the weakness. Several (Balazs 1964; Wakeman 1975: 43–4; Jacobs 1958: 84–8, 118–20; Wittfogel 1957; Weber 1951: 13–20) note Chinese cities lacked charters to serve as foundations for merchant autonomy. Others (Skinner 1976; Weber 1951; Murphey 1974: 54) note the divisive, particularistic character of merchant groups and their predominant mode of organizing into *landsmannschaften*, the German term for groups of fellow regionals called *huiguan*.

In addition to these lesser factors, most (Jacobs 1958; Moore 1966: 174; Wittfogel 1957: 255–6; Braudel 1972: 585–95) argue that the merchant class was weak because the state apparatus kept it that way. The state's power, these writers believe, was decisive in two ways. First, the direct power of the state, as exercised by officials, forcibly controlled commerce; state power, writes Balazs (1964: 41), was "all pervading". Second, the state was also an indirect force, because it set standards of prestige and gave direction to the aspirations of the able. The officially approved scale ranked the literati highest and the merchants lowest. Accordingly, wealthy merchants and especially their sons always turned from their class; they bought land and sometimes degrees, wore Confucian finery, and grew their fingernails long. They became non-productive gentry. Balazs (1964: 44), whose writing from the viewpoint of class theory is the most important and the most often cited, summarizes "the essential difference" between China and the West as follows: "While the Western town was the seed-bed and later the bulwark of the bourgeoisie, the Chinese town was primarily the seat of government, the residence of officials who were permanently hostile to the bourgeoisie, and thus always under the domination of the state."

Market theories of no capitalism

The market theories downplay the role of any particular class, and instead stress the workings and autonomous force of market factors. Various interpretations stress different factors and place different evaluations upon the growth of market economies. A Marxian reading, such as that by Karl Polanyi (1957; Polanyi *et al.* 1957), would find capitalism generated when the economic sector becomes separated from other institutional sectors and when land, labor, and capital become commodities. The growth of such a market economy forces the substance of the old order to give way and creates in its place capitalist institutions, institutions upon which new class privileges can be built. Structural functional theorists of modernization (Smelser 1959, 1963; Levy 1972; Eisenstadt 1973), basically in agreement with a Polanyi interpretation of the market's power to destroy traditional society, further maintain that this change is a necessary prelude to industrialization.

When used to pinpoint the reasons for China's poor economic showing, market theories locate China's recalcitrance quite differently from class theories. Whereas class theories stress weak merchant groups, market theories focus on market constraints, and on the absence of a free market. Market theorists, however, disagree among themselves as to the source of the constraints, as to whether China's traditionalism or Western imperialism bound the marketplace and prevented capitalism from developing.

Most sinologists (Feuerwerker 1958; Hou 1963, 1965; Skinner 1964, 1977; Elvin 1973; Murphey 1974; Myers 1980, 1991; Roxman 1981), including users of both Marxian and orthodox economic interpretations, find that market traditionalism held China back. They argue that China's economy, while market oriented, was unlike a capitalist market economy and that the West's economic influence in Asia throughout the nineteenth century was insufficient to upset traditional marketing patterns. These sinologists find three sources of market traditionalism. First, traditionalism came out of particularistic merchant groups, which developed rigid, guild-like organizations and monopolistic practices that stymied free market flows of commodities and hindered the development of capitalistic exchange relations. Second, traditionalism also stemmed from the marketing structure which, by late-imperial times, as Skinner (1964, 1977) shows, filled China's landscape with petty markets and complex systems of distribution that centered on regional urban hierarchies. Western encroachments were unable to eradicate quickly this extensive structure of intensive markets, as well as the practices and local culture nurtured by marketing communities. Third, the rapid population growth occurring during the last dynastic period (1644–1911) created conditions of increasingly reduced resources, which accelerated competition for available resources and produced a surplus of labor relative to the tasks at hand. These conditions favored the use of simple labor-intensive tools and hindered the adoption of industrial technology. These three factors maintaining traditionalism in the marketplace caused the late imperial economy to enter what Mark Elvin has called (1973: 298–316; 1972) a "high level equilibrium trap", a situation of "quantitative growth and qualitative standstill". In contrast with the West, these writers maintain, imperial China was economically static, an example of "growth without development" (Myers 1974: 77, 1980: 49; Huang 1980, 1985, 1990).[3]

Unlike those using class theory, those using some version of a marketing theory of capitalism find that the Chinese state was a relatively unimportant factor in China's backwardness. None the less, two noted scholars, Wallerstein (1974) and Fairbanks (1968), step back from scrutinizing the details of the market and take the longer view, namely that, even though the state did not interfere in the marketplace, it was still the state that controlled China's fate. According to Wallerstein, Chinese rulers opted toward maintaining the integrity of their empire and not expanding beyond the Chinese frontier to build state-supported networks of overseas trade. Western states, on the other hand, were small and competitive and had to rely on revenues from international trade to sustain their political regimes. World conquest meant little to the Chinese officials, but a lot to European rulers. On balance, says Wallerstein (1974: 63), China "was burdened by an imperial political structure".

The Protestant ethic theory of no capitalism

Of the three sets of theories used to explain Western capitalism and Chinese backwardness, Weber's Protestant ethic thesis is the least often used, and when it is pressed into service, it is usually secondary to class or market explanations. In this role, the thesis represents a pale imitation of the complex historical comparisons that Weber made between China and the West in both *Economy and Society* and his essay on China, and instead becomes equivalent to the simpleminded charge that Chinese values were not right for capitalism.

Weber's assessment of China was far more complex than this.[4] Weber analysed institutions and the social thinking and practices that went into making institutions. His essay on China was less concerned with Chinese developmental trends than with testing, through contrasts with China, the developmental trends of Western civilization. Weber had spent a lifetime trying to understand these trends; hence it is not surprising that he asked, "Why no capitalism in China?" in order to test his historical theories of Europe.[5]

In Weber's view, China and the modern West differed in all the major institutional spheres: in the economy, in social structure, in political organization, and in religious institutions. Some differences were relatively small (e.g., urban division of labor, Weber 1951: 96–7), some were larger and more significant (e.g. divided European vs. united Chinese rule, 1951: 33–62), but on balance all of them could be read as showing that, although in antiquity the West and China were similar in most regards, the West had since altered greatly in ways that China had not.[6] The explanation for Western trends consists of two parts. First, claimed Weber, in the West the structure of domination had changed from its patriarchal foundation, what Weber typologically termed "traditional domination", to a foundation based upon laws and formal modes of reasoning. But in China the patriarchal grip was unbroken. Second, in asking how it was that the underlying logic of domination in the West had altered, Weber found that Western heterodox movements, and sectarian ways of life, had repeatedly challenged the supremacy of institutions based upon orthodox principles, principles that kings and popes had used to justify their practices since antiquity. In China, heterodox movements never offered Confucian orthodoxy much of a test, because Confucianism was so much oriented to conduct in this world and so little directed to otherworldly matters. But in the West, believed Weber (1951: 237), "The great achievement of ethical religions, above all of the ethical and asceticist sects of Protestantism, was to shatter the fetters of the sib." Emerging from patriarchalism, the West formed new logics and new justifications for institutions. These institutional innovations, as it turned out, were necessary preconditions of capitalism. But China remained patriarchal and so without the conditions that might have been conducive to an independent origin to capitalism.

Weber's Protestant ethic thesis is hardly an equation of values and capitalism. Even so, many misread Weber and search for non-Western equivalents to Protestant asceticism or, quite simply, state that the Chinese were "burdened with the 'rationality' of its value system" (Wallerstein 1974: 63). Given the simplistic readings of Weber's thesis, it is not surprising that most scholars make this secondary to a class or market explanation for China's lack of capitalism. However, because Weber's theory is among the most complex ever offered for the origins of Western capitalism, it should also be seen as one of the most challenging explanations for China's lack of capitalism. But, this granted, Weber still offered an integrated historical interpretation only of Europe, and not of China.

Each of these three theories of Western capitalism suggests reasons why China did not follow a like course. Although it is true that such theories about the West help to delineate features of China's economy, it is also the case that these features, even when put together, do not produce a clear, unified understanding of how China's imperial economy actually worked. Instead, China emerges as a society with a strong state, with a traditional market, and with pacifying religions. So portrayed, China becomes stereotyped as the reverse image of the West. However valuable such insights may be, and in the conclusion to this chapter I will argue that they are more misleading than valuable, they none the less do not stack up to be a theory that explains the details of Chinese economic and social history in the same way that these theories of capitalism illuminate the details of Western history. In order to fashion a developmental history of the Chinese economy, the role of the state or the nature of market constraints might be important to examine, because they were certainly relevant in the West. But that they were important in the West does not mean that they are equally important in China or important in the same way.

To develop an analytic understanding of Chinese society that is comparable to our understanding of Western economies, one needs to develop concepts and theories in the same way that they were developed in the West, that is, through a close contextual analysis of the society in question. Once an understanding of the institutional conduct of the Chinese economy has been reached, then and only then is there a basis for cross-cultural comparisons designed to illuminate the Chinese economy.

The organizational structure of late-imperial Chinese commerce

How does one go about achieving an independent understanding of a set of social practices? Although there are many answers to this question, it is certain that at some point and in some way analysts should attempt to understand social practices from the participants' points of view. This is the much heralded and much criticised approach that Weber called *Verstehen*. In historical research, most criticisms of *Verstehen* suggest that analysts, removed from their subjects in time and space, cannot possibly know what historical actors had on their minds. Although this assertion is absolutely correct, it misses the level of analysis that Weber argued was necessary for good historical research. Weber did not want to know the private reasons that motivate people's actions; he always maintained that such reasons were diverse, often contradictory or uninformed, and, anyway, do not constitute a sociological level of analysis.[7] The level of analysis that Weber, as well as most historians, strove for was not individual knowledge, but rather the knowledge of a social world that participants share, what sociologists nowadays would call a normative framework. Weber was after public knowledge, the shared understandings that inform the actions of all genuine participants.

Looking at Chinese commerce as an institutional sphere in which there exists shared understandings of conduct, one is struck by three seemingly contradictory features, which I describe here as general conclusions reached by most analysts.

First, by all accounts, the Chinese domestic economy during most of the Qing period was exceedingly vigorous. Although it is impossible to judge its accuracy, a comment by Rhoads Murphey (1974: 23) is probably not an exaggeration: "The absolute levels of Ming and Ch'ing [Qing] commerce were extremely large. . . . What evidence we have . . . suggests even in per capita terms a level of inter-provincial trade equal to or greater than European levels as late as the beginning of the nineteenth century. The abso-lute total was of course far greater." The data that would allow such a conclusion are meager; for China we lack the documentation – the tax rolls and the merchant account books – that makes estimates for early-modern Europe, such as those of Braudel (1972), so impressive and revealing. None the less we do know that the bulk of trade throughout China was in daily necessities, in rice and other food stuffs, in cotton and silk cloth, in pottery and ceramics. There was a lively trade in luxury goods as well; this trade supplied the finery that was so important in marking the station of China's rural and urban elites, and these elites were spread throughout China and were not concentrated in a central city, in a London or a Paris. Even allowing for our inability to measure precisely the level of Qing commerce, we must still accept the conclusion not only that commerce was thriving, but, as a condition of its vigorousness, that it was also continuous and predictable.

It is this continuity and predictability that needs to be examined if one is to understand late-imperial commerce, but these become problems for expla-nation when matched with a second, equally well-established conclusion; namely, that the conduct of commerce in late-imperial China was a complex sphere of activity that established itself outside the normal jurisdiction of the imperial government.[8] Sybille van der Sprenkel (1977: 613) states this conclu-sion as forcefully as anyone has: "The magistrate's court was not the venue for the adjustment of commercial disputes. . . . Imperial law on [commerce] never having developed beyond the concern to enforce ethical norms and safeguard the public interest [left people] to pursue their activities locally with a minimum of interference . . . and without benefit of court adjudication. In other words much was left to unofficial social organization." Of course, the government played an active role in regulating commercial activity in its offi-cial monopolies on foreign trade, salt, porcelain (from the government factory), and several other lesser items. But in the main, and with the excep-tion of its official monopolies, the Ming and Qing governments did not determine the value of commodities, enforce contracts, set standards for weights and measurements, or even specify the medium of commercial exchange. The government played no significant role in establishing credit institutions, in creating commercial insurance, in setting acceptable interest rates, or even in backing its own paper currency. Beyond occasional attempts at taxation of commodities in transit (which was only institutionalized after 1853), government officially made no attempt to regulate the distribution or to tax the sale of goods. The imperial government did build and maintain the Grand Canal, which certainly stimulated commerce by allowing Beijing and northern China ready access to the products of the agriculturally rich areas in Central and South China. And state officials usually did uphold merchant codes when litigation involved them in disputes concerning merchants. But even so, the late-imperial state itself was relatively unimportant in establishing, implementing, and maintaining economic institutions in regard to the means and methods of production, distribution, and exchange.

Besides having little to do with the institutions of trade, the government also did little to control commercial participation.[9] It made no effort to define who would be a merchant or an artisan beyond the confines of its own monopolies. Laws of hereditary succession in some occupations, enforced as late as the early Ming period, gave way to a policy of non-interference. Nor did the government intrude into any aspect of commercial organizations, either in their rules or in their power over members and non-members alike, or in their control of the marketplace.

Those scholars arguing that the state controlled commerce make their case, for late-imperial China,[10] on the grounds that officials of the state regularly counted on liberal merchant bribes to supplement the squeeze from agriculture, and that merchants were powerless against such demands. Although it is true that merchants regularly paid bribes, the case for the state control of the merchant class is considerably overdrawn. In fact, the opposite view, that officials encouraged commerce, is probably more tenable. Because they had to rely heavily on revenues beyond land tax to finance district-level administration, officials usually tried to maximize their take by encouraging trade, by moderately squeezing it, and by themselves investing in it. But regardless of which side of the argument one favors, it still seems certain that neither the state through its policies nor the officials through their informal practices can be credited with creating and maintaining the institutional continuity and predictability of late-imperial commerce.

Juxtaposing these two conclusions – commercial vigor, continuity, and predictability, on one hand, and the lack of a government-backed framework for mercantile activities, on the other – one is struck by the fact that China lacked one of the foundations of European commerce: economic institutions defined by law and backed by the kings' courts. And from this, the sociological question takes shape: how were institutions of Chinese commerce created and maintained that would support such a vast economy?

The answer to this question is deceptively simple. What the imperial government did not provide, merchant associations did.[11] The techniques of trade, the establishment and enforcement of commercial codes, orderliness in the marketplace, regulation of commercial participation – all these and more rested squarely on the economic foundation supplied by regional associations. But this answer, which I will explain in detail, immediately leads to the more complex question as to how merchant associations were actually able to do all this.

This question leads to the third conclusion. Chinese merchant associations, variously identified as *huiguan* and *gungcuo*, were overwhelmingly groups of outsiders in their places of business. These were regional associations, or *Landsmannschaften*. Virtually every study about commerce and urban social structure during the late-imperial period shows that such regional associations were among the most prominent forms of urban organization and the principal type of merchant organization.[12] In fact, there is very little evidence to suggest that there were important groups of home-town merchants anywhere in China. In large cities as well as in small, in Beijing as in Shantou (Swatow), merchants organized as non-natives. In this regard, China has no counterpart to the denizen guilds of Europe or *chonin* associations of Japan.

That nonlocal merchant clannishness was an important feature of Chinese commerce seems fairly well established. However, taking this conclusion into consideration makes the sociological question about the continuity and predictability of Chinese commerce a more complex one to answer. Now the question becomes, how did a large number of very clannish merchant groups create and maintain economic institutions that supported China's vast commercial system?

One gets the first clues to an answer to this through empirically examining clannishness in relation to the membership criteria of merchant associations.

Clannishness and group boundaries

Recent work traces the source of particularism in regional associations to two features of life relating to marketing communities.[13] First, regional associations are based on fellow regional or *tongxiang* ties that arise from what G. William Skinner calls "local-system loyalties", loyalties that are created in one's home area. The commonalties generated by propinquity were used as "mobility strategies" to further the goals of local systems in higher order cities. Skinner (1977: 613), who first formulated this interpretation, writes that "native-place associations in economic centers were a manifestation of the struggle (of local systems) to monopolize or control an occupational niche" – hence the clannishness.[14] Second, the very act of sojourning from small towns up the marketing hierarchy produced the need for some type of association that would give the sojourner protection and assistance in an unfamiliar location.[15] According to Golas (1977: 556), "As strangers and outsiders, (merchants) often met with discrimination at the hands of the local populace and naturally preferred to associate with others who shared the same hardships." Hence, combined with local system dynamics, the process of migrating itself heightened the particularism of regional associations.

The data on merchant groups, however, do not support this characterization of clannishness. If, as Skinner assumes, urban regional associations are mainly manifestations of market town parochialism, or, as he puts it, "local systems loyalties", then one might predict that fairly stable networks of cohesive regional associations would be distributed throughout China. For instance, one might expect merchants from Shantou or Guangzhou (Canton) or some other city in Guangdong province to have established organized networks of associations wherever they traded, in China as well as in Southeast Asia. Such networks then could easily be seen as "mobility strategies", as the means to promote the interests of local marketing communities. But without denying the importance of parochialism in rural marketing communities, one finds more evidence to support an alternative hypothesis, that clannishness was more rooted in urban, commercial conditions than in the ecology of niche-finding local systems. The evidence suggests that regional merchant associations were, in the main, constituted anew in each location and that they had very changeable regional labels as criteria for membership. In other words, although regional associations might have been clannish, the regional definitions around which clannishness cohered – *tongxiang* or same-place identities – were highly variable and took shape in response to the conditions of trade in the location of one's work.

In theory, an individual's native place was fixed to a specific location, usually the site of the localized lineage. But, as a way to identify oneself when away from home, one's native place in practice formed a very flexible identity. Consider, for instance, the Guangdong merchants, the group identified by Peng Chang (1957) as the most powerful merchant group in late-nineteenth-century China.

Within Guangdong province, it was impossible to find a consolidated provincial merchant group. The commerce in every major city was handled by merchants who came from and retained their ties to districts in the city's rural hinterlands. For instance, in the treaty port of Shantou (Swatow), the Shantou guild (*Wannianfeng*) became well known to Westerners for its almost total control of the trade which came through the city (Morse 1909: 53–7).[16] Although composed of local people, the guild organization was based on *tongxiang* ties. It was a federation of merchants who came from the six districts surrounding the port city. The governing body of the guild was divided into two parts – those who represented the three districts south and west of the city (Jieyang, Puning, and Chaoyang) and those who represented the three districts north and east of the city (Haiyang, Chenghai, and Raoping). In addition to this guild, there were two smaller regional associations of merchants from Guangdong in Shantou. One was the *Bashu Huiguan*, which was composed of Hakka migrants and shop owners from several further outlying districts, one of which was in Fujian province (Xingning, Changle, Pingyuan, Zhenping, Dabu, and Fengshun in Guangdong province, and Yongding in Fujian province). The other guild, the least influential of the three, was the Guangzhou *Huiguan* for people from the Guangzhou area (*Decennial Reports* 1882–91: 537–40).

In Guangzhou a similar situation prevailed. Guangdong merchants were divided into many different groups from the surrounding districts, each specializing to some extent in certain businesses. In addition to eighteen or more *huiguan* associations of merchants from outside the province, there were at least seventeen different districts in Quangdong represented in formal *huiguan* associations (Rhoads 1974: 103–8). Besides these *huiguan*, there were over 100 different guilds in Guangzhou representing specific trades. Many of these guilds were divided in area-specific subgroups. For instance, the native bankers' guild, the *zhongxintang*, contained over four-teen different sub-groups which represented at least seventeen districts in Guangzhou's hinterland (Anonymous 1932: 187–90).

Outside of Guangdong province, the same situation prevailed. In nine-teenth-century Hong Kong, the leadership of the Chinese community was controlled by wealthy merchants, most of whom were from two districts in Guangdong: Dongguan and Zhongshan. These individuals organized mutual aid and charitable associations as well as occupational guilds (Smith 1971; Lethbridge 1971). Even on the small island of Chang Zhou, which is located near Hong Kong island, there were three regional associations representing four different districts in Guangdong (Dongguan, Huizhou, Chaozhou, and Si Yi) (Hayes 1963: 96). In the city of Wuzhou in Guangxi province there was a Guangdong *Huiguan* which was divided into guilds, some, if not all, of which represented a trade or skill specific to an area (*Decennial Reports* 1892–1901, 2: 333–4). In such major commercial and administrative centers as Suzhou, Shanghai, Hankou, Beijing, and Guilin, merchants from Guangdong divided into four or more different regional associations.[17] In less noted commercial centers, or those further away from Guangdong, *tongxiang* definitions became more general. In Tianjin, the merchants from Fujian and Guangdong belonged to the same organization (*Decennial Reports* 1892–1901, 2: 592), the *Minyue Huiguan*, but in Nanjing the Guangdong and Guangxi merchants joined each other in an association appropriately called the *Liangguang Huiguan* (Two Guang) (*Decennial Reports* 1892–1901, 1: 434). The *Liangguang Huiguan* was also found in Fuzhou, Tainan, and Suzhou.[18] In many places there was a general association for all those from Guangdong province, such as in Zhenjiang, Niuzhuang, Wuhu, Ningbo, Xiamen (Amoy), Qiongzhou, and Longzhou. But in the same places one was just as likely to find another *huiguan* for merchants from a particular region in Guangdong, and almost certainly one would find intra-organizational divisions between merchants from different areas of Guangdong.[19]

This example could be added to many others, all of which reveal consid-erable variation in how merchants and tradesmen would identify themselves by using their native place.[20] To explain this variation, two factors seem particularly important. First is the location of an association relative to the native place of its organizers. The closer individuals were to their native place, the more geographically specific the regional label became. For instance, a person in his native district capital would identify with those who came from the same village or standard marketing town. In this context, the regional association might well take the form of a surname association, an occupational guild, or both. A person migrating to the provincial capital might identify with those from the same district, prefecture or marketing area as his own. Further from the native place, the individual might well belong to a provincial *huiguan*, each member of which claimed a native place somewhere in that province. Being so variable, the regional label around which an association organized itself almost certainly did not reflect an established group located in one's native place.

A second factor that seems equally important is the occupation of the association's members. If one looks at the many exceptions to the above generalization (i.e., the further an association is from its region of origin, the more general its regional label) two hypotheses emerge. First, the more restrictive a specialized or monopolized occupation was in terms of the number of people capable of being employed, the more regionally specific an associational label became.[21] Second, the more a particular city could absorb migrants in a variety of occupations (e.g., a commercially active or rapidly growing urban area) the more specific the associational label was likely to be.

For example, individuals from Shaoxing prefecture in Zhejiang province obtained a reputation for their administrative ability and were frequently hired as private secretaries by administrative officials (Skinner 1976). Accordingly, in major administrative centers one finds regional associations exclusively for people from Shaoxing prefecture, as in Jiujiang, Shanghai, Hankou, Guangzhou, Hangzhou, Tianjin, and Wuhu (He 1966). In less noted administrative centers, they joined with others from their provinces in the Zhejiang regional association. However, in Beijing, the foremost administrative center, four of the eight districts in the prefecture formed separate regional associations (He 1966: 28). Other examples include the merchants from Huizhou prefecture in Anhui (Skinner 1976), and the Shanxi bankers (Yang 1937).

Typically, the hinterland areas of a city are the ones most likely to supply the majority of individuals for a variety of petty trading and piecework occupations, and thus individuals from such areas often form a regional association to distinguish themselves from other individuals from the same hinterland. In the treaty ports of Haikou (Qiungchow) and Beihai (Pakhoi) in south China, individuals from the hinterland prefecture of Gaozhou formed an exclusive regional association. In the former port they specialized in import-export businesses; in the latter,

> [t]he members of the Kaochou [Gaozhou] guild are a . . . humble class, consisting principally of petty dealers, porters and chair coolies, trade interests being subordinated to individual affairs. It is essentially a working-man's "club" and has little or no influence outside its own immediate radius . . .
>
> (*Decennial Reports* 1882–91: 635, 652).

Similarly in the northern port of Yentai (Zhifu), in the province of Shandong, individuals from hinterland prefectures and districts predominated in those occupational pursuits, ranging from iron mill laborer to local import-export businesses that were not easily monopolized by small groups. Those occupations that were capable of being so monopolized were held by outsiders, particularly the Shantou merchants.[22]

These examples support the conclusion that the variability of *tongxiang* labels for regional associations can be better explained by commercial conditions than by what Skinner calls local system loyalties. Were parochialism such an active force, one would expect less variation among, and more precise regional definitions of, these regional associations. This conclusion is supported by the fact that there are only a very few instances known where regional associations, formed in different places by individuals from the same native place, were organizationally connected.[23]

Clannishness, trustworthiness, and market stability

While not denying the importance of hometown parochialism or of Skinner's characterization of marketing structure, I believe there are other factors, urban and economic ones, that both help explain more fully the clannishness of merchant associations and provide the important clues in explaining the continuity of Chinese commerce. These urban factors are generally neglected, or if noted, only mentioned in passing. To describe these urban factors, consider for a moment the role of merchant associations in creating and enforcing an environment conducive to continuous predictable commerce – a matter, I might note, of great importance to those coming from the countryside for the sole purpose of making money.

If one believes what is written in the extant constitutions and bylaws of regional associations, then one thing is certain. Merchants and artisans understood that the role of their associations was to stabilize the marketplace by laying a basis for trustworthiness. Consider the *huiguan* constitutions collected by MacGowan. Could the foundation of commerce be stated more clearly than it was in the constitution of the Guangzhou *Huiguan* in Beihai (Pakhoi)?

> It is hoped that the rules we have adopted will lead to uniformity of action and unanimity of feeling among our members, who are bound by ties of townsmanship, and in this way secure ourselves against gradual degenerations, while it will teach those outside the Guild that being of one mind in our determination to oppose wrong, unscrupulous merchants and bad characters will seek to avoid us, and so avert their own discomfiture . . .
>
> (MacGowan 1886: 136)

The recurring theme in the constitutions of associations shows that merchants and artisans formulated and enforced rules and regulations in order "to secure the confidence of those with whom (they) deal, that all may like to trade with (them)"; "The principles of gain-getting are uniform and constant"; by-laws are inviolate "in order that none may be deceived, thus securing permanent concord between sellers and buyers"; "In establishing commercial regulation justice should be of a durable character in matters of selling and buying" (MacGowan 1886: 146–8).

These associational rules, it should be noted, were not private documents that circulated only among members. Rather, they were public documents. Associations usually submitted their rules and regulations to the magistrate's office, so that in cases of disputes involving association members, the magistrate could consult the document to make a ruling.[24] Moreover, associations quite often had their rules and regulations engraved in stone and displayed for all to see. In fact, some of the largest collections of late imperial stone rubbings pertain to just these activities of merchant and handicraft groups (S. M. Jones, see Mann 1976).

It is clear from reading these associational rules that associations took on the task of instilling trustworthiness in the marketplace by attempting to regulate the commercial conduct of their members. They seemingly did this in two complementary ways, by establishing reliable economic standards and by building regionalized reputations. At this point it is useful to distinguish between the class and status aspects of regional associations.[25] On the one hand, regional associations laid down rules to govern the performance of individuals in specific occupational roles; these rules will be termed class regulations. On the other hand, associations required individual conformity to prescribed standards of behavior, regardless of one's occupation; these will be termed status regulations. Whereas class regulations attempted to supply reliable economic institutions, status regulations attempted to heighten reliability by limiting participation to specific categories of people. The former spell out the manner of action; the latter, the manner of person performing the action.

The class regulations of merchant guilds were precise. A banking guild specified, among other things, the "touch" of silver: "The standard for shoe silver is fixed at 992 parts of pure silver and 8 parts of alloy, and no person shall be allowed to cast shoes of another standard" (*Decennial Reports* 1882–91: 35). A tea merchants' guild set standards for grading the quality and quantity of tea (MacGowan 1886: 151–6). A carpenters' guild fixed the type and quality of work customers should expect, and a barbers' guild the type of service (e.g., no "ear-cleaning during the last six days of the year") (MacGowan 1886: 177–8; *North China Herald*, Nov. 24, 1893: 823). Even the guild of blind entertainers in Beijing laid out its requirements in a set of regulations that Burgess (1928: 103) describes as "the most complicated and detailed of any guild in the city".

If one considers the fact that the late-imperial Chinese state took no part in standardizing weights, measures, or currency, then it is apparent that such class regulations were essential to business continuity and predictability.[26] Weights and measures varied by locality, and within a specific locality they varied by trade.[27] The *dou*, a capacity measure, varied throughout the empire between 176 and 1,800 cubic inches. The length measure, the *chi* (a foot), differed by trade, there being a carpenter's foot, a tailor's foot, a land foot and so forth. Each of these in turn varied by location.

According to Morse's calculations, the *chi* in China ranged from 8.6 to 27.8 inches. Area measurements, such as the *mou*, showed the same variability, ranging from 3,840 to 9,964 square feet. But he also noted that, in each location, merchant guilds would standardize the practices within their trades, so that they became "perfectly recognized and accepted as the custom of the trade and place" (Morse 1908: 171).

Status regulations, though often less precise than class regulations, were usually far more encompassing. They delineated membership criteria. Though fluctuating between locations, membership criteria in any one location were clearly spelled out. For instance, according to the commissioner of customs in Chongqing, potential members to a regional association had to "prove themselves *bona fide* natives of the province whose guild they seek to join, and must produce proof of having belonged to one or other of the minor societies existing at their native place" (*Decennial Reports* 1882–91: 120). The *Wanzhou Tungxiang hui* in Hangchow had a similar regulation and stipulated that "all those (from the same native place) who are staying in this provincial seat can be admitted as members if they are upright . . . have proper occupations, and pay the regular annual fee" (Zhuang and Chen 1941: 60–1). Such particularistic restrictions were seemingly the basis of building a reputation of economic trustworthiness.

Besides membership criteria, status regulations established the requirements for intra-organizational participation. At a minimum, this participation took two forms, financial and judicial. All regional associations about which I have information made financial contributions a condition of membership. Some required dues, some a percentage of profit, some a levy on assets. Whatever the form or combination thereof, the contribution acted as a stimulus for more active participation in other spheres of associational activity and as a means to get members to recruit others who were non-members. For instance, the *Hanyang Huiguan* in Yichang taxed all boats belonging to members, required "workingmen, such as tailors or carpenters' hands" to pay monthly dues in addition to an initial entrance fee, and extracted from the workingmen's masters a percentage of their profits and an entrance fee and made them responsible for their employees' contributions. The regulations then stipulated that "Any member not paying his subscription is dealt with in accordance with the gravity of the offense, and is either fined or reported to the officials for punishment. Anyone giving his support to such a member is likewise fined" (*Decennial Reports* 1882–91: 158–9).

The requirement of monetary contributions was one of the chief means of making the association an autocephalous economic organization – a self-regulating autonomous organization directed toward the establishment of economic order. The implicit theme running through this type of regulation is that members of regional associations had the duty to check on the conduct of their compatriots, whether members or non-members. At times, though, the theme was boldly stated, as in the case of the bankers' guild in Wuhu: "Any person who denounces to the guild a banker who has infringed the rules shall receive one-half of the fine of 100 taels, while the other half will go to the funds of the guild" (*Decennial Reports* 1882–91: 289).

The other condition of intra-organizational participation was the requirement that all disputes and illegalities had to be adjudicated by the association before any other action was taken.[28] The first – and usually the final – arbitration of justice resided in the association itself. The regulations applied not only to commercial disputes, for which the association was usually the law-making body, but often to criminal cases as well. For instance, a regulation of the Guangdong *Huiguan* in Fuzhou stated that "Members of the club offending public law shall be brought up for examination by the executive committee, and, if the offense is proved, shall be surrendered to the local authorities" (*Decennial Reports* 1882–91: 429). Even if the local magistrate was called upon to make a judgment, the magistrate often followed the *huiguan*'s recommendation.[29]

These two types of intra-organizational participation helped to create and to substantiate a regionalized reputation for trustworthiness. Outwardly, the reputation was pursued by demonstrating the group's suitability for performing a class role (e.g., the honesty of Shansi bankers) or the quality of the group's goods (e.g., the excellence of Fujienese paper products). Inwardly, however, a reputation was shaped by the control an association could place upon its members, a message which was clearly stated by the Guangzhou *Huiguan* in Ningbo as follows: "We came thither a long way by sea, and if we do not stand well here for straightforwardness, we can acquire no wealth" (MacGowan 1886: 148).

These efforts to lay a basis for trustworthiness reinforced urban status groups. Individual credibility in the marketplace was a function of one's accountability, which, in turn, was a function of one's membership in a group that could force compliance to established standards of conduct. Thus one's credibility was an element of one's integrity within an organized group as much as it was of one's honesty with customers. One's trustworthiness became a facet of one's regional status, one's interactional stance, one's "face", with one's compatriots. In Europe, where honesty had a legal as well as a moral meaning, compliance could be extracted from the courts. But in China, it could only be extracted from the group to which a person belonged.[30] Therefore, the crucial aspect of trustworthiness was the cohesiveness and identifiability of an *actual* group, a group into which a person's personal honor was vested. In this sense, to be trustworthy and hence commercially reliable was to be clannish.

Clannishness, cohesiveness, and competition

The necessity of having a group to ensure both one's trustworthiness and market stability produced what might be called, loosely, "responsible monopolies" – economic organizations which exclusively controlled a specialized area in the marketplace, but did so benignly. The thrust of group formation was the calculated possibility of group solidarity, the equalization of commercial opportunity, and mutual trust in providing for a predictable marketplace. This goal could only be accomplished through obtaining a position of economic power. But the acquisition of economic power aimed not so much at the maximization of gain as the monopolization of opportunities. Anyone who would enter a trade was forced to do so through the doors of the guild. Any out-of-towner who would find employment was forced by circumstances to go to his regional association. In so far as the guilds and regional associations were one organization, a regional group effectively monopolized the opportunities available in an occupation. In many occupations, however, the two did not overlap neatly. In some, there would be several regionally defined guilds for the same occupation, and in others, there would be one guild divided into regional cliques. None the less, the complexity of factors influencing group formation probably favored a condition in which they overlapped, with the regional label adjusting itself so that it could accommodate the majority of the profession.

The monopolization of the opportunities allowed the regional association to set standards and fix prices, but did not allow them to maximize profits. Though competition might have been intense in the association, in the marketplace it was attenuated. "The traveler in China", says a nineteenth-century resident,

> . . . is generally struck by the uniformity in prices prevailing throughout a town or even a district. The cost of certain commodities is just the same in a large general store as in a small trader's shop, but the explanation is simple enough, since all prices are fixed by the local union, and all traders in the same class of goods must belong to the union.
>
> (Jernigan 1905: 244)

The monopolization of employment opportunities, therefore, militated against price competition. The two, however, always hung in tenuous balance.

Clannishness: an assessment

A final word here will help integrate what has been discussed so far about the economic role of regional associations. Clannishness, the term so often used to characterize regional associations, is more the result of urban life than of rural parochialism. To be sure, patrilineality and other features of life in the countryside intensified one's identification with one's native place and kept one's native place located somewhere in the countryside, outside of large urban areas. These features combined to make one's urban life a sojourn, an opportune urban adventure of ideally limited duration. None the less, the solidarity of regional associations and the pride in non-local institutions that their members exhibited was a means, recognized as such by members, to provide the marketplace with reliable economic institutions and to attract customers to their wares. The show of parochialism was in part an affectation, an air, supplied to assure one's customers of one's impartiality and credibility.

In this sense, clannishness was to business success in China what religious affiliation was to business success in frontier America.[31] On the latter, Max Weber says:

> Admission to the congregation is recognized as an absolute guarantee of the moral qualities of a gentleman, especially those qualities required in business matters. . . . It is crucial that sect membership meant a certificate of moral qualification and especially of business morals for the individual. . . . A sect . . . is a voluntary association of only those who, according to the principle, are religiously and morally qualified.
>
> (Weber 1958: 305–6)

In an analogous fashion, a regional identification was a function of one's associational membership, rather than of one's native place. To customers and clients, it was a guarantee, the only guarantee, that a person's class roles would be performed creditably; it was an outward manifestation of a web of coercive and binding relationships which restrained an individual's cupidity and made him moral; and it was a sign of honor, a badge to be worn proudly, for it outwardly, if ambiguously, reminded its bearers and non-bearers alike that the ultimate reward for present scrupulousness would lie elsewhere.

To members, a regional identification meant something more. To the jobless, it meant an avenue to seek assistance; to employers, a way to recruit workers whose demands would be limited. To recent immigrants it meant friends; to not-so-recent immigrants, a means to disperse favors and to build alliances. To the poor, it meant comfort and possibly a way to gain wealth; to the rich, a way to extend their wealth and become notables in their own right. In so far as merchant identity was certified by one's membership in an association, the regional label of the association meant opportunity even more than it meant compliance. However, opportunity came only through compliance. And compliance demanded clannishness.

Conclusion

This analysis of merchant organization is the first step toward understanding Chinese economic institutions apart from Western theories of economic development. The most important implication of this effort is not to try to explain the reasons why imperial China failed to develop capitalism, but rather why China had a socialist revolution. This is a positive instead of a negative question to answer, and one that is ultimately more important and vastly more answerable. It is also a question in which the fate of the traditional Chinese economy figures prominently. The traditional Chinese economy did not hold firm; *huiguan* merchant organizations crumbled in the twentieth century under the weight of wars, revolutions, and a socialist state. *Huiguans*, as they existed in the Qing period, have today disappeared from mainland China, though they still exist in Taiwan and Southeast Asia. An analytic analysis of late-imperial merchant organizations, such as the one given here, adds to the knowledge of nineteenth-century China that is so important in understanding the cataclysmic events of the twentieth century.

To explain the late-imperial economy only in terms of its failure to develop capitalism is to ignore or misinterpret the very questions that give the most help. In fact, even so partial an analysis as this shows an institutional dynamic to Chinese commerce that cannot be grasped by answering negative questions. Moreover, the answers given this question, which I outlined above, contain misleading conclusions, which lead to two fundamental misunderstandings about the institutional character of the Chinese economy. To conclude, I want to outline these misunderstandings.

The first of these misunderstandings is the characterization of the imperial Chinese state, in light of Western economic theories, as either strong or weak, depending on which theory is being used. A more adequate view of the imperial state is to see it, when compared with Western states, as neither stronger nor weaker, but rather different. It differed from Western states in so many ways that a comparative verdict of strength or weakness in regard to merchants is really to misunderstand the institutional focus of the Chinese state. The state not only did not claim jurisdiction over commerce and merchants, but, as I suggest elsewhere (Hamilton 1984b), was not founded on the concept of jurisdiction that was so central in Western political philosophy. Much more than in the West, the state in China rested upon what Geertz (1980: 13–15) describes as the "doctrine of the exemplary center", a doctrine that built a moral, rather than a legal, order based upon ideas of roles and duties instead of upon ideas of jurisdictions and wills. In late-imperial China, the state let merchants define and maintain their own roles and duties, and in so far as the definitions and means to control their number did not undermine the state's own roles, officials supported merchants and their regulations. Therefore, to find economic "backwardness" in the absence of city charters and in the lack of merchant autonomy is to misunderstand the nature of Chinese political order and the place of commerce in that order. States differ in the conceptual foundations upon which people justify power and build order, and to ignore these differences is to ask why the apple tree does not bear oranges and to explain this deficiency by the differences in the color of the blossoms.

The second of these misunderstandings is the characterization of the Chinese economy, in relation to Western theories, as "traditional" and as being unduly and unnaturally constrained. Here again the biases of Western economic theory, based upon notions of free markets and the "laws" of supply and demand, result in a misreading of Chinese commerce. Contracts, property rights, commercial law, and the whole sphere of privileges, rights, and freedom relating to merchants are simply absent in China, while these, in the West, form the very basis of market predictability and continuity. These also become the condition of what Western thinkers describe as a free market, which is the only context in which "laws of supply and demand" make sense. In late-imperial China, clannishness did not bind the market, but rather was the condition of its freedom, if by freedom one means the predictability that allowed for a "free" flow of goods. As I have argued in this paper, clannishness was a key source of market stability because it provided, and merchants were purposefully organized in this way so as to provide, guarantees that market roles would be performed credibly.

These two misunderstandings center on the Western conception of the marketplace as a legally defined sphere of activity. But, as in all other areas of life, the marketplace in late-imperial China was defined in moral terms. Merchant and artisan uprightness was the cornerstone of commercial activity. To be upright, to be moral as a merchant, was to be a member of an actual group, and to uphold group standards. The groups themselves were regional associations; the bond that both tied people to these associations and defined their morality was clannishness; and clannishness rested on the Chinese moral conception of what constituted a fellow regional, a person joined to another by *tongxiang* ties. As Tou (1942: 58) put it, "The collective symbolism of native place associations is bred in a society which centers upon ethical relations, and hence native place associations were ethical manifestations of these relations." By virtue of its ethical nature, clannishness provided the foundation for late-imperial Chinese commerce and for the predictability and continuity that it enjoyed.

The misunderstandings I have outlined here arise from interpreting China as a negative case, as a society that did not develop capitalism. But China is not a mirror image of the West. Rather it is an independent vision of how a society can be put together, and it must be understood in its own terms. Cross-cultural comparisons are an important means to fashion such independent understandings, but China should be treated as the positive case (not the negative), and accordingly, the concepts and the theories for analysis should take their meaning from China's historical experience.

Notes

1   I want to thank Kwang-ching Liu for his encouragement and critical readings of this and previous drafts, and to acknowledge Kai-wing Chow's assistance on some of the Chinese sources.
2   A good discussion of eighteenth-century European ideas about China is found in Dawson (1967).
3   Not all would agree with this thesis of China's pre-modern market traditionalism. A few sinologists (Wakeman 1975; Bergere 1968) and comparative sociologists

(Moulder 1977; Moore 1966; Isaacs 1951; Lasek 1983; Huang 1980) claim that China's backwardness stemmed as much, if not more, from Western imperialism as from traditional patterns. Drawing on Wallerstein's work, Moulder, in particular, argues that the crucial difference between China's and Japan's historical trajectory into the modern world was China's early entry and Japan's late entry into the world economy. Both societies, she maintains, had similar pre-modern economies. But, because of its early, forced opening, China became a peripheral zone of world capitalism, while Japan, because it had the opportunity to develop its indigenous economy without outside interference, developed into a late-blooming sector of the industrial core.

4 For a more complete analysis of Weber's assessment of China, see Hamilton (1984b) and the references cited there.

5 It is worth noting that the Protestant influence on the origins of capitalism is only one of the many theories that Weber was attempting to test in his studies of world religions. See Collins (1980) for a well-rounded statement of Weber's analysis of capitalism.

6 Weber's most explicit statement to this effect is found in his essay on China (1951: 231): "In the traits relevant for us, the further back one goes in history the more similar the Chinese and Chinese culture appear to what is found in the Occident. The old popular beliefs, the old anchorets, the oldest songs of the *Shi Jing (Shih Ching)*, the old warrior kings, the antagonisms of the philosophical schools, feudalism, the beginnings of capitalist developments in the period of the Warring States – all of which are considered characteristic – are more closely related to occidental phenomena than are the traits of Confucian China." Also see pp. 242–3.

7 For a collection of readings on the controversy over *Verstehen*, see also Truzzi (1974) and Oakes (1977). For an example of Weber's distinction between the personal and normative levels of analysis, see, in particular, Weber's discussion of power and domination (1978: 53). Here he defines power in terms of personal interests, and domination in terms of norms, and then argues that "the concept of power is sociologically amorphous. All conceivable qualities of a person and all conceivable combinations of circumstances may put him in a position to impose his will in a given situation. The sociological concept of domination must hence be more precise . . . "

8 A large number of scholars make this point, but few explore its importance. For some of the most explicit statements to this effect, see MacGowan (1886: 186); Morse (1909: 20); Otte (1928); van der Sprenkel (1962: 89–90; 1977: 613); Yang (1970); Mann (1972: 77; 1981); and Myers (1974; 1980).

9 In pre-modern economies, state control of merchant participation is more common than state control of economic institutions. For some comments on this form of state–merchant relations, see Hamilton (1978a).

10 I should note that many scholars make this case in regard to merchant–state relations before the beginning of the Ming dynasty (1368). For the early period, the case is quite different and the state did in fact exert much more direct control over merchants and their activities. By the Ming and Qing periods, however, the relationship had greatly altered, which is a fact not sufficiently understood.

11 Fewsmith (1983: 618) even goes so far as to describe the role of merchant associations as "an extra bureaucratic group fulfilling regulatory functions beyond the normal reach of the bureaucracy", as "associations whose authority derived from and complemented that of the state". Although the state certainly permitted these associations to flourish, it is a misreading of the political institutions of late-imperial China to argue that the authority of merchant associations derived from the state, a point I will expand upon in the conclusion.

12 The chief source on *huiguan* is He Bingdi (1966) and on urban associations in general, Skinner (1977).

13 A number of analyses have appeared since the original publication of this article that largely explain Chinese sub-ethnicity in terms of one of these two features. See Hershatter *et al.* (1996), particularly Chapters 9–11, for a review of some of this literature.

14 Skinner makes this argument in a number of locations: in his analysis of marketing structure (1964–5; 1977), in his analysis of Chinese villages (1971), and in his analysis of migration and social mobility (1976).

15 I make a parallel argument based on organization of temporary migration (Hamilton 1979).

16 Morse (1909: 53–7) identifies this as an example of a native guild as opposed to a *huiguan*, but as can be clearly seen both are based upon *tongxiang* (fellow regional) ties.

17 Suzhou: *Decennial Reports* 1892–1901, 1: 552–3; Shanghai: He 1966: 49; *Decennial Reports* 1892–1901, 1: 525; Hankou: *Decennial Reports* 1882–91: 191; He 1966: 42–3; Beijing: He 1966: 32; Guilin: *Decennial Reports* 1892–1901, 2: 292.

18 Fuzhou: *Decennial Reports* 1882–91: 428; Tainan: *Decennial Reports* 1882–91: 494; Suzhou: *Decennial Reports* 1892–1901, 1: 552.

19 In Zhejiang there was one regional association of Guangdong merchants, the Guangdong *Huiguan*, which was controlled by people of two different regional guilds, the Guangzhou and the Chaoan merchant guilds (*Decennial Reports*, 1892–1901, 1: 462); Niuzhuang: *Decennial Reports* 1882–91: 38. In Wuhu, there were two regional associations for Guangdong merchants, one specially for rice merchants of Guangzhou and Zhaoqing prefectures and the other for any individual from the province (*Decennial Reports* 1882–91: 290). Ningbo: *Decennial Reports* 1882–91: 384; Xiamen: *Decennial Reports* 1882–91: 522; in Qiongzhou, Guangdong merchants organized into three different regional associations composed of merchants from Shantou, Guangzhou, and Gaozhou areas (*Decennial Reports* 1882–91: 635). Longzhou: *Decennial Reports* 1882–91: 662.

20 A thorough search of the literature on merchants, artisans, and regional groups did not turn up a single case in which the organizational boundaries of associations established by migrants from any specific area did not exhibit considerable fluidity.

21 He (1966), Skinner (1976), and others make this point a central part of their explanations about origins of *huiguan*, and correctly so. Undoubtedly many merchant associations form in a wide variety of locations around the selling of a product that is grown in the native area. But the important point here is to clarify the sources of variation. Zhuang and Chen (1941) show, for instance, that in large merchant and worker associations there were usually many smaller native-place *huiguan,* and in large native-place associations, there were many subdivided units organized around (1) merchants of the same trade; (2) handicraft workers of the same profession; and (3) labor of the same kind of work. Some of their variation is explained later in the chapter.

22 According to the port's Commissioner of Customs (*Decennial Reports* 1882–91: 46–7):

> The Shandong merchants are subdivided according to districts as follows: the Jinanfu merchants import ... Piece Good, but export little; the Dengzhou and Laizhou merchants sell Silk; Huangxian merchants deal in Vermicelli. The Shantou merchants form a flourishing, powerful body; they import Sugar from, and export Beancake, Vermicelli, and Salt Fish to Shantou, successfully crushing any competition as far as the trade with their native place is concerned. Shandong merchants have, however, taken the

trade with other places more into their own hands; for instance, the Guangzhou hongs trading between Yentai and Hongkong have fallen in number from twenty-two to eight, the Shandong firms having established branches in Hongkong. Still, as a rule, the import of the products of any place – such as Samshu and Paper from Ningbo, Beans from Niuzhuang (by junk), Sugar from Shantou and Amoy, Brass Buttons, Cassia Lignea, etc. from Canton – lies principally in the hands of, or is even monopolised by, natives of these places who have established firms here.

Of the petty occupational pursuits, the Commissioner says the following (*Decennial Reports* 1882–91: 54–5):

> The inhabtants (of Yentai) may be said to be constantly changing. Many natives leave the port for Tianjin and Niuzhuang, where they are employed as cargo coolies; others go to Vladivostock during summer to collect seaweed; others again, find employment as sailors on the vessels of the Beiyang Squadron. The vacancies thus caused are supplied by new-comers from all the surrounding districts, more especially from those of Laizhoufu and Tengzhoufu. . . . The iron-workers are chiefly natives of Liazhoufu, about 3,000 being boys from fourteen to twenty years of age.

23 See a discussion on this point in the record of the infamous Shantou (Swatow) Opium Guild case, *North China Herald*, Oct. 17, 1879, pp. 385–88.
24 Chang P. (1957: 28) cites some examples from Wuling merchant associations about merchants submitting their regulations to the local magistrate. The following is from tin utensil shops: "We now gather our fellow businessmen to discuss the selective re-establishment of previous regulations and the official has kindly permitted us to file our regulations with him for reference." Also see Tou (1942: 30).
25 I am using the terms "class" and "status" according to the definitions of Max Weber (1978: 926–39). Classes are categories of similar economic roles or similar positions in relation to the marketplace. Status groups or *Stande* are actual groups who share a specific "estimation of honor" and a "specific style of life".
26 For general discussions of currency in late imperial China see Yang (1952) and King (1965). The following remarks by the Blackburn Commission (Neville and Bell 1898: 179, 184, my emphasis) nicely summarize the currency conditions in nineteenth-century China and the sense of frustration that Westerners had in dealing with these conditions:

> The system of having a fixed weight of a given metal as a medium of exchange [sycee], is based on sound principles, but in China it is rendered intricate by confusing local variations both in the quality of the silver and the scale by which it is weighed . . . From this it will be seen that the value of a tael in one city may be much different from that in another, yet it is only by comparison that the tael varies, *for in each city the standard, both for purity and weight, is fixed and clearly defined* . . . So that in trading between province and province or city and city, all that is necessary is to take into account the difference in scale and the premium or discount, as the case may be, at which the local tael stands as compared with that of the place in which it is intended to transact business.

After explaining at length the difference between provincial sycee, they exclaimed:

> There is no space, nor is it necessary, to take note of the local variations in the tael and the cash in the small towns, for it will be seen from the above

brief description, in what a hopeless state of confusion the currency of China is.

The value of sycee (i.e., a determination of its weight and quality) was determined by the local banking guild, often in cooperation with other prestigious guilds. Thus if one wanted to know the value of his particular sycee in a specific location, he would go to the local *qianzhuang* (literally, money shop) which would determine its value. Sycee in the possession of prestigious guilds and banks was weighed, a "chop" (the guild's mark) was affixed to the silver certifying its quality and then passed without question. In many cases such chop marks became guarantees of quality.

27 Discussions of weights and measures are found in *Abstract of Information on Currency and Measures in China* (1889–90).

28 Of the numerous discussions of this point, the most important are Morse (1909) and van der Sprenkel (1962; 1977).

29 An example of this is cited in Tou Jiliang's study (1942: 35) of native-place associations. In Chongqing, "once the disputes between people of the same native place is settled by the joint committee of the Basheng [a federation of *huiguan* from eight provinces], the disputants would accept the judgment. But even if one did not accept it and appealed to the local government, the local official would still rule according to the judgment made by the Basheng."

30 In this sense, honesty was defined in terms of actual merchant group norms, and accordingly it was the group that had the duty to punish violations. In his usual decisive manner, Morse (1909: 27–8) summarizes the group's power over its members as follows:

> Their jurisdiction over their members is absolute, not by reason of any charter or delegated power, but by virtue of the faculty of combination by the community and of coercion on the individual which is so characteristic of the Chinese race. The method in which the jurisdiction is exercised is expressed in the rules of guild as follows: "It is agreed that members having disputes about money" (and, in practice, any other) "matters with each other shall submit their case to arbitration at a guild meeting, where every effort will be made to arrive at a satisfactory settlement of the dispute. If it proves impossible to arrive at an understanding, appeal may be made to the authorities; but if the complainant resorts to the courts in the first instance, without first referring to the guild, he shall be publicly reprimanded, and in any future case he may bring before the guild he will not be entitled to redress." This rule is expressed in modern language; a similar rule of another guild is more direct in its terms: "It is agreed that after a member of the guild, an individual or firm, has been expelled, all business relations with him shall cease, any member discovered to have had dealing with him, from sympathy or friendship, shall be fined 100 taels." In effect, sympathizers would also run the risk of being boycotted. The penalties for breach of the rules or unguild-like conduct range from a fine of candles for the temple, or a dinner of ten or a score or more plates, or a theatrical representation in the guild-hall or the temple, up to money fines of a considerable amount, and, in the last resort, to the cessation of business relations, the condemnation to trading catalepsy or death, the boycott.

31 Weber (1951: 99) also makes this connection in the case of China and America when he states: "In modern times, in equalitarian China just as in democratic America, the successful man has striven to legitimize himself socially by joining a highly esteemed club."

3   Chinese consumption of foreign commodities

A comparative perspective[1]

With considerable justification, Karl Marx and many later writers believe that a decisive factor in the nineteenth-century expansion of Western civilization was the distribution of commodities produced by capitalist factories. Marx (1959: 11) says, "Cheap commodity prices are the heavy artillery with which [the bourgeoisie] batters down all Chinese walls and forces the barbarians' intensely obstinate hatred of foreigners to capitulate. . . . It compels them to introduce what it calls civilization into their midst, i.e., to become bourgeoisie themselves. It creates a world after its own image". Nowadays, students of society seldom accept such simplicity in their explanations. None the less, most recent theories recounting the economic factors of modernization prominently include, as a causal mechanism, the distribution and sale of Western products in non-Western societies. The more sophisticated theories no longer rely exclusively on the difference in price between factory-made products and handicraft goods. Instead, they emphasize such factors as the restructuring of market relationships (e.g. Smelser 1963), the establishment of primary trading cities (e.g. Murphey 1969) and the subordination of non-Western producers (e.g. Frank 1967) – all of which are subsidiary to the creation of a world marketing system (Wallerstein 1974; Eisenstadt 1973). Despite such insightful and justified elaborations, *one* of the causal mainsprings by which this process of Western expansion *began* remains the non-Western consumption of Western goods.[2]

Granted the ubiquity of this causal theme, surprisingly little is known about the factors influencing non-Western use of Western commodities.[3] This chapter will explore some of these factors by focusing on what is regarded by many as a negative case – nineteenth-century China. It is well-known that the Chinese, during the height of Western commercial expansion (1860–1930), did not consume Western products readily or abundantly. It is equally well-known that the lack of Western influence in China goes far beyond the non-consumption of a few factory-made commodities. In fact, some suggest that, of all the non-Western agrarian societies in the nineteenth century, China was the least influenced by the impact of Western civilization (e.g. Jacobs 1958; Nathan 1972: Murphey 1974). Concentrating on a very narrow aspect of this impact (i.e., the lack of interest in Western products) can (1) suggest some factors that influenced the acceptance of Western commodities in non-Western societies, and (2) evaluate some approaches toward understanding larger, and obviously more complex, issues of Westernization during the nineteenth century.

Three sets of explanations will be outlined; each attempts to account for Chinese lack of interest in Western commodities: the "faulty marketing and merchandise", the "culture", and the "status competition" explanations. The "faulty marketing and merchandise" explanations contend that Western products could not overcome the competition of the traditional economy; hence the Chinese, being rational consumers, wisely purchased Chinese products. The "culture" explanations assert that China possessed a pervasive, socially integrating culture, whose symbols were known and approved by all; hence the Chinese, being highly ethnocentric and xenophobic, exclusively consumed tokens of their own culture. Nineteenth-century observers and modern scholars primarily use one of the two or both to explain Chinese non-consumption of Western goods. The "status competition" explanation – very rarely, and then only implicitly, encountered in the sources – maintains that the Chinese conception of high social status was more influenced by local and rural than by national and cosmopolitan standards, hence the Chinese preferred to consume commodities having established meanings of social status rather than those having exotic symbolic content. Each of these explanations will be examined from a comparative perspective in order to judge their usefulness in explaining the Chinese case. In order to approximate roughly the range of conditions within Chinese society, I will limit my comparisons to non-Western agrarian societies.

Limited space will confine my explanation to the non-Westerners' consumption of Western-made, primarily British, textiles. This choice is advantageous. Textiles rank as the most prominent export from nineteenth-century capitalist factories; textile production laid the initial industrial foundation for England and for other Western societies; and, most important, because the Chinese did not purchase much Western cotton, the Blackburn Chamber of Commerce (composed of Lancashire textile manufacturers) commissioned an investigation to discover the reasons. The report from this investigation gives the most detailed information available on the conditions of the textile trade in the interior of China.[4]

Consumption of foreign commodities during the Qing

That the Chinese did not purchase large quantities of Western products in the nineteenth and early twentieth centuries is a well-known fact. The extent to which they did not buy Western goods is not so well-known, and bears repeating briefly.[5]

One of the few quantitative measures of the consumption of Western products is the record of imports entering through specific trading centers. When used as an indicator of Chinese consumption, such statistics, even if completely reliable, represent the maximum figure possible. For China, however, these statistics are known to be greatly inflated for several reasons. First, because of extensive transshipment of goods between reporting stations, there is a significant but unmeasured amount of duplication in the figures. Second, Westerners and their staffs, who lived in the treaty ports, purchased a sizable portion of the imports. Third, as more treaty ports opened, the statistical coverage included previously unreported imports, thus exaggerating the rate of growth. Fourth, the value of imports was reported in Chinese taels, whose value declined between 1870 and 1930 by about two-thirds. Fifth, nearly a third of the total imports into China after 1920 went to Manchuria, a separate economic system developed and tightly controlled by the Japanese. Last, drugs and foodstuffs from Southeast Asia – such as rice, birdnests, and sharkfins – constituted between 20 and 30 percent of the total amount of imports.

Based upon these qualifications, Murphey (1974: 48–9) estimates that, although recorded foreign imports increased between the years 1870 and 1930 by a factor of thirty, the actual increase was "perhaps three or four times at most". Even if the statistics are not corrected to take these factors into account, the total dollar amount of imports places China on par with such countries as "Mexico, Chile, New Zealand, Brazil and the Union of South Africa, and far behind Argentina, Australia, Canada, Denmark, the Federation of Malaya, India, Indonesia, or of course any of the industrialized countries of the West, or Japan". If these figures are computed in terms of per capita consumption, then Murphey's assessment is not an exaggeration: "China's importation of foreign commodities remained negligible, and even at its peak probably smaller than that of any country in the world, including Tibet."

The faulty merchandise and marketing explanations

Although composed of many separate explanations, the faulty merchandise and marketing explanations category has a central theme: Western products were simply unable to overcome the competition posed by indigenous products. An important corollary to this theme maintains that the imposition of Western imperialism in China was incomplete. Western powers did not colonize China. Although they divided China into vast "areas of influence", Westerners lived in only a few coastal cities, such as Shanghai, and in China's capital, Peking. They did not disrupt the existing organization of the Chinese economy and used traditional means to market their products.

In elaborating this theme, the faulty merchandise and marketing explanations cover two overlapping, but analytically distinct, areas: (1) Western products were more expensive and of poorer quality than comparable handicraft products; (2) the traditional commercial system hampered the distribution and marketing of Western products.

Many analysts believe that the principal reason Western cottons sold poorly in China was that handicraft cottons were cheaper and better suited to the needs of the Chinese (Cooke 1858: 187; Neale 1862: 383; Nathan 1972; Reynolds 1974). The evidence presented by the Blackburn Commission, based largely on interviews and observations, seems to support this explanation. The Commission observed (Neville and Bell 1898: 256) that the majority of Chinese, the peasantry, engaged in outdoor manual labor and, therefore, required durable, warm clothing. Because they were tightly woven, using a fine thread, Western cottons lacked the durability and warmth of the coarser native cloth. A smart consumer, they reasoned, would purchase native cottons. Many modern students of China follow the same line of reasoning, describing the Chinese peasant as a "rational economic man": "A great deal of the Chinese reluctance to buy foreign goods or to adopt foreign business methods or technology *was entirely rational and not culture-bound*: traditional Chinese goods and methods were equal or superior especially in cost terms" (Murphey 1974: 30, emphasis added).

The quality of native cotton notwithstanding, the Blackburn Commission was especially concerned about its cheapness in comparison with the cheapest lines of Western fabrics. In seeking an explanation for this, the Commission made what they considered to be an important discovery: the relative cheapness of native cottons was the result of the importation of huge quantities of inexpensive cotton yarn from Indian cotton mills in Bombay (Neville and Bell 1898: 210–19, 234–5). The availability of this yarn had caused a "revolution" in weaving (Neville and Bell 1898: 27(1)). Wherever they traveled, the Commission found cotton handicraft industries, which once had been concentrated in the cotton-growing regions of the Yangtze river basin, spreading throughout China. Much of the increase in production, they discovered, was not for home consumption, but was for sale in the market-place. In some areas, such as South Yunnan, the Commission found that most of the local population, long accustomed to buying cloth in the marketplace, did not know how to weave before Indian cotton yarn became available. But with the importation of this yarn, many attended classes in weaving in order to take advantage of the sudden opportunity to profit from handicraft production (Neville and Bell 1898: 261–6). This increased the supply of handicraft cottons, causing their price to decline.

This explanation is appealing, for it would tend to support the contention that factory-made commodities were purchased because they were cheaper than handicraft goods, but when they were more expensive, they were not purchased. Hence in China, the exceptional society in which Western commodities were more expensive, they did not sell.

There are, however, some shortcomings to this explanation. It is questionable whether handicraft products, especially textiles, in other non-Western agrarian societies were more expensive than Western goods. Although information is limited, we do know that handicraft industries in many societies survived the nineteenth century and, indeed, some survive even today.[6] The important point here is not the cheapness of the commodities but who consumed them. The above explanation is designed to explain why the poorest Chinese, the peasants, did not buy Western fabrics. But in other non-Western agrarian societies, were peasants *the first, the only, or the most likely* consumers of Western fabrics? Platt (1973: 82) maintains that, during the nineteenth century, "For Latin America a large part of peasant consumption was met by home weaving, in cottons and especially in woolens. . . . " Morris (1968) makes the same observation for India. Based on this, it seems plausible that, in those societies where peasants lived more on the edge of subsistence than they did in China[7] and where the marketing system was less developed than it was in China, peasant populations would be even less likely to consume Western fabrics than were Chinese peasants. Moreover, based on ethnographic data, one has every reason to think that a great many peasants, Chinese and otherwise, would not be disposed towards the use of Western fabrics. For instance, we know that in many places peasant communities often used distinctive textile designs to differentiate their work from that of other peasant communities (e.g. Primov 1974). Nineteenth-century Western manufacturers did not attempt to imitate *most* of those designs.

This explanation seems even less reasonable, then, if one hypothesizes that it was the richer, not the poorer members of non-Western societies who were the first, and continued to be the most likely consumers of Western piece goods. Indeed, this hypothesis would agree with most nineteenth-century observations about who wore Western-style clothes. Though impressionistic, the documentary evidence is fairly clear that in Latin America, Turkey (the Ottoman Empire), Southeast Asia, and Japan, it was members of elite groups (e.g., the mestizos, the aristocrats, and the colonial indigenous leaders) who first dressed in Western fashions (e.g. Halperin-Donghi 1973: 85–90; Yanagida 1957: 9–30). Thus, one can suggest that Western textiles were initially luxury products whose comparative cheapness, when compared with other luxury fabrics, placed them within reach of other aspiring groups of individuals (e.g., merchants) who quickly emulated the dress of the socially higher ranked.[8]

If these qualifying remarks are accurate, then the fact that Chinese peasants did not buy Western piece goods because they lacked durability and were too expensive is also a fact among peasants in many other non-Western societies. Thus, it does not explain why China consumed fewer Western fabrics than other countries. In fact, it complicates the question considerably because one must now explain why the richer members of Chinese society, whose attire differed greatly from that of peasants, did not consume Western fabrics.

A possible explanation for why the more wealthy did not consume significant quantities of Western piece goods is that the traditional marketing system was simply too vast for Western goods to reach potential customers. Although one often finds this explanation in nineteenth-century sources (e.g. Cooke 1858: 202–6) as well as in modern studies, it contains some shortcomings when evaluated from a comparative perspective. Murphey (1974) and

Feuerwerker (1969), among others, argue that in China an important factor in the lack of foreign trade was the inability of Westerners to create a "modern" marketing system. Western commodities trickled into a fully-developed, well-supplied traditional economic system that was totally controlled by Chinese merchants. Western merchants were unable to obtain an adequate base from which to promote their products, so much so, says Feuerwerker (1969: 57), that "foreign trading firms [were] gradually transformed into Shanghai and Hong Kong commission agents serving the established Chinese commercial networks".

The reasoning behind making the correlation between China's exceptionally efficient traditional marketing system and the limited Chinese demand for imported goods is ambiguous, at best. During the nineteenth century in most complex agrarian societies, non-Western commercial firms gradually replaced Western commission agents in handling textile imports. What happened in China is in no way exceptional. Simply put, Western merchants typically did not venture beyond the major trading centers to establish wholesale or retail outlets. Native firms, which had formed the link between the Western commercial houses and retail outlets, began to deal directly with the manufacturing firms. This change occurred throughout the Ottoman Empire, Latin America, Russia, Africa, and Southeast Asia (Platt 1973; Skinner 1958; Wickberg 1965). Far from limiting the demand, the takeover by non-Western merchants intensified the distribution of Western cottons. Whether these developments in other non-Western societies mark the beginning of a "modern marketing system" or not begs the question.

For China, however, it is abundantly clear from the investigations of the Blackburn Commission that Western cotton fabrics and Indian cotton yarns were found throughout China, even in minor markets in the interior. Every other import that the Chinese showed they would consume (e.g., kerosene, cigarettes, matches) was likewise distributed throughout China. In fact, it should be argued that this vast and well-ordered traditional marketing system was better able to place Western imports in front of potential consumers than the marketing systems in most other non-Western societies, whether a "modern marketing system" or not. For the Westerners, the problem was that the Chinese simply would not accept much in the way of imports.

None the less, the traditional economic system did have a direct effect in lowering the amount of imports sold in China. The reason, however, was not that it limited consumer demands but, rather, that it increased the supply of products first imported from the West. Those imports the Chinese did accept were constantly subjected to competition from native products produced in imitation of the imported item. Indigenous production of cigarettes, opium, matches, kerosene, factory-made cotton yarn, cotton piece goods, and even particular economic services (e.g., steamship transportation) rapidly gained a sizable portion of the market in competition with the respective import (Murphey 1974; Feuerwerker 1969; Morse 1908: 343–50; Liu 1962: 151–6).

The productive capacity of the Chinese economy certainly limited the *amount* of foreign commodities imported, but not the *range* of imports the Chinese would accept in the first place.

In summary, the faulty merchandise and marketing explanations attempt to account for the non-consumption of Western goods in terms of a universalistic consumer decision model: economic man, rationally satisfying his needs, decides between competing items by weighing quality against cost – factors which, in turn, depend upon elements of production and distribution. When using this approach, one of course synthesizes a great deal of information about the Chinese use of Western imports. The approach, however, does not explain why the Chinese did not consume a wider range of Western products. What it does provide is a partial explanation for why the Chinese did not consume more of those items they found acceptable.

Perhaps one of the reasons for the limited explanatory value of this approach is because the question to be answered is essentially a comparative question: Why did the Chinese consume fewer and a smaller range of commodities than did people in other non-Western societies? In order to fashion a valid answer when using the universalistic consumer decision model, one must demonstrate that the economic factors influencing consumer decisions for the Chinese were *substantially different* from those factors in other societies. The faulty merchandise and marketing explanations do not demonstrate these crucial differences.

The culture explanations

Whereas the former explanations are based upon universalistic models, the culture explanations are based on a particularistic one. Explanations constructed from this model only apply to a specific culture – in this case, China. Of the three categories of explanation suggested in this paper, this category is the one most often used to account for the Chinese lack of interest in Western goods and, of the three, it is the most ambiguous.

The main tenets are easily described. China possessed a pervasive, well-articulated culture composed of a homogeneous set of institutionalized values emanating from the "Great Tradition" of Confucianism. Those who maintained this tradition were members of the upper class, educated and examined in its literature. This upper class, the literati, indoctrinated other societal members in its prescriptions and set an exemplary standard for other groups to emulate. Because of the widespread geographical distribution of the literati and because this class (the literati) was not hereditarily determined, Confucian culture formed an especially powerful value-integrating orientation. In this role, Confucianism supposedly provided the principles through which Chinese society functioned.

There are typically two ways that this and similar characterizations of Chinese culture are used to explain China's non-consumption of Western imports. First, the literati served as the model by which other Chinese judged appropriate behavior. Since it was in the interest of this group to consume the symbolic representations of Confucian culture, other social groups emulated their pecuniary canons of taste. Thus, this standard of consumption necessarily excluded Chinese interest in Western commodities. In this regard, says Wright (1962), "In China, where imports of consumers goods were predominant, there are no signs that these imports reflected an undermining taste for foreign luxuries or any desire to ape foreign ways. . . . The Chinese upper classes, being non-Western, serenely preferred the tokens of their own culture." The second and closely related variant of the culture explanation suggests that, because of the believed superiority of Chinese culture, the Chinese were extremely ethnocentric, disliking all foreigners and, by default, foreign-made commodities.

The Blackburn Commission gives considerable indirect evidence that would seem to support this explanation. They recommended that Lancashire manufacturers not try to produce cloth for poor Chinese. Instead, because Western cottons were cheaper than silks and the better grades of handicraft cottons, a more appropriate market should be upper-class Chinese. They noted, however, that wealthy Chinese thought Western cottons to be inferior when compared with these native fabrics; if purchased at all, they were used to supplement, not to replace, the more expensive native textiles. Decisive in this regard was the high status associated with wearing silks: "Every individual [wears] silken fabrics if the nature of his work and his means enables him to do so" (Neville and Bell 1898: 216). Thus, even though silk might sell at prices slightly higher than Western fabrics, its "consumer appeal" was much greater. The same sort of evaluation as that placed on silk also was placed on the best grades of handicraft cottons, especially those made entirely of Chinese cotton (Neville and Bell 1898: 255).

More important, the Commission recommended that the Lancashire cotton manufacturers give the Chinese precisely what they wanted. The Chinese, they maintained, patronized commodities because they met Chinese cultural standards, not simply because they were Chinese-made. Hence, the Commission strongly advised that Chinese designs be accurately reproduced.

> [O]rnament applied to woven fabrics is in all cases symbolical to the Chinese mind. . . . A descriptive classification is attached to all products of the weaver's art by the Chinese themselves, and unless our manufacturers of cotton brocades pay attention to such minute detail they cannot hope to maintain their interests in these markets. . . . It is no use attempting to give a Chinaman a three-toed dragon instead of one with five, or vice versa; it certainly is not a wise proceeding to irreligiously tamper with the traditional figure "motifs" of applied Chinese art.
>
> (Neville and Bell 1898: 288)

The Commission even found that the Chinese dyed or in some way refinished an extremely large portion of imported cloth sold in China (80–90 percent of

English-made bleached shirting), with most of the remaining imports being used "*for under clothing*, or as *linings* to the various garments" (Neville and Bell 1898: 289, emphasis added). Somewhat disheartened, they remarked "It is not that these goods lack anything in bleach or finish – they are as perfect as good machinery and highly-developed skill can make them, it is that though [bleached shirtings] approach the Chinaman's requirements most nearly of anything we send him, yet they are not exactly what he wants" (Neville and Bell 1898: 294).

The culture explanations are likewise appealing. They seem to account for why wealthier Chinese would not consume commodities symbolizing a non-Confucian way of life. The acceptable imports were thus those items which lacked cultural content (e.g., matches and cigarettes) or could be transformed into commodities having significance within Chinese culture (e.g., imported cotton yarn made into Chinese-style fabrics) or could be concealed (e.g., imported cotton cloth used as lining material). Yet, as acceptable as these explanations seem to be, they contain some ambiguities when examined from a comparative perspective.

The question is why Chinese culture, at this point in time, should *cause* more ethnocentrically-oriented patterns of behavior than did cultures in other non-Western societies. Was Chinese culture stronger or better articulated than were cultures elsewhere? The culture explanations are difficult to use in answering such questions because "culture" tends to be viewed as an indivisible whole. Inseparable aspects of the whole, such as the principles of propriety and filial piety, are considered unique to the particular cultural civilization. Thus, when comparing two cultures, one contrasts traits of two unique, holistic configurations. This makes systematic comparisons of similarities and differences impossible. Instead, what results from such comparisons is a tautological statement that people of particular societies do what they do because it is their cultural way to do so. In the case of Chinese culture, this problem of analysis is heightened by the belief that principles of Confucianism have had a continuous effect upon Chinese behavior for over two thousand years. In this role, Confucian culture becomes a "first cause", the unmoved mover of all that has happened in China. As Popper (1964) shows, for the purposes of analysis, such conceptualizations are useless because they cannot be falsified.

These objections notwithstanding, the culture explanations can be questioned on the basis of *intracultural contrasts*.[9] For well over the first thousand years of the imperial period, the Chinese regularly and widely consumed far more imports than they did during the last two dynastic periods, the Ming (AD 1368–1644) and the Qing (AD 1644–1912). Moreover, most students of China consider the Han (202 BC–AD 220) and particularly the Tang (AD 618–907) and Song (AD 960–1279) dynasties to be high points in China's political, social, and cultural achievements. The Ming and Qing periods, however, are often viewed as a long period of decline in all these respects.

Because of several excellent studies, we know more about the consumption of foreign commodities during the Tang than during the Han and Song dynasties. In the Tang period, quite unlike in the Qing, the Chinese consumed an extensive variety of imports whose very acceptance depended upon their exotic appeal, their "foreignness". According to Schafer's study:

> The Chinese taste for the exotic permeated every social class and every part of daily life: Iranian, Indian, and Turkish figures and decorations appeared on every kind of household object. The vogue for foreign clothes, foreign food, and foreign music was especially prevalent in the eighth century, but no part of the Tang era was free from it.
>
> (Schafer 1963: 28)

The staples of foreign trade during the Tang included many different kinds of foreign aromatics, drugs, woods, foods, and jewelry, and a host of spectacular esoterica ranging from foreign birds and wild animals to slaves, musicians, and dancers. Among the imports were foreign textiles and, more important for the purposes here, foreign clothing styles: "Fashions in the two capitals [of China] tended to follow Turkish and East Iranian modes of dress." Popular among men were such items as Turkish riding clothes, boots and "barbarian" hats, and among women, veils, fitted blouses, pleated skirts, "long stoles draped around the neck and even hair styles and makeup of 'un-Chinese' character" (Schafer 1963: 24).

The Tang dynasty may be considered atypical by some because of the extensive influence of non-Confucian doctrines then promulgated by the imperial rulers. But during the Song dynasties, at the height of both neo-Confucianism and literati authority, foreign trade was every bit as extensive as it was during the Tang. In fact, the records of Chau Ju-kua (Hirth and Rockhill 1970) and the fact that Southern Song obtained 20 percent of the total imperial revenues from foreign trade alone (Ma 1971) suggest that foreign imports may have increased between the two periods.[10]

Considering this striking contrast in the use of imports between the first half of the imperial period and the last half, the analyst faces a dilemma. If one uses the culture explanations to account for the lack of import consumption during the Qing, then why should these explanations not also apply to the Tang and Song eras? Does one account for the difference by suggesting that the culture changed, hence allowing for the validity of these explanations for the Qing? Or does one hypothesize that it is not Confucian culture but something else which determines the prevailing patterns of consumption, thus invalidating the culture explanations? This is not an enviable choice. To say that the content (i.e., the principal tenets) of Confucian culture changed flies in the face of evidence to the contrary. But to suggest that Confucian values did not influence Chinese consumer behavior seems equally untenable. A possible solution to this dilemma is to hypothesize that a change occurred in the way Confucian culture was maintained and interpreted within the context of Chinese society. In other words, the structure of Chinese society changed between the two eras and not necessarily the content of Chinese culture. This hypothesis is the substance of the status competition explanation.

The status competition explanation

The final explanation is one that emphasizes social structural parameters of consumption rather than economic or cultural factors. Although seldom encountered in the literature on the lack of Westernization in China, this explanation furnishes a basis for differential comparisons, which, in turn, provide an understanding of Chinese consumer logic.

The model on which this explanation rests is straightforward. In so far as they are able, individuals rationally purchase what they socially desire. Social desirability is a product of an ongoing situational process in which individuals choose the content and style of their consumption predicated on (1) what is available in that context and (2) how they view themselves in relation to their contemporaries. Thus, how a person decides on the social desirability of specific ideal and material goods is *in part* a function of that person's membership or aspirations of membership in what Weber (1978: 937) calls a "status group". "Status groups are stratified according to the principle of their consumption of goods as represented by special styles of life." From this perspective, consumption is directly related to a person's social status and his or her efforts to substantiate that status by consuming "a style of life" in agreement with or in opposition to significant others. Hence, the content and style of consumption can be seen as a component of status competition, in other words as competition in terms of ideal and material goods with significant others in the substantiation of one's status claims.

The task of analysis is to understand the composition and structuring of status groups in a particular context and to relate these two factors to an individual's consumption of goods. In this regard, Alexis de Tocqueville's distinction between aristocratic and democratic societies is useful. According to de Tocqueville, distinctive styles of consumption prevail in aristocratic societies.

> The rich in aristocratic societies, having never experienced a lot different from their own, have no fear of changing it; they can hardly imagine anything different. The comforts of life are by no means the aim of their existence; they are just a way of living. They take them as part of existence and enjoy them without thinking about them. The ... human taste for comfort being thus satisfied without trouble or anxiety, their faculties turn elsewhere and become involved in some grander and more difficult undertaking that inspires and engrosses them.
>
> (de Tocqueville 1969: 530–3)

However, in democratic societies very different styles appear.

> When distinctions of rank are blurred and privileges abolished, when
> patrimonies are divided up and education . . . spread, the poor conceive
> an eager desire to acquire comfort, and the rich think of the danger of
> losing it. A lot of middling fortunes are established. Their owners have
> enough physical enjoyments to get a taste for them, but not enough to
> content them. They never win them without effort or indulge in them
> without anxiety. . . . There is no question of building vast palaces, of
> conquering or excelling nature, or sucking the world dry to satisfy one
> man's greed. It is more a question of adding a few acres to one's fields,
> planting an orchard, enlarging a house, making life ever easier and more
> comfortable, keeping irritations away, and satisfying one's slightest needs
> without trouble and almost without expense. These are petty aims, but
> the soul cleaves to them; it dwells on them every day and in great detail;
> *in the end they shut out the rest of the world.*
>
> (Ibid., emphasis added)

I have quoted de Tocqueville at length because I think there is a clue
here in understanding the problem I have posed. Nineteenth-century China
was obviously not a democratic society, though nineteenth-century Western
observers frequently referred to it as democratic (e.g. Cooke 1858;
MacGowan 1886). None the less, in this period, Chinese society has many of
the structural characteristics of those societies that de Tocqueville described
as democratic. China did not have a hereditary elite but, rather, one whose
members obtained formal and informal power positions through achieved
means ranging from education to personal connections (Ho 1964).
Moreover, this elite was not a national elite. It was a local elite, locally determined through informal means and locally oriented in its exercise of power
(Ch'u 1969: 168–92).[11] The nexus of this elite was the locale—the standard
marketing communities (Skinner 1964, 1976), the district (Ch'u 1969), or
sub-district units (Freedman 1965). Although there is some scholarly
disagreement over the unit of the locale, it is agreed that the locale had a
considerable political and economic autonomy from the bureaucratic state.
In fact, Skinner (1976) insightfully argues that the influence of the locale in
determining the organizational parameters of Chinese society extended to
people of all income levels and was a principal factor in shaping "mobility
strategies" by which individuals could aspire to artisan, merchant, and official positions. These organizations (e.g., lineage associations, secret societies,
huiguan) existing at the local level typically, but not necessarily, cut across
class lines so that one could find both the wealthiest and the poorest
members of the local communities in the same organization.

Within this local society, a man measured his success in relation to the
success of others in his locale. Such a determination was always ambiguous
because there was no rigid hierarchy of formal positions denoting the attain-

ment of success other than office-holding, which, by regulation, could only occur outside one's local community. However, the assessment of one's relative success was very important because the ability to exert influence in local affairs was strongly associated with one's social standing (Ch'u 1969: 175–7). Hence, status competition was a complex and very serious undertaking that interlinked those recognized to be successful, those claiming success, those aspiring to success, and those clearly recognized to be unsuccessful. One of the best ways to demonstrate success or a claim of success was to practice a style of life that those along the continuum from the successful to the unsuccessful could agree revealed high social status. It is in this regard that Confucian culture is important because it contained those symbols of success – the accouterments of living the life of a gentleman – upon which all could agree.

In this context, as status competition grew more intense, the symbols of status became more fixed and the local inhabitants of all classes became more knowledgeable about the meaning of these symbols. In fact, one might hypothesize that the intensity of this competition helped promote the fad for domestic esoterica that was so prominent in the late imperial period but was less pronounced in earlier periods.[12] These esoteric items (e.g., snuff bottles, carved miniatures of all varieties, silk textile designs) were certainly luxury goods, but those with a "middling fortune" could afford many of the items and those with greater wealth could obtain the most exquisitely made. This love of luxury did not go unnoticed by the Blackburn Commission: "The Chinese everywhere emphatically has [a taste for luxury]. He may be trusted to buy luxuries to the full extent of his means" (Bourne 1898: 115). The Commission, however, saw this as an indication that the Chinese ought to be receptive to Western goods. As this analysis suggests, commodities having a Western symbolic content did not belong to those items which revealed a person's success.[13] Thus, to consume Western products was to put into question one's social standing, including one's influence in local affairs.

This line of analysis gains support from cross-cultural comparisons. In those complex agrarian societies accepting large quantities of Western goods (excluding such settler colonies as South Africa and New Zealand), one finds very similar structural configurations. In each society, considerable social distance separated vertically-ranked status groups. The membership in these groups tended to be ethnically, religiously, or hereditarily defined. For instance, in Russia a large number of Western products found ready acceptance simply because they were made in Europe, particularly in France. However, the Francophilia that seized Russia was restricted to the Russian nobility and their retainers. Western commodities had a symbolic value precisely because the class lines were so sharply drawn. Holding a vastly superior rank in comparison with peasants, the Russian elite had been consciously cajoled into this pattern of consumption by the centralizing monarchs, especially by Catherine the Great. Like France's Louis XIV, Russian rulers attempted to augment their power over the Russian nobility by increasing the prestige of their status while at the same time reducing their political authority. They were turned into a cohesive leisured class with wealth but not responsibility (Von Laue 1961).

South American elites likewise consumed Western products in large quantities but for slightly different reasons. In the revolutionary upsurge of the early nineteenth century, South American elites freed themselves from Spain's political domination. However, this elite group which had been formed during Spanish rule was ethnically categorized as *mestizo*; that is, the members spoke Spanish, belonged to the Catholic Church, and generally adhered to Spanish patterns of behavior as these patterns were implanted in the New World. Like the Russian elite, they were socially cohesive and distinct from the rest of the indigenous population who were categorized as Indians. Even though they might have owned haciendas in the hinterland, the elites were cosmopolitan and the Indians rural. Unlike the Russian elite, however, the South American social elites also were the political leaders who maintained invidious distinctions as one of the means of maintaining their hegemony. During the nineteenth century, the consumption of Western commodities, especially from England, symbolically signified elite status, so much so that the word *importado* became synonymous with quality and *nacional* synonymous with shoddy.[14]

In India, Western commodities were used by specific *jati* that in some way served the British, such as the Brahmin administrators and the Parsi merchants. In Thailand, which was never formally colonized, the Thai aristocracy Westernized in the mid-nineteenth century after Chulalongkorn centralized his administration in response to Western pressure. In the Philippines, and to a certain extent in Malaysia, Western textiles became an increasingly important item of consumption among the upper classes.

Of all the places in Asia, however, the craze for Western commodities was especially prevalent in Meiji Japan where "The very word for 'imported article' was uttered with a feeling approaching reverence, and [the use of] foreign things was a source of great pride" (Yanagida 1957: 288). According to one Japanese account in 1878, "Although imported goods appeared only ten years ago, one sees them in the house and on the person of every member of the urban upper classes. People want anything foreign, whether it is of value or not" (Yanagida 1957: 289). The consumption of Western textile products ranged from hats and caps, the former being worn by the upper classes and the latter by soldiers and merchants (Shibusawa 1958: 31), to gloves and all the trappings of formal Western attire. Although some of these products later spread to lower-class groups, the upper classes – the former aristocracy – were the first and the most frequent consumers of Western cloth and fashions, so much so that one analyst suggests that the use of Western clothing "simply emphasized the difference between the rich and the poor" (Shibusawa 1958: 25).

These and other examples strongly suggest that the consumption of Western commodities often reflected internal cleavages present in non-

Western societies before Western industrialization began. And in each case, the elites of the respective societies consumed in a manner not influenced by subordinate status groups. In short, status competition was class-specific; for the elite, it was a competition among gentlemen.

These remarks also apply to the Tang and Song dynasties in China. During these periods, Chinese society was much more hierarchically structured than it was during the Qing. Tang society is noted for its hereditary aristocratic families, which supplied the court with officials and enforced sumptuary laws for other groups in the society. As Elvin (1973) shows, the social distance between the peasantry and the elite at this point in time was so great that it is analytically justifiable to refer to a "serf-like" peasantry. The cosmopolitanism of the Tang and Song dynasties was in large part a reflection of social elitism, a response of an upper class without roots in the peasantry.

Although the status competition explanation allows for the use of differential comparisons, the testing of the explanation, none the less, presents some difficulties. For instance, it can be argued, on one hand, that since Russia and Latin America are part of the Western cultural complex, the receptivity of their elites to factory-made commodities is not surprising. This line of reasoning is an application of a culture explanation. On the other hand, the status competition explanation suggests that the Russian and Latin American elites, having weak ties to local society, were more open to exogenous influences from whatever source. In this respect, Westernization in Latin America would be analogous to the vogue for Chinese products in eighteenth-century Europe, when every manor house had its chinaware and other oriental luxuries. The demonstration that other aristocratic societies outside the Western cultural complex also welcomed Western commodities strengthens the status competition explanation, but this is not a definitive test. More research is obviously needed to refine the comparative testing of these explanations – perhaps by looking for elites who retained their native dress (as did the tribal leaders of West Africa and the Persian Gulf) or by finding variation in Westernization within societies that generally consumed Western products (as occurred in portions of Southern Mexico where elites, having strong affiliations within Indian communities, continued to dress as Indians).

Despite the difficulties in comparative testing of alternative explanations for a particular occurrence, there are few other approaches as useful in isolating possible causal relationships and in weighing the contribution of each explanation. As this case study has shown, each alternative has some merit, even though none of them alone is able to account for the non-consumption of Western goods in China. But together they form a composite answer to this question. The faulty merchandise and marketing explanations allow insight into a dynamic traditional economy that effectively was able to produce many Western commodities the Chinese found acceptable. That the Chinese did not import more of those acceptable items is accounted for, in part, by these explanations. The status competition explanation suggests some parameters of the situational logic by which individuals evaluated a range of possible consumer choices in relation to their relative social standing within the community. That the Chinese did not find exogenous commodities acceptable symbols of status is best interpreted by means of this explanation. The culture explanations provide an understanding of those commodities that did reflect one's success or claims of success.

Conclusion

If one narrowly defines "Westernization" as the adoption of Western styles and the purchase of Western commodities – thus analytically distinguishing this process from other processual aspects of Western expansion (e.g., political modernization, industrialization) – then some generalizations can be tentatively offered. This chapter's discussion suggests that Westernization would be more likely to occur in those non-Western societies in which there are established elite status groups. If these elite status groups also effectively controlled political power within their respective societies, as they did in Latin America, to a certain extent in Japan, and to a lesser extent in Russia, then one might further argue that Westernization can be regarded as an *indicator* of the maintenance of a pre-modern political and social structure. Thus, it is not unreasonable to alter Marx's prediction, quoted at the beginning of the chapter, to say that the purchase of Western commodities reproduces the old world in new dress.

This conclusion is, of course, in agreement with some recent efforts to show that contemporary Japanese and Latin American societies exhibit considerable continuity with the pre-modern period. However, in contrast to some of these efforts, the important point to be made here is that Westernization should not be viewed as necessarily antagonistic to the preservation of the old order, with historical continuity being maintained in spite of it. Rather, in such highly stratified societies, Westernization might be better viewed as a new way to signify, as an attempt to reaffirm, a traditional social order.[15]

The relative lack of Westernization in China, given its very different system of stratification, reveals substantially the same outcome as that experienced in most other societies, namely, the choice not to break decisively with the past. Thus – in theory, at least – China should not be seen as a negative case in terms of its rejection of Western influence simply because the Chinese failed to patronize the products of Western factories. The spread of Western civilization, even in an economic sense, is more complex and subtle than this. And Westernization, though significant and interesting, is hardly the whole story. In fact, it could and perhaps should be argued that the Chinese responded to Western economic expansion in more aggressive and positive ways than did individuals in many other non-Western societies. For instance, the Chinese, more than any other group of non-Westerners, became the principal retailers of Western products and exporters of raw products to the West throughout all of Southeast Asia and portions of the Pacific and the Caribbean. To call this collective action of millions "unresponsive to Western influence" is certainly dubious.

Therefore, if these suggestions have some validity, then the expansion of Western civilization is by no means an unambiguous process. Its analysis requires more than that which an economic, political or sociological perspective can alone provide. But, in combining these perspectives, one must strive for an analytic framework that facilitates the use of differential comparisons, for only by making systematic contrasts can one begin to disentangle the complexity of civilizational encounters.

Notes

1   This chapter is a revised version of a paper presented at the annual meeting of the International Society for the Comparative Study of Civilizations (U.S.), April 1976. I am indebted to Ben Orlove, C. K. Yang, Pierre van den Berghe, Benjamin Nelson, Gilbert Rozman, and two anonymous reviewers for their useful comments on the earlier version.

2   This causal mechanism is illustrated in such studies as Wallerstein's (1974), where Eastern Europe (the periphery) buys manufactured commodities from and sells agricultural products to Western Europe (the core), and Gallagher and Robinson's (1953), where England builds an informal empire out of non-colonialized countries (e.g., Latin American) by maintaining commercial suzerainty over the territory, thus ensuring an overseas market for British goods.

3   The lack of interest in this area can be explained, in part, by the sociologist's general lack of interest in the process of consumption. As Smelser (1976: 131–40) remarks, "consumer behavior" typically has been a topic of interest only for economists. There are, of course, some exceptions. Besides those sociologists mentioned below, Veblen (1953) and Fallers (1966) provide notable contributions to the sociology of consumption. (For more recent work on consumption from a viewpoint that is similar to the one taken in this chapter, see Douglas and Isherwood 1979. Also see Chapter 5.)

4   Members of the Blackburn Commission traveled some 4,300 miles through the interior of south and central China between October 1896 and June 1897. They collected detailed information on all factors relating to how the Chinese met "their own wants in the matter of textiles", including material on marketing, distribution, indigenous handicraft production, taxation and "local customs and usage as they might affect our textile industry" (Nevilie and Bell 1898: Preface). The report was published in two lengthy sections, one written by H. Neville and H. Bell and the other by F. S. A. Bourne (Bourne 1898), a member of the British Consular Service, under the title *Report of the Mission to China of the Blackburn Chamber of Commerce.*

5   For these comments, I am closely following the discussion of Murphey (1974: 47–9); also see Feuerwerker (1969).

6   In many parts of the world, handicraft production thrived until well after World War Two, for example among the highland Indians of Central and South America (Orlove 1974), throughout sub-Saharan Africa (Plumer 1971), in Indonesia (Adams 1969), in Thailand (Ingram 1955: 118–23) and in India (National Council of Applied Economic Research 1959; Morse 1908; Raychaudhuri 1968).

7   Although the point is certainly subject to debate, recent research shows that the Chinese per capita income was quite high by world standards, perhaps as high as

that in any society in the world prior to the Industrial Revolution. See, for example, Murphey (1974: 324), Myers (1970) and Perkins (1969).

8 From this perspective, the textile handicraft industries supposedly ruined by Western capitalism were the ones that produced the more expensive fabrics consumed by the upper classes. This hypothesis also accords with such information as we possess. For instance, in South Asia the large textile handicraft industries which were hurt by Western competition were those that produced fine fabrics for the export and local elite markets (Chandra 1968: 52–2; Raychaudhuri 1968: 93–4; Halperin-Dongh 1975: 54). Too often this handicraft industry is mistakenly equated with the handicraft industries producing for peasant consumption, some of which survive today.

9 In the following temporal comparison, I am not suggesting that the political, social, and economic organizations of the two periods were essentially the same. I am suggesting that culture explanations need to be specified. Whatever their shortcomings in this respect, temporal comparisons are a way to hold culture constant, thus aiding specification.

10 A short description of clothing styles during the late Song period given by Gernet (1962: 127–32) indicates some foreign influence on the style of dress, but certainly not as much as that which prevailed during the Tang dynasty.

11 Duara's study of the structure of rural areas in northern China (1988) very nicely substantiates the argument made in this section about the close relation between local power and a consuming status order.

12 Connoisseurs of Chinese art often describe late Qing art as being primarily composed of heavily stylized copies of the art of earlier dynasties. In contrast, Tang and Song art is seen as more free flowing and original, though lacking the technical perfection achieved in the Qing period.

13 This point is well illustrated by Chen's observations in the 1930s of the style of life adopted by Chinese returning to China after working abroad, and presumably having been exposed to Western styles, for many years. According to Chen (1940: 111), successful returnees made an "effective display of pride" by showing "evidences of taste and culture. . . . [Their] ideal of 'complete happiness' . . . is not in fact anything new the emigrants bring back with them from abroad, but embodied in the folkways of the countryside. What they do contribute is financial ability to gratify these tastes." Watson (1975) makes identical observations in his excellent study of a contemporary single-lineage village in the New Territories of Hong Kong.

14 The best summary of these patterns is found in Halperin-Donghi (1973: 82–94). In regard to the use of Western textiles in Latin America, he (p. 86) writes, "From Mexico to Buenos Aires women began enthusiastically to accept the dictates of fashion which not only took for granted the acceptance of a new style, but above all that of periodically changing styles which increased the consumption of imported cloth. The process was not restricted exclusively to the upper classes. In a society which ever since colonial times had been divided into only two sectors according to criteria which were not exclusively economic, any woman who did not wish to be associated with the lowest stratum had to use her ingenuity to follow the changing moods of fashion." An important point he makes, which also applies to Japan (Shibusawa 1958: 21–7), is the rapidity with which the people of these societies accepted Western clothing. In Mexico, the changeover occurred between 1824 and 1827, and in Japan between 1872 and 1884.

15 This hypothesis implies a slight but significant alteration in the posited (e.g. Frank 1967) direct relationship between Western capitalism and underdevelopment in the third world. The implication here is that the relationship is not direct but, rather, is mediated through political and stratification systems, in which variance would produce different outcomes at different times and places.

4 The importance of commerce in the organization of China's late-imperial economy

(Co-authored with Chang Wei-an, with the assistance of Chi-kong Lai)

Asian business networks have been much in the news. For the past decade or so, many observers of Asia's rise to prominence have written about the importance of these networks to Asian economic success. The Japanese *keiretsu*, the Korean *chaebol*, and the Chinese family-owned conglomerate – these business groups, many writers believe, are at the core of Asia's capitalist transformation. To explain these groups, the same writers touted the significance of the government in creating and making them flourish. In the Asian business crisis of 1997–98, reportage about these networks abruptly switched from praise to damnation. All types of Asian business groups and the government–business relationships supporting them suddenly became examples of cronyism and crony capitalism, and were seen to be the harbingers of Asia's unanticipated economic collapse.

In most of these writings, regardless of their tone, there is a tension between accounting for the origins of these business groups, on the one hand, and explaining how these groups organize the economy and with what effects, on the other hand.[1] Many analysts seem to think that, by explaining why groups form, they have also explained how groups operate economically. The nurturing of these groups ostensibly explains their nature. For instance, a significant number of writers explain the present configurations of business groups in terms of proximate causes – a government policy, an alliance based on old school ties, the lack of adequate capital markets – all happenstance or historical preconditions for their emergence. Another set of analysts make business networks arise from a timeless culture. They are the embodiments, respectively, of Japanese or Korean or Chinese ways of life, in which the past is refurbished for use in the present. Either way, these analysts imply that the social or political origins of such groups simultaneously summarize their economic roles and economic consequences. For example, groups with once and continuing political ties are judged as examples of political intervention into the marketplace and, in the extreme, cronyism. Groups founded on social connections among owners, managers, or employees may be seen as examples of embeddedness, a condition where shared values increase trust among participants and reduce the cost of doing business.

The reason that it seems so natural to conflate the origins and operations of economically active groups is typically due to the presence of an underlying theory of economies that would seem to explain the connection between the two. For instance, when analysts demonstrate the political origins of groups, they implicitly or explicitly contrast this observation with an essentialized neo-classical theory of capitalist markets, and thus reach the conclusion that the organization of the economy in these societies does not reflect market forces, and hence market outcomes must be politically influenced, if not mandated.

This ongoing comparison between the origins of groups and an underlying theory of economies produces a curious outcome when it comes to doing a historical analysis of economies.[2] The organization of economic groups becomes coterminous with the types and duration of economies in which they are active. In the case of modern Asian business groups, most writers make them historical outcomes, but provide no actual histories of their origins or functioning before the capitalist era began. In most accounts, business groups, except for those in Japan, started after World War Two. Occasionally a writer will push the timeline further back, as far back as the late nineteenth century, but at this point the writer is really examining the source, the headwaters of the capitalist river that has flowed forth in the late twentieth century. By this logic, capitalism in Asia, including capitalist economic organization, could have no possible history apart from the history of Western capitalism. With a lineal conception of history, how could it be otherwise?

The same logic extends to the period before Western capitalism spread to Asia. The history of pre-capitalist economic organizations typically ends with the coming of capitalism, in whatever guise it appears: colonialism, imperialism, dependent development, or commercial capitalism. For imperial China, some crude versions of this thesis are found in Marxian theories of pre-capitalist economies. The despotic state dominated the weak economy, making merchants an appendage of the state and subject to the arbitrary power of China's patrimonial bureaucracy. The organization and operation of the economy are subsumed within and understood to be a part of China's pre-capitalist classifications: "Asiatic mode of production", "Oriental despotism", and "hydraulic societies". This characterization immediately stops when Western capitalism enters the scene, at which time China's economic organization is shaped by the global economy, becomes classified as semi-colonial, and is subject to the withering effects of Western imperialism.

Although not so blatant, quite sophisticated interpretations of China's pre-nineteenth-century economy make the same leap from origins to organization via a theory of capitalism.[3] As we outline in this chapter, most interpretations of China's economy before the capitalist era are based on a comparison between ideal-typical models of markets derived from the analysis of European capitalism and abstracted forms occurring historically in China. Several writers (Hamilton 1985a; Wong 1997) have argued that this approach – attempting to understand China's late-imperial economy through applying theories of capitalist origins derived from the Western experience – is, in methodological terms, questionable and often produces pernicious results, but no one has made the point earlier or more clearly than Perry Anderson:

> Asian development cannot in any way be reduced to a uniform residual category, left over after the canons of European revolution have been established. Any serious theoretical exploration of the historical field outside . . . Europe will have to supersede traditional and generic contrasts with it, and proceed to a concrete and accurate typology of social formations and state systems in their own right, which respects their very great differences of structure and development. It is merely in the night of our ignorance that all alien shapes take on the same hue.
>
> (Anderson 1974b: 549)

As Anderson's "procedural lesson" implies, the methodological problems arise when the pre-modern, non-Western economy becomes a negative case, a case stereotyped negatively against the positive components of theories explaining the rise of Western capitalism. According to this approach, the Chinese economy is not treated as an independent case that has an organizational logic grounded in the subjective understanding of the participants. The classificatory schemes generated by Western capitalism bestow the nature, organization, and economic effects on whatever organized forms might appear within the pre-modern economy.

In opposition to this type of historical interpretation, recent work in economic sociology demonstrates that the way economies are organized and operate on a day-to-day basis directly reflects the way societies themselves are organized. Today's capitalist economies are quite different from one another. For instance, the organizational foundations of capitalism in Germany differ from those in France, and consequences of those differences are substantial (Hollingsworth and Boyer 1997). Even the organizational differences in two parts of the same national economy, say between U.S. Silicon Valley and East Coast high technology firms in the 1980s (Saxenian 1994), can also lead to sizeable differences in economic outcomes. In order to explain these differences, it is not helpful to argue that France is more or less capitalistic than Germany or that West Coast firms are more or less market-oriented than East Coast firms. Instead, one should argue that capitalism has neither an inherent nature nor essential features and that these examples indicate substantively different versions of how industrial economies in the modern world can be effectively organized.[4]

This perspective has implications for the historical analysis of economies as well. The divide between capitalist and pre-capitalist economies may be more theoretical than empirical and more conceptual than real. How economies are organized and operate is institutionally rooted in ongoing societies. Societies do not stop suddenly, and start again when some innovations, however momentous, appear. Instead people integrate those new ways of doing things into fully packed, ongoing, subjectively understood patterns of existence. Without a doubt, from the sixteenth century forward, the economies of Western Europe, expanding beyond the borders of the continent, spearheaded a still-continuing transformation of economies round the world. But essentializing the capitalist transformation, giving it conceptual exactitude beyond time and place, masks the continuities in the social organization of economic activity, even in Europe. In fact, it is one of those paradoxes of history that the continuities in society – those things that we hold dear or cannot change or do not even recognize because they are so much a part of our taken-for-granted existence – these things give direction to changes. Long-term transformation may have very subtle beginnings, for it is often the organization of ongoing activity and not the subtle beginnings that leads society along one trajectory or another and that nurtures and accelerates the change.

What are some of these continuities in the Chinese economy? We argue that there are significant parallels between the organization of the late-imperial economy and the organization of the modern capitalist economies in Taiwan and Mainland China (cf. Ka and Selden 1986). This parallel cannot be explained as a function of some linear sequence of events – of one thing coming after another. In fact, these parallels that we describe are disconnected in time and, to some extent, even in space. We should think of these parallels instead as having emerged from similar (but by no means identical) shared understandings of social organization and from similar (but by no means identical) structural conditions confronted by economically active participants, such as relations of power and authority. Framed in this manner, we believe that a comparison between modern and pre-modern, between capitalist and non-capitalist economies, can help solve some persistent problems in the understanding of both modern and pre-modern economies. In particular, we show that an analysis of the organizational patterns in the late-imperial Chinese economy helps to clarify some key theoretical issues in the analysis of global capitalism today. Unsurprisingly, the reverse is also true. The bundle of theoretical concepts created to explain today's economic transformations is very useful in interpreting some of the most significant characteristics of China's own extraordinary imperial economy, many organizational patterns of which continue to shape China's economic development today.

Let us begin with a summary of our thesis: In late-imperial and early-modern China, commercial organization, that is the organization of marketing products, shaped the patterns of commodity production, in our case the production of cotton textiles. Using Gary Gereffi's commodity chain approach (Gereffi and Korzeniewicz 1994), we argue that the production and distribution networks represented by cotton textiles approximate that of a "buyer-driven chain" and that the production end of this chain can be accurately characterized as a "flexible production system". Substantiating this claim for historical China forces us to reassess those "up-to-the-minute" factors that most theorists view as the essential causative elements in today's global economy, namely information and work process systems, high technology, and global merchandising. Such factors may not prove to be as decisive as they are touted to be after all, but merely contributory to the economic patterns that we observe today. Our conclusions points to an alternative explanation, in line with the embeddedness approach for which Granovetter (1985) and others have argued: recurring patterns of social organization shape the ways that people come together to engage in economic activities, and, in our case, we show that these patterns of "doing things together" (Becker 1986) shape both modern and pre-modern Chinese economies.

The "sprouts of capitalism" debate

One of the most persistent and complex debates about the Chinese economy in imperial times is whether it exhibited capitalistic characteristics. There are two important versions of this debate. One version features scholars from the People's Republic of China[5] who argue whether "feudalistic" China harbored nascent capitalist tendencies. This is known generically as the "sprouts of capitalism" debate, but the second version might as well be called that too, because the basic issues are very similar. The second version rages primarily among Western scholars (Elvin 1973; Huang 1991; Myers 1991; Feuerwerker 1992; Wong 1992, 1997; Brook and Blue 1999; Pomeranz 2000). Wanting to put some distance between themselves and the Marxist slant taken by the first group, the second set of scholars address a Smithian version of the question, by asking whether or not the commercial expansion of the Chinese imperial economy constitutes "genuine" economic development.[6] As academic disagreements go, both versions of the debate are quite heated.

The debate hinges on a paradox. On the one hand, by any measure, the late-imperial Chinese economy was an extraordinarily large economy. Remember that, based on "purchasing-power parities", the International Monetary Fund ranked the mainland Chinese economy in the late 1990s as having the third largest Gross Domestic product (GDP) in the world. By comparison, the imperial economy through much of Ming and Qing times (1368–1911) was undoubtedly the largest domestic economy in the world well into the nineteenth century. Absolute size of this economy is, however, not so indicative of development if the economy was based primarily on household and village self-sufficiency. All disputants in the debates, however, agree that this was not the case, though they differ on the levels of commercialization and commodification and on whether these levels differ from those in Western Europe in the same period (e.g. Wong 1997; Pomeranz 2000). As the starting point in the debate, they recognize that the imperial economy contained exceedingly sophisticated and organizationally complex economic regions. In this regard, nearly everyone acknowledges Skinner's

(1964, 1977, 1985) research in defining the major regions in the late-imperial economy. These regions consisted of densely integrated marketing structures that connected all parts of the region to a hierarchy of urban marketing centers. At the imperial level, all the regions were integrated by means of a vibrant inter-regional trade in both luxury goods and many basic commodities, such as rice, salt, tea, sugar, and the inputs to make clothing (including the raw cotton and silk, dyed and undyed yarn, and bolt cloth) (Rowe 1984: 54–62; Mazumdar 1998). As Mazumdar (pp. 51–9) stresses, we should not overstate the amount of China's internal trade. Although "the domestic market for all commodities remained restricted" and although the average peasant family consumed few traded commodities, the absolute level of trade was none the less very high.[7]

Wu Chengming (1985) gives one of the best-informed, though still very rough, estimates of the scale of this trade, as shown in Table 4.1.[8] From the table, it is difficult to interpret the level of consumption that this internal trade represents. Wu gives an added indication that about 14.3 percent of the total output of cotton cloth was internally traded in mid-nineteenth century (cited by Mazumdar 1998). Mazumdar (p. 57) notes that Wu's calculations understate the level of domestic trade because they exclude commodities sold for tax payments. Moreover, if we add trade in cotton and cotton yarn, which most peasant families had to purchase in the marketplace in order to weave

Table 4.1 Estimates of the important commodities in China's internal trade in 1840[1]

Commodity	Volume[2]	Value (1,000 taels)	% of total value
Grain	24.5 billion catties (JIN)	16,333.3	42.14
Cotton	2,555,000 piculs (DAN)	1,277.5	3.30
Cotton fabric	315,177,000 bolts (PI)	9,455.3	24.39
Silk	71,000 piculs (DAN)	1,202.3	3.10
Silk fabric	49,000 piculs (DAN)	1,455.0	3.75
Tea	2,605,000 piculs (DAN)	3,186.1	8.22
Salt	3.22 billion catties (JIN)	5,852.9	15.10

Source: The table is reproduced from Chao 1977: 173

1   The data for this table are found in Yen (1963: 83).
2   During the late-imperial period, China's weights and measures were not standardized, but rather varied widely throughout China. See, for instance, *Abstract of Information* 1889–90, and Morse 1908. We can obtain only the roughest idea of the amounts represented by the table with the figures provided by Mazumdar (1998, pp. 413–17)): A catty equals about 1.33 pounds; a picul equals 100 catty or 133.3 pounds. A tael equals approximately 1 ounce avoirdupois of silver. At the time, 3 taels equaled U.S.$4.00.

their own cloth and make their own clothes, then this level of trade is very substantial. If we also add to these figures the extraordinary maritime trade in which Chinese merchants engaged and for which peasant produced goods (Hamashita 2003), then we must conclude that the domestic trade was a very large and very significant component of China's late-imperial economy. In fact, Pomeranz (2000: 165) argues that China's internal trade rivaled, and perhaps even exceeded, Europe's trade as late as the late eighteenth century.

Despite such a huge volume of internal trade in basic commodities, the late-imperial economy showed, on the other hand, very few signs of advanced production techniques for any commodity, including the production of cotton cloth. In fact, outside of the imperial workshops, where fine porcelains and silks were manufactured, the levels of technological sophistication in many areas of production did not approach the levels one finds in Europe and Japan during the same period, a point made by a number of scholars (Elvin 1973; Jones 1981, 1988; Huang 1985, 1990; Goldstone 1996).[9] Their general argument is that cheap peasant labor, supplied by the rapidly expanding population, drove out the possibility of technical advances and thus removed the possibility of an independent origin to industrial capitalism. As Mark Elvin (1973) put it, despite being the largest economy in its day, the Chinese economy was unable to get out of its population-induced "high-level equilibrium trap", a Malthusian condition that resulted in "quantitative growth and qualitative standstill".

This debate and, in particular, the concept of a "high-level equilibrium trap" epitomize the use of Western models of capitalism to characterize China's late-imperial economy. The participants in the debate argue about the causes of China's perceived lack of economic development in contrast to a catalog of factors causing capitalist development in Europe.[10] This contrast makes China into a negative case, where the focus of explanation is the absence of something – in this instance, the absence of increasing levels of centralized, factory-based production. The absence in China of what was present in eighteenth-century Europe is then explained by evoking the opposite of what was present in the positive case. The "high-level equilibrium trap" is an unexamined assertion for China of a supposed opposite truth in Europe, namely that the aggregate effects of population density diminish wages and reduce demand to the point that there is no incentive to centralize production, as occurred in Europe. Therefore, the verdict on China's late-imperial economy is rendered "quantitative growth and qualitative standstill".

Cotton textiles, by far the largest handicraft industry in late-imperial China, form the most significant point of reference in this debate. According to Philip Huang:

Cotton lies at the heart of the story of commercialization in the Ming–Qing Yangzi delta. In 1350, no one in China wore cotton cloth; by 1850, almost every peasant did. The dramatic spread of cotton, replacing hemp, affected every household and powered a host of related changes. Its story dwarfs those of all other crops and industries in importance for this period.

(Huang 1990: 44)

Those who argue for economic dynamism suggest that cotton production illustrates the roots, if not the actual sprouts, of capitalism. In the course of the Ming and Qing dynasties, cotton textile production expanded tremendously and became increasingly rationalized, with substantial differentiation in the chain of production (Dietrich 1972). Growing, spinning, weaving, dyeing and calendering, wholesaling, and retailing – all became separate steps in the manufacture and distribution of cotton textiles. Different people predominated at different stages in the production process, a process characterized by a sophisticated division of labor that required considerable skills in some stages of production and relatively simple skills in other stages. Whole regions became known for their cotton production and entire villages for their specialization in one or another of the stages. As the production of cloth became rationalized, the system of distribution widened, so that an integrated, highly competitive market in cotton textiles existed throughout the empire (Myers 1991: 615).[11] This cotton trade extended into Southeast Asia, and some Chinese-manufactured cotton cloth, called Nankeen, even made it to Europe and the Americas in the eighteenth and early nineteenth centuries as one of the export items in the China trade. The presence of a vibrant textile industry in late-imperial China is indisputable.

On the other side of the debate, however, are some other equally indisputable points. Despite considerable sophistication in the marketing of cotton textiles, at the production end of the process, especially in growing, spinning, and weaving, there is a well-documented devolution in production technology (Elvin 1972) and an "involution" in economic development (Huang 1990). The critics show that, as commercialization increased and distribution widened, the technology of production did not advance and, in fact, even simplified. For these writers, the Song dynasty is the high-water mark of China's economy, a point in time when China's technology was advanced beyond that of contemporary Europe (Elvin 1973; Jones 1988). Despite technological sophistication, China's economy did not take off; economic development did not occur. Mark Elvin (1972, 1973) argues, for example, that China, as late as the fourteenth century, possessed water- or animal-powered spinning machines that were in wide use and technologically more advanced than anything in Europe before the eighteenth century. Yet, by the beginning of the seventeenth century, these machines had disappeared from China. Replacing these more complex machines were simpler, more labor intensive devices suitable for use by women and children inside the household. As a result of this devolution, Elvin further argues, China moved in the opposite direction, away from a large, integrated factory system, as occurred in Europe and the United States, and towards the asserted "high-level equilibrium trap".

To these critics, a growing sophistication of production (i.e. where "output expands faster than labor input", Huang 1990: 11) is the essence of capitalist development. Without such sophistication, they argue, no industrial revolution, no genuine sprouts of capitalism, occurred in China. Instead, with commerce serving "as a substitute for management" (Elvin 1973), China supposedly experienced only a long steady devolution into increasing poverty and immiseration.

Although this debate is considerably more varied and the argumentation more complex than we have portrayed here, it is none the less obvious that some of the aspects of the debate seem very similar to some of the issues confronting observers of modern global capitalism. Is the only type of industrialization one that is indicated by the presence of large factories? To this question, analysts today would quickly and resoundingly answer "No". Complex forms of industrialization (defined here as the "ization" of industry, namely the development and systematization of an area of production) occur outside of large-scale, technologically sophisticated factories, as many studies in contemporary Asia, Europe, and the United States clearly reveal. The catch-all label for such non-vertically integrated systems of production is "flexible production" or "flexible specialization".

Flexible production in pre-industrial China

Given the fact of flexible production systems in modern capitalism, can we argue that late-imperial China is an example of industrialization in the absence of factories, an example of flexible specialization on a mammoth scale? The first reaction to such a suggestion is that the idea is absurd. Neither the literature on flexible production systems in the contemporary times, nor the literature on late-imperial China, would support such an implication.

In their seminal book, *The Second Industrial Divide*, Piore and Sabel (1984) do connect pre-modern craft traditions to the development of flexible specialization. But their argument is that Fordism, in the form of large-scale, vertically integrated factories, drove out craft industries in most societies except in peripheral industries where the markets were "too narrow and fluctuating to repay the specialized use of resources of mass production" (p. 206). In a few places, however, such as in northern Italy, a craft tradition persisted, and in the wake of a crisis in Fordist production, this craft tradition revitalized and was so transformed that it became the leading edge of a totally new form of capitalist production. What made flexible specialization new and different from both Fordist production and the pre-industrial craft tradition was the ability to use the most advanced technology, to create complex subcontracting arrangements to match product specification and product demand, and to develop new products using the flexible production techniques (Piore and Sabel 1984: 215). As a consequence of these innovations, modern small firm networks shifted "toward greater flexibility [in] provoking technological sophistication – rather than regression to simple techniques" (p. 207). Although there is a substantial literature criticising various aspects of Piore and Sabel's conception of flexible specialization,[12] critics do not argue that this shift from a pre-industrial craft tradition to the small firm networks in the world economy today was anything other than an economic transformation. From this literature, therefore, it seems difficult to argue that the textile industry in late-imperial China is an instance of flexible production, because this is a clear example of a regression toward simpler technology.

The literature on cotton production in imperial China offers no help in rebutting this conclusion. The descriptions of textile production in the Ming and Qing periods shows that the initial steps in production, namely spinning and weaving, were not concentrated in cities, but rather in the countryside (Xu 1981, 1988, 1992). Moreover, despite some examples to the contrary, these descriptions also make it clear that these initial steps, including growing cotton, were largely subsidiary agricultural industries, which supplied additional income to peasant households. Women and children who did most of the spinning and weaving within the households were themselves scattered throughout the cotton-growing regions and beyond. What this literature shows is that the initial steps in production were so decentralized and, seemingly, so uncoordinated that it is difficult even to speak of a "system" of textile production. Hence, the only conclusion that seems possible is that this is not only not an example of flexible production, but also not even a good example of a "craft" industry, if by that term we mean, following Piore and Sabel (1984), a sophisticated, artisan-based handicraft tradition that draws on cooperative community traditions.

This is where most analysts end the discussion: late-imperial production is simply labeled as "traditional", and, despite a few insignificant continuities, modern production is entirely different in spirit, in organization, in all regards. Our examination of imperial China's textile industry, however, raises some problems with the old formula that radically severs the past from the present.

The first thing we notice is that there are too many similarities between the organization of economic activity in late-imperial China and the post-World War Two industrialization process in both Taiwan and now the People's Republic of China (PRC) to simply brush them aside. Outside the state-controlled sectors in both economies, the industrialization process has been concentrated in the countryside in small and medium-sized firms, and, in the initial phases at least, draws on subsidiary household labor. In Taiwan, the household, in the form of family firms, was and remains the basic unit of production, and the technology of production matches the resources of the producers, and hence is different, if not simpler, than it would have been in large, economy-of-scale factories (Hamilton and Biggart 1988; Hamilton and Kao 1990; Orrù *et al.* 1997). Even in Taiwan, in some areas of production, particularly in intermediate goods, such as plastics and chemicals, where the firms have grown very large and have become diversified business groups, the businesses remain fundamentally family-owned and controlled. In the PRC, restrictions on private ownership still favor some form of collective ownership, but even in this context, township enterprises contain some of the dynamics of family-controlled firms, especially in regard to personalized and centralized decision-making and the necessity to cultivate inter-personal ties (Lin 1995; Wank 1999).

These and other similarities would be superficial ones were it not for a more fundamental parallel between modern and pre-modern Chinese economies that make the economies in the two different periods organizationally very similar. Examining how the economies in both periods actually operate in both economic and organizational terms reveals that the distribution sectors of the economies drive the entire structures. These economies are organized "backward" from distribution rather than "forward" from production.

Our understanding of the significant effects of commerce on commodity production builds on a widespread agreement among the disputants in the "greater" sprouts-of-capitalism debate that, from at least the middle Ming into the twentieth century, the commercial sectors of the imperial Chinese economy steadily developed and reached considerable levels of organizational complexity, so complex in fact that some analysts simply write the whole commercial system off as being confusing, particularistic, and detrimental to economic growth.[13] The same writers (Huang 1990; Myers 1991), however, acknowledge that the commercialization of the late-imperial economy resulted in remarkably efficient markets in those basic commodities that were widely traded.[14] A curious aspect of this literature, however, is that none of the disputants causally connects what happens at the production end with what happens at the distribution end. It is as if the two ends of the production chain bear no causal relationship to one another.

This omission is less pronounced in the most recent and richly detailed discussions of commodity production that builds on a dialogue with the literature on proto-industrialization in Europe (Wong 1997; Mazumdar 1998; Bray 1999; Pomeranz 2000). These scholars consider at length the conditions of peasant producers of sugar, cotton, and silk who are incorporated in merchant-led putting-out systems, and recognize that "small peasant producers were not able to set prices any more than they were able to choose which market to sell in" (Mazumdar 1998: 329). Even so, the most recent work still does not connect the effects of regional merchant groups, whose economic power also controls the national distribution of these commodities, with the conditions of production. For example, in Pomeranz's extended analysis (2000) about why the economies of late-imperial China and early-modern Europe diverged from each other in the late eighteenth and early nineteenth centuries, he barely touches on merchants or merchant organization. Concerning primarily the macro-economic factors, he (2000: 207) instead draws a linear and non-reflexive relationship between production and distribution, thus concluding that production of goods amounted to nothing more than a "proto-industrial cul de sac, in which even with steadily increasing labor inputs, the spread of the best known production practices, and a growing commercialization making possible an ever-more efficient division of labor, production was just barely staying ahead of population growth".

At the theoretical level, this omission can be explained in large part because the literature on economic theory and economic history, on which they draw heavily, exhibits the same reluctance to connect distribution and manufacture. From Marx and Smith to Coase and North, economic theorists have been predominantly theorists of production. Distribution, marketing, and consumption are relegated to a secondary position.[15] Only in the most recent economic theorizing does the distribution end of the process start to have a backward effect on the production end.

One of the clearest characterizations of these linkages is found in Gary Gereffi's formulation of global commodity chains (1994a and 1994b; also Gereffi and Hamilton 1996).[16] Gereffi argues that production should not be analysed in the absence of knowledge about the entire chain – from the basic inputs to the final consumption of a product. Using a wealth of empirical data, Gereffi shows that the organization of production is very different if it is "driven" from the distribution rather than from the manufacturing ends of the chain. By "driven", Gereffi means that, in some but certainly not all cases of commodity production, a firm or a set of firms is able to coordinate the most significant steps in the production of a product, directly through ownership or indirectly through its economic power in controlling some aspect of production or distribution. The crucial determinants in whether firms are able to control multiple steps in commodity chains are the barriers to entry at any point in the production and distribution process.

For some products that are very difficult to produce because, for instance, of the level of technology or required capital, the firm that controls the production is often able to coordinate most steps in the chain. Commercial aircraft manufacturers, such as Boeing, and automobile manufacturers, such as Toyota and General Motors, are examples of what Gereffi calls "producer-driven commodity chains". Some firms either vertically integrate the entire production sequence inside the firm, thereby owning and authoritatively controlling the significant steps in a commodity chain. Other larger producers, such as the Toyota group, form very large networks of independent firms, some of which the Toyota group partially owns and some of which it does not. Those firms that the group does not own, however, are still eager to produce under Toyota's direct guidance simply because of Toyota's great economic power.

The organizing influence of large, vertically integrated firms and inter-firm networks is easy enough to envision. Alfred Chandler (1977, 1990), for one, has described the very great influence of large firms to integrate forward in the chain to control distribution or backward in the chain to control production, and in so doing to reshape the organization of entire economies. It is the absence of such firms and of the tendency to develop such firms that prompts many analysts to reject any claims of a nascent form of capitalism in late-imperial China.[17]

Gereffi's research, however, shows the equally important but very different effects of merchandising on production. Using many examples of consumer non-durables, such as footwear and garments, Gereffi shows that in the last several decades large-scale retailers and brand name merchandisers, which he collectively calls "big-buyers", have begun to dominate their respective sectors. Toys 'Я' Us, Home Depot, Office Max, Ikea, Costco, and Sam's Club are all examples of discount retailers that do not own or directly control the firms that supply their goods, but that have such large-scale purchasing power and the ability to shape buyer preferences as to be able to exert tremendous influence over quality and pricing of the goods they buy. Nike, Reebok, The Gap, Liz Claiborne, Gateway Computers, and Dell Computers are examples of brand-name retailers that do not own or directly control the factories that make the goods they sell. The brand name merchandisers are:

> . . . technically . . . not "manufacturers" because they have no factories. Rather, these companies are "merchandisers" that design and/or market, but do not make, the branded products they sell. These firms rely on complex tiered networks of overseas production contractors that perform almost all their specialized tasks. Branded merchandisers may farm out part or all of their activities – product development, manufacturing, packaging, shipping, and even accounts receivable – to different agents around the world.
>
> (Gereffi 1994b: 221)

As Gereffi (p. 221) makes clear, both sets of companies do not make their profits from "scale, volume, and technological advances" but rather from "unique combinations of high-value research, design, sales, marketing, and financial services that allow the buyers and branded merchandisers to act as strategic brokers in linking overseas factories and traders with evolving product niches in their main consumer markets". Product differentiation is the key strategy of merchandising, a strategy aimed at creating niche markets for specialized products in which the merchandisers can reduce competition and approach monopolistic control. The economic power of mass retailers and brand name merchandisers is achieved by creating such barriers to entry at the marketing end of the commodity chain that the actual producers of goods have no choice but to fall in line with the demands of these firms. The backward organization of production then, assuming equal quality, goes to the least-cost providers of the product. If there are multiple providers of a product, then the big buyers drive the production cost down by playing one producer off against the others. The backward power of commercial organization on producers competing in the same markets forces these producers to create ever cheaper and therefore simpler forms of production, given acceptable levels of quality.

Not every location is equally suited for this low-cost production. It is, therefore, no coincidence that big buyers have had a clear preference for subcontracting in economies dominated by small and medium-sized independent firms which, outside the PRC, are typically family-owned. Research makes it clear that the industrialization of modern Taiwan, Hong Kong, and the PRC (after 1978) has resulted mightily from export production of batch-manufactured products purchased by big buyers.[18] From bicycles, footwear, and garments, to components for computers and televisions, networks of small and medium-sized Chinese firms have led their respective economies in the production of items sold around the world under the brand names of one kind of merchandising firm or another (Chen 1994; Hamilton 1997). It is also clear that this form of production has become increasingly rationalized so that these small-firm economies progressively get better at being efficient, flexible producers (Gereffi 1994b; Chen 1998; Kao and Hamilton 2006). Indeed, modern Chinese economies are among the best examples of flexible production systems in the world today.

Consumerism, brand names, and product differentiation in pre-industrial China

What do such buyer-driven chains have to do with late-imperial China? Surprisingly, the answer is, we believe, about the same as it is for China in the late twentieth century.[19]

The economy in late-imperial China was not only vastly larger than in either medieval Europe or pre-industrial Japan, but it was also organized differently along three important dimensions: (1) the social structural conditions of consumption: (2) the affinity between these conditions and the development of a system of mass merchandising: and (3) the organization of the distribution end of the commodity production. Before the mid-eighteenth century in both Europe and Japan, the buying power of a relatively small, disproportionately wealthy aristocracy directed the efforts of the best craftsmen. In Japan, the samurai class, constituting about 10 percent of the total population, was largely urban-based and set the standards for consumption until they became increasingly impoverished in the late-eighteen and nineteenth centuries (Hanley 1997). In Europe, again before the eighteenth century, aristocratic families, which were becoming increasingly urbanized from the sixteenth century on, also established the fashions of the day and had the power to exclude most other classes from imitating their style of life (McKendrick *et al.*1982; Campbell 1987). The hereditary upper strata in both locations also directly or indirectly controlled the economic decisions of many handicraft and agricultural producers, as well as resident merchant groups (Hanley and Yamamura 1977; Pratt 1999). Hereditary elites and their agents vied over and controlled much of the land and most economically active towns and trading routes. In both Japan and Europe, urban-based merchants and artisans gained some independence, primarily by organizing in trade and handicraft associations (Sheldon 1958; Pratt 1999), so much so that Weber referred to European cities as being illegitimate enclaves in the midst of the *oikos* economies of the Middle Ages (Weber 1978: 1212–338). Free peasants in Western Europe did not emerge until the rise of great monarchies after the devastating Thirty Years War, and did not rise at all in Central and Eastern Europe until nearly the twentieth century. In Japan, until the mid-eighteen century, peasants were tied to the land and largely cut off from participation in regional and national markets. After that time, a rural elite largely emerged that began to link rural areas to national markets, but this elite also controlled peasant participation in proto-industrial activities (Smith 1959; Pratt 1999). Therefore, indirectly through their buying power and demands for conspicuous consumption, and sometimes directly through incorporating artisans in their patrimonial households, the upper strata in Europe and Japan shaped the efforts of handicraft producers, pulling them toward a system of production based on creating finely made, one-of-a-kind products. This is a handicraft tradition of relatively few buyers, restricted markets, and conspicuous products.

By contrast, starting as early as the sixteenth century, Chinese peasants and artisans produced for impersonal mass markets for which they made the ultimate decisions about what they produced and how they produced it. The major consumers for peasant-produced agricultural and handicraft products included a wide range of people from non-hereditary landowning and administrative elites to even rather poor peasants. The elites, however, were clearly the principal consumers. However, elite status was not hereditary, and because of partible inheritance, the landowning wealth was constantly being reshuffled. Tenure as an imperial administrator was short-lived, was based on merit in the examination system, and could not be directly passed on to one's heirs. Unlike their Japanese and European counterparts, the consuming elites in China were located in urban areas and small marketing centers scattered throughout imperial China and not concentrated in disproportionately huge primary cities, such as a Paris, London, or Tokyo. Contending for power and privilege, Chinese elites needed to consume conspicuously in relation to peers in their locale, but not so sumptuously as to separate themselves in status from others in local society with whom they maintained alliances.[20]

We have simplified the differences between China on the one hand, and Japan and Europe on the other hand, in order to suggest that the social structure in late-imperial China created an affinity, an opening if you will, for a pre-modern equivalent of mass merchandisers. In order to illustrate this affinity, we want to cite Alexis de Tocqueville's (1969) comparative model to explain the differences in manufacturing he observed between aristocratic Europe and the democratic United States (which not coincidentally contained, as did late-imperial China, a significant landowning elite in the midst of a fluid class system).

Craftsmen in aristocratic societies work for a strictly limited number of customers who are very hard to please. Perfect workmanship gives the best hope of profit. The situation is very different when privileges have been abolished and classes intermingled and when men are continually rising and falling in the social scale ... [The fluctuation in family fortunes creates] a crowd of citizens whose desires outrun their means and who will gladly agree to put up with an imperfect substitute rather than do without the object of their desire altogether. The craftsman easily understands this feeling, for he shares it. In aristocracies he charged very high prices to a few. He sees that he can now get rich quicker by selling cheaply to all. Now, there are only two ways of making a product cheaper. The first is to find better, quicker, more skillful ways of making it. The second is to make a great number of objects which are more or less the same but not so good. In a democracy every workman applies his wits to both these points. ... Craftsmen in democratic ages do not seek only to bring the useful things they make within the reach of every citizen, but also try to give each object a look of brilliance unconnected with its true worth.

(Tocqueville 1969: 466–7)

Tocqueville's mental experiment is useful here in understanding the complex social structural differences between the late-imperial Chinese economy and other pre-modern economies with which it is usually compared. Tocqueville clearly sees the backward linkages between the consumption and production of goods, and recognizes that the consumption of goods is directly shaped by the awareness of consumers whose situational logic reflects their positioning in the social order. Knowing the Europe of his day well, he saw that craft production in the United States appeared to have a very different orientation in relation to the consumer. We would extend this model one step further by suggesting that the activities of merchants (literally "merchandising") built from and accentuated the same structurally induced situational logic.

Tocqueville's portrait of the United States has a number of features in common with late-imperial China, although they are obviously very different societies. First, both late-imperial China and nineteenth-century America were societies with ambiguous class structure, with few legal or formal barriers to class mobility. Both societies had considerable intergenerational mobility, as is well illustrated by land divisions in China (Rowe 1985), and in both locations there were powerful socially embedded logics that prevented freezing class boundaries. Second, both societies were strongly decentralized with vibrant regions and with elites integrated into the status structure at local and regional levels, more so than at national levels. Third, both societies had vast domestic economies, and moreover, outside of the American South, the orientation of both economies was towards domestic but not exports markets, unlike Britain and to a lesser degree France. These conditions set the stage for the development of an economic system oriented to producing differentiated products for mass markets. In late-imperial China, these affinities encouraged a handicraft tradition to produce for impersonal mass markets. In the United States, these same affinities provided the entrepreneurial conditions for creating, after the Civil War, large, vertically integrated firms – producer-driven commodity chains – to produce products for mass markets.

The similarities between China and the United States are broad structural ones, which helps specify some of the distinctive features of China. One of the key points of difference between the economic organization in China and in the U.S.A. concerns the ability to create and maintain large businesses in the private sphere. Large businesses in the U.S.A. emerged only in the post-Civil War period, when the courts interpreted shareholding companies as a legal "person", which limited the liability of owners to assets of the company. This legal change coincided with the organizational revolution that transformed every sphere of American society. Administered bureaucratically, large groups in both public and private spheres became the order of the day. By contrast, in late-imperial China, only the state and political contenders (e.g., the Taiping rebels) could organize large, centrally controlled groups. Outside of the political sphere, the family was the primary medium for setting groups boundaries (Fei 1992). In late-imperial China, and to a large extent in modern China as well, the combination of partible inheritance shaping property owning and property "rights" (which undermined the formation of large groups outside of those created by the state) and the aggressiveness and success of non-family-based economic organizations, such as merchant associations, limited the size of businesses and pushed these businesses towards commodity production based on merchandising, that is, on pre-industrial equivalents of buyer-driven commodity chains. The ever-present tendency to segment property holdings across generations, and the presence of effective long-term networks controlling trade, meant that the crucial "barrier to entry" in producing commodities for China's vast domestic economy was the distribution of those commodities to mass markets, rather than their actual manufacture.

To better understand how such barriers to entry operated in the Chinese economy, one needs to examine both the products being sold and the organization of buying and selling, or what is termed in Chinese the organization of *maimai*. The products themselves were genuine commodities in the modern sense of that term. Increasingly from the mid-Ming on, most widely traded commodities were differentiated products, in the sense that they were distinguished from like products through brand names and other differentiating markers. The use of brand names has been verified for a wide range of products, including cotton cloth, garments, porcelain, boots, tea, wine, medicine and herbs, scissors, needles, copper locks, copper mirrors, gold and silver bullion, hair ornaments, jewelry, jade items, writing brushes, writing paper, ink sticks, ink stones, lacquerware, books, and bank drafts. Widely available throughout the empire, many of these branded products were associated with their regional origins, including, for example:

> Shaoxing wine, Jianzhou tea, Luchou silk piece goods, Xiangxiu (Hunan
> embroidery), Yuexiu (Guangdong embroidery), Shuxiu (Sichuan
> embroidery), Suxiu (Suzhou embroidery), Shujin (Sichuan cotton cloth),
> Huizhou ink stones and brushes, Fuzhou paper, Suzhou New Year
> prints, Yixing teapots and cups, and Jingdezhen porcelains (Quanguo
> Mingte Chanpin 1982). Such regional distinctions are not simple area
> designations. These products were widely available in most large urban
> centers, and in the richer regions of China, many could be found even in
> small markets.
>
> (Hamilton and Lai 1988: 258)

This kind of product differentiation was minutely developed for cotton
textiles as well as for other goods. Cotton fabric production was mostly
centered in Songjiang prefecture, which is located in the Yangzi River delta.
According to Ye Mengzhu (1981: 157–8), a native scholar of Songjiang
living in the seventeenth century, Songjiang cloth was classified into three
categories by width. The widest cut of cloth, called *biaobu*, was shipped to
Shaanxi, Shanxi, and the capital, Beijing. The middle category of cloth,
labeled *zhongji*, was made for markets in Hunan, Hubei, Jiangxi,
Guangdong, and Guangxi. The narrowest cut, measuring about one foot
(*chi*), was called *xiaobu*, and it was marketed only in Raozhou and other
districts in Jiangxi. Besides being classified by width, Songjiang cloth was
also differentiated by various types of woven patterns and by merchant
seals. Even in remote areas, such as Guizhou, some cloth included advertisements (e.g., "A fine product circulated in Beijing") woven directly into the
fabric itself (Lai and Hamilton 1986). According to the 1512 edition of
Songjiang fuzhi, the prefectural gazetteer, "As for cotton cloth ... every
(manufacturing) village and market town has its own varieties and names;
the list is inexhaustible" (quoted in Nishijima 1984: 49). The edition goes on
to list, in a special section on cloth, fifteen different types. Within the
distinctions made by producing regions, there was also an additional variation based upon the quality of the weave. The most expensive cotton weave
was known as "three shuttle cloth". One bolt of this cloth could be
exchanged for one bolt of silk, both of which sold for about two taels per
bolt. Ordinary cotton cloth sold from .3 to .4 taels per bolt (Wiens 1976;
Nishijima 1984).

In addition to these distinctions made by producing communities, there
were also those made by distributors. Cloth merchants, usually buying from
producers in local market towns, were known by the quality of cloth they
handled. To certify the cloth they would sell, in turn, to far distant
merchants, they made a mark, known as a *jitou* (loom-head), at the end of
each bolt of cloth they collected for resale.

The importance of these *jitou* brand names, and how they worked, can be gleaned from a late-Qing novel, *Sanyi Bitan* (1827). In the story, Wang Yimei was one of the largest cloth distributors among the famous Xinan merchants (i.e., merchants from Huihou, Anhui Province). On his firm's signboard, he used his given name, *Yimei*, and he paid *jihu* (families involved in textile production) to place "*Yimei*" at the end of each bolt. Using this method, Wang developed a national market for his product and sold one million bolts annually. Although fictitious, the example is backed up by stone inscriptions showing that, for the late-imperial period, long-distance cloth merchants made their decisions about which cloth to buy based on merchant marks; firms having a reputation for honesty and quality would have their mark accepted above those of uncertain reputation (*Shanghai beike* 1980: 84–8). Undoubtedly, because cloth marked with certain merchant chops would bring higher prices, the stone inscriptions also record complaints that some merchants using fraudulent marks would try to sell inferior cloth (*Shanghai beike* 1980: 202–3). Considering this sort of brand name proliferation, it is not surprising that, according to one source for late Ming (cited by Fu 1957: 15–16; Li Renpu 1983: 199), there were forty-two different kinds of cotton cloth available in the market of Yanshan, a small town in Jiangsu.

A contrast with Europe accentuates the extraordinary character of brand names in China. Very few students of industrializing Europe mention the presence of commodities bearing brand names. What little research has been done is primarily in marketing and advertising research (e.g. Borden 1947; Coles 1949; Davis 1967) and in historical studies of patents and trademark laws (e.g. Schechter 1925; Dutton 1984). More recently, however, a few historians and social scientists have started looking more closely at patterns of consumption in Western societies (e.g., Jones 1973; Ewen 1976; McKendrick *et al.* 1982; Fox and Lears 1983; Marchand 1985). The uniform conclusion of these studies is that analysts regard the origin and widespread use of brand names as being an aspect of capitalist development.

Two types of studies are particularly important in this regard. First, several scholars mention the absence of brand names in medieval Europe. The most cited study is that by Schechter (1925). Schechter explains in his history on trademark laws that merchant and artisan marks were not brands names in the modern sense of the term. Instead:

> ... the characteristics of the typical craftsman's mark of the Middle Ages were: (1) that it was compulsory, not optional; (2) that its purpose was the preservation of gild standards of production and the enforcement of gild or other local monopolies rather than the impressing on the mind of the purchaser the excellence of the product in question and thereby the creation of a psychological need for that product; (3) that, consequently, while the modern trademark is distinctly an asset to its owner, the medieval craftsman's mark was essentially a liability.
>
> (Schechter 1925: 78)

Schechter explains that the difference between modern and medieval commodity marks results from differences in production and distribution systems between the two eras, particularly in the relations between producers and consumers. For the majority of people in medieval society, "wants were comparatively few and unchanging". People "were supplied by neighboring craftsmen; consumer and producer stood in direct relation with one another". Each town of any size had its own merchants and artisans, who in turn organized guilds through which they sought to monopolize production and trade. The guilds "strove by every means at their disposal to prevent 'foreigners' – as the merchants coming from a town five miles away might be described – from competing with their gild" (pp. 41–2). Merchant and artisan marks were the devices by which guilds sought to exclude outsiders and to control the economic activities of insiders. Although Schechter's thesis is dated and rather simplistic,[21] historians of marketing and advertising (e.g. Borden 1947; Coles 1949; Davis 1967), based largely on references to Schechter's study, argue that brand names start only in the modern era.

This thesis largely coincides with recent scholarship on patterns of consumption in modern society. A growing number of studies discuss the appearance, in the eighteenth century, of differentiated consumer products and the importance of these products for the success of Western capitalism. Mokyr (1977), Jones (1973), McKendrick *et al.* (1982) and Brewer and Porter (1993) argue that the eighteenth-century English economy became commoditized in response to changing patterns of consumption. An expanding middle class, according to their analyses, began to require affordable items of fashion and comfort in order to emulate the accoutrements of the elite. McKendrick in McKendrick *et al.* (1982: 13) believes that this shift in demand is of such importance as to proclaim a "consumer revolution" in eighteenth-century England. "[C]onsumer behavior was so rampant and the acceptance of commercial attitudes so pervasive that no one . . . should doubt that the first of the world's consumer societies had unmistakably emerged by 1800." This demand for fashionable products created an opportunity for manufacturers to explore ways to streamline their production and to market their products. Accordingly, such individuals as Josiah Wedgwood, the mass producer of English porcelains, began to create and to advertise brand-name products designed to distinguish their wares from similar lines produced by competitors (Jones 1973; McKendrick *et al.* 1982; Brewer and Porter 1993; Fine and Leopold 1993).

Research on later periods of Western capitalism (e.g. Ewen 1976; Fox and Lears 1983; Marchand 1985) uniformly emphasize the interrelations of mass consumer markets, the growth of large corporations, and advertising and marketing based upon products having brand names. Consumerism and brand names, so the theory goes, went hand-in-hand to produce capitalist production as we know it today.

Even though their significance can certainly be debated,[22] that brand names are an important feature of modern Western capitalism can hardly be disputed. It is certain, however, that England was not the world's first consumer society and that consumerism does not only occur under conditions of capitalism.

The organization of merchant networks

Widespread distribution of differentiated commodities in late-imperial China implies vast merchandising networks. As described in Chapter 2, these merchandising networks certainly existed. Moreover, they emerged without the institutional support of the late-imperial state. The Ming and Qing state did not standardize weights and measures, support a fixed currency, create commercial codes, or guarantee contracts – all of which formed the bedrock of Western economies. This absence of state-supported economic institutions helps to explain why there were such formidable barriers to entry at the distribution end of commodity chains. What the state did not provide, the merchant and artisan groups did, and in so doing they restricted access to marketing products. It was only through these merchant groups that China's vast domestic economy actually worked. But, more than that, the control over commerce established by merchants and artisan groups not only shaped trade, but also moved backwards to structure commodity production as well.

How were these merchants groups organized so that they created these backward effects on production? A contrast with Europe and Japan is again revealing. Merchant associations in Europe and Japan were divided between resident guilds and non-resident traders. The guild structure in most urban areas allowed resident merchants exclusively to control the commerce of the locale. Non-resident merchants were, in essence, wholesalers but not retailers. The ability of guilds to restrict commercial competition meant that such guilds could limit the widespread distribution of common products and could force consumers to buy what was locally produced or distributed. This situation prevailed until the guild structure broke up in the seventeenth and eighteenth centuries. The division between local and non-local merchants remains, even to this day, in the form of the distinction between wholesale and retail.

In China, however, the resident/non-resident categorization did not serve as the foundation for merchant and artisan organizations. Regardless of their length of residence in a locale, when merchants and artisans defined themselves collectively, they did so in terms of some combination of occupational specialization and regionality. This regionality, loosely linked to a lineage homeland somewhere outside their city of business, was very flexibly defined, and could be expanded or contracted based on the situational needs of the group.

These economic groupings provided the institutional underpinning of Chinese commerce. These commercial activities were centered in *huiguan* or *gongsuo*, which were places, much like club houses, set aside for anyone who came from a defined region in China to meet and to do business. Every *huiguan* and *gongsuo* had its own rules, rules that applied to fellow-regionals or to people in that line of business. These were rules of personal conduct, as well as rules for the businesses in which the fellow regionals specialized. These groups specified such things as the weights and measures for the line of business, the type of currency accepted, the quality and price of the products or services that they sold. Those who did not abide by the rules, the leaders would sanction – sometimes by fines, but the leaders could go so far as to drive violators into bankruptcy and out of business.[23]

By serving all these functions, regional groups created the institutional environment in which trade flourished. From the point of view of individuals, these merchant associations provided a structure of restraint and coercion to which individuals had to conform in order to realize their economic opportunities. From the point of view of the economy as a whole, these groups created an institutional environment in which buying and selling (*maimai*) was made into predictable and routine activities (see Chapter 2 for details).

Day-to-day normality and predictability was socially manufactured through the operation of trading networks. To an extent not appreciated by most scholars today,[24] Chinese merchants and artisan networks promoted competition within and among networks. These networks form the interpersonal structure of merchants and artisan associations.[25] Economically, however, they created an equivalent of a commodity market in which buyers and sellers met repeatedly, made deals, and set prices self-consciously and reflexively in the company of other buyers and sellers of the same or similar products. In this context, transactors tried to make the best long-term deals for themselves. Short-term maximization, in which fellow regionals and their regular consumers would short-change each other, would not serve as well as long-term deals that would insure longevity for all transacting parties. In his account of the activities of Chinese traders in Indonesia, Geertz describes the manner in which Chinese merchants in China also traded. The merchant, he said, typically wants:

> . . . to spread [himself] thin over a very wide range of deals rather than to plunge deeply in any one. Putting all one's eggs in a single basket is not a favored mode of procedure . . . As a result, large, or even moderately large, single deals with only two people involved are very rare, even in cases where the traders are large enough to handle such deals alone. Both large and small transactions usually involve a multiplicity of people, each making a small contribution and each taking out a small return. A trader contracting even a fairly petty agreement will look for others to go in with him; and, in fact, there is widely felt normative obli-

gation on the part of traders to allow other people to cut into a good thing. . . . The individual trader, unless he is very small indeed, is the center of a series of rapidly forming and dissolving one-deal, compositely organized trading coalitions.

(Geertz 1963: 40)

As Geertz describes, each investment is split into many parts and distributed to others in the network.

Merchants and artisans formed similarly organized groups at each step in the final production and distribution of a product. Such groups created mini clearing houses for goods and services, which assured everyone in the group that no one person could dominate the group and that the general rules of trade would be fair, mutually agreed upon, and collectively enforced.[26] The groups, in effect, created price-efficient markets in goods and services at each step in a commodity chain, effectively segmenting each chain and encouraging different groups of people to handle each step. The segmentation maximized leverage at the merchandising end of the chain.

The market power of regional merchant networks

We can set these organized economic activities into motion by showing how the textile trade worked. The important point to emphasize here is that the organization of the late-imperial economy is not a static system, but rather an evolving one. We will divide our discussion of late-imperial commercial organization between the periods before and after 1850. Before 1850, China was a net exporter of commodities (e.g., teas and silks) and an importer of bullion. Although both the exports and imports had important effects on China's economy, the internal organization of trade was largely insulated from the diffusion of Western goods. After 1850, with China's defeat in the Opium Wars, Western products, technologies, and organizational forms were introduced into China, where they began to reshape the organization of the Chinese economy.

Long before 1850, Chinese merchants had gained control of both the collection of textiles from producing areas and their final dispersal to local sellers throughout the area of distribution. The same is true for other products as well. While it is the case that, in the mid-nineteenth century, long-distance trade was in the hands of different sets of merchants in different places, all the merchant groups seemed to work in much the same way (Rowe 1984). The groups specializing in textiles, for instance, would attempt to make connections in particular producing regions and would concentrate their distribution in other areas. Merchants typically went to regional markets in the producing areas and bought cloth from commission agents or petty merchants who had collected the cloth in smaller markets from producing households in the region. Merchants then delivered the cloth to groups specializing in finishing the cloth by dyeing and calendering.

According to Craig Dietrich (1972: 130), the merchants would give the cloth, together with "calendering contracts", to a set of people called *pao-tou*, or bosses. These bosses, in turn, would hire independent artisans who rented their equipment from the bosses and worked under their supervision.

> The merchants exercised considerable control over the calendering industry without assuming any direct managerial responsibility ... The whole organization resembled a modified putting-out system, wherein merchants entrusted raw material (cloth) to laborers through the intermediary of bosses. After processing, the laborers returned it, through the same intermediary, to the merchants. The importance of merchants was not confined to the calendering industry. Since the activities of the innumerable spinners and weavers were not integrated with one another in any organizational structure, it was the merchants, both local and regional, who held the industry together and allowed it to function as a system.
>
> (Dietrich 1972: 131)

As nearly as we can tell, over the course from mid-Ming to late Qing periods (1500 to 1850), regional merchant networks gained a progressively stronger hold on China's economy, and then after 1850 these networks spread to Southeast Asia where they also dominated the domestic economies in the region. The data are not sufficient to say whether these early changes in networks occurred gradually or in spurts. But it is clear that the organization of commerce changed during the 350-year period. At the start of the era, and perhaps for the duration of the Ming period, local markets were controlled by local brokers (*ya hang*) who had licenses from the government to act as intermediaries between peasants selling goods in official markets and long-distance merchants who would bring in goods to sell and who would buy local products to sell elsewhere (Mann 1987). In large cities, brokers set up branches (called *shu chuang*) in the countryside to deal with peasant producers more directly, but such branches could only sell to licensed brokers. Even during the Ming period, however, non-local regional merchant networks had the resources and the connections to final markets and therefore probably had the upper hand in dealing with market brokers. A Ming dynasty poem says as much: "Brokers treat outside merchants like kings, because to oppose them means war".

By the start of the Qing dynasty in the mid-seventeenth century, the balance of power had swung decisively towards long-distance trading networks (Xu 1992). In early Qing, peasants could sell directly to long-distance merchants without going through market brokers. As a consequence, long-distance merchants began to patronize buyers in the countryside (*zuo chuang*) who collected goods directly from peasant producers. Such collection strategies put regional merchants directly into competition with market-based brokers.

By mid-Qing, the economic power of non-local merchants had overwhelmed locally based merchants (Xu 1992). The brokerage system, which was relatively powerful in the Ming, had lost its significance and had been largely replaced by non-local merchants, the most successful of whom began to establish brand-name stores (*zihao*). At the same time, specialization in the textile trade occurred so that different steps in the production of cotton cloth were now systematically farmed out to different groups. Local traders or local representatives of regional networks would collect raw cloth that had been woven by peasant households and would sell it to brand-name stores. Very similar to OEM (original equipment manufacturing) production today, where branded products (e.g., Nike, Dell) indicate the merchandiser and not the maker of products, the merchant owners of these stores would farm out the cloth to dyeing mills. The mills would return the dyed cloth to the brand-name stores with the brand name dyed into each bolt of cloth. A typical brand name would read "Manufactured by the Lin Family". At this point, the merchandiser had become by far the most powerful link in the chain, powerful enough to shape all the backward links.

By late Qing, the regional merchant networks controlled all the links in the cotton textile commodity chain (Hamilton 1977a; Xu 1992). The broker system declined over the long term and eventually disappeared. The local merchants who had previously been brokers gradually became long-distance traders themselves. Capitalizing on their local connections, they extended their trading networks to other locations. By late Qing, the great bulk of China's commerce was handled by regionalized trading networks, which in any one urban setting might have sufficient density to be represented by merchant associations that had been established by non-local merchants from this or that region. By late Qing, the invidious distinction between local and non-local merchant and artisan groups had all but disappeared, when virtually all groups became enmeshed in one or another form of non-local grouping (Hamilton 1985a). Moreover, by the late nineteenth century, as Mark Elvin (1973) and Ho Ping-ti (1966) show, these regional merchants had greatly expanded; regionally organized migrants had gained control not only of commerce but also of most occupations in China's cities, everything from sailors to barbers; even the beggars in Beijing (Burgess 1928) had a regionally-based organization.

The growing importance of regional merchant groups in the 19th and early 20th century

In the 1840s, losing the first round of skirmishes with Western states, China was forced to open its borders to Western traders and Western commodities. By 1850, British cotton textiles began to flood Chinese markets. Eyeing China's millions, the British had expected Chinese consumers to buy great quantities of British-made cotton goods, as had so many other consumers in other parts of the world. In fact, Sir Henry Pottinger, the British representative at the signing of the Treaty of Nanking in 1842, had forecast that "even the total output of Lancashire would not be sufficient to satisfy consumption in a single province in China" (Chao 1977: 168). This prediction matched the belief in Europe, echoed by Marx (1959: 11), that "[c]heap commodity prices are the heavy artillery with which (the bourgeoisie) batters down all Chinese walls and forces the barbarians' intensely obstinate hatred of foreigners to capitulate." This perception colored the interpretation of the Western impact on China for years, as many analysts (e.g. Isaacs 1961) reported that Western imports had destroyed China's handicraft industries. That view, however, has now been thoroughly revised (Feuerwerker 1970; Chao 1977). But what is less understood is the role played by China's merchants in creating a new system of handicraft cotton textile production that competed successfully with Western cotton textile imports. The new system, based on the importation of foreign yarn, unambiguously shows a continuation of the backward linkages of merchandising on cotton textile production.

From 1850 to the 1930s, when the Great Depression and the Japanese invasion irrevocably disrupted daily life in China, Chinese handicraft cotton textile production not only survived the onslaught of Western and Japanese imported textiles, but in fact thrived. This, in fact, was the heyday of China's handicraft production. Chinese hand-made textiles not only supplied most of the domestic market with cloth, but also became a flourishing export commodity. As Table 4.2 shows, the export of Chinese native cloth grew about 80-fold between 1870 and 1925, and millions of households were engaged in making cloth from yarn, and, in addition, thousands of small factories emerged to weave, dye, and finish the cloth (Chao 1977: 169–217; Xu 1992).

The impetus for this remarkable growth in China's cotton handicraft industry was the ready availability of large supplies of cotton yarn imported largely from India and Japan between 1860 and 1920, and subsequently provided by mills in China as well. China's pre-1850 cotton handicraft production had been concentrated in the cotton-growing regions in the lower reaches of the Yangtze River. The demand for cotton textiles was in part limited by the supply of cotton and, more importantly, by the control of merchant networks whose economic power structured the whole system of production. Although competitive within networks, only a few regional merchant networks had access to raw cotton. These, in turn, had control over the national distribution of cotton cloth. When Chinese markets were opened to foreign trade, different sets of merchants all across China could suddenly purchase cotton yarn cheaply and could promote and manage their own production networks. Demand for yarn boomed. After 1850, every province in China began to produce hand-made cottons (Chao 1977), and cotton-growing areas began to produce more cotton as well. In an effort to explain the dismal reception of British cotton cloth in China (Britain did not sell yarn overseas, only cloth), troubleshooters from Lancashire reported that even in the peripheral provinces of Yunnan and Guizhou yarn imported from India had created thriving handicraft industries where none had existed before. Women even attended classes to learn how to weave (Neville and Bell 1898: 261–6).

What remained crucial for the expansion of production was the ability of merchants successfully to merchandise and sell hand-made cloth in competi-

Table 4.2 Exports of Chinese native cloth, 1871–1930 (5-year total)[1]

Period	Quantity (piculs)	Value (1,000 haikwan taels)
1871-75	3,903	193
1876-80	9,328	487
1881-85	12,917	526
1886-90	28,086	1,037
1891-95	88,528	3,289
1896-1900	139,188	5,855
1901-5	129,932	6,124
1906-10	178,346	8,548
1911-15	221,917	11,454
1916-20	258,596	15,698
1921-25	315,516	19,737
1926-30	201,486	13,494

1 The table is reproduced from Chao, 1977, p. 173. The data for this table are found in Yen (1963, p. 83). For approximate conversions of piculs and taels to Western measures, see foot-note 28.

tion with Western and Japanese imported cloth. Here, too, the Western opening-up of China, which introduced new and cheaper means of trans-porting goods (e.g., railways and steamships) greatly enhanced the ability of Chinese merchants to distribute their goods and hence to compete with Westerners. But it was organization of commerce that created the potential and led the system of handicraft production to new levels.

In the post-1850 period, increasing opportunities to participate in the cotton trade led Chinese merchants to rationalize the existing system of production and distribution, but not to transform it. The number and size of putting-out systems of production greatly increased, as did the efforts to merchandise finished cloth, but each step in the chain of production remained segmented, as it had before 1850. Chao (1977) gives several exam-ples that cause one to realize that handicraft production was not a throwback to a traditional system, but rather was a competitive alternative to a factory-based system. One example he gives is of the emergence of a new handicraft industry in Wei district in Shandong province. In the early years of the twentieth century, Wei district was linked, by a railroad built in

1904, to Qingdao, a new treaty port opening in 1899. Taking advantage of this new opportunity, a number of merchant firms organized a putting-out system based on providing credit to households to buy simple handlooms and cotton yarn and return cotton cloth. In ten years, they had organized over 100,000 looms producing cotton cloth:

> During the peak years about 150,000 persons were involved in the production of native cloth, with a maximum annual output of ten million bolts. . . . Although gray goods and bleached cloth remained as the prominent products throughout, the quantities of colored and patterned cloth were sufficiently large to justify the establishment of factories specializing in various finishing processes. According to a survey made in the early 1930s, there were 30 dyeing factories, 7 calendering factories, and 3 packing companies. The products of Wei Xian enjoyed a nationwide market.
>
> (Chao 1977: 196)

As is the case with most analysts, Chao describes the system of production in greater detail than the system of merchandising and distribution, but he does recognize the importance of the merchant end of the endeavor (1977: 206–17). Arguing that merchants decisively affected the rise and fall of centers of handicraft production, he cites some examples of merchant organization. For instance, a study of cotton handicrafts in Hebei province in 1934 showed that "a total of 25.7 million bolts of native cloth were produced in 89 xian (districts) in the province, of which 89 percent were sold to other places through cloth merchants". These cloth merchants were not consolidated into huge firms, but were rather divided into many small firms, each handling, calculates Chao (p. 204), about one hundred weaving households. The largest firms he came across managed 4,000 looms. These putting-out firms organized production in the following ways:

> (1) buying factory yarn in large quantities from big cities, (2) distributing the yarn to individual hand weavers and setting specifications for the products, (3) collecting cloth from weavers and performing finishing works if necessary, and (4) transporting the goods to other cities for sale.
>
> (Chao 1977: 204)

Xu Xinwu (1992: 365–8) substantiates that the same patterns that were observed in the Ming and early Qing continued in the 1920s.[27]

Conclusion

The interpretation of China's handicraft industry travels the same path as the greater "sprouts of capitalism debate". Historians have not viewed China's handicraft production in the Ming, Qing, and Republican eras –

right up to the Japanese invasion in 1936 – as an example of capitalism, of industrialization, or even of modernization. Most analysts see it as evidence of continuing traditionalism and of spreading commercialization without genuine development. As such, most conclude that China's handicraft tradition at last came to an end with destruction caused by World War Two and the post-war economic reorganization that occurred as a consequence of the Communist Revolution on the mainland.

The thesis in this chapter is different. By overemphasizing the capitalism–no capitalism, development–no development debate, analysts ignore the organizational features, and particularly the strength and dynamism, of the Chinese economy as well as the evolution of the system over the past 500 years. If we push our analysis back to an even earlier period, to the economically sophisticated but rigidly stratified (Northern and Southern) Song dynasties, we see that the economic organization of the Song differed greatly from what emerged in the Ming and Qing periods. Song commerce was urban-based with relatively little penetration of the rural areas (Shiba 1970). Merchants were rooted to urban locales. They were urban resident merchants and not non-local regional merchants, and commodity production was equally urban and not rural. The economic organization of Song China was more similar to that of late-medieval Europe and Tokugawa Japan than to what emerged in Ming and Qing China, in large part because the social organization of society promoted that form of economy.

The commercial transformation of late-imperial China grew out of the intense reorientation of Chinese society that occurred at the end of the Yuan and beginning of the Ming dynasties. In the Ming, a relatively decentralized, rural-based society emerged. Elites were centered in and mainly circulated in local society, grounded there, in part, by the growth of powerful, local lineage groups. Centered on the mobility of households, the class structure became "fluid", as Ho Ping-ti (1964) put it. The commercial system that developed in the mid-Ming reflected the features of that society. Although the society certainly changed during the last 500 years, from the sixteenth century to the early twentieth century, the changes were largely matters of degree rather than of kind, and consisted of systematizing the patterns that were already prevalent and important. By the late Qing, the commercial system of China was the tail that wagged the entire structure of China's economy outside of the state sector, and, for much of this period, the state sector was concerned with taxation and the redistribution of grain through the granary system developed by the Qing state (Will and Wong 1991). Although the state sector collapsed in the final decades of the nineteenth century, the economic organization of the private was not transformed into some other economic stage or system when Western and Japanese powers forcibly opened China, but rather grew along a trajectory established in the pre-1850 period. The opening of China's markets to Western traders merely quickened this earlier process of change by expanding the range of economic opportunities that Chinese people could grasp, a conclusion echoed by Sherman Cochran (1980, 2000) as well. This outcome occurred despite the changes wrought by Western and Japanese imperialism (Brandt 1989).

The advances in this commercial system during the late-imperial period directly contributed to the simplification of technology when contrasted with production of the same products elsewhere round the world, particularly in Europe and the United States. There is no culprit in this process, no direct or indirect agency that blocks economic development in China, no high-level equilibrium trap that Mark Elvin (1973) discussed, no economic involution that Huang (1985, 1990) talks about, and no peasant-induced barrier to development that Mazumdar (1998) ends up with. The merchandising power at the commercial ends of China's economy pushed the deployment of simple technology at the production end of the economy; and as production became centered in the household, then gender and kinship dynamics controlled the labor force. Often confined to households, women and young girls became primary producers of many handicraft goods.[28] But population pressure and cheap labor are not the reasons for these developments. What happened in the large picture also happened in the small. "A puzzling fact" that Chao (1977: 182) noted is that, in the early part of the twentieth century when both foreign yarn and a range of alternative looms were readily available, the first ones to disappear were the "native spinning wheels with 3 or 4 spindles". The most common loom in use was also the most primitive one, a "single spindle wheel so simple that a girl of seven or eight would learn to operate it".

As we argue here, China's system of production and distribution was an alternative to the Fordist systems of production that emerged in the nineteenth and early twentieth centuries, systems with well-organized, producer-driven commodity chains. But the absence of these types of chains does not mean that China's economy was antagonistic to capitalism. Quite to the contrary, China embraced the new economic order. China's economy was extensively and intensively organized and was deeply rooted in Chinese social institutions. The buyer-driven features of the economy gave the economy momentum and direction, and as economically active Chinese took advantage of new opportunities introduced by the opening of China to the outside world and as they incorporated Western organizational forms (e.g., limited liability companies) and material technologies, they simply reinvented their traditions. A large part of the Chinese economy, especially in the coastal areas, seamlessly became integrated in global capitalism, and indeed became a competitive form of capitalist production. This is simply to say that the Chinese ways of doing business were sophisticated, were oriented to profit, and could compete successfully in almost any market. Even in the late nineteenth and early twentieth centuries, in the struggle for economic success, Chinese merchants and industrialists usually came out on top (MacPherson and Yearley 1987; Hamilton 1996; Cochran 2000).

If one were to examine the organization of the textile industry in Taiwan and China in the past decade, or the footwear industry or the garment industry or the bicycle industry or even the high technology industries, as we have done elsewhere (Orrù *et al.* 1997; Hsing 1998; Kao and Hamilton 2006), it would be apparent that the economic organization in all of these sectors shares the organizational features of putting-out systems of production that existed a century earlier. This observation does not imply that there is a linear chain of events that connects the two eras. At this particular historical moment, the big buyers pulling the greater Chinese economies are the same big buyers who now shape the global economy, and these are not predominantly Chinese-owned firms. Instead, the globally oriented discount houses and brand-name merchandisers referred to on page 105 are largely, but not exclusively, Western-owned. Like a century ago, the production networks shaped by these big buyers emphasize piecework (referred to as batch-production system) and flexible work routines. These factors give advantages to factories with low overhead (such as small and medium-sized family-owned firms) and to flexibility in organizing production networks that can expand or contract with changing demand (Shieh 1992; Chen 1995). The technology used in such factories must necessarily match the manufacturing jobs being done and the resources available to those running the businesses. Inevitably, the technology used in such circumstances is simpler and less costly than that deployed in large, vertically integrated factories. To be sure, some differences currently exist between the organization of Taiwan's and the Chinese Mainland's economies, but in the vibrant export of the Mainland economy, production systems intermingle Taiwanese, Hong Kong, and PRC firms, often resulting in even greater flexibility than that found solely in Hong Kong or Taiwan. Indeed, the boundary lines between the economies of Hong Kong, Taiwan, and the PRC have virtually disappeared, creating what Barry Naughton (1997) calls "the China circle".

The point is that the technology in use reflects the way the economy is socially organized, as well as the product being made. That young girls made cloth on single-spindle looms a century ago, or that the women (and often men too) in households gather around the dining table to assemble computer parts today, does not indicate economic involution or capitalistic ineptitude of any kind. But it does indicate that we cannot understand how economies work unless we understand how they are organized in some holistic way.

Notes

1 For a more developed discussion of the theme of this paragraph, including the pertinent literature, see Hamilton *et al.* (2000) and Feenstra and Hamilton (2006).
2 Recently a number of scholars have made similar observations, including Brook and Blue (1999), Wong (1997), and Pomeranz (2000).
3 Much the same can be said for many interpretations of the rise of capitalism in other locations in Asia, in Southeast Asia, and especially in Japan. In the

Japanese literature, however, there is also an equal effort on the part of some scholars to discover the pre-modern origins of Japanese capitalism in functional equivalents to the prerequisites for Western capitalism, as for instance Bellah (1957) did a number of years ago and as Collins (1999) did more recently.

4   There are, of course, limits to this type of comparison. Clearly, European nations are more oriented to capitalism than are most African nations. But the point is that many economic differences result from differences in how economic activity is organized and institutionalized in a particular social environment, and not whether the economic configuration is more or less capitalistic. The latter makes capitalism into an ideal condition, the difference from which can be measured precisely.

5   For reviews of this literature see Rawski (1991), Feuerwerker (1992), and Brook (1989).

6   In his discussion of China's economy, Wong (1997) uses the adjective "Smithian" to describe the market dynamics of an essentially agriculture economy. He opposes Smithian markets with commercial capitalism. Our use of Smithian conforms to the more orthodox economic connotations of Adam Smith's work to mean market dynamics, whether capitalist or not (Hamilton 1985a). We argue in this paper that Wong's distinction between Smithian commerce and capitalistic commerce is not particularly meaningful when applied to nineteenth- and twentieth-century China.

7   For an excellent comparison of the levels of consumption in China and Western Europe in the nineteenth and twentieth centuries, see Pomeranz (2000: 114–65).

8   Also see Pomeranz's more recent estimates (2000: 138–41, 327–38), which appeared after this chapter was first completed.

9   Literati paraphernalia are exceptions, but even these were often modest in contrast to the finery and accoutrements of Western and Japanese elites.

10   The most recent and thorough participant in this debate is Pomeranz (2000), whose book is an extended analysis of "The Great Divergence" between China and Western Europe.

11   Wu Chengming (1985: 260–2) has shown that, in the Ming Dynasty, cotton production was centralized in Jiangsu Province:

> The main type of cloth produced [in this region] was called *biao* and *leng* [later called *shi* cloth]. About 150 to 200 million bolts of this cloth were shipped and marketed throughout a wide region of China connected by means of long-distance trade. In the Qing Dynasty, the areas of cotton production expanded, to include cloth from Sung-jiang, Chang-shou, Wu-shi, all of which was collectively called the Su-sung production area. Apart from these, there were also some smaller centralized production regions in north and central China. The long-distance shipping and marketing of this cloth increased over that which occurred in the Ming dynasty.

For a similar description, see Nishijima (1984: 526).

12   For some of the more recent contributions to the assessment of this literature see Lazerson and Lorenzoni (1999), Storper and Salais (1997), and Vallas (1999).

13   The interpretation of this commercialization is, however, disputed. The Marxian advocates for the sprouts of capitalism view commercialization as evidence for the bourgeoisification of feudalism, a necessary step for the eventual revolution. The critics of this interpretation argue that, despite commercialization, no independent merchant class developed, and hence no capitalism. The Smithian advocates for a sustained economic development in late-imperial China see commercialization as evidence for the creation of price-setting markets that allowed industrious peasants gradually to raise their standard of living through participation in the market. The critics of the Smithian interpretation argue that

no improvement in the standard of living resulted from this commercialization, which instead led to involution and peasant immiseration.

14 In opposition to evidence given by Rawski (1989) and Brandt (1989), Wong (1997: 66) questions how efficient China's markets really were, but without giving any evidence to support his contention.

15 Some might be inclined to think of Adam Smith as the theorist who connected both ends of the commodity chain together, in his concept of supply and demand. Although he theorized demand, Smith's work transformed thinking about production. To some extent neo-classical economics, as a production-led theorization of markets, has followed this lead ever since.

16 The concept of global commodity chains was first suggested by Terence Hopkins and Immanuel Wallerstein (1986), but Gereffi (Gereffi and Korzeniewicz 1994) is most responsible for its recent reemergence and importance.

17 It is worth noting the Western bias in the thinking of many analysts of the imperial Chinese economy, who assume that vertical integration, whether backward or forward, naturally occurs in the process of industrialization, when in fact many writers, including Chandler, show that different outcomes occurred in different locations.

18 It is worth noting that significant portions of the PRC's export economy is organized through the direct investments and involvement of entrepreneurs from Hong Kong and Taiwan, who have moved their firms or branches of their firms to the Chinese Mainland and who have subcontracted portions of their production to local firms.

19 This section draws heavily on the arguments made in Hamilton and Lai (1988).

20 For more detail on these patterns of consumptions, see Hamilton (1977a).

21 Recent research on medieval markets (e.g. Berger 1980; Hilton 1985; Biddick 1985) show greater market penetration into the countryside than previously believed, but they do not fundamentally alter Schechter's characterization.

22 The economic literature on brand names is largely confined to marketing research (e.g. Pilditch 1970). There are, however, relevant economic studies about product differentiation. Economists (e.g. Scherer 1970; Chamberlin 1950) have investigated theoretically the conditions producing product differentiation. According to Scherer (1970: 324), brand-name differentiation occurs when producing firms "strive to differentiate their goods and services from rival offerings". Given this competition, firms rationally plan strategies to create products that consumer will buy.

23 It is significant to note that *huiguan* and *gongsuo* all but disappeared in between during the Mao era in the PRC. After the economic reforms of the late 1970s, they have started to reappear.

24 We are struck by the tendency to interpret Chinese merchant associations as examples of collusion, monopoly, cronyism, and cartels without really examining how these associations operated economically. This tendency is reminiscent of the 1879 civil suit by Western merchants against the Swatow Opium Guild, in which the Westerners brought charges of unfair trade, collusion, and conspiracy against Chinese merchants. The Chinese merchants defended themselves successfully by showing that Westerners had imposed their own conceptions of guilds onto Chinese behavior. Not only was there no collusion, there was also no guild, merely a place where fellow-regionals meet to discuss business and enjoy each other's companionship (Hamilton 1977a; also see Hamilton 1985a).

25 It should be emphasized that merchant groups in late imperial China, the *huiguan*, were unlike Western guilds, to which a person either belonged or not. *Huiguan* are meeting places and not formal organizations. As places, they fostered economically active networks that rested on common social relationships. The commonality allowed the network to be socially binding, because

normative rules existed on how one should treat others bound by a *guanxi* tie. Merchants' associations of out-of-towners formed for many reasons, such as when the critical mass of fellow-regionals was sufficient to support building a meeting hall, when the competition among networks was great enough to promote greater coordination, or when local opposition to non-local merchants merited a common front. But merchant networks, resting on both economic opportunity and some social basis for moral, if not physical, coercion, operated whether a physically located *huiguan* existed or not.

26 The structural similarity between trading in a commodity market and trading in a situation where transactors engage in long-term repetitive trading is striking. For a detailed analysis of commodity, bond, and equity markets that is very similar to the account of Chinese traders given by Clifford Geertz, see Abolafia (1997).

27 Xu (1992) concludes that brand-name products were crucial to how the cloth market functions. Much of the cloth business revolved around the ability to obtain credit, and the better known the brand the easier it was to obtain the credit essential for creating a putting-out system, and the easier it was to sell the cloth to merchants who would resell the cloth in other places. Cloth merchants would grade their cloth and give a different brand name to each grade. The merchants would, in turn, register their brand names with the cloth merchants' trade associations, which would protect the brand names and take such actions as were necessary to punish violators. Xu reports that then, as now, brand-name piracy was a problem.

28 It is worth noting that the large spinning factories that emerged in Shanghai during the 1920s and 1930s, producing cheap yarn, partially supported the spread of handicraft production.

Part II
Chinese capitalism in Asia

5   Hong Kong and the rise of capitalism in Asia

In the early 1980s, British and Chinese diplomats began secret negotiations that would lead to the signing of the Sino–British Joint Declaration in 1984. This agreement set the route by which the two governments and the people of Hong Kong would travel in the thirteen-year journey to 1997. The back-drop to these negotiations, as well as this unprecedented change of sovereignty, has been Hong Kong's status as one of the world's premier cities in the global economy. Any understanding of Hong Kong today has to begin with the capitalist transformation that has made it the global city that it has now become. Most writers treat Hong Kong's rise to prominence as a post-World War Two phenomenon, and explain its success as a triumph of free market capitalism. In this chapter, however, I want to argue that Hong Kong's role in the global economy needs to be situated in history and under-stood as integral to Asia's capitalist trajectories, which developed in the nineteenth century.

This topic is large and complex enough that I will be able to develop only a broad outline of a single theme in this chapter. Before I summarize this theme, however, please consider the two key terms that underlie this chapter: capitalism, and Hong Kong. For capitalism, keep in mind three dimensions. First, don't think of capitalism in terms of countries, but rather in terms of people, firms, money, products, industries, and the interrelationships among these. Second, think of capitalism as ever-changing movements of these things in time and space, as having historical and geographical characteris-tics. Third, think of capitalism, this movement in time and space, as complex economic activities that people try to control in some fashion. Entrepreneurs try to organize these activities, often in competition with each other; workers want to limit them so they don't dominate their lives too much; government officials try to regulate them, usually in opposition to somebody; bankers try to channel them, always to their own advantage. The idea, of course, is that capitalism represents contested economic movements in time and space that are always organized to some degree.

Now consider Hong Kong. Do not think of Hong Kong as an NIC, an NIE, an Asian tiger, a little dragon, or one of the flying geese. All these acronyms and metaphors that are used to characterize Hong Kong are so biological, so functional in the sense of a closed system, that they make Hong Kong seem like a type of economic species that was born or hatched and that may grow to maturity someday. Instead, think about Hong Kong as a place where there is an ever-changing mix and an ever-contested but still organized movement of people, firms, money, products, and industries.

Having conceptualized capitalism and Hong Kong in these ways, I now want to put before you a thesis that summarizes my understanding of Asia's capitalist transformation and of Hong Kong's roles in this transformation. There are two indigenous "great traditions" of organized capitalist development in East and Southeast Asia that began in the nineteenth century with the opening of East Asia to a Western-dominated world economy. These two great traditions are the Japanese and the Chinese modes of organizing and controlling the economic opportunities in the region. As I will explain, the Japanese mode is one of corporatized political economy, and the Chinese is one of entrepreneurial deal-making. These two modes of economic organization have led to two broad, path-dependent trajectories of development. Path dependence, a currently fashionable term, means that history makes a difference. Where you end up depends very much on where you start. This thesis is especially accurate in collective endeavors. Past patterns of collective action always shape but do not necessarily determine the present, as well as the future patterns of action. Chinese and Japanese modes of seizing economic opportunities in the nineteenth century launched two distinct, more or less organized capitalist trajectories of economic development. Greatly altered by World War Two and its aftermath, these trajectories, I maintain, nevertheless re-emerged in the second half of the twentieth century.

I will argue that Hong Kong, as a place, was and continues to be at the organizing center of Chinese-led capitalism. Hong Kong assumed this role shortly after its founding in the nineteenth century and continued it until World War Two. Then, after the war and the Chinese revolution, Hong Kong was the first location where Chinese capitalism re-emerged, although in a somewhat changed form.

In the bulk of this chapter, I will give some supporting evidence for this thesis. In arguing that history makes a difference, I will concentrate mainly on the pre-World War Two period. Then in the last section of this chapter I will discuss in what ways Asia's post-war industrial boom represents a continuation of pre-war trajectories.

Two trajectories of Asian capitalism[1]

Most people date the development of Asian capitalism in areas outside of Japan to the period after World War Two. Certainly, this is the era in which we see Hong Kong, Singapore, and Taiwan begin their rapid industrial ascent. But let me argue that such a dating ignores the fact that the groundwork for this ascent was already prepared well in advance of the war. Chinese entrepreneurs throughout the region were already "capitalistic", if by this we mean that they were already aggressively profit-oriented in their private pursuits and were eager to seize opportunities to make more money. This capitalistic acquisitiveness was in place before the skylines of Hong Kong, Singapore, and Taipei filled with skyscrapers; these cities – the cities that we see today – are the consequences, not the causes, of capitalist development throughout the entire region.

The post-war dating also ignores another fact. The economic changes in these locations were not isolated events, but rather occurred in a rapidly developing capitalist world economy that was producing economic changes in many locations. In fact, the success of capitalism in Chinese and ethnic Chinese-dominated economies outside the Peoples Republic of China – the economies of Taiwan, Hong Kong, Singapore, and many Southeast Asian countries – cannot be understood apart from the dynamics of this global economy. Because Chinese modes of capitalist acquisition are based on bottom-up individual and family-based strategies of seizing opportunities wherever they exist, rather than on top-down corporatist strategies of linking state administrative capabilities with elite economic opportunities, Chinese capitalism is integral to world capitalism itself.

It is the absence of a politically framed domestic economy that makes Chinese forms of capitalism so elusive. Most interpreters of Asia's recent past see no genuine capitalistic development in late-nineteenth and early-twentieth-century China. In fact, it is conventional to argue that, whereas Japan industrialized in the late nineteenth and early twentieth centuries, China remained economically backward. To substantiate this thesis, most scholars simply point to the obvious early industrial capacity of the Japanese – particularly in heavy industries such as iron and steel, and in related products such as ships, trains, trucks, and automobiles – and the lack of these industries in China. With these industries, so the interpretation goes, the Japanese developed modern armies and navies that won wars against the Chinese in 1895 and against the Russians in 1905. By contrast, the Chinese attempt to industrialize did not fare so well. While it is true that the Chinese developed some state-owned, merchant-run heavy industries in the nineteenth century, these industries were not particularly successful (Liu 1962; Feuerwerker 1958), and besides the Chinese lost every war they fought with an outside power from the time of the Opium Wars in the 1840s until World War Two, when it was outside circumstances that defeated the Japanese.[2] Based upon these obvious comparisons, the Japanese industrialized and the Chinese did not.

But if we take another look at these "obvious" comparisons, I want to show you that they are not very persuasive because the time frame is too narrow and the definition of capitalism too rigid. If we made exactly the same comparisons today, that of industrial capacity based upon heavy industry, we would reach nearly the same conclusions: Japan is an industrial power, whereas Taiwan, Hong Kong, and Singapore are relatively undeveloped. The three Chinese-dominated economies do not have much in the way of heavy industry. But does that mean that today they are not industrialized or capitalistic? This is, of course, nonsense. Even so, it is still true that none of these locations has yet made a car for export.[3]

Chinese-dominated areas in the world economy are not characterized by heavy industries; by comparison, the Chinese manufacturers specialize in small and medium-sized firms. These modest-sized factories normally make consumer non-durables – products such as clothes, shoes, TV sets, calculators, computers – manufactured items that fill houses throughout the United States and Europe, as well as in Asia. Economists know that one cannot compute a country's rate of economic growth and its GNP based only on the output of one or two industrial sectors. Why, then, should historians and sociologists, with their comparisons between Japanese and Chinese economies, implicitly do that for the nineteenth and early twentieth centuries?

Even if we were to take all the sectors into account, the historical comparison between Japan and China would still be clouded by the political dimension. China neither won its wars nor developed a successful political economy, and therefore, so the judgment goes, failed as an industrializing society.

This point brings us to a key question. Is political power, in the form of a strong state in war and peace, necessary for or even synonymous with capitalism, with the economic movement of people, firms, capital, products? Most analysts of economic development confidently conclude that centralized political power and capitalistic success are causally interrelated.[4] Indeed one can list numerous examples where the two are interrelated, such as the capitalist development of South Korea, but can one not also envision successful forms of capitalism without a state structure and without an integrated political economy? Let me submit to you that the Chinese forms of acquisitiveness represent such a case.

Consider again the two Asian cases – Japan and China in the late nineteenth and early twentieth centuries. What we see in this contrast is not the presence of capitalism in the one and the absence of capitalism in the other. Rather, I would argue that we see two different versions of capitalism emerging more or less simultaneously with the opening of these economies to global economic and political influences. These same two versions of capitalism have intensified and have taken their places among the dominant forms of global capitalism in the late twentieth century.

Japan's corporatized political economy

Let me compare the institutional beginnings of these two forms of capitalism, so that their differences are clear. Japanese capitalism is largely an indigenous transformation. It is a product of political economy. The record is absolutely clear on this score. For instance, during the Meiji era (1868–1912), the political elites of Japan formulated a comprehensive development plan, thirty volumes, covering every aspect of the Japanese economy.[5] Published in 1884, the plan was based on a thorough investigation of

European economic and corporate institutions undertaken by elite Japanese who went to Europe, lived there for a while, observed, asked questions, and returned to Japan to develop an economic plan to catch up with the West, the first of its kind in the world. Even more amazing than the plan itself is the fact that most of the plan's ten-year targets "were in fact accomplished" (Tu *et al.* 1991: 79).

Another and an even more impressive example of changes in the Meiji period comes from Eleanor Westney in her book *Imitation and Innovation, The Transfer of Western Organizational Patterns to Meiji Japan* (1987). Westney shows that, in the first fifteen years of the Meiji period (roughly from 1868 to 1883), the Japanese political and economic elites organizationally transformed the Japanese state and society. They created, among other things, Western-style armies and navies, postal and telegraph systems, an educational system ranging from primary schools to universities, a unified banking system, and a national police force organized bureaucratically. With each of these organizational innovations, Japanese government officials and private elites imitated Western practices, borrowing freely – sometimes exactly, sometimes loosely. As Westney (1987: 6) insightfully points out, "the distinction between copying and inventing, between imitation and innovation, are false dichotomies: the successful imitation of foreign organization patterns requires innovation". By the end of the Meiji period, Japan was well on its way toward becoming an explicitly, self-consciously organized society, literally a society of organizations, and 100 percent Japanese.

In this context, it is important to see that Japanese industrialization was part of an evolving, but always coordinated political policy. A part of this policy was the creation of an industrial structure made up of competing enterprise groups, each composed of large, quasi-independent firms organized collectively, known as the *zaibatsu*. Mitsui, Mitsubishi, Sumitomo, among others, had all developed diversified holdings, systematic interlinkages among firms, and administrative management techniques before the end of the nineteenth century.[6]

In every arena – in politics, in business, in education – Japanese elites had sufficient authority within Japanese society to implement their policies successfully. This ability rested on a system of internal controls that permeated the social order. This system of social control relied on intricate intersecting relationships that created, beyond kinship, intense structurally embedded duties and obligations, which, from the participants' points of view, were demanding, even oppressive, but not necessarily centralized and authoritarian. This system of control gave the Japanese elites the ability to mobilize and manipulate vast human and material resources. At this point in time, in those early years of global change, this ability to mobilize also gave the Japanese an opening, a passageway by which to propel themselves collectively into the global scene, economically as well as politically.

Why did the Japanese elites pursue this route? Professor Hamashita (2003) of Tokyo University presents a convincing thesis that Japanese officials selected this course of action because they recognized their own limitations vis-à-vis their chief opponents in Asia, the Chinese. In the middle of the nineteenth century, with the Qing Dynasty still holding firm, Japanese officials felt that commercial expansion in Asia was not a viable strategy. Largely due to the Sinocentric tribute system that existed throughout Asia until the middle of the nineteenth century, Chinese merchants controlled commercial exchanges in almost every Asian port, including those in Japan. The Japanese determined that they could not beat the Chinese at their own game of being Asia's chief merchants, and so they began, instead, to develop internally, using their human resources and organizational capabilities to implant a form of Western capitalism in Asia.

Therefore, in Japan, during the nineteenth and early twentieth centuries, the primary carriers of capitalist development were coalitions of political and economic elites.[7] Japanese capitalism was not a creation of the merchant class, although a few merchants participated in the elite coalition. Nor was Japanese capitalism a creation of the peasants, although peasants certainly changed their productive and labor outputs drastically. By comparison with the Chinese case, as we will see, Japanese capitalism is a creation of political economy, of a mutually reinforcing system of governmental controls and elite economic privileges. In a very short period, the Japanese were able to shift from small-scale production of handicraft goods to large-scale production of industrial products, from small factories to hierarchies of bureaucratically controlled corporations organized into conglomerate networks.

Chinese entrepreneurial capitalism

The nineteenth-century institutional foundations of the Chinese forms of capitalism – politically, economically, and socially – were nothing like those of Japan. In the period between 1850 and 1890, it is impossible to imagine the Qing court sending large groups of scholars to Europe and the United States to learn about Western ways. The small efforts that were made largely failed (Kuo and Liu 1978: 537–42). It is impossible to imagine the court creating and then implementing detailed plans for economic development. Even the much vaulted "self-strengthening movement" in the 1860s and 1870s was confined largely to military reforms, and those were crushed in military defeats inflicted by France and Japan. It is even more difficult to imagine the court successfully enforcing a policy of borrowing organizational patterns from the West and implementing them successfully in local society. Listen to the words of Li Hung-chang, China's dominant modernizer in the nineteenth century:

> Although I have never been in Europe, I have been inquiring and investigating Western political and cultural conditions for nearly 20 years, and I have formed some general ideas. I have stated in detail the necessity of

opening coal and iron mines, of building telegraph lines and railways, and of opening schools for pursuing Western knowledge and sciences in order to train men of ability . . . Prince Kung agreed with my suggestion, but said that nobody dared to promote such actions [at court.]. . . . [In any event] the gentry class forbids the local people to use Western methods and machines, so that eventually the people will not be able to do anything. All these undertakings have been promoted by me alone; but it is as difficult to achieve a result as it is to catch the wind. Scholars and men of letters always criticise me for honoring strange knowledge and for being queer and unusual. It is really difficult to understand the minds of some Chinese.

(Quoted in Li 1967: 108–9)

The Qing rulers could not establish a national capitalist-oriented political economy as the Meiji reformers were able to do. Although the Manchus ruled a great empire, their domination did not extend into their own local society. Below the administrative veneer of the imperial regime were politically elusive villages and market towns organized through kinship and status. Even had they so desired, the political elites could not mobilize China's vast human and material resources. To Chinese in local society, "Heaven is high and the emperor is far away".

Although China did not develop a state-based capitalism in the nineteenth century, there was none the less a capitalist transformation among the Chinese. The carriers of Chinese capitalism were not political elites, but rather the heads of households who wanted to achieve some wealth and local renown. These heads of households were peasants, merchants, artisans, and occasionally scholars; they were not organized as distinct classes of people; but rather they were family heads who moved into and out of ambiguously defined social and economic roles. The organizational medium for this Chinese economy rested largely on individual entrepreneurs and family firms embedded in extensive regional commercial networks, networks of fellow-regionals.[8] This was an economy organized through institutions controlled by people embedded in local society. From the time of the Ming Dynasty (1368–1644), the Chinese economy has always been a triumph of local society, never of the state.

Family, kinship, and regionally based institutions shaped economic activity and nurtured distinctive forms of enterprise structure. Because the household, the *jia*, was the critical unit in both community and kinship organization, the Chinese did not make a rigid separation between the household and the firm.[9] Accordingly, firms were like households, and, like households, Chinese enterprises were usually small in size. If the family businesses were really successful, however, the firms, like the households of prominent scholars, grew larger as more relatives and friends were included in the expanding circles of household members. Huge businesses, however, were very rare, because most wealthy businessmen did not try to create larger and larger horizontally or vertically integrated firms, as occurred in Japan or the United States. If they remained economically active at all and did not retire to the countryside, as so many wealthy businessmen did, they invested in extensive networks of family members and friends running small and middle-sized firms, often covering several areas of business and in diverse locations.

The reasons for this strategy were several. The first reason is the effects of inheritance upon shaping business practices (Wong 1985). Japanese inheritance practices rest on the centrality of the stem family (the *ie*) and upon the practice of primogeniture. A large firm could be passed on intact to one son, usually the eldest. By contrast, Chinese inheritance practices rest on the importance of maintaining the patrilineage and hence on partible inheritance, with each son receiving an equal share of his father's estate so that each son can establish an independent household. If the father worked to create a single large business, it would almost certainly be broken up and the assets divided (*fenjia*) after his death. A more reasonable strategy would be to start multiple small businesses that could be passed on intact to the sons after the father's death. This inheritance pattern is reinforced by an institutionalized system that creates economies of scope and scale, not from individual firms, but rather from networks of interconnected firms. Business people use these networks, based on reciprocal relationships (*guanxi* networks), to raise investment capital, secure the necessary labor, manufacture products, and distribute commodities.[10] Building and rebuilding these networks creates an economy based on deal-making entrepreneurship.

This type of entrepreneurial economy, composed largely of small and medium-sized family firms linked together through various types of competitive as well as cooperative social relationships, is not conducive to developing heavy industries, and certainly was not in the nineteenth century. Instead, this household-based economy produced a type of petty commercial capitalism.[11]

You might ask what is capitalistic about the petty commercial practices of the Chinese in the nineteenth century. This would be a good question, because there is nothing essentially capitalistic, in the Western sense of the term, about these practices at all, except for the fact that the Chinese used them very successfully to make a lot of money. In fact, we can trace many of these commercial practices back to economic expansion that occurred during the Ming dynasty. But the fact is that these economic practices were very flexible, did not rely on state patronage, built communities of trust among close colleagues, and were readily adapted to seizing economic opportunities. Founded squarely on institutions of family and locale, these flexible economic practices offered the Chinese their opening, their passageway into a world economy that was just then in the process of becoming globally integrated.

On this score, the record is also absolutely clear. Less than ten years after the opening of China and the founding of Hong Kong, Chinese peasants, merchants, and artisans began to migrate around the world in search of their fortunes. In absolute terms, this migration was extremely large in its day, probably the largest free migration in the world during the nineteenth century. The migration was widely dispersed throughout the world, although the majority of the migrants went to Southeast Asia. The migration was also, from a comparative perspective, quite extraordinary. It was a temporary migration and, like the economic activity itself, was well organized through fellow-regional relationships. The majority of the emigrants planned to and eventually did return to their hometowns.[12]

By contrast, in this same period, the Japanese hardly migrated at all. The only other country in Asia besides China that produced many migrants in these years was the British colony of India, whose people migrated to other spots in the British Empire. The Chinese, however, migrated all over the world wherever money was to be made.

The Chinese searched for gold in California and in Australia in the 1850s and 1860s, and were very successful, but when the mines dried up, they turned to other pursuits, such as digging canals and building railways; they also founded and operated small businesses. However, as we have said, the Chinese migrated mainly to Southeast Asia. Some Chinese had lived in Siam, Java, and the Philippines for a long time, serving the rulers of those countries as privileged merchants and tax farmers. In the last half of the nineteenth century, these Chinese were now joined by hundreds of thousands of newly emigrating Chinese, who poured into every corner of Southeast Asia. Most were wage laborers, but a sizeable minority became very successful businessmen. These Chinese businessmen organized networks of interconnected small firms to collect and process such primary products as timber and rice and to distribute sundry goods throughout the countryside. By the second decade of the twentieth century, the Chinese dominated the service and manufacturing sectors of the local economies throughout the entire region and were major figures in trade between Asian countries and the West.[13]

By the beginning of the twentieth century, Chinese merchants and small-scale manufacturers largely dominated the most modernized parts of the Chinese economy as well (MacPherson and Yearly 1987). In every sector, except in heavy industry, local Chinese were able to outdo Westerners in the production and sale of consumer products for the Chinese. The Chinese bought very few cars, tractors, or trains, but they did buy a lot of textiles, cigarettes, matches, and small household items. Moreover, with a few notable exceptions, the Chinese controlled banking, retailing, and wholesaling, and by the 1920s, when department stores became important, the Chinese controlled the department stores, too (Chan 1982).

Hong Kong was the center of this capitalist expansion. One observer (Remer 1933: x, cited by Hicks 1993: xxxiii) in the 1930s unambiguously said that Hong Kong was "the economic capital of the overseas Chinese". The business structure of Hong Kong in the period before and during World

War Two consisted of firms owned by people coming from or still living in districts in the Canton delta, such as Taishan, Nanhai, Zhongshan, and Xinhui (Chung 2004). These people jointly owned sets of firms that often included hotels, restaurants, insurance companies, import/export companies, banks, and investment and loan companies – all designed to aid the flow of human and material resources from Guangdong, through Hong Kong, into the rest of the world and then back again.

In the years before World War Two, Hong Kong served as a capitalist funnel. Hundreds of thousands of Chinese emigrants from the Guangdong and Fukien hinterland left from and returned to Hong Kong every year (Hicks 1993: 18–20). Billions of Chinese dollars flowed through Hong Kong banks and remittance centers. Some money left China for investments in distant places, but the larger portion flowed into China in the form of remittances – wages and profits from work performed elsewhere. The money flowing into China fueled the commercialization of South China in the period before World War Two.

What is frequently forgotten is the fact that Hong Kong played the same role in the economy of China as it did in the economies of Southeast Asia. In the early twentieth century, organizing their commercial activity largely through Hong Kong, the Cantonese were the largest group of businessmen in Shanghai, and they largely controlled the distribution of imported sundry items throughout China.

While Japan's more or less closed economy was gearing up for the war in Asia, the economies in which the Chinese predominated opened up to global trade. These economic advances occurred in China and in Southeast Asia without the support and the coordination of a strong state. In Japan, the state legitimized capitalism, coordinated elite interests, and resolved conflicts among the elites. In the same period in China, the state collapsed. That, however, did not hinder as much as it freed Chinese entrepreneurs to create networks that spanned political boundaries, and that worked despite, not because of, politics. The weakening and ultimate defeat of the Chinese state opened commerce and industry on the China coast and connected the Chinese with capitalist developments elsewhere. Chinese migration resulted from these conditions. Moreover, with the decline, collapse, and disintegration of the Chinese political order, the real forces of Chinese capitalism, the household entrepreneurs, moved to where money could be made – to such safe havens on the coast as Shanghai, Canton, and other treaty ports, and overseas to Southeast Asia, Hawaii, and the American West Coast.

To summarize, then, in the century before World War Two, the Chinese had integrated themselves into the expanding global economy; they rode the waves of capitalism around the world – in Shanghai, California, Australia, England, the Caribbean, and Southeast Asia. Based upon their flexible networks and hard work, they monopolized selected economic niches in many countries throughout the world. In contemporary terminology, we would say that they monopolized segments of the service sector in the world economy in the late nineteenth and early twentieth centuries. They were retailers, wholesalers, and financiers; they were the world's most prominent capitalist merchant group. Though integrated in and dependent on the global economy, this household-based form of capitalism was independent from any one political order.

On the other hand, after a short period of embracing all things Western, the Japanese elite successfully resisted becoming dependent on international trade. Instead, they created their own internal markets and built their own version of a strong corporate-oriented political economy. They started as industrialists producing for local and regional markets, and from there expanded into the service sectors by organizing their own banks and trading companies, and only then did they gradually begin to integrate themselves into the world economy. The Japanese and Chinese responses are separate reactions to the spread of Western imperialism; both were equally capitalistic and both have led historically to distinct trajectories of economic development.

Economic development in the second half of the twentieth century

In a rather schematic way, I have described the patterns of capitalist development in Asia before World War Two. Now, I want to ask, did World War Two end these trajectories? Or, despite the interruption caused by the war, have these trajectories resumed in the last half of the twentieth century? I want to offer here an answer to these questions by listing five observations concerning post-war development that point to the resumption of the two trajectories of development.

First, if we think historically, it is clear that the Japanese pre-war capitalist trajectory quickly reasserted itself after the war. Japan was able to restore its form of capitalism because it was able to restore its political economy. The Japanese economy was rebuilt in the 1950s. The Cold War had forced the United States to see Japan as its primary ally in East Asia and to support its economic reconstruction. Shortly after the American occupation ended, the new Japanese government, centered on administrative agencies, began to refurbish Japanese-style capitalism by rebuilding a system of political economy in tune with the world as it existed in the post-war era.

One of the first steps of this administrative government was to create a new industrial structure. The American occupation forces had outlawed and disbanded the family-centered enterprise groups, the pre-war *zaibatsu*, by making each firm in the group independently owned and eliminating the family-owned holding company at the center of each group. But shortly after occupation ended, with the blessing of the Japanese bureaucracy, the firms in the former *zaibatsu* renewed their economic alliances and created a new system of business groups without family ownership. Capitalizing on opportunities presented by the Korean War and the Cold War, these enterprise groups, often referred to as *keiretsu*, worked hand-in-hand with the government and quickly resumed their economic domination over the domestic economy.[14] The huge production networks that resulted from these alliances manufactured products that would sell both domestically and internationally. By the mid-1980s, the sales of just the largest firms in these enterprise groups represented 81 percent of Japan's Gross Domestic Product (Hamilton, Zeile, and Kim 1990). In the 1980s, sheltered by an umbrella provided by the state, the manufacturing *keiretsu* led the Japanese form of capitalism to a world prominence that it had never enjoyed before the war.

My second observation is that, whereas the Japanese state easily rebuilt Japan's corporate capitalism, the entrepreneurial base of Chinese capitalism was much more difficult to restore quickly for very obvious reasons. The first thirty-five-year period, from 1945 to 1980, was one of intense political change in Asia. With the exceptions of Hong Kong, Thailand, and a few Himalayan kingdoms, every location in Asia in the decade after World War Two not only had new governments but also new forms of government. For most locations, direct colonial rule ended and independence was declared. China, of course, received its new government through revolution, and Japan through defeat and occupation. Whatever their forms, however, new governments never have an easy time. Civil wars occurred in Korea and Vietnam, and rebellions, coups d'état, repressions, and insurgencies were the rule elsewhere.

This political turmoil caused two major changes in how Chinese entrepreneurs were able to do business. First, the greatest change in the immediate post-war period came as a consequence of the Chinese revolution. In pre-war days, the Chinese mainland, even more than Japan, had been the core of Asia's integration in global economy. Hong Kong and Shanghai were at the center of this core. Suddenly, the Communist Revolution cut off Mainland China, economically and politically, from the rest of the world.

A second and equally important change came with the dismantling of colonial rule in East and Southeast Asia. Throughout pre-war Asia, colonial connections had driven many lines of trade and manufacturing in which the Chinese were directly or indirectly involved. The war and its political aftermath destroyed these trade patterns. The leaders of the new nations wanted new economies that were separated from colonial dependencies. Following the economic thinking of the time that recommended import substitution, most of these new leaders tried to create their own largely independent domestic economies. They nationalized many industries and started numerous other state-owned or state-controlled enterprises. They also tried to create classes of domestic industrialists. They tried to regulate and organize the flow of economic activities within their own borders. Therefore, by the end of the 1950s, the pre-war commercial connections had mostly been severed, and new ones had not yet formed.

The Japanese war, decolonialization in Southeast Asia, and the communist revolution on the mainland had essentially destroyed the commercial capitalism of the pre-war period. Therefore, with only one exception, the Chinese living outside the People's Republic in Asia between 1945 and the early 1960s came under intense pressure to nationalize their economic and political interests. Governments throughout the region watched the activities and questioned the loyalties of first-, second-, and sometimes third- and fourth-generation Chinese businessmen. In the first thirty years after the war, throughout almost the entire region, Chinese entrepreneurialism was directly challenged and channeled by changing political fortunes in the post-war period.

My third observation is that Hong Kong was the only exception to this rule during the immediate post-war period, and it is in Hong Kong where Chinese entrepreneurialism first re-emerged as an independent force in world capitalism. The normal explanation for Hong Kong's post-war industrialization is its extraordinary post-war circumstances. Immediately after the war, the British colonial government tried to resume business as usual in a very unusual time. By 1950, virtually all economic exchanges with the Mainland had come to an end, and Hong Kong ceased to be an entrepot. But, as if to compensate for this sudden end to trade, Hong Kong found itself awash in money, laborers, and entrepreneurs. In the 1950s, investment money, some fleeing from China before the revolution and some in the form of remittances from Southeast Asia that were cut off from entering China, arrived and stayed in Hong Kong. Refugees escaping communist domination built squatter settlements all over the colony, thus supplying a low-wage labor force. And some prominent entrepreneurs from Shanghai moved their factories there. Most people argue that this combination of factors allowed Hong Kong quickly to shift its economy from that of trading entrepot to industrial enclave.

Although these resources certainly contributed to rapid growth, let me argue that the underlying reason for Hong Kong's industrialization was Chinese commercial entrepreneurialism, a resumption of Chinese involvement in the world economy. Chinese businessmen in Hong Kong had to find markets for products that were or that could be produced in a small enclave cut off from normal trade patterns and with no natural resources other than its people. Unlike Japan, Hong Kong, even in the earliest stages of post-war growth, did not have sufficient local markets to consume the goods produced in its factories. As Wong Siu-lun (1988b: 74) notes in his seminal study on the Shanghai industrialists in Hong Kong, marketing was always the biggest problem faced by textile manufacturers, so important in fact that factory owners themselves or their closest representatives "usually traveled in person to look for potential markets and to negotiate face-to-face with their clients".

The markets that Hong Kong entrepreneurs found were part of and integral to a rapidly changing global economy. Fueled by post-war consumerism in the United States and Europe, department stores and "dime stores" were springing up all over both regions and were offering "ready-to-wear" clothes, toys, simple electrical appliances, and other fairly inexpensive household items. Using their commercial know-how and a lot of hard work, Hong

Kong entrepreneurs began to link up with what Gary Gereffi (1994b) calls the "big buyers", purchase agents who represented these large retail and wholesale firms in the West, such as Sears, Montgomery Ward, J. C. Penney, Marks and Spencer, and the Bon Marché.

This pattern of doing business began with rattan furniture, plastic flowers, and textiles, but was soon repeated with a broad range of household non-durable consumer goods – garments, watches, toys, transistor radios, you name it. The firms manufacturing these items were modest in size, tiny as compared to the production networks in Japan, and they were not organized in huge industrial configurations. Rather, grouped often in small, loosely organized subcontracting networks that were reminiscent of pre-war commercial networks, Hong Kong firms became the manufacturing links in long commodity chains that began in the West with designs, orders, and specifications and ended back in the West with marketing, retail, and consumption.

These buyer-driven commodity chains overwhelmingly originated in the United States, Great Britain, and Germany. The trade statistics show this pattern very clearly. Throughout the 1950s, export trade with the United States and Europe was at a very low level and was steady or declining slightly. The upward trajectory of export trade started in 1961 and has grown rapidly since that time. But until the early 1980s the export trade of Hong Kong was overwhelmingly accounted for by trade with just three countries: the United States, Great Britain, and Germany. In 1975, for instance, these three alone accounted for nearly 60 percent of Hong Kong's total exports. In the same year, Hong Kong's exports to Japan accounted for only 4.2 percent, Singapore for 2.7 percent, and Taiwan for less than 1 percent (Cheng 1985: 177).

The old Southeast Asian-centered trading patterns had vanished, and a new set of trading patterns had appeared. But despite these changes, continuity in organization and control remained. Hong Kong entrepreneurs let the markets pull products. Networks of small firms hunted for and then responded to that market demand (Turner 1996). Such a system of commercial capitalism is very different than the Japanese form of capitalism in which large manufacturing corporations create products and push those products into markets. The Japanese system is demand-creating and the Chinese system is demand-responsive.

My fourth observation is that, while Chinese entrepreneurs in Hong Kong began to reconnect with the global economy, Chinese entrepreneurs in Singapore and Taiwan were still embedded in nationalist regimes. In other words, Hong Kong was exceptional, but Singapore and Taiwan were not, at least not until about a decade later. It was not until Singapore declared independence in 1965 that there was any long-term security for Chinese economic interests anywhere in Southeast Asia. Remember that between 1959 and 1968, anti-Chinese pogroms occurred in Indonesia and as late as 1969 race riots occurred in Malaysia. The Chinese everywhere in Southeast Asia lived under the shadow of nationalist politics at least until the 1970s, and some still do today.

Perhaps for this reason, when political officials in Singapore initially formed their industrial policy, they elected not to encourage Singapore's own Chinese entrepreneurs. Instead, they decided to develop many state-owned enterprises and to encourage a broad range of multinational firms from the United States, Europe, and Japan to build manufacturing and service operations in Singapore.

On Taiwan, the great majority of the Chinese – the Taiwanese Chinese – also came under intense pressure to nationalize their interests, but since Taiwan was ruled by Chinese, the ethnic dynamic in Taiwan was to be Chinese rather than to be something else. In the 1950s, however, Taiwan's import substitution policies blocked most attempts by local businesspeople to trade beyond the state boundaries.[15] It was not until the early 1960s that this pattern began to change, and when it did, the initial entrepreneurial linkages were with Japanese trading groups and Japanese manufacturers.[16] For a time, Taiwanese manufacturing firms served as the subcontracting ends of the production networks of Japanese business groups, which is a very different position in the global economy than the one assumed by Hong Kong firms.

My fifth and final observation is that it was not until the early to mid-1980s that the entrepreneurial foundations of Chinese capitalism were fully re-established outside the People's Republic of China. In the late 1970s, political stability came to the core countries of Southeast Asia – Thailand, Malaysia, Indonesia and Singapore. All of them began to relax their economic nationalism. At the same time, mainland China started its economic reforms and opened its economy to outsiders. Soon thereafter, China and Southeast Asia began to attract huge amounts of direct foreign investments. Much of this investment came from firms in Japan, Taiwan, and Hong Kong, all of them looking for cheaper sources of labor and other economic advantages.

These crisscrossing investments were fueled by a new retail revolution that was occurring worldwide, fueled in turn by the development of mall shopping, super discount stores, and brand-name merchandisers such as The Gap, The Limited, Nike, Reebok, Dell Computers, and Mattel Toys, – all of whom were these manufacturers without factories. Computerized inventory systems, rapid sea and air transportation, and saturation advertising accompanied these trends in mass merchandising.

Chinese entrepreneurs quickly took advantage of these new opportunities. They manufactured the newest products, bought the choicest real estate, and made the best deals of anyone doing business in Asia. The new Chinese entrepreneurs from Taiwan, Hong Kong, and Southeast Asia were no longer petty capitalists and no longer bound by considerations of region and lineage.

Their success in Hong Kong, Taiwan, and Southeast Asia came quickly, in part because they were economically the most agile and the most mobilized segments of the population. Often Western-educated, they recognized the opportunities presented by changing political and economic environments. Their success allowed them to assume positions of great economic power in their home economies. In Hong Kong, the deal-making Chinese entrepreneurs bought out most of the British *hongs*. In Taiwan, the private firms owned by ethnic Taiwanese eclipsed the state- and party-owned firms. Throughout Southeast Asia, the ethnic Chinese gained control of the most dynamic sectors of the economy. Chinese entrepreneurs became the super-capitalists of Asia.

Hong Kong is again at the center of this capitalist development. Hong Kong's manufacturing base is now in Guangdong, and Hong Kong is again the capitalist funnel through which human and material resources move into and out of China. The largest investors in China are from the Chinese-dominated economies outside of China: Hong Kong, Taiwan, and Singapore. Until the Asian business crisis, the largest multinational firm in Thailand, the Chaeron Pokphand Group, an enterprise group owned and controlled by ethnic Chinese, was also the largest single investor in China.

Unlike in the pre-World War Two period, the Chinese state is resurgent, but the Communist regime, for all its bravado, is quickly and surely losing control of the economic activities of Chinese local society. The tension, even the contradiction, exists between the regime at the center and the authority vested in local institutions (Wank 1999). If the accounts of Chinese development are correct, then it seems, once again, that the state continues to contribute much less, and local society much more, to capitalist expansion. Moreover, the commercialization and industrialization of China is being aided by money flowing in from Chinese living outside of China. In shape, if not in substance, the capitalist trajectories of Asia have returned to their pre-World War Two forms.

Hong Kong is now a part of China and has begun the 50-year experiment of "one country, two systems". I, of course, do not know what is going to happen as a result of this protracted political experiment. But I will confidently predict that the change in Hong Kong's sovereignty will not bring an end to the trajectory of Chinese-led capitalism that I have described in this chapter. Nor do I think it will mark a new beginning. The past is too much with us for that.

Notes

1 In this section I draw freely from my earlier essay, "Overseas Chinese Capitalism" (Hamilton 1996b).
2 I should perhaps qualify this statement by noting that, while China lost all its wars with outside powers, it continued to have some success in battles in inner Asia.
3 Taiwan's government has tried to create automobile exports, but to date has had no success, even though there are a number of automobile-producing firms in Taiwan. On Taiwan's automobile industry, see Gregory Noble (1987).
4 One of the first statements of this point was made by Alexander Gerschenkron (1962) and more recently by Amsden (1989).
5 Henry Rosovsky discusses this development plan in Tu *et al.* (1991, p. 79–80).
6 For a fine description of the formation of the *zaibatsu* in the late nineteenth century, see Morikawa (1992).

7 For additional background on the formation of capitalism in Japan, see Garon, (1987); Samuels (1987); Smith (1959), and Westney (1987).

8 A classic statement of the relationship between enterprise and family is found in Fei Xiaotong (1992), chapter 12; also see references in Hamilton and Wang's "Introduction" to Fei's book.

9 This point needs further research. For useful beginnings in this direction, see Wong (1985) and Redding (1990).

10 For more on the importance of *guanxi* in business, see relevant chapters in Hamilton (1991a).

11 Yen-p'ing Hao (1986), characterizes the late imperial economy as "commercial capitalism". The term is adequate for the nineteenth century because a great deal of the economic expansion that occurred then in China was indeed commercial and not industrial. But the term "commercial capitalism" is inadequate now because similar family principles and similar types of networks are still being used, but this time to put together small firms to manufacture industrial products – the garments in Hong Kong and the bicycles in Taiwan.

12 For an excellent discussion of Chinese migration in the pre-war period, see Hicks (1993).

13 The literature on the Chinese in Southeast Asia is substantial. A basic text, though quite old, is still Purcell (1965). Also see Skinner (1957); Wickberg (1965); Lim and Gosling (1983); and Wang (1991).

14 For a discussion of the dissolution of the *zaibatsu* during the American occupation, see Hadley (1970). For a discussion of the state role in restoring Japan's political economy, see Johnson (1982).

15 In the 1950s the Taiwanese state pursued a policy of import substitution, first by nationalizing Japanese-owned firms in agriculture and manufacturing, and later by creating new firms for steel and petroleum production. The state also promoted private-sector production, largely for local markets, in critical import-substitution industries such as textile and chemical production. The state also controlled exports.

16 Before the war, Japan had relied on agricultural products from Taiwan. In the 1950s, Japanese trading groups re-established these ties with Taiwanese-owned firms. Serving buyers of Taiwanese products for the Japanese market, these groups soon expanded the range of goods that they traded. In the same period, a group of Taiwanese manufacturers began subcontract production for firms in Japanese enterprise groups, firms that included Toshiba, Sony, Sharp, and Matsushita. Such Taiwanese firms as Tatung and Sampo began by assembling, or manufacturing parts for, household electronics products, primarily radios and TVs. Today one of Taiwan's largest producers of consumer electronics, Tatung, produces under license from Toshiba. Sampo, another of Taiwan's largest makers of consumer electronics, produces parts for Sony and Sharp. Matsushita, Japan's largest maker of household electronic products, started an independent firm and sponsored subcontracting and product assembly networks in Taiwan in the early 1960s. A look at Taiwan's export and import trade statistics demonstrates this link to Japan. In 1955, Japan received 59 percent and North America 4 percent of Taiwan's total exports. Ten years later, in 1965, Taiwan producers still sent 30 percent of all their total exports to Japan and only 21 percent to North America. It was not until 1967 that the U.S. overtook Japan as the leading buyer of Taiwan products. The import statistics are equally revealing. Taiwan has run a very large trade deficit with Japan every year since 1960. In fact, since record-keeping began in 1952, Japanese imports have always ranged between 20 and 40 percent of Taiwan's total imports. For a discussion of the Japanese role in Taiwan's early industrialization, see Gold (1986).

6 Remaking the global economy

U.S. retailers and Asian manufacturers[1]

(Co-authored with Misha Petrovic and Robert C. Feenstra)

Introduction

In every presidential election of the past two decades, the state of U.S. manufacturing has been a campaign issue. In the most recent election, John Kerry repeatedly accused the Bush administration of sending American jobs overseas. The furor began when the head of the president's Council of Economic Advisers, N. Gregory Mankiw, said that outsourcing is "a good thing", is simply "a new way of doing international trade". Sensing an issue, Democrats immediately proclaimed that the Republican administration was pushing firms to send offshore significant parts of their U.S. business. Campaigning in the upper Midwest, candidate Kerry most often referred to this outsourcing as a decline of American manufacturing, but most of the actual news about outsourcing featured service sector jobs, such as call centers, which were moving to India. While the Democrats continued to pound the issue, most economists and business analysts dismissed the claims. Following the standard line, Daniel Drezner (2004) called the controversy "the outsourcing bogeyman". Even economist and diehard anti-Bush *New York Times* columnist Paul Krugman said the outsourcing issue was a non-starter.

Although confident in their claims, most economic analysts did note the continuing decline in U.S. manufacturing. Some even note that the U.S. has been losing manufacturing jobs since the 1980s. Drezner, for example, calls attention to the fact that U.S. manufacturing jobs have "declined for 43 consecutive months", but he, like most others, says that there is no cause for worry because many higher-paying, knowledge-intensive jobs are being added to the U.S. economy, even as the more standardized, and hence tedious and lower-paying, jobs are moving to other regions around the world. Confident that the "laws of comparative advantage" apply to the future of American competitiveness, many economists believe that, in the long run, every nation's economy is better off if trade occurs in a borderless world.

A prominent part of this debate is the role of the state in ensuring the economic welfare of the nation. On one side of debate, the so-called neoliberals argue that states need to create and maintain an institutional infrastructure ensuring that markets work openly and without undue interference from any source. Such an infrastructure necessarily includes a financial structure – banks and regulated markets for stocks, bonds, commodities, and money – that operates in a transparent fashion, allowing all players access to all relevant information. The entire system operates to ensure that prices of goods, services, property, and capital are established by market mechanisms of supply and demand. To the extent that all nations have such infrastructures and that these infrastructures are equally open to people, locals as well as foreigners, then in principle prices structures will reflect global markets. And if global markets work as the advocates of comparative advantage suggest they work, then, in the long run, all nations will have an advantage in something. From this point of view "global", rather than "international" trade is the ideal.

The other side of the debate is one articulated through the lens of political economy. Here issues are defined in terms of competitive, instead of comparative, advantage. According to this view, each government has an obligation to maximize its nation's competitive advantage, and thereby to increase the national share of world trade. The state's role in increasing the nation's competitive advantage is also to establish an economic infrastructure, but in this case the infrastructure works to increase a nation's productive capacity and to monitor and regulate economic activity in order to position national firms advantageously relative to firms of other nations. Officials can increase a nation's productive capacity by targeting industries for special financial incentive, by funding research in selected areas, or by raising the level of education for all citizens. They can monitor economic activity through creating government departments that collect relevant information, analyse economic statistics, and develop economic policies to further growth in the targeted industries. The political economy perspective cares little about global markets, but a lot about international trade. From this point of view, the flow of international trade is an aggregated outcome of global competition among nations and national firms, and the most aggressive nations win in this competition, while less proactive nations diminish.

This on-going debate about markets and states harks back to the controversy about the causes of Asian industrialization. Free trade advocates line up on one side of this controversy, and developmental state advocates line up on the other. The free traders argue that Asian states opened their respective economies to unrestricted global trade, and because of cheap Asian labor and other comparative advantages, the products manufactured by Asian firms were competitive in global markets. Critiquing the free trade position, political economists contend that the Asian states planned and managed economic development and "governed the markets" throughout the region. The Asian states created their competitive advantage *vis-à-vis* other nations, and obtained a disproportionately large share of the international trade in manufactured goods.

We could, quite appropriately, push back this market–state debate to Adam Smith's critique of state-led mercantilist policies based on his notion of the natural laws of supply and demand. Indeed, there is considerable continuity in this debate about the role of markets. In Smith's theory, as in the theories of comparative advantage today, markets are assumed to work effortlessly and without cost according to the invisible hand of supply and demand. In principle, supply and demand are both equally important, but in fact most economic theories have a decided bias on the supply side, in particular in specifying the costs of production (including transaction costs) and the factors that might impede or distort production. In fact, in the continuing discussions of the "Asian Miracle", the entire market side of the debate focuses on the factors relating to supply and none to demand (e.g. World Bank 1993; Stiglitz and Yusuf 2001).

Political economists make the same mistake. In nearly all studies of the competitive advantage among nations, the analyses focus on production and factors relating to production. Some writers emphasize government policies and others social and economic institutions, as well as business organization or more generally the business environment. It is rare for any analyst to examine the influence of demand on the organization of production.[2] This production bias is nowhere more obvious than in the debate about what caused post-World War Two Asian industrialization. The works cataloging the economic policies of the Asian developmental states (Johnson 1982; Cumings 1984; Gold 1986; Wade 1990; Woo 1991; Woo-Cumings 1999; Evans 1995) and the business activities of state champions (i.e., firms selected by the state for special support) (Amsden 1989, 2001) are comprehensive and detailed. Throughout this entire literature about the causes of Asian industrialization, there is hardly any reference to how demand might have influenced production. It is, therefore, ironic that those developmental state theorists who are most critical of market explanations simply assume that market processes prevail at the demand end: somehow all those Asian manufactured and exported products find overseas buyers. Robert Wade (1990: 148), who discusses the Taiwanese government's economic policies in meticulous detail, seems to speak for most theorists when he writes that the "marketing side of Taiwan's export growth . . . remains a mystery".

Despite Wade's comment, the marketing (or demand) side of Asian export growth is not a mystery. Likewise, the reasons U.S. manufacturing jobs are declining is also not a mystery. Moreover, the rise of Asian and the decline of U.S., manufacturing are two aspects of the same trend. This trend can best be identified as the rise of global retailing and of retailers as global market-makers. The transformation of the global markets for consumer goods has had the most profound consequences for the restructuring of the global economy in the last forty or so years, and of the part upon which Asian industrialization is based. The part of our story that we present here starts in 1965, at the time when the first global markets for mass produced consumer goods were created, and focuses on the relations between American general merchandise retailers and their Asian suppliers. These two types of firm have been, arguably, the most important global market-makers for all consumer goods except for cars and food in the past thirty years.

In the first section we provide a brief historical background, by retracing the pre-1965 evolution of the U.S. retailing sector. After that, we divide the developments between 1965 and 1997, the year of the major financial crisis that shook the foundations of the East Asian economies, into three distinct, roughly ten-year periods, and dedicate one section to each of these. As we describe in the final section, changes in the relations among global retailers and Asian manufacturers before 1997 were the main drivers leading to the emergence of export-oriented industrialization in mainland China in the years after 1997.

Before the retail revolution

In 1981, Barry Bluestone (Bluestone *et al.* 1981), writing with a group of colleagues, used the words "retail revolution" to describe the changes in the American economy that they saw occurring in the decades immediately following World War Two. In the thirty years between 1950 and 1980, they observed that the entire retail sector had gone through a "total restructuring". Viewing the sector from the vantage point of a new century, we would have to argue that what they described as the retail revolution in 1981 was, in fact, a global transformation just beginning. Today, less than twenty-five years later, it is apparent that the retail revolution has changed, and continues to change, not only in the U.S., but also in the global economy.

Bluestone and his colleagues' use of the term "retail revolution" was not, however, the first. Indeed, analysts have been talking about revolutions in distribution since the emergence of the first department stores in Paris in the 1850s. The term was used again at the beginning of the twentieth century to describe Montgomery Ward's and Sears and Roebuck's mail order catalogue businesses and the sophisticated warehousing systems that supported them. It was also used for the rapid expansion of the chain store format in the 1920s, for the spread of supermarkets in the 1930s, and the rise of general merchandise discounters around 1960. In fact, ever since the beginnings of industrialization in Europe and the United States, large retailers have been prominent in all advanced market economies. Moreover, most of what we viewed as retailing and distribution innovations in the second half of the twentieth century, many of which are summarized by the term "lean retailing", such as point-of-sale information, supply-chain management, and automated inventory and warehousing systems, had clear counterparts in the first half of the twentieth century.[3] We must be careful, therefore, not to overstate the distinctiveness of retailing in the most recent decades. That said, however, we want to stress that, from 1965 onward, transformation in retailing has been rapid, global, and qualitatively different than that which preceded it.

The national organization of U.S. retailing between 1945 and 1965

The consolidation of and concentration in retailing in the United States occurred at different times and for different reasons than had occurred in manufacturing. In the decades before World War Two, the manufacturing sectors of the American economy had already gone through several periods of mergers and massive consolidations that not only resulted in vertical and horizontal control over processes of production, but, by virtue of the economic power of manufacturing firms, also allowed them to control the distribution and retailing of their products as well (Chandler 1977). For instance, the automobile manufacturers developed franchised retail outlets, as did some consumer appliances makers (e.g., RCA and General Electric). More often, manufacturers dealt directly with wholesalers that in turn distributed products to many small retail stores, most of which were independently owned. These changes in American manufacturing are nicely described and much debated in a series of books and articles starting with Chandler (1977, 1990) and proceeding on to Fligstein (1990), Lazonick (1991), Roy (1997), Prechel (2000), Perrow (2002), and Langlois (2003).

Despite the preponderance of small, independently owned retailers, a number of large retail chains began to emerge before World War Two. The mail-order mass retailers, such as Sears and Roebuck and Montgomery Wards, were very prominent before World War One, and in the 1920s, with the growth of cities and the decline of rural America, these same firms began to establish chain stores in urban cores throughout the United States. Also, the largest retailer before World War Two was A&P (Atlantic and Pacific), which had established a national chain of grocery stores early in the twentieth century. These chain stores, however, were important exceptions to the rule, as most retail firms, whatever the type of product they sold, continued to be small, regionally concentrated and privately owned. Clothing, shoes, groceries, hardware and building supplies, household appliances, as well as most other consumer products were sold through such locally or regionally owned stores, and these stores obtained their goods through supply lines that they neither directly controlled nor could indirectly influence through their buying power. Therefore, with only a few exceptions before World War Two, there was a stark contrast between the relative concentration of manufacturers in their respective sectors (Chandler 1990) and the relative lack of concentration of retailers in their respective sectors (Bluestone *et al.* 1981).

The divergence between manufacturers and retailers was further exacerbated by state and federal legislation known as "fair trade laws". These laws "(technically Resale Price Maintenance statutes) were the legal mechanism that permitted manufacturing firms to set a minimum price that retailers (and wholesalers) could charge for the products they produced" (Bluestone *et al.* 1981: 124–5). Although these laws were not well enforced or very effective in maintaining price levels for most products, they none the less reduced the enthusiasm and probably the capacity within the retail sector for widespread expansion and consolidation.

Immediately after World War Two, therefore, the large-firm model of corporate capitalism predominated (Prechel 2000). In the United States, the

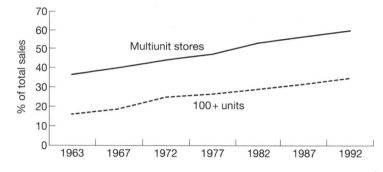

Figure 6.1 Growth of chain stores in the retail sector, 1963–92

position of General Motors, Ford, IBM, General Electric, Westinghouse Boeing, and a long list of other large corporations in nearly every economic sector seems unassailable (Chandler 1990: 638–732). Likewise in early post-war years, mammoth business groups in Europe and Japan, such as Daimler-Benz, Volkswagen, Mitsubishi, and Mitsui, re-emerged stronger than they were before the war, and new giants, such as Toyota and Sony, suddenly entered the scene.

While manufacturing firms had built dominant positions in their respective industries before and immediately after World War Two, retail firms (e.g., department stores and supermarkets) only started the process of concentration in earnest in the 1950s (Bluestone *et al.* 1981). (See Figures 6.1 and 6.2.) Although fair trade laws continued to favor manufacturers over retailers, such large-chain retailers as Sears, J. C. Penney, and Montgomery Ward,

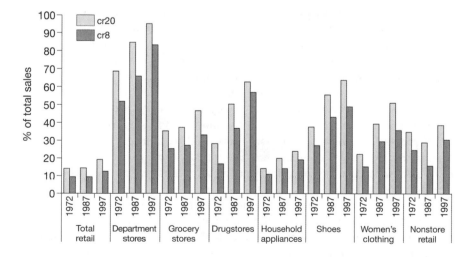

Figure 6.2 Concentration in select retail sectors in top 8 and top 20 firms, 1972–97

went through a period of rapid expansion and began to dominate department store retailing. These national chains became so dominant, in fact, that many small, independently owned department stores simply went out of business in the face of the centralized buying power of these national stores.

One of the great advantages of the large department store chains was their ability "to escape price-maintenance regulations by selling private-label products, such as Sears's Kenmore line produced by Whirlpool". In fact, "the proliferation of private labels reduced the efficacy of fair trade laws to the point where active support almost disappeared" (Bluestone *et al.* 1981: 126). By the mid-1960s, most states no longer actively enforced these laws, and by the mid-1970s the laws had been repealed throughout most of the United States. In 1981, when Bluestone and his colleagues examined the retail structure of the United States, the retail revolution was in full swing. "Repeal (of fair trade laws)", they (1981: 126) concluded, "precipitated a virtually total restructuring of the retail sector."

The initial set of changes, occurring in the late 1950s and 1960s, were, in large part, a consequence of three interrelated factors: tax policies on commercial construction, the construction of interstate highways, and suburbanization. First, in 1954, the U.S. Congress passed, and President Eisenhower signed into law, the Internal Revenue Code of 1954. These tax laws provided for accelerated depreciation of commercial buildings, among other business investments. This loophole in tax laws allowed investors to make much higher returns on commercial construction than on equities, and so the shopping-center construction boom began, stimulated not by the demand of consumers for convenient shopping locations, but rather by the money of speculators (Hanchett 1996). At the end of 1953 there were about ten major shopping centers in the country, but beginning immediately in 1954 there was a surge not only in the more common strip malls, of which there were about 500 in 1954, but more importantly in the construction of large shopping centers. In 1964, ten years after the initial surge of the shopping center development, there were 7,600 shopping centers in the United States, including nearly 400 large regional shopping malls, and accounting for almost 30 percent of total retail sales (Bucklin 1972; Cohen 2002). All of these shopping centers not only needed anchor stores, which were usually general retailers such as Sears and Macy's, but also specialty stores that could bring in niche consumers.[4] Most major retail chains of this period expanded rapidly in size, especially those that were already large and well capitalized. Sears, J.C. Penney, and Federated Stores (Macy's) were among the clear winners in the contest to become the standard anchor stores in the new malls being built.

By the 1960s, however, the supply of available additional retail space created opportunities for a whole new lineup of specialty retailers, retailers that began to appeal to the main currents of the Vietnam and post-Vietnam War era: growing youth and sports subcultures fed by television programs and advertising, the rapid increase in women working in professional jobs, counterculture movements that led to alternative lifestyles and niche fashions. These new specialty retailers, such as The Gap and The Limited, started operation in the 1960s, expanded rapidly and went public in the 1970s, and joined the exclusive Fortune 500 group of leading U.S. companies in the 1990s.

The second major driver of the retail revolution was another act of government, the Federal Highway Act of 1956, which established the inter-state highway system, including ring roads around major American cities. By the 1960s, high-speed interstate highways connected all major urban areas in the country. These highways facilitated not only suburbanization, which is our third factor, but also the ability of firms efficiently to use trucking as their primary form of product distribution, which in turn led to more developed logistical systems of distribution.

A closely related third driver was the suburbanization of America's urban population. The mass migration to the suburbs that started in the late 1950s and continued through the 1980s led to massive home construction and to widespread home and automobile ownership. It also provided consumers for the shopping centers that had been built around every major urban area. These consumers increasingly became able to choose among the niche-market lifestyles that specialty retailers began to target. Each enhanced the other. By the late 1970s, in response to the boom in home construction and the rise in home ownership, the traditional sector of hardware and home building supplies experienced a rapid reorganization, led by home improvement retail chains such as Home Depot.

These three drivers of the initial phase of the retail revolution paved the way for two sets of changes, both occurring in the 1960s and 1970s: the emergence and rapid widespread adoption of value merchandising and, at nearly the same moment, the split in value merchandising between general merchandisers and specialty retailers. As Table 6.1 (page 154–5) shows, it was during this period and shortly thereafter that most of the now promi-nent stores in both categories began operations or converted to value merchandising. In one year alone, 1962, only months apart from each other, Wal-Mart, Kmart, Kohl's and Target first began operations as self-service discount department stores.[5] Specialty retailers, as we have seen, date from this period as well. Both categories of value merchandisers, as well as the national department store chains, would increasingly source the goods they sold from Asian manufacturers.

By 1965, therefore, the supply of retail space was large and was rapidly growing, growing perhaps even faster than the demand for goods that retailers were selling. Also by 1965, a diversified lineup of strong regional and national retail chains was starting to emerge: general department stores, discount department stores, specialty retailers of many varieties, including clothing, sport goods, toys, grocery and drugstore chains, all to some degree competing with each other and all requiring predictable supply lines.

Table 6.1 U.S. retail firms with revenues over $5 billion, 2001. (Ordered by founding year.)

Name	Industry	Fortune rank	Revenues 2001	Founded
Sonic Automotive	Automotive	288	6,337	1997
AutoNation	Automotive	101	19,989	(1996/99)
United Auto Group	Automotive	292	6,221	1990
Office Depot	Office Products	173	11,154	1986
Staples	Office Products	178	10,744	1986
BJ's Wholesale Club	Warehouse Club	331	5,280	1984
Costco Wholesale	Warehouse Club	44	34,797	1983
Home Depot	Home Improvement	18	53,553	1978
Nike	Apparel Market	204	9,489	1972
Gap	Apparel	149	13,848	1969
Best Buy	Electronics	131	15,327	(1966/83)
CVS	Food and Drug	93	22,241	1963
Limited	Apparel	208	9,363	1963
Rite Aid	Food and Drug	132	15,297	(1962/68)
Wal-Mart Stores	General Merchandise	1	219,812	1962
Target	General Merchandise	34	39,888	1962
Kmart	General Merchandise	40	36,910	1962
Kohl's	General Merchandise	253	7,489	1962
Toys 'Я' Us	Toys	175	11,019	1957
Dollar General	General Merchandise	326	5,323	1955
Circuit City Stores	Electronics	157	12,959	1949
Winn-Dixie Stores	Food and Drug	160	12,903	(1939/55)
Albertson's	Food and Drug	38	37,931	1939
Dillard's	General Merchandise	230	8,388	1938
Publix Super Markets	Food and Drug	133	15,284	1930
Federated Dept. Stores	General Merchandise	118	16,895	1929
TJX	Apparel	179	10,709	1929
Safeway	Food and Drug	45	34,301	1926
Lowe's	Home Improvement	94	22,111	(1921/61)

(Continued on next page)

Table 6.1 (cont.)

Name	Industry	Fortune rank	Revenues 2001	Founded
J. C. Penney	General Merchandise	50	32,004	1902
Walgreen	Food and Drug	78	24,623	1901
Nordstrom	General Merchandise	314	5,634	1901
Saks	General Merchandise	297	6,071	(1900/24)
VF	Apparel Market	320	5,519	(1899/1951)
Sears Roebuck	General Merchandise	32	41,078	1893
Kroger	Food and Drug	22	50,098	1883
May Dept. Stores	General Merchandise	143	14,175	1877

For our purposes, the most distinguishing feature of this emerging retail lineup before 1965 was the fact that it was supplied with products almost exclusively from American manufacturers. As Figure 6.3 shows, from the time of the Great Depression in 1929 through 1965, U.S. imports of foreign goods were at historically low levels. The period of depression reduced the demand for, and the destruction of Europe and Asia during World War Two reduced the supply of, foreign goods. Therefore, in the years immediately after World War Two, American manufacturers not only supplied goods for American consumers, but also created markets in Europe and Asia for

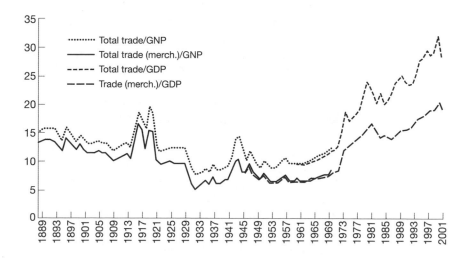

Figure 6.3 Trade in GNP, 1889–2000

American-manufactured products, especially capital goods needed to rebuild the economies around the world. The 1950s were definitely the heyday for American manufacturing.

The globalization of supplier markets for U.S. retailers after 1965

In 1965, the United States ran its first post-war trade deficit with Japan. The deficit was rather small, $334 million, and did not represent a major cause for concern, especially in comparison with the massive $6.3 billion trade surplus with the rest of the world. A large increase in the imports of steel, the main category in overall U.S.–Japan trade, could have easily been attributed to temporary difficulties of the domestic industry in a labor contract negotiation year. The rest of Japanese exports – radios and monochrome TVs, small motorcycles, low-end fabrics, apparel, and footwear, toys and glass products – while occasionally provoking vocal complaints from affected domestic industries, seemed to reinforce the widely held opinion that Japanese manufacturers still had a long way to go before they could compete with the technological sophistication and industrial power of their American counterparts.

In retrospect, however, the beginning of the U.S. trade deficit with Japan could easily be interpreted as a telling, even if only symbolic, indicator of the new era in the evolution of the U.S. economy, characterized by persistent trade deficits with Asian economies and the flooding of domestic markets by foreign manufactures. In sharp contrast with the previous period, the structure and dynamics of the post-1965 U.S. economy have been profoundly impacted by its rapidly developing links with the global economy. In 1965, the ratio of total U.S. international trade (imports and exports) to its GDP stood at a relatively modest 10 percent, a little bit over half of what it was at its all-time high in 1919 and still lower than in the years before the Great Depression. Fifteen years later, in 1980, it reached 24 percent. In the same period, the U.S. economy turned from a net exporter, the position it held since the 1870s, to a net importer, with trade deficit in 1980 approaching $20 billion.

Trade figures from 1965 on show that imports in most major categories of manufactured goods constituted a growing percentage of U.S. consumption. Figure 6.4 shows that, in 1965, imports accounted for less than 10 percent of total U.S. consumption in all major categories of manufactured consumer goods, but import penetration in all categories of consumer (non-grocery) goods rose rapidly after that. Where did these imports come from? Figure 6.5 shows that the East Asian countries (i.e., Japan, South Korea, Taiwan, Hong Kong, and China) accounted for over 50 percent in almost all categories of imports from 1975 on.

We will now disaggregate these trends decade by decade to show the dramatic shifts that occurred from 1965 to the present time.

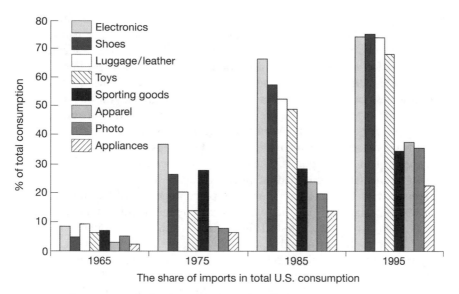

Figure 6.4 Import penetration in general merchandise

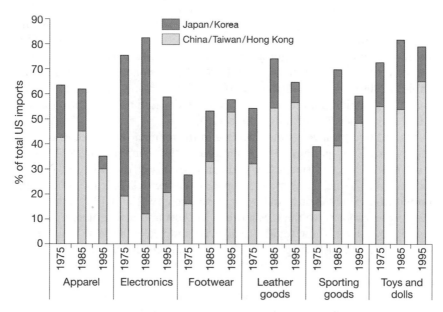

Figure 6.5 Imports of general merchandise from Asia

1965–1975: Creating Asian suppliers for American retailers

Beginning around 1965, U.S. imports of foreign goods started abruptly to rise. Between 1965 and 1972, the data on foreign imports have to be pieced together from a variety of sources, but from 1972 on the data are extraordinarily detailed and allow a definitive description of what these imports are.[6] These trade data show that Asian exports to the United States began from a very low base but grew at an increasing pace through the rest of the century. U.S.-bound exports from Japan and Hong Kong started first, but only in several categories of goods. As noted, Figure 6.4 shows that in 1965 imports constituted a very low percentage of total U.S. consumption in all the major categories of imported goods. The only import above 10 percent of total U.S. consumption was an intermediate product, Japanese steel.

However, in the next five years this percentage jumped dramatically, so that by 1972, the first year that we can examine the detailed data, some clear trends begin to emerge. First, Taiwan and South Korea joined Japan and Hong Kong as the principal Asian economies exporting to the U.S., with Singapore coming somewhat later and providing smaller quantities of a narrower range of U.S. imports than the other Asian NICs. In 1965, imports from Taiwan and South Korea were almost non-existent, but, starting around 1968 for Taiwan and 1970 for South Korea, the exports jumped suddenly. We will concentrate primarily on these two economies, because, by 1985, they are the two pivotal economies in the region, their total exports in the 1980s exceeding Japanese exports to the U.S. in most categories except for automobiles and consumer electronics.

Second, from a U.S. perspective, during the first decade (1965–75) these countries contributed only a very small percentage of total U.S. consumption, even in the fastest-growing categories. But from the perspective of the exporting economies, these goods exported to the U.S. accounted for a very large percentage of the total growth of these economies (Feenstra and Hamilton 2006). This was especially true for Hong Kong, Taiwan, and South Korea, all of which maintained low levels of domestic consumption during the first several decades of industrialization.

The third trend is a very rapid increase in the number of categories of items being exported. Assuming that the pattern of U.S. imports in 1972 reflects emerging trends that started a few years earlier, we see from Figure 6.6 a very rapid increase in the number of seven-digit custom classifications for items exported from South Korea and Taiwan between 1972 and 1988. Already by 1972, Taiwan exported to the U.S. more than 2000, and Korea more than 1000, categories of goods. These totals rapidly rose and peaked in 1985 and 1986, at levels approaching 6000 categories for Taiwan and 5000 for South Korea.

The fourth trend shows that, throughout the period, despite the wide variety of exported goods, a very high percentage of their total value was concentrated in only a very few product categories. As Figure 6.7 reveals, the highest concentration for both countries occurs in the earliest period, with

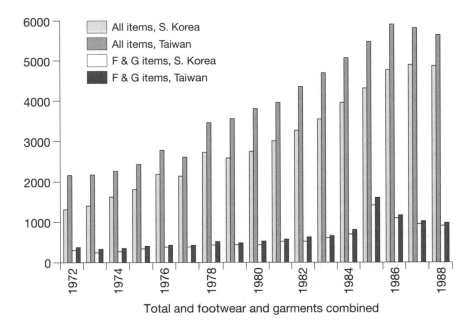

Figure 6.6   Number of categories of imports, total and footwear and garments combined

nearly 50 percent of the value of Korea's exports to the United States and 25 percent of the value of Taiwan's exports to the United States being contained in only ten categories of seven-digit categories. Indeed, in 1972, nearly 90 percent of the value of Korean exports, and nearly 80 percent of the value of Taiwan's exports, was in the top 100 categories. In other words,

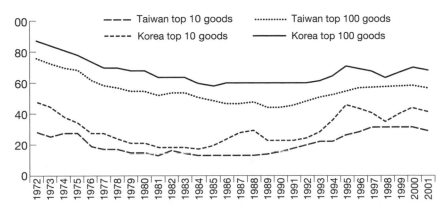

Figure 6.7   The share of top 10 and top 100 categories of goods in total value of exports to the United States, 1972–2001

in the early years of industrialization both countries exported very large batches of only a few items.

What are these items? As we will describe more fully in the next section, the products are typically quite specialized types of footwear, apparel, consumer electronics, and an array of other goods. We can get a general picture of the full array of these goods with the following "export land-scape" from both countries. Imagine the product classification used by the U.S. customs (from 1972 to 1988 this was the seven-digit TSUSA classifica-tion), arranged on along a plain from 1000000 to 9999999. If we group all products to the first three digits and aggregate the total value of goods in these three-digit categories exported to the U.S. over the entire period the classification was in use, then we obtain for each country a picture of the goods exported to the U.S. These are shown for South Korea and Taiwan in Figures 6.8 and 6.9. From these landscapes, it is apparent that most of the export value from these economies is primarily in just a handful of major categories and that, with a few exceptions, the export landscapes of the two countries look very similar. Going from left to right, the peak categories above two billion U.S. dollars in one or both export landscapes are plywood (TSUSA 240), garments (381–4), steel (610), machinery and component parts of machinery (646), (653), (661), (676), electrical appliances (684), elec-tronic products – television and radio (685), (687), transportation vehicles and parts (692), footwear (700), luggage and related products (706), furniture (727), bicycles (734), (737), rubber and plastic products (772), and leather products (791).

If we examine these landscapes year by year and disaggregate the general categories product by product, then a fifth trend emerges. In the years before

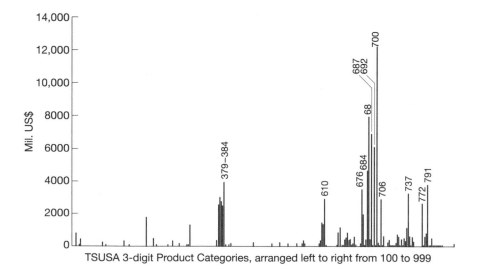

Figure 6.8 US imports from South Korea, 1972–88

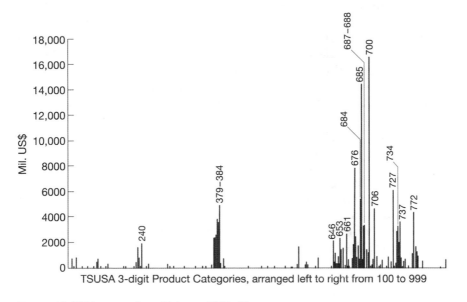

Figure 6.9 US imports from Taiwan, 1972–88

1975, the exported goods were very similar among the exporting countries. For example, before 1975, garments exports were among the highest categories of exports from both countries, with garments providing about a third of the total value of Korea's exports to the United States and a quarter of Taiwan's. Among the 263 and 345 types of garments that South Korea and Taiwan, respectively, exported to the United States in 1972, the top five items provided 42 percent of the total value of garments from Korea and 39 percent from Taiwan. Three of the top five garment items are the same for both countries, namely specific types of sweaters, knit shirts, and trousers, all for women and girls. As we will see in the next section, however, after 1975 the products being exported began rapidly to diverge.

For the period before 1975, what explains these five emergent trends? Instead of the usual inchoate supply-side stories used to explain the Asian Miracle, most often in terms of developmental states, smart and trusting entrepreneurs, and free trade regimes, we should see that these particular trends are the direct results of the emergence of global intermediaries and their ability to create supplier markets, often including suppliers themselves, for retail products to be sold in the United States. Therefore, rather than simply asking what comparative advantages these few Asian economies had in this period, we should ask instead why did most of the major U.S. retailers begin to source products in East Asia between 1965 and 1975?

First of all, we know that most of the major retailers did begin to source during this period. They developed networks of buying offices (or contracted with major sourcing firms) in Hong Kong, Taiwan, and South Korea in the late 1960s and early 1970s, and they quickly ramped up their orders from these countries in the following years (Gereffi and Pan 1994). For example, Sears established its buying office in Taiwan in 1967, Kmart and J. C. Penney in 1971, and Associated Merchandising Corporation (which bought for Dayton-Hudson, Federated Department Stores, and Target, among many others) and Mast Industries (a wholly-owned subsidiary of The Limited) in 1973 (Gereffi and Pan 1994). At about the same time, most of these U.S. retailers opened offices in South Korea (Jung 1984).

The reason they came to Asia in the first place was their rapid expansion and intense competition in the United States in the late 1960s and early 1970s.[7] In response to the Fair Trade Laws, many of the largest department stores began to develop private-label clothing that they could use to undercut their brand-name competitors. The department stores first bought their private-label clothing from American-based manufacturing companies located in the South, but when orders rapidly expanded, these Southern manufacturers began to arrange for a portion of their manufacturing to be done in Asia (Bonacich and Waller 1994). Their ability to source goods in Asia was facilitated by Japanese trading companies, especially Mitsui, which served as intermediaries between the American firms that ordered the goods and the Asian firms that manufactured them.

In the earliest years, the role played by Japanese trading companies is absolutely crucial and almost entirely overlooked. Known as *sogo shosha*, Japanese trading companies were instrumental in facilitating the re-industrialization of Japan after World War Two. The nine top trading companies, generally one for each of Japan's largest business groups, handled most of the trade into and out of Japan from the early 1960s (Yoshino and Lifson 1986; Tsurumi 1984; Kojima and Ozawa 1984). These same companies also served an identical role within the domestic economy where they brokered trade among firms both within and between business groups. Within Japan, says Okumura (1991: 222), the trading companies "serve as intermediaries for intercorporate trading", and handle most exchanges among firms of all sizes. This use of trading intermediaries created "a very large web of reciprocal dealings in Japan" and thus created a dense network of cooperating firms.

In the 1960s, just as the retail revolution was occurring in the United States, Japanese trading companies began to expand their operations outside of Japan. Partly in response to opportunities presented by U.S. retail firms, these firms began to establish manufacturing firms for the specific purpose of making products for export. Eighty percent of these firms were located in developing countries, mostly other countries in Asia (Kojima and Ozawa 1984). These manufacturing firms were usually organized as joint ventures, which represented some combination of a Japanese firm, a local firm, and the trading company. According to Kojima and Ozawa,

This geographical concentration reflects the fact that most of these ventures produce standardized products in highly labour-intensive operations, both for local markets and for export, by capitalizing on low-cost labour in Third World countries. It is also in the developing countries that the trading companies' ability to provide business-infrastructural services is in great demand and can create profitable opportunities for direct investment.

(Kojima and Ozawa 1984: 43)

Before 1975, Japanese trading companies handled the lion's share of exports from Taiwan, South Korea, and Hong Kong (Feenstra and Hamilton 2006; Fields 1995; Wade 1990; Jung 1984; Rhee *et al.* 1984). They were able to accomplish this feat by developing vast communication networks that allowed them to match orders on the one side of the Pacific Ocean with manufacturing capabilities on the other side. In the 1970s, Mitsui and Co., for example, had established "the most comprehensive sophisticated system, called a 'global on-line network system'; telex-cum-computers are strategically installed in five key cities around the world. The daily volume of telex communication can amount to as many as 80,000 dispatches and receipts, a volume far larger than that handled by any other trading company" (Kojima and Ozawa 1984: 25).

With the initial success of Japanese trading companies in creating competent suppliers, it soon became apparent to all concerned, however, that neither the Japanese trading companies nor other types of go-betweens were needed any longer to match U.S. retailers to non-Japanese Asian manufacturers. The general department stores and, more importantly, the new generation of discount and specialty retailers, especially those specializing in fashion apparels and footwear, eliminated the middlemen and began directly to arrange their own contracting relationships in Asia. (As we noted above, all the major general retailers opened buying offices in the key Asian countries during the decade between 1965 and 1975.) They were helped in this matchmaking effort by local firms and business groups that established their own trading companies to represent local manufacturers and to negotiate with U.S. retailers. In South Korea, with government encouragement, the top exporting *chaebol* established their own trading companies in 1975 and soon afterward the top five controlled over 50 percent of all exports from South Korea (Feenstra and Hamilton 2006). In Taiwan, whose export economy was dominated by small and medium-sized firms, most small networks of manufacturing firms (called satellite assembly systems) were also represented by trading companies, albeit much smaller than their Korean counterparts. Between 1973 and the mid-1980s, the number of Taiwanese trading companies jumped from 2,777 to over 40,000 (Levy 1991; Fields 1995; Hsing 1999; Feenstra and Hamilton 2006).

By 1975, Asian supplier markets had been created, partly by Japanese multinationals and partly by local efforts, and a model of how to do contract manufacturing in Asia (and elsewhere) was in the process of being developed and institutionalized. From the beginning, contract manufacturing spawned a relationship between retailers and manufacturers that did not exist in the United States. Beginning on a small scale in the early 1960s, but then accelerating rapidly after that, retailers started to directly source batches of differentiated goods specially ordered for sale in niche markets. The standard reason given for the early contract manufacturing in East Asia is the cheap labor, which of course was a factor. But even more important was that American-based retailers, engaged in hot competition in their home markets, began to develop and organize manufacturing directly without owning factories and without the corporate and labor negotiations that would be involved in subcontracting with American-based firms. This model of brand name merchandising blurred the distinction between retailing and manufacturing, so much so that many manufacturing firms, such as The Gap, The Limited, Nike, and later Dell Computers, began to appear that did not actually manufacture anything, but rather focused almost entirely on building and assessing consumer demand, designing products for consumer niches, merchandising those products to the targeted markets, and building relationships with Asian manufacturers that would supply their goods.

During this same decade when the American retail sector was beginning its transformation, the East Asian countries were developing the capacity to respond quickly to the needs of intermediary buyers for reliable infrastructures for international trade. The East Asian NICs founded extensive trade and manufacturing associations and built world trade centers, all to facilitate the matching process between buyers and potential manufacturers. At the same time, these countries began rapidly to establish the physical and financial infrastructure that would facilitate international trade (e.g., ports, shipping, containerization, fast freight forwarding, railways, highways, as well as banking, credit markets, stock markets, and corporate insurance). These infrastructure projects and market institutions allowed global intermediaries to develop the industries and to create competitive supplier markets throughout East Asia, and allowed Asian manufacturers to become increasingly more responsive to big-buyer demands.

1975–1985: Diversification of supplier markets for U.S. retailers

The rapid expansion and growing diversity of retailing in the United States, and the equally rapid expansion of Asian manufacturing during the period from 1965 to 1985, are two aspects of the same economic phenomenon. After the first ten years, by 1975, the retailers, the various sets of intermediaries (trading companies), and the Asian manufacturers had provisionally worked out the basic method of contract manufacturing. Supplier markets for products to be sold by U.S. retailers had been created. Moreover, the governments and industrialists in the key areas (i.e., Japan, Hong Kong,

Taiwan, South Korea, and Singapore) had built sufficient economic infrastructures to facilitate this type of long-distance manufacturing.

At exactly this moment, around 1975, the United States slipped into a
severe recession. The Vietnam War had ended precipitously and the first
oil shock had occurred, and then a few years later, in 1980, a second oil
shock happened. The traditional retailing sector and U.S. manufacturers
both declined rapidly during the period. As occurs in most economic
downturns, in this recession many American consumers saved money by
shopping where they could find the lowest prices. It was in this period that
competition between the new discount and specialty retailers, on the one
hand, and the older, more traditional retailers, on the other hand, came to
a head, and set off a wave of mergers and acquisitions, resulting in even
greater consolidation within the U.S. retail sector. The number of mass
discounters was reduced from over ten to four major chains. Moreover, the
major department stores, such as Macy's and the Bon Marche, curtailed
their in-store brands and began to build mini-boutiques within their stores,
featuring such brand-name apparel manufacturers as Polo and Anne
Klein. In addition, many of the same brand-name manufacturers began to
open factory outlet stores in scattered locations around the United States
and elsewhere.

The rise of the new retailers stocked with many items manufactured in
Asia contributed to a reorganization of U.S. manufacturing that occurred in
the late 1970s and early 1980s. Many analysts of the period (e.g. Bluestone
and Harrison 1982) began to worry that American firms were no longer
competitive. Many older and well-established manufacturing firms were
forced into bankruptcy and many survivors had to restructure, including
IBM among many others. The Upper Midwest, formerly renowned as the
industrial heartland of America, became widely known as the "Rustbelt"
(Bluestone and Harrison 1982; Harrison and Bluestone 1988). An important
cause of this crisis in American manufacturing was that many of the traditional retailers had maintained their American-based supply lines and
stocked their shelves with more traditional types of products, but as these
retailers lost customers because of their competitors' low prices and the availability of new products carried by other retailers, the orders with American
manufacturers declined even as the imports of foreign products surged.

The need to cut costs and to restructure led once-powerful manufacturers
to join the ranks of the factory-less brand-name merchandisers. Beginning
in the late 1970s and continuing through the 1990s, such firms as Schwinn
(bicycles), Eddie Bauer (specialty outdoor clothing), General Electric and
Westinghouse (household appliances), and Compaq (computers) closed all
or most of their consumer product factories in the United States and began
to contract all or a large part of their products overseas, mostly in East Asia.
In the same period, the last surviving large manufacturer of televisions and
radios, Zenith, gave up its American factories in favor of Asian contractors.
For a time, in the 1980s, even automobile makers such as Chrysler and

General Motors sourced entire lines of automobiles from Japan and South Korea.

In making the move to Asia, many American firms actually invested in and helped to organize the Asian production of their branded goods. Others played a more passive role, letting the Asian manufacturers perform the primary entrepreneurial functions. In both regards, these businesses simply followed in the footsteps of the earlier firms, copying the first-comers' techniques of contract manufacturing and direct sourcing of component parts and finished goods. What started in textiles had by 1985 spread to almost every category of consumer goods, including a full range of high technology products, most of which were never mass produced in the United States. In fact, the Asian supply lines for high technology products had been sufficiently developed by the early 1980s that Dell Computer Corporation and Gateway, two companies that owe their successes entirely to contract manufacturing, much of which is centered in Taiwan, started their businesses in, respectively, 1984 and 1985.

During the decade from 1975 to 1985, American retailers and brand-name merchandisers, a group that Gary Gereffi calls "the big buyers", directly shaped the patterns of Asian manufacturing. Before 1975, the big buyers were just figuring out how and what to order. It was a period before special-ized buying strategies and specialized manufacturing strategies had emerged, a period when buyers were making their first big orders and when local manufacturers were engaged in intense competition to obtain these orders. For this reason, there was a lot of overlap in the goods that Hong Kong, South Korea, and Taiwan were exporting in the earliest years of industrial-ization. The big buyers simply had not learned sufficiently about the manufacturing capabilities of their Asian partners, and the Asian factory owners had not yet learned what they could best and most profitably produce. In the next decade, all the initial problems in global matchmaking were sorted out.

Starting around 1975, the pattern of production began to change. This is the period when intermediary demand for Asian goods dramatically increased, largely reflecting the success of new retailers and merchandisers in the United States. The surging demand led these big buyers to figure out their ordering strategies for different products. As orders began to build in volume, the composition of products in each category of each country's export landscape began rapidly to increase, so that larger quantities of many different types of products were being ordered and produced. At the same time, the actual products being manufactured in each country began to diverge. Trade data show that, during this decade, a division of labor emerged among the countries of East Asia. Each country began to specialize in particular products within each category.

In some cases, such as footwear, specialization appeared very early in the process, as is clear from Figure 6.10.[8] This figure shows that, even from the

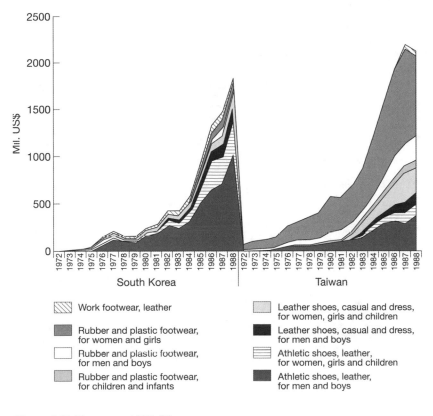

Figure 6.10 Footwear, 1972–88

very first period of our data in 1972, Taiwanese and South Korean footwear exporters were producing somewhat different types of footwear, even though they shared some of the same products (a type of soft-soled vinyl shoes for women). However, as new categories emerged by the mid-1970s, a clear division of labor between Taiwanese and South Korean footwear manufacturers was established and continued to grow throughout the entire period, with Taiwanese manufacturers specializing in rubber and plastic shoes and those from South Korea specializing in leather shoes.

Rubber and plastic products, which are important export items for both countries throughout the period, show another variation of these two trends. Before 1975, both countries predominantly exported rubber and plastic clothing, largely rain gear, to the United States, but, as Figure 6.11 (page 168) shows, after 1975 Korea increasingly specialized in exporting various kinds of tires – tires for cars, trucks, buses, and bicycles – while during the same period Taiwan's exports in this category expanded to include an array of products in addition to plastic clothing: religious articles,

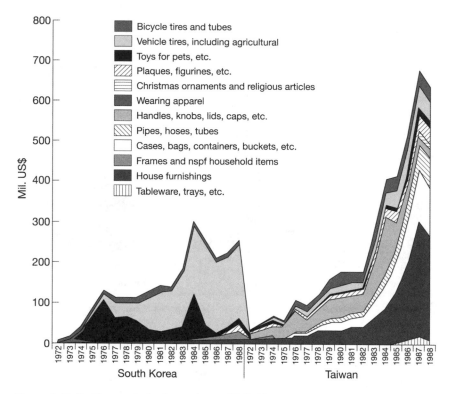

Legend:
- Bicycle tires and tubes
- Vehicle tires, including agricultural
- Toys for pets, etc.
- Plaques, figurines, etc.
- Christmas ornaments and religious articles
- Wearing apparel
- Handles, knobs, lids, caps, etc.
- Pipes, hoses, tubes
- Cases, bags, containers, buckets, etc.
- Frames and nspf household items
- House furnishings
- Tableware, trays, etc.

Figure 6.11 Rubber and plastic products, 1972–88

household furnishings, curtains, Christmas tree ornaments, as well as some bicycle tires.

These two examples indicate that, during this fifteen-year period leading up to 1987, products within categories gradually begin to segment, with South Korean exports in most categories increasingly consisting of products that could be mass-produced in large Fordist factories (e.g., in garments: men's shirts, as opposed to women's fashion garments), and often, but not always, that were final products ready for consumer use, such as microwave ovens, video machines (VCRs), tires, and automobiles. In contrast, within the same three-digit product categories, Taiwanese exports tended to be component parts, goods having short product cycles (e.g., in garments: women's clothes), and some fairly complex final products that can be assembled from standardized components (e.g., computers, TVs, and bicycles), this was in addition to a considerable range of relatively inexpensive simply-made consumer products (e.g., luggage, household products made of plastic). Figures 6.12 and 6.13 depict the clearest examples of this trend: household appliances and transportation parts and equipment, including bicycles and bicycle parts.

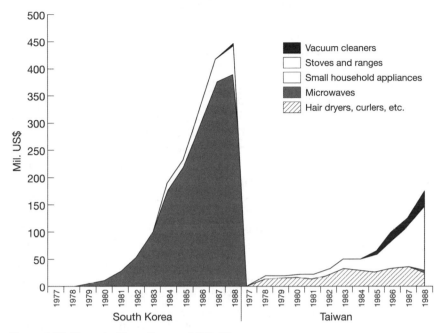

Figure 6.12 Household appliances, 1972–88

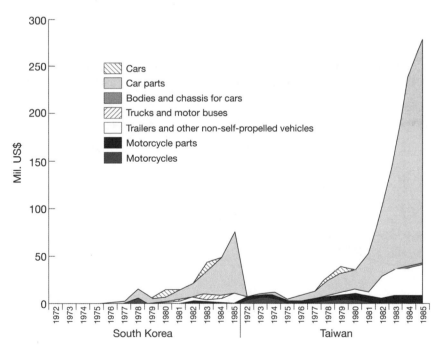

Figure 6.13 Transportation, 1972–85

From 1975 on, the general trend (see Figure 6.14) has been for these Asian economies to specialize, and therefore to diverge in what they produce. The reason for this divergence results from the system of production that emerges in each economy in response to repeat orders from big buyers that, in turn, reinforces what was ordered there.[9] South Korea, for example, started the industrialization process in the late 1960s with a few large and competitive business groups, and, as the orders began to come in, these large groups, known locally as "octopi", gobbled up most of the opportunities presented by foreign buyers. The result was that the big business groups, the *chaebol,* controlled the flow of orders and vertically integrated to prevent other *chaebol* from obtaining the orders. By contrast, in Taiwan, which began the industrialization process with many small firms competing for the early orders and no major players that could monopolize the opportunities, businesspeople began from the outset to specialize in products that small firms, interlinked in small networks, could profitably produce. As the orders began to flow, Taiwanese small and medium-sized manufacturers became experts at producing a wide variety of products in batches, and the largest private-sector enterprises, usually family-owned business groups, became suppliers of intermediate goods (e.g., plastics, synthetic yarn, textiles, chemicals) and business services (e.g., shipping, insurance).

The big buyers in those locations quickly became sophisticated in sourcing their products with those entrepreneurs who could best produce them. For instance, Nike ordered very large runs of low-end standardized running shoes in Korea, and their high-end and more specialized shoes from Taiwan (Levy 1988). In the industrializing countries of East Asia, the ordering system reinforced the competitive dynamics that drove the divergence in the industrial structure of each country, quite apart from anything that the government of that country did. By 1985, the basic organizational

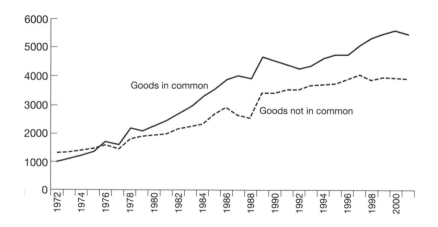

Figure 6.14 Similarity between South Korea and Taiwan's export landscapes

trajectories of these economies were firmly in place and dependent on their continuing linkages with U.S. retailers and merchandisers.

1985–1997: Rationalization of global supply lines

Two developments occurred in the mid-1980s that would forever restructure the organization of Asian economies. The first was the Plaza Accord signed in 1985, and the second was the global implementation of "lean retailing", a development that started in the previous decade but was only gradually implemented in Asia in the late 1980s and 1990s.

On 22 September 1985, at the Plaza Hotel in New York City, after years of running trade deficits with South Korea, Japan, and Taiwan, the United States completed negotiations on a currency reform measure that all parties signed. The Plaza Accord, as this currency reform became known, removed the pegged trading range of East Asian currencies with the U.S. dollar and allowed the Asian currencies to appreciate. Within two years, Taiwan's currency moved from 40 to 30 New Taiwan dollars to 1 U.S. dollar; Korea's currency appreciated more moderately. These revaluations immediately made the export goods from both economies more expensive in the United States, and accelerated the shift out of labor-intensive products towards more high-skilled and capital-intensive exports that had already begun in both economies. The revaluation also made goods manufactured in the United States less expensive relative to Asian economies, and for a time in the 1990s American manufacturers seemed to bounce back. Though short-lived, their rejuvenation was linked to the second development.

The second development was a comprehensive reorganization of global supply lines that resulted from the U.S. retailers' implementation of what is known as "lean retailing". The initial elements of lean retailing began obscurely in the 1970s with the development of the Uniform Product Code (UPC), barcodes, and scanning devices. A group of food manufacturers (including Heinz, General Mills, and General Foods) and grocery store owners (including Kroger, A&P Tea Company, and First National Stores) first met in 1969 to discuss the development of product codes to make the management of grocery store inventories more efficient. The committee completed their work in 1974, the same year the first item bearing a UPC symbol, a package of Wrigley's chewing gum, "crossed the scanner at Marsh's Supermarket in Troy, Ohio" (Brown 1997: 5). The UPC committee anticipated that "there would never be more than 6,000 registrations", but the registrations soared, numbering over 110,000 distinct UPC symbols by 1994, twenty years later. By 2002, the figure had doubled again.

Barcodes, scanners, and more generally "electronic data interchange" (EDI) became the medium to continue the trend towards the globalization of supply lines that was already well begun in the late 1960s and 1970s.[10] A core principle of value merchandising – for discount retailers, brand-name merchandisers, and specialty retailers – is to match as closely as possible the number and types of goods on hand to the number and types of goods that consumers will actually buy. This involves a precise calculation of consumer demand. In the 1960s and 1970s, however, value merchandisers and department stores could only anticipate consumer demand, and to hedge their risks they would buy limited quantities of a limited range of each type of differentiated goods – so many in extra-large sizes, so many in pink, and so forth.

The development of high-powered mainframe computers and database software suitable for inventory control, both of which did not become widely available until the early 1980s, quickly made barcodes and scanners the preferred instruments of assessing consumer choice at the place and time of purchase. By the late 1980s, these innovations allowed retailers and merchandisers to rationalize their supply chains.

Abernathy and his colleagues (Abernathy *et al.* 1999) describe the "four building blocks" of this effort to rationalize supply chains, the total configuration of which they call "lean retailing". As already discussed, the first building block of lean retailing is standardized product codes, barcodes, and scanning technology. Second, based on UPCs and barcodes, merchandisers and retailers created computerized inventory management systems. "Mass merchants have 150,000 SKU (stockkeeping units) and department stores may have over a million, indicating the variety of styles, colors, fabrics, sizes, and products that constitute . . . sales. Bar codes permit organizations to effectively handle the kind of vast product differentiation that would have been prohibitively expensive in an earlier era" (Abernathy *et al.* 1999: 61). Computerized inventory systems facilitated the development of electronic data interchange, which allowed retailers and suppliers to communicate in a common, standardized way. Using a common communication interface, contract manufacturers obtained real-time information about how products were selling and which items needed to be reordered, thereby expediting "purchase orders, shipping invoices, and funds transfer" (Abernathy *et al.* 1999: 62).

Third, merchandisers and retailers adopted state-of-the-art distribution centers, which rely on "sophisticated equipment like scanners and automated conveyer systems" to manage the flow of goods (Abernathy *et al.* 1999: 64). These modern distribution centers are the retailers' equivalent of the just-in-time inventory systems pioneered by Toyota and other Japanese manufacturers in the 1970s. Applied to retailing, they are basically transfer points, instead of the traditional warehouses that national department stores had depended on in earlier years.

Fourth, lean retailing relies on enforcing "standards across firms" (Abernathy *et al.* 1999: 69–70). Standardization across firms and across networks of firms in such things as sizes, colors, weights and measures, operating systems, communication devices, and any number of other matters allows multiple firms and multiple networks of firms to work together in a seamless way. Standardization creates a common world of work processes, or what Abernathy and his colleagues call "packages", within and between industries, permitting firms in different sectors of the economy (such as manufacturing, retailing, and shipping), and whose personnel never meet face-to-face, to coordinate their joint endeavors. For instance, by adopting standardized packages, retailers supply manufacturers with all the necessary information to make the product "floor-ready". Packaged in the right box, affixed with the right retail price for a given location and with the right barcode and tracking information, the product can be shipped from the manufacturing site, tracked along the way, delivered to a distribution center and then to the specific store where the item is needed ready for display, with no further effort on the part of the retailer.

The innovations first designed for grocery stores were, in the 1980s, commandeered by other types of retailers. At first, however, the adoption of UPCs was uneven. Many of the older retail firms, such as Sears, not only had predominantly American supply-lines, but also had already made large capital investments in developing proprietary, automated inventory systems, and were reluctant to make additional and even larger investments to adopt universal product codes and standardized scanning devices. But after Kmart and Wal-Mart both adopted the technology in the early 1980s and "began to demand that their vendors adopt the U.P.C" as well (Dunlop and Rivkin 1997: 5), most other retailers not only had to adopt the new technology, but had to rationalize their supply lines, making them more efficient and competitive and cutting costs wherever costs could be reduced.

This rationalization of retailer supply lines brought all domestic and global suppliers into a common, price-sensitive frame of reference. For the first time, all segments of value chains, both in the United States and overseas, could be scrutinized and examined for ways to further streamline operations and cut costs. At first, lean retailing gave an advantage to those American manufacturers that could meet the demands of the big-box retailers. Starting in the late 1980s, Wal-Mart's "Buy American" campaign, for example, was not merely a patriotic effort to purchase locally, but was, more accurately, Wal-Mart's effort to reorganize its supply chain by directly integrating suppliers into Wal-Mart's automated restocking system, the implication of which is spelled out in another location (Petrovic and Hamilton 2006). American manufacturers enjoyed the benefits of propinquity and easy access to computerization.

This push into lean retailing occurred at the very time currencies in the leading export economies in Asia were being revaluated upwards relative to the U.S. dollar (except for Hong Kong, whose economy remained pegged to the U.S. dollar). In the span of just a few years, the Japanese, Taiwanese, and, to a lesser degree, South Korean economies went through a momentary period of jubilation, a period when everyone felt much richer and many began to make extravagant purchases at home and abroad. The period of jubilation ended quickly, however, when domestic manufacturers realized that they could no longer meet the price points that the U.S. retailers and merchandisers required.

For the moment, Asian manufacturers in Japan, South Korea, and Taiwan lost their advantage and had to fight to maintain contracts with their big buyers. Based on interviews made in Taiwan at the time (Kao and Hamilton forthcoming; see also Chapter 7), leading manufacturers lowered their own profit margins to the point of breaking even, and had to relentlessly squeeze other firms in their production networks. They complained of working harder for longer hours and for less pay than they did in the early 1980s, when it seemed like everyone was getting rich. By 1990, in both Taiwan and Japan, the property and stock-market bubble collapsed. Japan entered a long, deflationary recession, from which, fifteen years later, it has yet fully to emerge.

The currency revaluation stopped the Japanese economy in its tracks, but not its main exporting firms. By the late 1980s, Japanese industries were major OEM suppliers in only just a few products (e.g., microwaves, computers). Instead, many of the largest Japanese business groups had gone to considerable effort to build their own globally recognized brand names (e.g., Sony, Panasonic, Toyota) or to use their technology to develop upstream products, such as Toshiba's LCD panels and Shimano's bicycle gears, that they then could sell to all makers of the respective products. In order to remain competitive in terms of price and quality, the many major Japanese companies transferred their final assembly sites, along with some production, to other countries. The automobile makers went to the U.S. to achieve cheaper costs and avoid tariff barriers (Kenney and Florida 1993), and also invested heavily in Southeast Asia, especially in Thailand (Doner 1990). The huge consumer electronic conglomerate, Matsushita, transferred much of its manufacturing and assembly to Malaysia, where it contributed about 5 percent of Malaysia's GDP. The effect of these foreign direct investments on the domestic economy was widely reported in Japan as the "hollowing out" of the Japanese economy.

Unlike Japan, South Korea and Taiwan were able to escape severe recession, and they even were able to increase their exports, but they did so in quite different ways. By 1985, the four largest South Korean *chaebol* (i.e., Hyundai, Samsung, Lucky Goldstar, and Daewoo) dwarfed all the other business groups in South Korea in size and sales, and virtually monopolized exports from South Korea (Kim 1997; Lim 2002; Feenstra and Hamilton 2006). After the currency evaluations, these behemoths began to follow the precedent set by the largest Japanese business groups, establishing global brand names and developing higher-quality, up-market products. They extended the scope and scale of their enterprise groups in Korea, and they began systematically to globalize their business. They built manufacturing plants in cheap labor areas, such as Indonesia and Central America, for shoes and garments, as well as in locations near their targeted markets, such as automobile plants in Eastern Europe. They established an array of differentiated products – Samsung and LG in consumer electronics, Hyundai and Daewoo in automobiles – that undercut the prices of their Japanese competitors. This strategy led these business groups to disengage from the commodity chains of U.S. branded goods, but still allowed them to market their products with American retailers, in competition with all other brands.

In the wake of the Plaza Accord, many of Taiwan's export manufacturers faced a serious dilemma (Hsing 1998; see Chapter 7). They had OEM contracts for goods that they needed to deliver to U.S. retailers, but they could not produce those goods profitably. If they failed to honor their contracts, the retailers and brand-name merchandisers would easily find other manufacturers to make the products. If they stayed in Taiwan and honored their contracts, they would likely go bankrupt and lose the contract anyway. After several years of hesitation, those small and medium-sized firms making garments, bicycles, footwear, and other types of similar consumer goods moved their manufacturing operations to China. The move occurred suddenly, like a stampede, in a matter of just a couple of years. The abrupt departure of so many exporters shows up clearly in the trade statistics, as Figures 6.15–6.18 show. In some industries, such as bicycle manufacture, most of the production networks moved to China when the lead firm moved, but in other industries, such as footwear, toys, furniture, and garments, only the lead firm moved, and, once in China, they vertically integrated their production, making most component parts of their products in-house. Many firms producing for export, however, split their operations, with low-end mass production going to China and high-end batch production staying in Taiwan.

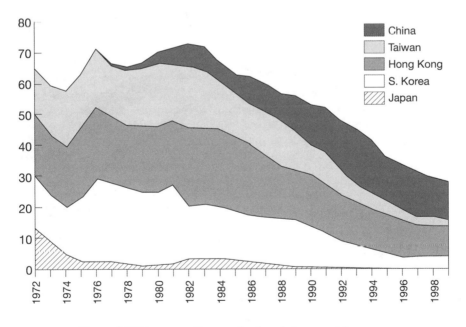

Figure 6.15 Share of US imports of apparel, select Asian countries

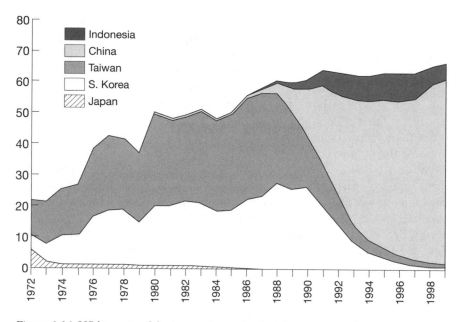

Figure 6.16 US imports of footwear, share of select Asian economies

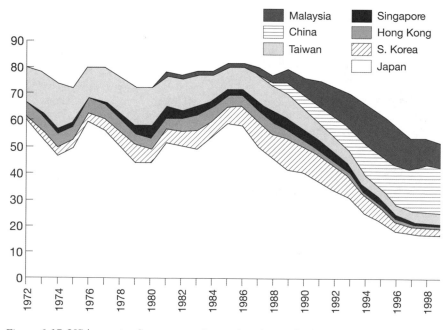

Figure 6.17 US imports of consumer electronics, share of select Asian economies

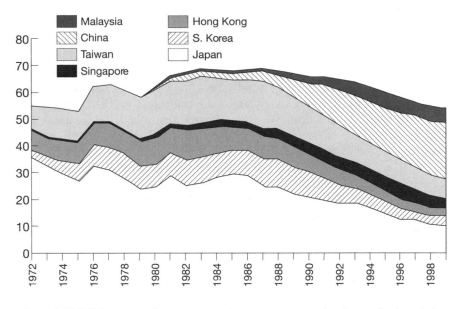

Figure 6.18 US imports of non-automotive consumer goods, share of select Asian
economies

In the late 1980s and early 1990s, at the same time that Taiwan's most
successful export manufacturers were contemplating moves to China, or
perhaps to Southeast Asia, the high technology boom occurred in Silicon
Valley. Taiwan's high technology industry was closely linked to Silicon
Valley through multiple connections (Saxenian 1999). Early on, Taiwanese
manufacturers were leading producers of PC peripherals and component
parts, but as the boom in the U.S. progressed, Taiwanese manufacturers, in
their own Silicon Valley outside of Hsin Chu in north-central Taiwan, began
to produce more and more standardized PC components and founded a
number of leading PC firms, most notably Acer Computers. Along with a
handful of other firms, Acer became one of the world's leading OEM
producers of inexpensive PCs. The high technology boom in Taiwan was
also fed by the establishment of semiconductor foundries (upstream firms
that make semiconductor chips to order for any downstream firm that
designs and wants to use those chips in dedicated products). The first and
most important of these foundries was the government-sponsored Taiwan
Semiconductor Manufacturing Corporation (TSMC).

Major retailers and brand-name merchandisers, such as Dell Computers,
Hewlett Packard, and Gateway, were primary drivers of Taiwan's high technology industry. As the demand for these American branded products rose,
so too did the productive capacity of Taiwan's high technology manufacturers. The success of these firms was not based on, and did not lead to,
efforts to develop their own brand names; rather they continued to upgrade

their capabilities as high-level contract manufacturers deeply integrated in industries led by U.S. retailers and merchandisers.

The period between 1985 and 1997 was characterized, then, by the further divergence of national development strategies, initiated in response to the reorganization of the U.S. demand for consumer goods. At the same time, however, the whole region was rapidly becoming more integrated, and was beginning to show an increasingly elaborate pattern of intra-regional trade, investment, and production. We have already mentioned the Japanese and Korean strategies of organizing production in ASEAN countries, and Taiwan's shift of low-tech manufacturing to Mainland China. During the same period, Hong Kong emerged as the business service and financial hub for the region. By the mid-1990s, any attempt to classify national economies in East Asia as to the level of their industrial development was of little use. While Japan may still be a clear leader in advanced consumer electronics, as well as in the automotive sector, sizeable portions of its production and assembly are organized outside of its borders. South Korea and Taiwan both managed to reshape their economies after the Plaza Accord, although in very different ways. Both have also maintained their strengths in many categories of lower-value export products, the pattern particularly characteristic for Taiwan. Newly developing economies of the 1990s such as Indonesia, Thailand, Malaysia, and the Philippines did not experience the same pattern of industrial upgrading as Japan, Taiwan, and South Korea; instead, they rapidly developed a presence in high technology sectors while at the same time maintaining traditional strengths in non-manufactured exports, such as rice, rubber, and palm oil.

1997 to the present day: convergence in China

By the mid-1990s, many of the Japanese, South Korean, Hong Kong, and Taiwanese manufacturers had re-established their labor-intensive export businesses in new locations. At home, new businesses had been started, often manufacturing products that had been unknown only a few years earlier and rarely manufactured in the U.S., such as cellphones, digital cameras, laptop computers, and DVD players. Although many Asian firms continued to hold contracts with U.S. retailers and brand-name merchandisers, they also worked diligently to obtain new orders from retailers and merchandisers in Europe and Latin American, as well as all across Asia. The U.S. share of Asian exports declined throughout the period, although the absolute values of exports continue to rise (Feenstra and Hamilton 2006). Also by the mid-1990s, U.S. big-box retailers no longer simply purchased goods in Asia; they began actively to integrate Asian manufacturers into their supply chains. Again, American manufacturers continued their long, gradual decline, driven in large part by the eagerness of American retailers to unify and simplify their supply lines around the least-cost producers, mostly Asian ones in all areas of consumer goods except for food and cosmetics.

What seemed at the time to be an endless expansion, like a Pacific Century dawning, came to an abrupt halt in 1997. Starting in Thailand in the summer of 1997, the financial underpinnings of economies all across Asia crumbled. The financial and property markets in Indonesia, Malaysia, Singapore, the Philippines, Hong Kong, and South Korea were all deeply shaken, each for slightly different reasons; all of these countries also suffered sudden and serious declines in exports and domestic production. Although still mired in what was nearly a decade-long recession, Japan was less affected by the Asian financial crisis.

Among all the countries of Asia, Taiwan and China fared the best. Along with South Korea and Southeast Asian countries, Taiwan devalued its dollar against the U.S. dollar, but, because the corporate debt was low, Taiwan did not suffer a financial collapse; its exports merely became less expensive in the U.S. China resisted all attempts to devalue its currency, in part because such a move might have devastated China's debt-ladened banking system. The exports from both countries, as well as their total economies, continued to grow. The reason for this continued growth is simple enough. Both economies were pulled forward by their integration in U.S. supply chains (see Chapter 10).

When the financial crisis occurred in Asia, the U.S. was in the buoyant years of the dot.com boom and the run-up to the Y2K scare, which led computer owners to upgrade for fear that their computers' internal clocks would be unable to register the new millennium. These were the years when high technology merchandisers, such as Dell, Gateway, and Hewlett Packard, cemented their ties with Taiwanese manufacturers, and when Taiwanese manufacturers began to relocate their low-end PC production to China. These were also the years when Wal-Mart, Target, and Kmart began establishing superstores across the U.S. and when Wal-Mart was beginning its global expansion. U.S. demand for the full range of consumer goods was at an all-time high, and outside of those areas most affected by the crisis, global demand was also picking up, especially in China.

First the Asian financial crisis and then the 2001 bursting of the dot.com bubble in the U.S. led businesses worldwide to reconsider their Asian strategies. In 2001, U.S. demand for high technology consumer goods suddenly and precipitously declined, which also led to an economic slowdown in Taiwan. But China's economy continued to grow. Encouraged by the Chinese government and by China's membership in the World Trade Organization, businesses around the world began to look to China as both its manufacturing platform and its next big market. The largest investors in China were its closest neighbors: Hong Kong and Taiwan continued their large scale investments in the Mainland, but now they were joined by large investments from Japan and South Korea. The four countries together account for 70 percent of the total direct foreign investment in China (Lardy 2003). The convergence of Asian firms developing manufacturing sites in China prompted retailers to establish buying offices there as well. As one

Wal-Mart buyer explained, retailers followed their Taiwanese suppliers: "The only reason [manufacturing] moved from Taiwan was China's low level of wages. 'We didn't have any trouble in China, because the Taiwanese went into China and built their factories. We were dealing with the same people' " (Hornblower 2005).

Recognizing the potential of China as the single best low-cost provider of goods, and as representing a huge domestic market in its own right, Wal-Mart executives established in 2001 their direct buying office (that later turned into Wal-Mart's global sourcing headquarters) in Shenzhen, China, just across the border from Hong Kong, and in 2003 another buying office in Tianjin. In 2004, Wal-Mart exported over $18 billion of goods purchased from China, which amounts to 10 percent of all U.S. exports from China. Wal-Mart alone accounts for 30 percent of all foreign buying in China. Besides exporting from China, Wal-Mart is also in the midst of a huge expansion of retail stores in China; they will be opening dozens of stores there in the next few years. Wal-Mart is not the only major retailer to combine foreign buying with a domestic presence in China. The giant French firm, Carrefour, the second-largest retailer in the world, is the largest foreign retailer in China and is well ahead of Wal-Mart. Not far behind the front runners are the German retail chains Metro and Ahold.

China is now emerging as the world's premier manufacturing platform for a large range of consumer goods. It is also one of the world's largest consumer markets. Some large U.S. manufacturers, such as General Motors, are making huge investments in joint ventures producing for China's domestic market. But the largest U.S. investments in China are likely to be made by America's largest companies, the retailers and in particular Wal-Mart, a firm that has now become one of the few truly global market-makers.

Conclusion

Along with many other firms, Wal-Mart has invested in the China's manu-facturing capacity, and, based on this investment, Wal-Mart has consolidated its global chain, reducing the number of principal suppliers and forming a global alliance with the top 50. These investments having been made, will Wal-Mart and other retailers and merchandisers soon – or easily – abandon China for some other location, such as India or Southeast Asia? Even if China's prices rise, perhaps through an upward revaluation of China's currency, will China's manufacturing platform become less impor-tant than it is today? Of course, these questions are for the future to answer. But one thing should be clear from the above narrative: both the compara-tive advantage of locations in global markets and the competition advantage of nations in international trade are not decided by the impersonal workings of costless markets. Real firms, creating and maintaining real markets, competitively determine both comparative and competitive advantage in the global economy today. As the global retail sector consolidates, as it has been doing for the past 50 years, there is every reason to conclude that a relatively small number of very large retailers will become the hub of the global economy, and will become the makers of both consumer and supplier markets throughout the world.

There is much yet to understand about the role of retailers in the global economy. We end this chapter, therefore, with three propositions that we hope will fuel future research. First, we conclude that markets do not emerge spontaneously, in order to ensure the match between global demand and global supply, but are rather created and shaped by real economic players, and the most prominent players making markets in the global economy today are retailers and brand-name merchandisers. These actors are true intermediaries (Spulber 1996, 1998; Rauch 2001b, 1999), not only because they link producers with consumers, but also, and more accurately, because they actively create supplier markets on the one side, while simultaneously creating consumer markets on the other side. The conventional theories of comparative and competitive advantage contain no market intermediaries, no explicit treatment of demand, and only a supply-side interpretation of the comparative costs of production or the developmental edge given by state policies. However, once we add global intermediaries into this mix, then we not only incorporate a demand-side dimension into our analysis, but are also able to address the logistics of global trade, i.e. the actual way that global supply meets global demand.

This leads us to our second major proposition. Global markets cannot be reduced to the operation of an abstract, costless price mechanism. Instead, they consist of a rich, increasingly complex patchwork of institutions that shapes and enables international trade. Where these institutions have been established for a while, and operate in a smooth and predictable manner, they may indeed appear to all parties in exchange as *mechanisms*: for finding, engaging, and keeping trade partners, for pricing and contracting, and for getting the products into and through the market. These mechanisms, as has been pointed out so many times by economists and politicians, can, and quite often do, benefit all trade participants. This, however, should not conceal the fact that these mechanisms are made and reproduced by large business firms, which typically dedicate a substantial amount of their organizational resources to such "market-making" activities, not for the universal benefit of all or to approximate the economist's model of perfect competition, but rather to maximize their own trading opportunities. Actual markets, then, always bear the imprint of their creators, and their current form often reveals a rich history of changes and conflicts over the shape of their institutions.

Finally, we propose that global markets do not, and should not be expected to, balance firms, regions, and nations in a state of productive equilibrium. There is also no reason to conclude that the most proactive, bureaucratically administered state policies will result in a national economy actually achieving some advantage in international trade over other nations with less developmentally oriented state systems. How economies actually develop depends on many factors, not the least of which are the accumulated results of many choices that result in increasing returns in some locations and decreasing returns in others (Krugman 1996). Although institutionalized markets do generate a fair amount of stability and predictability, that fact alone does not necessarily ensure optimal, efficient, or universally beneficial outcomes. However, rather than viewing such outcomes as examples of market failure, as distortions from the ideal form of competitive market, we should understand these outcomes as the result of many knowledgeable actors making successive choices about how to position themselves in global markets. Increasingly such choices involve working with one or more of the global market-makers or finding a niche where one can grow one's own business apart from their influence, and increasingly those niches are becoming harder and harder to find.

Notes

1   This chapter summarizes portions of chapters 6, 7, and 8 of Feenstra and Hamilton, *Emergent Economies, Divergent Paths: Economic Organization and International Trade in South Korea and Taiwan* (2006).

2   The works of Gary Gereffi (1994b, 1999; Gereffi, Humphrey, and Sturgeon 2005; Gereffi, Spener, and Bair 2002) and of a small group of other scholars (Appelbaum and Smith 1996; Bonacich *et al.* 1994) investigating global commodity chains are among the only exceptions, and even here the emphasis remains on the organization of production, rather than on how firms, as market-makers, link supplier and consumer markets.

3   By 1906, Sears's Central Merchandise Building was able to process 27,000 orders an hour and ship goods within 48 hours of receiving an order. By 1915, Montgomery Ward and Sears kept files on four–six million customers and used them to analyse consumer markets segmented by demographics and socioeconomic status as well as their past shopping behavior with the company.

4   From the late 1950s through the 1980s, investment in retailing grew at a faster rate than the growth of sale or the GDP (Regan 1999: 399).

5   Leading the fight against fair trade laws (Bluestone *et al.* 1981: 125), discount retailers began to compete directly with full-service department stores by sourcing items that they regularly stocked and that were not necessarily branded (e.g., children's clothes, toys, tools, kitchenware) and by working closely with brand-name merchandisers to sell products that were branded (e.g., household electronic products such as TV and stereos). Kmart (as Kresge) opened its first discount store in 1962, in 1976 it changed its name from Kresge to Kmart, and rapidly expanded after that. In 1969, according to Kresge's Annual Report, only 5 percent of the company's sales was from imported items, but it planned to expand "imported merchandise from the Orient" in the "near future". Kmart established buying offices in Taiwan in 1971 and by 1992 had placed over $500 million U.S. worth of orders from Taiwan alone, where approximately 40 percent of its foreign orders were placed (Gereffi and Pan 1994: 137). Toys 'R' Us opened as a toy supermarket in 1957, adopted discount methods in the 1960s, became a publicly listed firm in 1970, and grew quickly to be the dominant retailer of toys in the United States; many of their lines of toys were sourced in East Asia. Wal-Mart opened its first discount store in 1969, its first distribution center in 1970, and went public in 1979 with one billion dollars worth of sales.

By 1990, both Wal-Mart and Kmart had replaced Sears and J. C. Penney as the top U.S. retailers. Home Depot, now the world's largest home improvement retailer, started in 1978.

6 Previously unused for this purpose, the detailed data come from the International Trade and Investment Program at the National Bureau of Economic Research. The director of the program, Robert Feenstra, compiled a comprehensive database of all U.S. imports from 1972 to 2001, and even more recently has updated the database to the year 2004.

7 This database contains the most disaggregated trade data available. Collected by the U.S. Custom Service, the data report the country of origin for U.S. imports at a seven-digit level known as the Tariff Schedule of the U.S. Annotated (TSUSA) from 1972 to 1988, and at the ten-digit Harmonized System (HS) level from 1989 on. Both of these are fine enough to distinguish between four-wheeled and three-wheeled baby carriages, or between bicycles having wheel sizes between 55 and 63.5 centimeters and those having wheel sizes 63.5 centimeters and larger, or between parts of almost any export product and the whole product itself. For instance, in 1985, listed among Taiwan's 6,257 categories of export products sold to the United States were 1,691 distinct types of garments and 127 distinct types of footwear.

8 During this period, the Vietnam War was accelerating, and trade between Japan and the United States grew, in part in response to the wartime availability of Japanese goods in U.S. military commissaries. Watches, stereos, and tape recorders that were made by such Japanese companies as Seiko, Sony, and Aiwa and purchased by soldiers stationed overseas, were instrumental in introducing Japanese-made goods to American consumers. Soon afterwards, Japanese automobile makers, such as Toyota, began to export to the United States.

9 In order to depict this trend graphically, we included all seven-digit categories of footwear whose total value exceeded $10 million U.S. in any year period between 1972 and 1985.

10 According to the Uniform Code Council, EDI is "A standard format for computer-to-computer transmission of business information and transactions between trading partners, such as invoices and purchase orders."

7 Reflexive manufacturing
Taiwan's integration in the global economy

(with Kao Cheng-shu)

The adage, "What you see depends on where you look", certainly applies to the disciplinary gaze given to explaining Asian capitalism. In the past two decades, the leading explanations of Asia's economic ups and downs split between market and state theories, with economists generally advocating the former and political scientists the latter. This interpretive standoff between disciplinary perspectives continues a controversy started in other sites, particularly Europe and Latin America. However, with their rapid and pervasive economic successes, the countries in East and Southeast Asia became the ideal testing grounds for theories of economic development.

In the 1970s and early 1980s, the empirical observations of economists seemed more persuasive. Some economists made bold statements about developmental inevitability of free markets, but most area-oriented economists (Little 1979; Scitovsky 1985; Kuo *et al.* 1981; Galenson 1979) gave nuanced explanations that included political and social factors, but that none the less focused squarely on macro-economic data: interest and currency rates, per capital income, total factor productivity, bilateral trade flows, and so forth.

With the publication of Chalmers Johnson's influential book on MITI (1982), the point of view began to change. Johnson persuasively argued that Japan's economic success arose, not because of free markets, but rather because of the state's careful planning and its capacity to implement those plans within the economy. Johnson's book was followed by a number of important works that generalized his conclusions to other political regimes, particularly those in Asia. In fact, with the work of Cumings (1984), Deyo (1987), Amsden (1985, 1989), Woo (1991), Wade (1991), and Evans (1995), South Korea and Taiwan became the epitome of the developmental state, and other regimes, even the Japanese one, were seen as less successful versions. Like the economists before them, these political scientists developed nuanced explanations that included a range of other non-political factors, including social and economic ones, but their disciplinary gaze remained centered on the "primacy of politics, as carried out most particularly by a nation's governmental bureaucrats and technocrats" (Pempel 1999).

Market economists focus on macro-economic patterns, and political economists on regime characteristics and industrial policy. Although other factors enter into their explanations at the periphery, what they see is largely a function of where they look. Strangely, however, neither set of theorists look squarely at what is, ostensibly, the object of their investigation – the industrializing economy itself, particularly how the economy is organized and how it operates. In his meticulous analysis of the state's role in creating Taiwan's industrial economy, Robert Wade (1990: 70) confesses this exact point:

> I should stress that the organization of firms – their size, the way they grow, their methods of doing business, and the relationships between them – is a major gap in the argument of this book. Any discussion of an economy's development should give a central place to the organization of firms and industries. But since little evidence is available on this subject for Taiwan, and since my primary interest is the uses of public power, I say little more about it.

Market and state theories of Asian industrial growth presuppose, respectively, that global market forces and the economic policies of strong states effectively create a society's industrial organization, which in turn leads to economic performance as measured by rates of growth. In the recent Asian business crisis, the same pattern of explanation continues: macro-economic forces (e.g., exchange rates and money flows) and cronyism in political regimes were offered as the effective forces causing economic decline, but what suffered and often went bankrupt were the businesses themselves. In explaining both the rise of and the later crisis in Asian economies, the organization of the economy, the intermediate variable, is left unexamined, is a taken-for-granted and effective outcome of the primary causes.

A third group of researchers has been examining the organization and operation of Asian economies. Very broadly, these writers engage in what is known as institutional analysis, but their perspectives range broadly from political economy (Evans 1995; Fields 1995; Haggard *et al.* 1997) to economic sociology (Kim Eun Mee 1998; Kim Hyuk-Rae 1993, 1994, 1998; Lew and Park 2000; Orrù *et al.* 1997; Whitley 1992, 1999) and economic geography (Mitchell 1995; Yeung 1997, 1999; Yeung and Olds 1999). Although this institutional perspective concentrates very broadly on economic organization, particularly on such topics as governance, these writers rarely examine, for the economy as a whole, the organizational qualities of interaction among firms. They prefer instead to look at the institutional background rather than at the organizational foreground.

In this chapter, we suggest that the organization of market activity should not be seen exclusively in terms of background institutional factors or as the exclusive outcome of either state or macro-economic forces. Instead, our view is that the organization of economic activity has emergent features that are not fully accounted for by exogenous factors (such as state power or macro-economic forces) or by background institutional features of society (such as family and kinship institutions). Instead, we conclude that such exogenous institutional factors are socially constructed and reconstructed in the context of on-going action, which is intrinsically shaped by the organization of interactions. In other words, the past, as well as the future, only has relevance in the context of present action.[1]

Using this organizational perspective, we want to rethink the fundamental structure of Taiwan's economy. We will focus not on industrial policy, financial flows, or political and social institutions, but rather on the Taiwanese entrepreneurs themselves, their firms, and their interpersonal networks. Using this focus, we can see the organizational characteristics of this economy and can understand the dynamics of this economy apart from other factors, all of which are important in the mix, but none of which explains how the economy grows and changes over time.

For this analysis we draw on the intensive interviews done over a twelve-year period by the research teams of the Institute of East Asia Societies and Economies (IEASE) at Tunghai University in Taiwan. These teams have interviewed over 600 Taiwanese entrepreneurs who own or manage firms in Taiwan and China. Over 50 entrepreneurs were interviewed several times. Most interviews lasted for more than two hours and some lasted over four hours. All the interviews have been transcribed.[2]

Since these interviews cover nearly a fifteen-year period, we cannot treat them as a sample on which we can perform statistical tests. Indeed, it is difficult statistically to compare the same firm at two different points in time, because, except for continuity of owners, some of them radically changed their products, networks of colleagues, locations of manufacturing, and nearly everything else. More fundamentally, the firm is not the basic unit of the economy, in the way that the corporation appears to be in the United States. In Taiwan, all firms, of whatever size, are embedded in networks of other firms. Therefore, in order to understand the organization of Taiwan's economy, it only makes sense to examine how firms operate in a network of other firms and how changes occur over time in qualitative terms and from the point of view of the firm owners. In this chapter we will refer to our interviews in general terms, sometimes citing work that has concentrated on subsets of the interview material and sometimes giving examples from the firms we interview.

Using these interviews as our point of entrance into Taiwan's economy, we will show that Taiwan's export-oriented entrepreneurs organized their early participation in Taiwan's economy through the medium of family-owned small and medium-sized firms. They had little direct assistance from the state, although indirectly the state-provided infrastructure and upstream supplies (such as electrical energy and petroleum), and some state policies (such as land reform in the mid-1950s) unintentionally contributed to economic growth in the 1960s. These entrepreneurs also had very little direct assistance from large Taiwanese businesses, some of which received government subsidies. In the early years, several levels of economic players (e.g., small and medium-sized firms, big business, state-owned enterprises) coexisted with very little direct interaction among the levels. It was not until the late 1970s and early 1980s that a more or less integrated economic system emerged, a system in which all the economic levels began systematically to interact. It was at this time that the small and medium-sized firms became the tail that wagged the dog, became the productive force around which the rest of the Taiwanese economy was progressively more organized. The large firms began to target the input needs of the small and medium-sized firms, and later the state planners fell in line and also began to support the infrastructure and financial needs of smaller firms. The small and medium-sized firms retained relative independence, while the rest of the country became increasingly intertwined with their needs.

In the early years, though, owners of small firms initially drew on their social relationships to develop manufacturing networks that could effectively produce batches of goods on demand. From these beginnings, Taiwan's entrepreneurs began, aggressively and with increasing sophistication, to position themselves in the global economy as specialists in OEM (original equipment manufacturing) production of components and whole goods that were distributed and merchandised globally by non-Taiwanese firms. Because this system of production responds directly to external orders for goods and adjusts its production capabilities accordingly, we call this system of production "reflexive manufacturing". It is our conclusion that the state had very little direct influence in creating this system of production, but once it became a going concern the state then adjusted its goals and altered its own directives to complement and further rationalize this system of production. This chapter recounts the rise and rationalization of Taiwan's system of reflexive manufacturing. In order to have a better understanding, we have to put this developmental process back into its historical context.

The rise of small and medium-sized enterprises (SMEs) in Taiwan: the importance of the initial stage

The fundamental importance of SMEs to Taiwan's economy could not have been anticipated in the early years after World War Two. The legacy of Japanese colonialism was a dual economic structure. The large Japanese-owned *zaibatsu* dominated Taiwan's predominantly agricultural economy from the beginning of the colonial period in 1895 until its demise in 1945. Outside the state-owned sector were small Chinese-owned businesses, which were relatively unimportant producers of manufactured goods in Taiwan. In this regard, they were much like small business elsewhere in the world economy in the immediate post-war period. In 1945, China's Kuomintang government simply took over the large firms that the Japanese created and made them the foundations of a large, state-owned segment of the Taiwanese economy, a segment that continues strongly today. In 1948, fleeing from Communist victors, the Kuomintang government retreated to Taiwan and began a nearly twenty-year effort to return its military forces, consisting of a standing army of 600,000 men, to Mainland soil.

In this period, roughly from 1948 to 1968, the Chinese Nationalist government's primary goals were political and not economic. Stability in Taiwan was the first priority, and the government used repression to attain that goal. State-directed resources for SME development were non-existent. Through their connections to the government and their domination of the Kuomintang, Mainlanders controlled access to state resources, and some of these connections were instrumental in starting a few large businesses, particularly party-owned businesses in communications (e.g., newspapers, radio, and television). Also, a few entrepreneurs with state backing, such as Wang Yung-ching, the founder of Formosa Plastics, started import substitution manufacturing.

On the whole, however, the government's expensive military and foreign policy reduced the amount of resources that could be used for the development of the domestic economy. The main substantive economic goal in the 1950s was to create a self-sustaining rice-based system of agriculture, which would be needed in the event of war and blockades. Invoking the people's livelihood doctrine (*mingshengjuyi*), which is one of Sun Yatsen's People's Three Principles, the Kuomintang government stressed relative equality within society and limited monopolistic tendencies in the private sector. To this end, the government embarked on land reform, reallocating land to small farmers who actually tilled the soil in exchange for non-controlling shares in a few large, party-owned and state-owned enterprises given to former landowners.

Land reform created an agriculturally-based freeholder economy, in which individual households could decide what crops to grow and how to allocate labor and capital. Although rice remained an important staple, farmers also began to raise other types of cash crops, so much so that agricultural products became Taiwan's principal export sector in the 1950s. This trend continued through the 1960s as well, particularly during the Vietnam War, when Taiwanese farmers were one of the primary suppliers of fresh agricultural goods for the American forces in Vietnam (Ho 1978: 198–200). "We grew lettuce," one person recalled, "but we didn't eat it."

The reminiscences of some of the earliest successful entrepreneurs make it clear that one of the unintended consequences of land reform was to nurture a densely networked local society. The Kuomintang encouraged local networks by establishing rural cooperatives and local party organizations, both of which many farmers joined. At the same time, the Kuomingtang removed the former landlords from economic as well as political power. This reform was a move to consolidate their power at the local level, which actually encouraged factionalism. Although the Kuomintang encouraged local networks, the state gave no support for non-agricultural pursuits. None the less, people in rural areas began to explore other ways to expand their ability to make money beyond farming. We heard many accounts of how the earliest entrepreneurs, often the sons of farmers, had migrated for a time to nearby cities to learn skills that later became instrumental in starting their own businesses in the countryside. The capital used to start these new businesses usually came from their savings and from family members or friends engaged in a part-time farming. Our interviews largely correspond to Tai-li Hu's account of her mother-in-law's rural village, Liu Ts'o, where no firms were started during the 1960s, but where many villagers had gained sufficient skill in nearby Taichung City to return to Liu Ts'o in the 1970s to establish, "all of a sudden", 20 small-scale factories. Indeed, Ho (1978) makes the claim that, throughout Taiwan, rural industrialization was an extraordinarily important feature of Taiwan's economic development. Our interviews make it clear that the earliest entrepreneurs, in Taichung City in the 1960s and throughout the entire region in the 1970s, relied heavily on raising capital and recruiting labor from the social networks that developed in the aftermath of land reform, a point also acknowledged by others as well (Ho 1978: 172–4; Speare 1992; Liao and Huang 1994).[3] These networks based on locale and kinship enabled the agriculturally-based rural society to generate enough resources for a few entrepreneurs to start modest businesses in the late 1960s and early 1970s. By the mid-1970s, these early beginnings mushroomed into a full-scale manufacturing boom, a boom that would transform Taiwan's local society.

The backdrop to this manufacturing boom was the transformation of Asia's role in the global economy. Deeply involved in the Korean War as well as the Cold War, the United States encouraged Japan to rebuild their economy after World War Two using exports to global markets as the basis for their reindustrialization. Japanese businesses, particularly the trading companies, quickly renewed ties to Taiwan,[4] and agriculturally rich Taiwan began to export food products to Japan. In addition, a few large Japanese electrical appliance firms began to do some subcontracting in Taiwan (Gold 1986). About 50 percent of Taiwan's very modest exports during the 1950s went to Japan (Ho 1978: 392). By the late 1960s, the Vietnam War had further increased the U.S. involvement in the region and had encouraged wholesale buyers to locate products in Asia for sale in the United States and Europe. In part stimulated by the availability of high-quality manufacturing in Japan and Hong Kong, retail outlets and mass merchandisers in the United States and Europe discovered that they could buy set amounts of manufactured products (e.g., garments, toys, and consumer electronics) in East Asia for resale elsewhere. This period marked the beginning of OEM production in Asia.

Taiwan's export economy took off in the 1970s. This initial stage of industrialization is tremendously important, because it shaped the basic structure of the Taiwanese economy and set the economy on a trajectory of development that continues today, thirty years later. The beginning of export production started in agriculture and textiles but quickly expanded to other areas. Small and medium-sized firms began as the primary manufacturers for exports. These firms could buy some of their inputs from Taiwan's import-substituting large firms that had been subsidized by the government, but they also bought inputs from Japan and the United States as well. Our interviews are clear on one point: contrary to what Amsden (1985) and Evans (1995) have suggested, there was never a formal or even a long-term informal relationship between the upstream producers of intermediate goods, such as the producers of plastics and textiles, and the SMEs, the producers of finished products. Even though the SMEs needed these intermediate goods, they would happily buy from anyone offering them the right combination of price, quality, and availability. The success of the SMEs depended on their autonomy from large upstream firms and the organizational flexibility in linking with each other.

From the beginning, small trading companies, each consisting of only a handful of employees, brokered deals between foreign buyers and local networks of SMEs. The research teams at IEASE interviewed about forty entrepreneurs who started or managed such trading companies (Chen 1994). The interviews revealed that most owners of trading companies have a modest education and are able to speak a little English. Many of these entrepreneurs, sometimes with no advance contacts, simply went on the road, sample suitcase in hand, going from one wholesale firm to another in the United States and Europe. The trading companies they owned were known colloquially as *pibao gungsi*, "suitcase companies". The entrepreneurs served as compilers of information about trends in consumption, collectors of samples for reverse engineering, and matchmakers between foreign buyers and local manufacturers. Once they had orders in hand, the traders actively participated in establishing manufacturing networks for the ordered products. Even though entrepreneurs drew on their social relationships, the production networks they put together were temporary, functioning only as long as the contracts lasted. As such, the networks were not static. Rather their composition changed dramatically over time. As orders increased, the organizing entrepreneurs would increase their production by subcontracting parts of the manufacturing process to others. Building around production, the networks grew more complex as production became more complex. Networks segmented and proliferated, with some specializing in one type of product or a specific type of manufacturing process (e.g., metal-working). Geographic concentrations grew. For instance, in the area around Hemei, in central Taiwan, hundreds of firms participated in the manufacture of cotton textiles and garments (Chen 1997). In Chiayi, in southern Taiwan, the six plants located there manufacturing hydraulic jacks dominated the world's production of hydraulic jacks.

This model of doing business was easy to learn and easy to adapt to the manufacture of most types of products. Entry for bottom-end subcontractors was easy and required little capital. Once the process of manufacturing was mastered, a subcontractor could venture out on his own, finding a new product to make or a better way to make an existing product. Hence once this model of doing business was a proven success, foreign buyers began to seek out manufacturers to make the products that they wanted to merchandise. Trade shows set up by the government helped to showcase selected firms, but the real links between global demand and local production were the thousands of small trading companies and entrepreneurs willing to go out and find buyers (Levy 1988).

By the late 1970s, an accelerating and self-reinforcing cycle of production had begun, fed in large part by the accelerating retail boom in the United States. By this time, the Vietnam War had ended and mass merchandising of brand-name products had begun in earnest. Many people nowadays forget that the most common brand names for consumer non-durables date only from the 1970s. Such footwear companies as Nike and Reebok, and such clothing companies as Esprit, Ann Kline, and The Gap began in the 1970s as manufacturers without factories, as designers and merchandisers that subcontracted the manufacture of their brand-name goods. Gary Gereffi (1994b) terms these merchandisers and mass retailers "big buyers", and calls the types of manufacturing arrangements they established "buyer-driven commodity chains". From the outset of their deployment, Taiwan, Hong Kong, and South Korea had very large shares of the big-buyer subcontracts. When such buyer-driven chains proved fabulously successful, Taiwan's manufacturing model became self-perpetuating.

Whether successful or not, Taiwan's entrepreneurs drew on their knowledge of everyday society to create their production networks. The knowledge they used to make the economy work was the tacit social knowledge they already possessed. At least initially, they needed little special training to become entrepreneurs. They had, most of all, to know how to "do society". This outcome was neither an intended consequence of government officials, who left local society alone as long as there was stability and not too much speculation, nor an intended outcome of Taiwan's big businesses, which increasingly oriented their own business strategies to fulfilling the demands created by export-driven SMEs. Instead, the network organization of Taiwan's economy rested squarely on the patterns of activity reconstructed from the patterns of Taiwan's local society.[5]

The economic organization of the SMEs: the connections of global economy

It would be a mistake, however, to conclude that the organization of Taiwan's economy is due simply and entirely to its embeddedness in Taiwanese society. Social institutions certainly shaped these networks by giving them everyday social meanings as well as a style-of-life orientation (Chen 1994, 1995). But when these networks became the medium of a system of production that could successfully compete in the global economy, the network organization grew increasingly economic and increasingly directed towards improving the global competitiveness of entrepreneurs. The interviews with entrepreneurs make this point very clearly: they are not in business in order to "do society" (i.e., "to be sociable") but rather they were "sociable" in order to make money from their business. They are business-people first and foremost, and as businesspeople they are not only socially embedded, but also economically embedded in a system of production in which they are players and in which they can be entrepreneurs, but over which they have very little control.

Seen in this way, the network organization of the Taiwan economy has two levels of activity: the activities of entrepreneurs and their firms and the activities of networks. Entrepreneurs and their firms are not autonomous actors, but rather they are collective players in a system of production, a system they helped create and of which they are a product. Socially, such firms are, *ipso facto*, family firms because these entrepreneurs are part of a society in which family and kinship relationships form the organizational medium by which all activities outside of the state sphere are organized (Fei 1992; Hamilton 2000). The heads of such businesses are *laoban*, a word conventionally translated as "boss". But *laoban* means more than a boss; it means the person in charge. The head of Formosa Plastic is a *laoban*, as is the owner of a peddler stand selling "rotten" tofu. The *laoban* of a business is the counterpart of the head of a household (*jiachang*), and in fact the person in charge of the business is usually the acknowledged head of the household. Therefore, business decisions are often family decisions, as Kao (1999) has demonstrated in his study of the importance of the "boss's wife" (*laoban niang*) to the everyday operation of entrepreneurial firms, large as well as small ones. But a full understanding of how these firms actually operate and transform economically is only achieved by examining how they become a part of a system of production.

In order to survive economically, entrepreneurs must be socially and normatively connected to each other and, more importantly, their firms must be integrated into one or more production networks. We have spent many years, through observations and interviews, trying to understand how these networks operate as economic organizations. Looking at the networks from the entrepreneurs' point of view (including that of the bosses' wives), we see that family units constantly learn and relearn how to be a part of production networks. Being in a network, or networking, is a process rather than a state of being. Networking is part of a constantly changing economic world in which networks are dynamic vehicles through which productive activity is carried out.

We have come to see these networks as "functional hierarchies". The social counterpart of these economically oriented and often very specialized hierarchies is the continuing round of banquets in which all the *laoban* engage. The inviter hosts the meal for the invited, and all eaters observes the etiquette of the round table, where equality and hierarchy are subtly blended. Similarly, most production networks consist of firms that have been invited to participate. The networks form around the manufacture of a product. Typically, the inviting entrepreneur, often but not necessarily connected to a trading company, organizes a production network which is made up of independent firms. Each firm corresponds to the actual requirements to manufacture a specific product. Some firms may be large, some medium, and some small, depending on the inputs and manufacturing sequence. Even though in reality inequalities among entrepreneurs may be considerable, in a formal sense, every firm in the network is independent and every *laoban* an independent operator. However, for each production network there is an organizer, who invites others in, who serves as a host, who coordinates the activities of the network, and who serves as the person in charge.

For products having large and long-term orders, manufacturing networks typically grow better at networking and often are quite stable over time. Firms increase their technological sophistication; inefficient firms are weeded out tactfully, and more efficient firms are integrated into the network. For short-term orders, production networks form and reform around each new order and each new product being produced. Network organizers also shift over time. Having experience as a subcontractor, an entrepreneur may try his hand at organizing a new production network around the same or similar products. Viewed from the standpoint of the economy as a whole, the dynamism and flexibility of the Taiwanese economy is easy to understand. The ability of the Taiwanese economy to respond quickly to changing global demands, to be reflexive manufacturers, was present early in Taiwan's economic development.

The networking dynamism has internal as well as external causes. The internal causes arise from a tendency of economic networking to incorporate new firms in expanding areas of production (often through subcontracting and outsourcing) and to diversify across product areas as demands change. The proliferation of firms leads to product development and product differentiation. In fact, the level of product diversification in Taiwan's economy is nothing short of amazing (Feenstra *et al.* 1999), even when compared with much larger economies, such as South Korea and, for some product areas, even Japan. It should be noted that government support is not among the internal causes. The government has provided the SMEs with no protection, few privileges, and little guidance. The government has provided a friendly environment and limited support for the development of selected upstream and midstream industries. But the SME's export successes, their organizational flexibility, and their manufacturing capacities cannot be adequately explained by policy directives or by the actions of government technocrats, however competent they may be (Hamilton 1997).

The external causes of Taiwan's networking flexibility and dynamism are equally important to, and complementary with, the internal ones. These

causes are directly linked to the global economy and to the rationalizing pressure constantly placed on the organization of the economy. We can understand
the pressure towards rationalization by understanding the price structure
within which Taiwan's networks function. Although the entrepreneurs may
want to increase their profits over the long term, the real pressure to rationalize production networks usually comes from the big buyers, who find
themselves in global competition with other merchandisers offering similar
products. The big buyers constantly squeeze production networks with each
new round of orders, and the functional hierarchies respond by further rationalizing their production chains. In this sense, networking and price structures
are intimately linked and integral to the same economic system. As we will
discuss in the next section, production networks frequently reach a point where
no further systemization will allow the networks to reach the price targets set
by outside buyers within an acceptable level of profit as demanded by participating firms, and an acceptable level of quality as demanded by buyers. At this
point, networks collapse and are only re-established under very different
circumstances, such as producing different products or producing the same
products under very different conditions of production.

The post-Plaza Accord transformation of Taiwan's economy

In the 12 years between the signing of the Plaza Accord in 1985 and the
onset of the Asian business crisis in 1997, Taiwan's economy was transformed. In this period, Taiwan went from being one of the world's leading
exporters of footwear and garments to an economy that exports very little in
the way of either product (Hsing 1998; Gereffi 1994b). In the same period,
Taiwan became one of the world's leading manufacturers of an amazing
array of high technology products. From the late 1980s to the early 1990s,
Taiwan also experienced a severe crisis and emerged from that crisis as one of
the world's most resilient and dynamic economies, an economy specializing
in reflexive manufacturing. It was this reflexivity that allowed Taiwan to
emerge relatively unscathed from the 1997 crisis that forced most other Asian
economies into near bankruptcy.

In the twenty-year period between the late 1960s and the late 1980s,
Taiwan's economy flourished. Early on, OEM manufacturing was very profitable and an exceedingly wide range of products came to be manufactured
in Taiwan's production networks. As the years passed, the production teams
had to work harder and harder to maintain the same level of income.
Networks could only absorb so many accelerating demands from the global
markets. And within Taiwan, every successful sector of production had also
generated many competing networks, which, when added to competition
from other locations in Asia, only made matters worse. Production networks
could not indefinitely cushion declining profits.

These complaints about declining profits and unending work were ubiquitous themes from our interviews during this period. But other factors

influenced Taiwan's economic environment at this time. By the late 1980s, demographic changes in Taiwan's society were having a full effect on its economy. Family planning had been so successful that the birth rate dropped precipitously. At the same time that the birthrate was falling, the government extended the length of mandatory education through twelve grades, further keeping people out of the labor force, and those entering the labor force with education often wanted new types of jobs. Accordingly, the labor market tightened as fewer and fewer young people entered the labor force at the bottom of the ladder. Additionally, the government directives banning the entry of foreign laborers did not help to alleviate the problem. The rate of unemployment reached the lowest point ever just as the demand for cheap labor increased.

After years of running trade deficits with Korea, Japan, and Taiwan, the United States negotiated a currency reform measure and, in 1985, all parties signed at the Plaza Hotel in New York City. The Plaza Accord, as this currency reform became known, removed the pegged trading rate of East Asian currencies with the U.S. dollar and allowed the Asian currencies to appreciate. Over the period of a year, Taiwan's currency moved from 40 New Taiwan dollars to 1 U.S. dollar to 27 New Taiwanese Dollars to 1 U.S. dollar. The revaluation had an immediate effect on the cross-market price structure within Taiwan's economy. Momentarily everyone was much richer when computed in U.S. dollars. The price of imports fell considerably, and local consumption and styles of life rose quickly. Real estate prices, which had been rising, now took off, and money poured into property construction. Stock market speculation also increased.

After a short lag time, however, the cost of labor in Taiwan grew prohibitively high and, accordingly, Taiwan's exports became more expensive in world markets. By the late 1980s, the real estate bubble burst, the stock market collapsed from a high of about 14,000 to a little over 2,000, and rising exports began to taper off. Suddenly, in 1988, Taiwan's outward investment skyrocketed. In a two-year period, 1990–92, Taiwan's most profitable manufacturers – those specializing in footwear, textiles, and garments – were out of business or moved the site of their assembly operations to China and Southeast Asia. Those entrepreneurs who stayed in Taiwan began to look for new products to manufacture.

Our interviews reveal that the initial impetus to relocate the site of manufacturing came from the big buyers (i.e., brand-name manufacturers such as Nike, and mass retailers such as Home Depot) who told their manufacturers to move or lose their contracts. There was no government policy that encouraged this movement or assisted it in any way. Quite to the contrary, the government forbade the transfer of funds to the People's Republic. The owners of the SMEs, however, openly ignored the governmental restrictions and moved huge amounts of capital, machinery, and intermediate inputs to China by transshipping them through Hong Kong. Once a core group of entrepreneurs began to move, every competitor and would-be competitor also had to move. The interviews show that, win or lose, most entrepreneurs felt they had no choice. An SME stampede to China ensued, and as soon as the SMEs had established a China beachhead, some of Taiwan's large firms, supplying intermediate inputs to the small firms, began to set up subsidiary firms in China, too. (However, having greater control over large firms, the government was able to block many of them from moving.)

Once in China, Taiwanese entrepreneurs found they could not duplicate the production networks they had had in Taiwan. Similar to Hsing's (1998) findings, our interviews with Taiwanese firms in Guangdong Province show that they were forced to integrate many of the operations into the trans- planted firm that had been done formerly by independent firms in the network. Quite a few entrepreneurs, especially those making footwear and garments, had to establish factories in China many times the size and employing many times the workers than they had done in Taiwan. The scale of production meant that they needed massive amounts of intermediate inputs, much of which they continued to buy from manufacturers in Taiwan. Accordingly, Taiwan's exports to Hong Kong and then transshipped to China zoomed upward. Many firms kept their headquarters in Taiwan, had their manufacturing sites in China, and shipped their exports out to the rest of the world from Hong Kong.

The transformation of Taiwan's reflexive manufacturing

This hollowing out of the Taiwan economy in only a two-year period did not, however, spell an end to Taiwan's manufacturing boom, as one might have predicted it would. Instead, after a downturn of several years, Taiwan's manufacturing exports resumed again, more strongly than ever. How can the resumption of, and even increase in, Taiwan's manufacturing prowess be explained? We believe that Taiwan's reflexive manufacturing system best explains this remarkable restructuring that has occurred in the last decade.

Interviews show that Taiwan's entrepreneurs followed one of two strategies to upgrade their businesses. First, many entrepreneurs simply did not want to abandon their homes and their families to establish new factories overseas. They decided to remain in Taiwan making the same products, but now targeting the very high end of the market. Where one firm had been making bicycles for mass consumption, they now began to make titanium and carbon composition bicycles for select enthusiasts who would pay premium prices.

The second strategy for many organizers of manufacturing networks, especially those in traditional labor-intensive industries, was to split their business into low-end and high-end segments. They moved low-end labor- intensive segments to areas outside of Taiwan, and resumed production on existing or new contracts in the new location. For the high-end segment, they typically tried to move production to a higher level of quality with more capital intensity than was the case previously. This often meant that they needed to find some new products to make, which were hopefully not totally unrelated to the previous products. They wanted to retain their manufacturing expertise but to find a new market in which they could excel. One entrepreneur described his efforts as a "search and discovery mission". Entrepreneurs would read trade magazines and go to trade shows. They would travel to their markets in the United States and Europe to get ideas. Once they hit upon a new product, they would recombine previous resources, put together a new production network, reinvest their own money, and then begin again. In this search and discovery, one entrepreneur, who had made shoes for twenty years, ended up successfully making high-end craft tools. Another entrepreneur, who had made model airplanes as toys, began making turbo jets for foreign governments. In more than a few cases, however, entrepreneurs decided just to close their businesses, usually without formally claiming bankruptcy. They sold their property and used the money to invest elsewhere.

In the late 1980s, a new period of rapid growth began, this time in high technology industries. The entrepreneurs creating these new industries were a new group of people quite different from the first round of entrepreneurs. These were more highly educated, many receiving their education in Taiwan, but an important few had gone to school in the United States, had worked in Western high technology firms, and then moved back to Taiwan to start businesses or manage existing ones.

This new set of entrepreneurs built on a previous high technology industry that had arisen in Taiwan in the early 1980s, but that had remained small and relatively unsophisticated. According to the accounts that these entrepreneurs gave us, the PC industry in Taiwan developed accidentally and with no direct assistance from the government. The government indirectly helped, however, by banning the manufacture of gambling machines. With the government prohibition, those firms that had been making these machines needed to find something else for its production network to manufacture. Drawing on their expertise, they decided to make PC clones and copies of the Apple II. When asked how he could make a computer from scratch, one entrepreneur replied with the Chinese saying, "We have no experience with horses, but we have ridden a donkey". From this beginning, PC factories in Taiwan grew to become the main OEM suppliers for such American PC computer companies as Compaq and Dell. Taiwan became the third largest manufacturer of PC-related products, behind the United States and Japan.

The new beginning for the high technology firms occurred in the early 1990s. Demand in the United States for computer components and periph-erals was high, and many U.S. firms were in hot competition with each other to offer the latest PCs to consumers who were just developing an appetite for fast computers with lots of memory. The area of deepest concentration of software and hardware producers was in Silicon Valley. Saxenian (1994, 1998) shows that these producers were highly networked, and from the beginning Taiwanese and Chinese American entrepreneurs had an impor-tant presence among Silicon Valley firms. Many of the hardware firms were eager to locate high-quality and low-cost OEM producers for components that had very rapid product cycles. Drawing on their connections in both California and Taiwan, a number of Chinese high technology engineers started manufacturing firms in Taiwan, many adjacent to one another in the Hsinchu Science-Based Industrial Park.

At this time, Taiwan had no silicon wafer semiconductor factory. The Taiwan government decided Taiwan's economy needed to be competitive in high technology industries, but did not want to compete head on with firms in the United States and Japan. Private entrepreneurs (Morris Chang, a former executive at Texas Instruments, being the most prominent one) persuaded government officials to follow the pattern of other large firms in Taiwan, namely to be upstream providers of intermediate inputs that SMEs could then use to manufacture exports. Joining with Philips Electronics, the government established the Taiwan Semiconductor Manufacturing Company (TSMC), the world's first dedicated independent semiconductor manufacturing foundry. A semiconductor foundry is simply an OEM manufacturer of semiconductor chips designed and merchandised by other firms, in much the same way that garments and footwear had been in Taiwan. In fact, TSMC's charter prevents the company "from designing or making our own brand-name IC products. TSMC therefore is a partner, not a competitor with other semiconductor companies" (TSMC Annual Report 1998: 7).

TSMC's success epitomizes Taiwan's new surge in reflexive manufacturing. From the beginning, TSMC began to work cooperatively with small chip design firms that would create special purpose chip sets for export products. The design firms, in turn, worked with export manufacturing firms, some located in Taiwan and some elsewhere. The key feature of the semiconductor foundry business is its integration into a manufacturing system whose foremost characteristic is its quick response to external demand, the essence of reflexive manufacturing. The approach proved successful, and soon other entrepreneurs started foundries in competition with TSMC. The foundry business took off. Today, semiconductor foundries form an extremely important segment in global high technology development, in which Taiwanese foundries have a commanding lead, producing over 80 percent of the global demand for foundry-made chips. With foundries, every high technology firm can have their own "virtual fab". They can be designers and merchandisers of products that they do not produce. Increasingly the global high technology industries are becoming "buyer-driven chains", and increasingly Taiwan's organizational capacity for reflexive manufacturing has pushed global high technology in this direction.

Besides the big semiconductor companies, other PC and PC-related high technology industries share the similar characteristics of reflexive manufacturing as well. Although they are new firms, we also see many continuities in the patterns of network production between the newer and the older industries. We want to be clear here: Taiwanese high-tech companies are not organized in exactly the same manner as they were with footwear and other similar products. None the less, decentralized but well-connected production networks serve as the basic organizational pattern in both the new and the old industries. Businesses in Taiwan are accustomed to decentralized networking instead of vertical integration. The major difference in the high technology industry is that the entrepreneurs are more highly professionalized than they were in the previous networks of *laoban*. Notwithstanding this difference, it is still apparent that there is an affinity between the global high technology industry and network production systems. It is not surprising, therefore, that Taiwanese manufacturers played such an important part in the formation of this industry. The Taiwanese entrepreneurs have mobilized existing local conditions and efficiently integrated them into the global division of labor. They are able to achieve mass production and flexibility simultaneously. It is the transformed network production system that makes reflexive manufacturing possible and successful.

A final word is needed about the role of the state in the development of high technology industries. Unlike in the older industries, in the new high technology industries the state plays a more active role, but that role is still largely restricted to providing infrastructure, for instance in the form of developing science parks, and investment capital for large, capital-intensive endeavors that serve as upstream suppliers of intermediate inputs for export manufacturers. In this role, the Taiwanese state does not act like the mythical "developmental state" so often discussed in the literature, but rather reacts to, and is merely a sustainer of, the reflexive manufacturing system that is well institutionalized and that powers Taiwan forward.

Conclusion

What you see depends on where you look. In this chapter, using the insights we have gained from twelve years of intensive interviews, we have looked at the organization of Taiwan's economy from the point of view of those who organize it, the entrepreneurial owners and managers of firms. Based on our interviews, Taiwan's entrepreneurs do not see the government as their partner. State planners are often more than willing to take credit for Taiwan's spectacular industrial successes, and some are even willing to call Taiwan's capitalist transformation an economic miracle. But the entrepreneurs interviewed by the research teams at IEASE never used the word "miracle" to describe what they have done and they saw very little governmental effects on the products of their labor. Most entrepreneurs ignored government programs and complied with government regulations only if it was convenient to do so. Their world is a world of business and for them the government is largely outside of this world, and is certainly not its shaper.

Analysing their words and actions, we have come to understand that the entrepreneur's world is complexly organized, and that the government has very little role in creating it or shaping it. The organization of Taiwan's economy is shaped by the social and economic life of those who run it. It is a world that runs by socially interpreted rules of family and friends, but it is also a world that is thoroughly economic and calculable in those terms. There is no boundary between the social and the economic; the boundary is kept purposefully ambiguous. Both the social and economic worlds are intimately and intricately bound up in one reality. That reality is grounded in the routines of everyday life and thus is distinctively Taiwanese. It is also historical in that it has evolved and grown over time. But it is also a reality that is now intertwined in global economic forces, which the Taiwanese entrepreneurs were active participants in creating, but over which they, as individuals, have very little control. For them, the market is not an invisible hand that works automatically towards beneficent ends. Instead, the market is filled with real things, real products, real money, real families, real decisions, and real futures, none of which will necessarily lead to good ends. They see bankruptcies and failures, as well as wealth and successes, all around them. They know that the paths to wealth and success are tried and tested, and have become institutionalized processes in an economic system constantly recreating itself in the light of new and ever-changing ways to make money. This encompassing economic system, which constitutes the world of Taiwan's entrepreneurs, is what we have identified as a system of reflexive manufacturing. It is through this system of manufacturing that Taiwan has become integrated into the global economy.

Notes

1   This premise is a foundational element in the work of such pragmatist social scientists as Mead (1932) and James (1907), and has been reconstructed somewhat for use in modern social science by Giddens (1979) and others (Strauss 1991). Although philosophically sound, the premise has had little relevance in empirical research because most social scientists do not use frameworks that are sufficiently organizational and interactional, both elements that are necessary to capture the contingent, developmental, and emergent qualities of social action.

2   The chapter is part of a book project in which the two authors are engaged. Because of space limitations, we use very few quotations in this chapter for the interviews. For a fuller description of these interviews and for other analyses of SMEs based on these interviews, see Chen 1994, 1995 and Kao 1999.

3   Hu (1984: 212) argues, however, that in her case study "the capital accumulated for the development of rural small-scale industry was not mainly from agriculture". Our interviews indicate that, although rural-based capital accumulation might have been modest, the use of rural resources, including the land and labor of those living in the countryside, was substantial and facilitated the rapid growth of industries that occurred in the 1970s and early 1980s.

4   The Korean War limited products that Japan could buy from Korea but at the same time increased the demand for exports. In the post-war period, the Japanese trading companies quickly re-entered the Taiwanese economy, but, in part because of the war and in part because of the lingering animosity from the colonial era, Japanese trading companies were less successful in Korea.

5   For an extensive analysis based on the interviews done by the Tunghai team, see in particular the two books written by Chen (1994, 1995), which reached these same conclusion as well.

8 Asian business networks in transition, or what Alan Greenspan does not know about the Asian financial crisis

In January and February of 1998, Alan Greenspan (1998a, 1998b, 1998c), the chairman of America's Federal Board of Reserve, made a number of presentations before committees of the United States Congress. In his testimony, as well as in the question and answer session afterward, he explained the reasons for the economic crisis that had gripped Asia since the previous summer. He also outlined a rationale for congressional support for the International Monetary Fund's (IMF) so-called aid packages to Korea, Thailand, and Indonesia. The reasoning in his speeches echoed that expressed in many articles – really editorials and thought pieces – by other economists that appeared in many major newspapers and magazines beginning in October 1997.[1] The economic reasoning that Greenspan and other writers used to interpret the first year of Asia's financial crisis draws on a set of images of how the capitalist world economy works and of how the Asian countries got themselves into such an awful fix.

Many students of Asian societies, myself included, interpret Asian economies, and also the Asian crisis, in a very different way. In this chapter I use Alan Greenspan's interpretation as a proxy for the general views of the most prominent economic analysts, and contrast this rather conventional economic interpretation to what I believe is a more realist interpretation of the economic and social background – the so-called secondary causes – that shaped the crisis without actually causing its occurrence. I argue that the crisis results from fundamental shifts both in the organization of global capitalism and in the integration of Asian economies into this global system.

What Alan Greenspan predicts

In asking the U.S. Congress for money to support the IMF, Greenspan predicted that the Asian business crisis would have two positive long-term consequences. The successful resolution of the crisis would first bring an end to crony capitalism and, second, hasten the convergence of capitalism into one global pattern, or what Greenspan (1998b) referred to as "the Western form of free market capitalism". Both predictions hinge on what he means by the two crucial terms, "crony capitalism" and "free market capitalism".

The term *crony capitalism* is an interesting one. When the seriousness of the crisis became clear, Greenspan, in chorus with many other observers, began to use it retrospectively to interpret crucial organizational dimensions of Asian economies before the crisis began to single out these dimensions as the fundamental cause of the current emergency. To economists, the term *cronyism* generally implies that collusion of any kind undermines market processes. In the Asian context, the meaning is more nuanced. These observers charge that there are two forms of cronyism at work.

The first form of cronyism is a systemic linkage between government and business. Such linkages are so strong and so unidirectional that they amount to straightforward government interventions into the marketplace. Until the crisis, political economists often praised such interventions as the source of the Asian miracle. Remember Alice Amsden's proclamation (1989) that Korea's success came from the government's "getting the prices wrong", and Robert Wade's (1990) persuasive argument that Asian states were able to "govern the market" and thereby to create their own success? Now these same scenarios, we are told, create what economists call *moral hazard*, "situations in which someone can reap the rewards from their actions when events go well but do not suffer the full consequences when they go badly" (Greenspan 1998b: 2). Most commentaries, including Greenspan's, use South Korea as the key example of moral hazard. The Korean state officials targeted industrial sectors for rapid growth. Korean banks, largely controlled by the state, gave huge loans to those businesses selected to develop the targeted sectors. Such government support also signaled other investors, both local and foreign, to lend large sums of money on the assumption that everyone could share in the profits when times were good, but that the government would cover the loans if times turned sour. Such no-lose situations of government-induced moral hazard, reiterated the economists, resulted in very high levels of firm indebtedness (leverage as a ratio of debt to equity) in South Korea, Thailand, and Indonesia. The high levels of leverage made the firms vulnerable to currency fluctuations, thus precipitating the crisis.

Most commentators, however, see crony capitalism as something more than collusion between government and business. It is also a term they apply to the inter-firm networks that made up the business groups for which many Asian economies are so well known. The *keiretsu* in Japan, the *chaebol* in South Korea, the overseas family-owned Chinese conglomerates in Southeast Asia – these are all cited as prime and undifferentiated examples of "crony capitalism". The logic that establishes them equally as examples of cronyism is subtler than for the blatant government intervention in the economy. In the case of business groups, accusations of cronyism arise from the common practice of firms in a group owning each other's shares and loaning each other money, creating a web of interlocking ownership and indebtedness. In such cases, says Alan Greenspan (1998b: 10), stocks are purchased and loans are made "on the basis of association, not economic value". It is at this point that the analysts begin to equate cronyism with *guanxi*, that ubiquitous term meaning, in Chinese, relationship or connection. Equating cronyism and *guanxi* implies that networks based on interpersonal associations look a lot like market-distorting cartels.

In his statements before the congressional committee, Greenspan predicted that the Asian business crisis would have the effect of lessening, if not ending, crony capitalism in Asia. The IMF-imposed economic reforms would spell an end to artificial government supports, an end to cross-holding, and, most important, an end to Asian forms of capitalism, all of which rest on some form of cronyism. An end to these kinds of market distortions, he further predicted, would encourage the major Asian economies to converge towards one pattern of global capitalism, which Greenspan identified as the Western form of free market capitalism.

The free market capitalism that Greenspan described in his presentation has four clearly defined features. These features would, supposedly, become more obvious in Asia as crony capitalism recedes. First, transparency in accounting and in public disclosure of information is an "essential" element of free market capitalism. The broad "dissemination of detailed disclosures of governments, financial institutions, and firms, is required if the risks inherent in our global financial structures are to be contained". Without clear signals about "product and asset prices, interest   rates, debt by maturity, detailed accounts of central banks, and private enterprises, . . . a competitive free-market system cannot reach a firm balance except by chance" (Greenspan 1998b: 9). Second, when there is transparency in the economic system, both "private transactors and government policymakers" can "discipline" themselves, meaning they can accurately assess the risks before them and act prudently. Third, this discipline leads to price structures in credit, equity, and product markets that reflect "true" value, rather than "distorted" value based on some form of moral hazard. Fourth, and finally, "an effective competitive economy", said Greenspan (1998c: 8), "requires a rule of law" that would limit arbitrary government intrusion in commercial disputes and establish a regulatory system to structure the incentives of economic players.

Greenspan's picture of global capitalism

In Greenspan's portrayal of the Asian crisis, there is a clear indictment of Asian business practices and a valorization of Western economic institutions. There is an equally clear presumption that, were Asian economic institutions more like the Western ones, the crisis would have been much less severe, if not averted altogether. This portrayal is, of course, not Greenspan's alone, but rather is a view that many commentators share. If we examine this view closely, we see that it is based on a set of assumptions that form a more or less coherent image about the nature of global capitalism.

Let me quickly sketch out the main features of this portrait. The first thing we should note is that this picture of global capitalism has a very clear foreground and a very fuzzy background. In the clear foreground are the institutions of capitalism, and in the blurred background are the economic activities of manufacturing, distributing, and consuming. If we set this image in motion, Greenspan's narrative of the Asian crisis directs our attention only to what happens in the foreground. The picture of global capitalism that we get is the following:

First, capitalism is perceived to be a country-based phenomenon. Free market capitalism is equated with clearly defined and relatively stable economic institutions, which one might call "institutionalized markets", rather than the less well-defined and ever-changing economic activities of manufacturing and distributing products. In the foreground, we see that capitalism corresponds to a system of ownership (equity systems are a market for ownership), a system of banking and credit, an established and distant relationship between governments and markets, and a country-based means to monitor these institutions. If these conditions are met, then the presumption is that the economy will be free market capitalism. In this system of capitalism, price-setting occurs in markets for ownership, in markets for money, in markets for labor, and in markets for undifferentiated products (e.g., commodity markets, ranging from gold to orange juice).

Second, this country-based capitalism is presumed to rest on market institutions that are objective and neutral with respect to society and culture. In this view, institutions are systems of incentives that can be engineered to produce transparency and market discipline. Such systems of incentives are, in essence, sets of rules that constrain all economic actors in the same way, regardless of their social and cultural affiliations. Keeping the institutional rules in the foreground and the society and culture in the background provides the level playing field that American trade negotiators so often find missing in Asian economies.

Third, it is assured that free market capitalism automatically arises if the incentive structures are correctly constructed and strictly and fairly enforced. The intent of the IMF bailout is to impose such incentive structures in each of the troubled economies. The outcome of these measures will be to install economic institutions that are similar, if not identical, everywhere in the world. When economists talk about the global convergence toward free market capitalism, the capitalism they have in mind is the capitalism that presumably flows from creating consistent foreground institutions – call it *institutionalized free-market capitalism*. Markets are only "free" if the incentive structures are constructed and institutionalized that way and if the participants, as well as the system as a whole, are strictly and fairly monitored, hence a capitalism of "institutionalized free markets".

A fourth feature of this image of capitalism occurs in the fuzzy background. The actual activities of manufacturing, distributing, and selling products are not in clear view, but are assumed to occur somewhere out of sight, more or less automatically, and to follow the laws of supply and demand.[2] Even though economic activities, as well as price-setting processes, occur out of view, most analysts would argue that the conceptual fuzziness is not a problem because economic activities are inherently dynamic and ever-changing. The principles of efficiency and profit and the laws of supply and demand parsimoniously drive the system of global capitalism, making predictable what would otherwise be uninterpretable and chaotic.

Using this interpretation of global capitalism, Greenspan locates the sources of the current crisis in the foreground features of Asian economies: in the lack of transparency (which is only a feature of institutionalized markets), in unformed or weak markets for credit, in an excess of government intervention, and in inadequate equity markets that might buffer currency fluctuations. In most analyses, including Greenspan's, the background factors – the actual processes of making and selling products – are hardly mentioned.

What is missing in this vision of capitalism?

Greenspan conceives of capitalism in terms of the paraphernalia of economic activities, rather than in terms of the economic activities themselves. He focuses on the institutional structures that frame business activities. In his view, free market capitalism is a particular kind of institutional framing that, when correctly built and strictly monitored, clarifies all economic activities, making them transparent, without artificially constraining them. This framing supposedly produces reliable economic outcomes that faithfully reflect the laws of supply and demand and the principles of efficiency and profit, so much so that those activities may be left in the background.

Writing as an economic sociologist and not an economist, I find that the features missing from this image of capitalism are the very features without which capitalism would not exist at all: industrial production and mass consumption. For me, these are the core features of capitalism, the up-front characteristics, but for many (though by no means all) economists, they are the background factors, blurred and indistinct.

Even more importantly, the country metaphor used to conceptualize global capitalism is perniciously inadequate. Capitalism cannot be characterized, even metaphorically, as a state-based economic system in equilibrium. As a sociologist, I see capitalism as a moving story, a historical narrative. The main protagonists are not countries but people, firms, products, capital, institutions, and the interrelationship among all of these. The setting of the story is not confined to national boundaries but rather follows the protagonists wherever they move in time and space. Finally, I see the narrative as being shaped by active attempts to control the working of all these things. In other words, capitalism is complexly organized through the efforts of people, firms and governments, each attempting to control the actions of others. Alan Greenspan's free-market institutions are forms of control that one set of actors (e.g., the state or the IMF) tries to impose on other sets of actors, sometimes against their wishes. The point is that capitalism is always contested terrain. The notions of movement, change, organization, and contestation are all missing in the Greenspan version of capitalism.

This is not the place to discuss the theoretical differences between these two versions of capitalism. The reader, however, should keep in mind what I mean by *capitalism*, for the simple reason that Greenspan's characterization misses the very things that have been driving globalization in the first place, the very things that have integrated Asian economies into the world economy: the spread of capitalistic activities in the form of industrial production and mass consumerism. These are non-cyclical changes, and cannot be viewed as aspects of a larger equilibrium that has now gotten out of kilter. Rather, these transformations in production and consumption have occurred worldwide and have resulted in profound structural changes in most of the world's economies, particularly those in Asia. Do we, as analysts of Asian economies, really believe that the Asian crisis was simply the result of inadequate institutional framing? Or do we believe that the current crisis has something to do with these worldwide capitalist transformations?

Transformations in the global economy

What are some of these transformations? There have of course been many changes, but two *organizational* changes that have occurred at the level of the global economy in the past twenty years seem particularly important: the rise of demand-driven economies and the creation of reflexive manufacturing systems.[3]

Not so many years ago, most capitalist economies in the world could be characterized as producer-driven, in the sense that consumers largely bought what large manufacturing firms produced (Chandler 1977, 1990; Chandler and Daems 1980; Piore and Sabel 1984). In the immediate post-World War Two era, very large vertically integrated corporations and business groups supplied the major consuming regions of the world with whatever manufactured goods were consumed. The first great manufacturing enterprises were American, but by the 1960s the German and Japanese corporations became effective competitors. These manufacturing giants are the General Motors, IBMs, General Electrics, Boeings, Volkswagens, Sonys, and Toyotas of the world economy. The major economic contests occurred between these giant producers; by and large, what they produced, we consumed. They defined the product and manufactured it mainly from within their own firm or group of firms, and we, the consumers, purchased whatever they made. As Piore and Sable (1984) observed so insightfully, adopting an economy-of-scale, Fordist production system was the only viable route to major economic success for most firms.

In the 1960s and early 1970s, an alternative approach to manufacturing began small and then accelerated (Piore and Sable 1984; Harvey 1990;

Gereffi 1994b; Gereffi and Korzeniewicz 1994; Saxenian 1994; Harrison 1994).[4] Largely because of technological advances in mass communications (e.g., television), firms that emphasized retailing and merchandizing – for example, department stores such as J. C. Penny, Wal-Mart, and Kmart, and brand-name merchandisers, such as Calvin Klein and Nike – started to appear. These firms specialized in the selling of fashion goods and goods with rapidly changing product cycles, such as televisions and computers. Department stores have been around for a long time, as have brand-name producers, but this time brand-name producers began to merchandise products that they did not make. They did not own factories; they designed the goods, subcontracted their manufacture, and then merchandised them through their own retail outlets (e.g., Gap) or outlets that someone else ran (e.g., the Bon Marche and Norstrom). This type of manufacturing started with the demand side, with what would sell, with products whose qualities were purposefully constructed for carefully selected segments of the mass market. Emphasizing the products themselves, as opposed to how, where, or by whom the products were made, created an awareness of niche markets – an awareness of demand. By the late 1970s and early 1980s, merchandisers computerized their inventory systems, based on such innovations as barcodes, so that they could reduce inventory and cut costs. They would only design and order from their subcontractors products that appeared to be selling. This manufacturing process started in textiles, but entrepreneurs, understanding the way the logic behind this type of manufacturing worked, soon began to apply these techniques to almost every category of consumer goods.

Consider this alternative approach to manufacturing. The shift involves a fundamental transfer of economic power from the manufacturing end to the merchandising and distribution end of the commodity chain.[5] The principal barrier to entry into the making and selling of goods shifted into the hands of merchandisers and retailers. The marketability of products was all that mattered. Quality, of course, counted, but quality was guaranteed through the branding and the retailing process. If Nike's name was on the shoe, then of course the shoe was good. If Wal-Mart or the Bon Marche sold the goods, then of course they would stand behind the quality. The importance of manufacturing in and of itself began to recede, relative to the product that was being made and merchandised.

In the 1980s and 1990s, the effects of this trend so intensified that no part of the global capitalist economy remained unaffected (Dicken 1992; Castells 1996). One should remember the crisis that shook, and to some extent still shakes, the industrial structure of the United States (Harrison 1994). It was in the late 1970s and early 1980s that the industrial heartland of America became known as the rust belt, when such world-renowned companies as IBM and Chrysler almost went bankrupt, and when a number of core American cities did, in fact, go bankrupt and had to be bailed out, such as Detroit, Cleveland, and New York City (e.g. Bluestone and Harrison 1982).

It was during this period of profound industrial restructuring in the United States that the U.S. economy began to shift from being a producer-driven to a demand-responsive economy, an economy in which super-discount retailers and brand-name merchandisers emerged victorious (Gereffi 1994b; Gereffi and Hamilton 1996).

This shift toward demand responsiveness led to the creation of what I call *reflexive manufacturing systems.*[6] Once the product is designed and the niche market targeted, then demand is calculated. Based on calculated demand, a manufacturing process is put together that will result in the targeted price and quality. This requires that merchandisers standardize the product (e.g., the hamburger, the cup of coffee, the running shoe, the computer) and then design a manufacturing process that achieves the desired goal. Because the merchandisers do not own the factories, this requires backward engineering, or reflexive manufacturing, which segments the production process into explicit steps whose efficiency and profitability can be calculated in advance of production so that each step can be allocated to a least-cost producer.

The creation of reflexive manufacturing capabilities occurred gradually. Initially, coordination between the merchandisers and the subcontractors was difficult, and few service providers could handle the intermediate and subsidiary steps in getting a product made and delivered to the merchandisers. But it was not too long before the intermediate roles – the shippers, the fast-freight forwarders, the custom handlers, the banking services – were identified and filled, and the whole process of reflexive manufacturing was made routine.

The changing integration of Asian business networks into the global economy

What do these trends have to do with Asian business networks and the Asian business crisis? The answer is, a great deal.

The story of Asian economic development is not a country-by-country story, is not a story told through such bestiary metaphors as tigers, dragons, or flying geese. Most analysts emphasize Asia's export-led development, but when they explain how the development occurred, they give country-by-country accounts of industrial policies designed to capture foreign direct investment, or of infrastructural and institutional factors that attract or put off would-be investors.[7] As evidence for their accounts, the same analysts typically present macroeconomic data that have been collected by individual countries, such as bilateral trade flows and foreign direct investment. This mode of analysis tends to push the understanding of economic development patterns toward the state-centered, "institutionalized free market" model of capitalism that I outlined earlier.[8]

What analysts do not often examine, however, is the actual organization of a country's or region's economy and the integration of that economy into the organization of global capitalism. The trade figures are there, and so the integration is merely assumed. But if Asia's integration into the global economy is looked at carefully, it becomes apparent that the linkages in the manufacturing and distribution of goods within and between Asian and Western economies are complexly organized. The linkages are organized globally through processes of manufacturing, merchandising, distributing, and consuming, and not merely through constraints imposed by political economies. A close examination would also show that these interlinked commodity chains simultaneously are embedded in the social and political institutions of locales and are extremely sensitive to such global conditions as price and currency fluctuations.[9] Because they are so sensitive, the economic power in many of these global commodity chains has shifted from producer-driven to demand-responsive. As I show in the following discussion, this shift is not a simple case of changing competitive advantage, but of what Nicole Biggart and I (Orrù *et al.* 1997: 97–110) have called *societal competitive advantage*, a situation in which distinctive and nontransferable social patterns lend themselves to particular organizing strategies that subsequently become integral elements in highly competitive manufacturing and distribution chains in the global economy.

Large Japanese business networks were the first of Asia's business networks to achieve global significance. As is well known, post-World War Two Japanese enterprises organized themselves by creatively reconstructing the patterns of the pre-war business groups, the *zaibatsu*. In the 1950s and 1960s, when the new Japanese business groups, the new *zaibatsu* – the intermarket groups, such as Mitsubishi and Sumitomo – first began to organize themselves, their major competitors were the vertically integrated corporations in the United States and Europe. The Japanese countered those industrial giants by creating some of their own.

These new business groups, composed of tiers of independent firms, were more flexibly organized and more all-encompassing than were their American counterparts in the 1960s and 1970s (Gerlach 1992; Fruin 1992; Aoki and Dore 1994; Westney 1996; Orrù *et al.* 1997). The Japanese groups created horizontal synergies by linking upstream firms that produced intermediate goods, such as steel, to downstream assembly firms that manufactured such things as ships and automobiles. They also created vertical synergies in each area of final production by developing *kereitsu*, vertically tiered hierarchies of firms that constituted "one-setism", the principle of self-sufficient production systems (Gerlach 1992: 85–6; Westney 1996). To make this economic organization work as a self-sustaining system, they situated financial services – banking and insurance – and trading companies at the center of each group. Ownership of the business groups was accomplished collectively through jointly holding each other's shares, a practice that protected the group from hostile incursions from the outside. The main banks coordinated the loans for member firms, and, because equity holding conserved ownership in the group, bank indebtedness became the way to finance growth and daily operations (Sheard 1986;

Gerlach 1992). The trading companies handled most transactions among member firms and served as the main trading arm, selling products produced by the group to the rest of the world. Although group structure draws its models from Japanese social organization (Aoki 1992), these groups are examples not of cronyism, but of vertical integration carried to its logical conclusion. That there are six or more groups so organized, and that these six groups hotly compete among each other for domestic and global market share, means that are not monopolies, but rather vertically integrated groups geared first, last, and always to the production and distribution of goods (Westney 1996).

By the 1970s and 1980s, the Japanese business groups had become so institutionalized in their practices and so adept at manufacturing that they succeeded in capturing a sizeable share of the global market in many product areas, from automobiles to high technology electronics. To a large extent, the success of these giant business groups precipitated the industrial crisis in the U.S., which, in turn, promoted the shift of American corporations from vertical integration to product creation, reflexive manufacturing, and merchandising (e.g., Bluestone and Harrison 1982; Prestowitz 1988; Womack *et al.* 1990; Reich 1992; Harrison 1994)

At the same time that Japanese industrial might was rising, the economies in South Korea, Taiwan, and Hong Kong were also developing. But if we look closely at these economies, we see considerable differences in how they were linked to global capitalism. Beginning in the early 1960s, South Korean state officials decided to industrialize the Korean economy by supporting the development of large enterprises that could compete with Japanese firms in the same global markets that the Japanese were selling their products. The story of the *chaebol* is well known (Amsden 1989; Woo 1991; Kim 1997, Orrù *et al.* 1997). The government selected key entrepreneurs, favored them with preferential loans, allowed their enterprises to grow into very large, diversified and vertically integrated business groups, and then attempted to control them through the state's control of the banking system and a system of perpetual indebtedness.[10] By the late 1970s, the top five *chaebol* were so large that their output alone represented approximately 20 percent of the valued added in the Korean economy, or nearly 70 percent of the economy if their sales are represented as a ratio to the Korean GDP. By the 1980s, the state-of-the-art production facilities of the *chaebol* had successfully challenged the dominance of Japanese firms in the same product lines at a price point that was slightly cheaper and at a level of quality that was slightly lower than the Japanese products themselves – challenged so much so that some writers began to ask "Is Korea the next Japan?" (Kang 1989; Amsden 1989).

Japanese and Korean manufacturers are examples of producer-driven mass production systems. Capital-intensive, heavily subsidized, and highly leveraged, both enterprise systems rely very heavily on government infrastructure to allow them to encompass the industrial structure of each country.

The network structure of these enterprise groups allows for considerable flexibility in the organization of export production, but the interdependent network of the firms themselves was a fixed, not a flexible, feature of both Japan's and South Korea's enterprise system. Speaking of Japan, Ronald Dore (1986) described this system as "flexible rigidities": flexible production and organizational and structural rigidities. Amsden (1989) implies much the same conclusion for South Korea.

The organizational rigidity in these enterprise systems arises from their being doubly embedded in their respective societies, first in social institutions and second in an institutionalized political economy. The organizational structures of enterprises are socially constructed, metaphorically, on norms of kinship and community, the main tenets of which are reconstructed and reified in the course of making these enterprises work economically (Aoki 1988, 1992; Orrù *et al.* 1997). Embedded in the social organization of these societies, the enterprise systems also become institutionalized into the larger political economy of the societies, so that the different segments of the society become mutually supporting (Whitley 1992; Brinton and Kariya 1998). The internal organization of these economies, in turn, structured the integration of each country's export-led trade regime. The goal of this regime was for the major Japanese and South Korean business groups to compete head-on with other business groups in their own societies so that they could be particularly competitive with major manufacturers elsewhere in Asia and in the West. This strategy worked extremely well for a while.[11]

Whereas Japan and Korea developed their own forms of industrial giantism, entrepreneurs in Taiwan and Hong Kong adopted a very different approach to building their respective economies. From the outset, Chinese social organization, based on differentially structured relationships among family and friends, made it difficult for entrepreneurs to create large, vertically integrated firms that were similar in scope and scale to those in Japan and South Korea (Wong 1985; Redding 1990; Chen 1994, 1995). Elsewhere, I have described at length some of the reasons that it is so difficult for Chinese to create such enterprises (Hamilton and Biggart 1988; Orrù *et al.* 1997), so I will not repeat myself here. It is enough to say that the push toward individual ownership and toward certain forms of interpersonal cooperation within and between families led to economies in Hong Kong and Taiwan that were composed primarily of modest-sized firms in the manufacturing sectors. Large firms do exist in both Hong Kong and Taiwan, but they are primarily producers of intermediate goods, such as polyurethane or textiles, where advantages associated with economies of scale allow firms to grow large and where some vertical integration in the upstream production process is possible. Large firms are also found in the property and services sectors, for different reasons. But, by and large, small and medium-sized firms predominate in the sectors specializing in manufacturing final products.

Given these propensities, Chinese entrepreneurs never thought they could or should compete with large, vertically integrated corporations elsewhere. Instead, outside of the state-dominated sectors, Chinese entrepreneurs began to produce products and parts of products that would be merchandised by others (Shieh 1992; Hamilton 1997). By the 1960s, Hong Kong manufacturers were producing garments, a range of plastic products, and fairly simple electrical appliances for American and European retailers (Wong 1988b). Taiwan manufacturers also specialized in textiles and garments, but in addition served as small-time subcontract manufacturers for Japanese enterprises (Gold 1986). By the 1970s, when the first merchandising boom started in the United States, Hong Kong and Taiwanese entrepreneurs began to play important manufacturing roles in the reflexive manufacturing systems that Western retailers and brand-name merchandisers were just figuring out how to create (e.g. Turner 1996; Gereffi 1994b). The availability of flexible manufacturing options in Taiwan and Hong Kong, as well as the OEM production in Korea and Japan, promoted the ability of Western firms to figure out how backward-engineered manufacturing might work. Textiles, garments, footwear, and high-technology products are all examples of Western-merchandised, brand-named goods that Korea and Japan, on the one hand, and Hong Kong and Taiwan, on the other, began to produce not only in competition with each other, but also within commodity chains that were organized in very different ways (Levy 1988, 1991). Whereas Korea's and Japan's vertically integrated commodity chains produced finished export goods, Taiwan's and Hong Kong's small and medium-sized firms produced parts of export products that could be flexibly assembled in many different locations.

As the demand-responsive trend accelerated in the 1980s, the competitive advantage of Taiwan and Hong Kong nearly equaled that of Japan and Korea, as is shown dramatically by rapid increases in exports from Taiwan and Hong Kong and by the fact that Taiwan took Japan's place as the holder of the world's largest foreign reserves. In 1985, on the eve of the Plaza Accord (the agreement that forced most currencies in East Asia to float against the U.S. dollar), Japan and Korea, on the one side, and Taiwan and Hong Kong, on the other, represented alternative systems of production that were in demand in the global economy.[12] With the signing of the Plaza Accord, however, the relative advantages of each alternative shifted suddenly.[13]

In a matter of a year, East Asian currencies increased their value, in some cases by nearly 40 percent. In Taiwan, the currency shift soon created an economic crisis. In a relatively short time, the stock market lost nearly 75 percent of its value, the property bubble burst, and bankruptcies were everywhere. Faced with much higher labor costs, networks of Taiwanese manufacturers making garments, footwear, and household appliances could not produce at the price points demanded by Western buyers. Many of the networks abruptly dissolved. In some cases, they were reconstituted in very different ways in the People's Republic of China and Southeast Asia, where labor costs were much lower (Hsing 1998). Those entrepreneurs who remained in Taiwan searched for new partners, for new products to make, or for new and lower-cost ways to make what they had previously made (Chen 1995). In Hong Kong, exempt from the Plaza Accord then as well as now, so that the HK dollar remains pegged to the U.S. dollar, wages had still moved high enough that most labor-intensive manufacturing moved out of Hong Kong into the Guangdong hinterland. The movement of industry out of Hong Kong rapidly accelerated after 1985 (Naughton 1997; Soulard 1997).

These changes in Hong Kong's and Taiwan's business networks were quite profound and amounted to a comprehensive industrial restructuring (Hsing 1998; Naughton 1997). At first, this restructuring seemed to disadvantage the Hong Kong and Taiwanese manufacturers, many of whom had to relocate and to reorganize their businesses. In just a few years, triangle manufacturing systems were created (Gereffi 1994a) in which Western buyers continued to placed orders with the Hong Kong and Taiwanese manufacturers they had used before. Now, however, these manufacturers had shifted the site of production to affiliated factories in China and Southeast Asia, and the production networks grew even larger and more cost sensitive. The restructuring, therefore, had the consequence of increasing Chinese involvement in the global development of Western-led subcontract manufacturing. Entrepreneurs from Taiwan and Hong Kong became specialists in and carriers of reflexive manufacturing techniques. They became better at producing in batches and more integrated into global manufacturing than ever before. In the 1990s, for example, the high technology industry swung decisively towards Taiwan's globalized manufacturing system, because they became indispensable component and OEM suppliers for such high-technology merchandisers as Dell and Gateway. For another example, the People's Republic of China is now the largest exporter to the United States. Nearly 44 percent of China's exports come from Guangdong province, are produced in networks of firms coordinated by Hong Kong and Taiwanese entrepreneurs, and are trans-shipped out of Hong Kong with the help of services provided in Hong Kong (Naughton 1997).

A careful analysis of the underlying causes of Asia's 1997 financial crisis reveals that the difficulties of Korean and Japanese manufacturers today should be traced to their unwillingness, and perhaps their inability, to respond organizationally to currency fluctuations that began in 1985 and that continued with China's currency devaluation in 1991. The immediate effects of currency adjustments in 1985 in Japan and South Korea were much smaller than in Taiwan and Hong Kong, but the long-term effects have been much more severe. In the five years after 1985, Japanese manufacturing groups, suddenly richer than ever with upwardly valued money, and seemingly invincible, began investing heavily and often unwisely around the world. Oblivious to valuations, global investors, including Japanese investors, pushed the Japanese stock market to unparalleled heights. By 1990, however, the Japanese bubble had reached its limits.

Although a few global firms (e.g., Sony and Toyota) continued to excel for a time, the profitability of the underlying system of production could not sustain the overhead network structure of Japanese business groups. The currency revaluations increased the costs of domestic labor and reduced the competitiveness of locally produced goods as export products. Pricing their goods high in relatively closed domestic economies, Japanese businesses kept the prices in global markets near or even below those of their international competitors. Some businesses also began to figure out how to produce the same goods in low-cost ways, usually by investing heavily in overseas capital-intensive production facilities (Hatch and Yamamura 1996). At the same time that Japanese business groups embarked on strategies of massive outward investment, Japan's domestic economy began to contract. The stock market collapsed, the property bubble began to deflate, and Japan slipped into a recession from which it has yet to emerge (Asher and Smithers 1998).

Finding some lucrative global niches, the four or five top Korean manufacturing groups remained highly competitive and even profitable in some sectors. These *chaebol* embarked on a tripartite strategy to upgrade existing products, to find new, higher-value products to mass-produce, and to relocate labor-intensive factories to foreign sites where labor was cheaper. They had sufficient low-cost borrowed capital to pursue this global expansion. Funded by ample loans from government and private sources, the top Korean *chaebol* built factories both locally and globally to mass produce such products as semiconductor chips and automobiles. But for many of the *chaebol* outside of the huge top five groups, profit margins declined, and series of bankruptcies of lesser groups began to occur even before the 1997 financial crisis (*Financial Times*, 8 August 1997, p. 17; *The Wall Street Journal*, 10 September 1997, p. A18).

The massive outward investment to reconstruct vertically integrated networks of Japanese and Korean business groups on a global, instead of a national, basis had two consequences. Domestically, raising money for foreign investments lifted the debt leverage of firms and extended the search for additional capital to foreign banks and foreign credit markets. Internationally, the direct foreign investments were targeted for only a few locations, with Southeast Asia among the principal sites for investment. Beginning in the early 1970s, but accelerating in the 1980s, Matsushita developed its production facilities in Malaysia, where it alone accounts for about 5 percent of Malaysia's GNP. Finding the Thai government very amenable, Japanese automobile firms moved many labor-intensive manufacturing plants to Thailand (Doner 1990). Korean garment and footwear firms primarily went to Indonesia. Many other Japanese and Korean firms began to follow suit. They were joined by other manufacturing firms and service providers from other locations around the world that wanted to get in on the action in Southeast Asia. Institutional investors (e.g., pension funds and banks) began to pour money into local stock markets, buying shares in those few Southeast Asian firms in which there was sufficient liquidity, and into local property markets. The result of this massive inflow of investment was too much money chasing too few opportunities. A speculative bubble emerged in stocks, property, and financial services. The influx of capital led to a huge demand for imports, some for intermediate goods for manufacturing final products, but also a lot for luxury goods, such as cars and cognac.

Another, and equally important, consequence of the extended and greatly increased flow of funds to and from Asian countries, especially the funds from institutional investors, was the development of globalized financial institutions. This is an irony of the crisis. East Asian industrialization had been largely accomplished from local money administered through locally embedded financial institutions. For instance, the state-owned banking system controlled Korea's industrial development for most of the period from the 1960s to the early 1990s (Amsden 1989; Kim 1997). Foreign investors had only limited ability to invest in Korean firms and only limited ability to take money out of Korea. In Taiwan, investment capital for small and medium-sized firms came from the informal economy, in large part because the state-owned banking system would not readily loan money to small firms (Lee 1990; Lin 1991). Before the 1990s in Southeast Asia, a lot of the investment capital for businesses owned by the ethnic Chinese came from local banks that were also owned by ethnic Chinese. These banks were only loosely connected to international financial networks. By the 1990s, however, the desire of international investors to invest their money in Asia pushed forward a series of liberalization measures that gradually opened Asian economies to the flow of Western money. Most Asian countries implemented globally standardized rules for stock exchanges, for banking, and for other financial institutions, and connected local financial organizations to globalized ones. The globalization of local finance set the stage for the Asian leg of the global crisis.

The crisis

The proximate cause of the so-called Asian financial crisis in 1997 was another currency fluctuation, followed this time by an all-out panic. Running out of reserves to back its currency, the Thai government allowed the baht to float against the U.S. dollar. Recognizing their investments were at stake, nearly everyone abandoned their assets in baht. As investors of all types moved their money into safe havens, in essence stopping the flow of money, the stock market crashed, currency plummeted, and credit vanished. Companies needing capital could no longer get it, and those owing money had nowhere to turn, and many went bankrupt in the process.

The same initial scenario quickly was repeated in one country after another. Among countries with convertible currencies, only Hong Kong successfully defended its currency from devaluation. Because the Chinese yuan is not yet convertible, China did not have to support its currency. But the crisis was a general one, and global stock markets all developed what many referred to as the "Asian flu".

However, the crisis did not play itself out in the same way in every location. In Taiwan, the panic was short-lived; Taiwan firms soon took the opportunity to expand at the expense of others. As the general period of economic decline extended through Asia, turning from slowdown to recession, Taiwan's economy suffered a crisis of falling demand. Otherwise the economy remained sound and only a few major bankruptcies occurred. In Hong Kong, the very high price of property receded and the stock market collapsed. The Hong Kong government intervened to slow the slide in property values and actively propped up stock prices by buying shares of major companies. Although shaken, manufacturing in both locations goes on unimpeded. Falling demand in Asia and elsewhere is the greatest danger, and, if the recession is a prolonged one, a new and potentially more serious crisis may emerge. In these places, the crisis in its earliest phases was relatively slight and was confined to the most speculative parts of the economy.

But in Korea and in Japan, the initial crisis was very large indeed, and has continued to reverberate through both economies. The reason for the severity is that the financial nature of the crisis went straight to the heart of the industrial structure in both countries. The business groups, the *chaebol* in Korea and the *keiretsu* and intermarket groups in Japan, have found that they cannot sustain the debt-financed system of vertical integration that they had in the past. This inability to sustain these systems intact started before the recent crisis, but now it appears that these two economies will have to find solutions to correct a manufacturing system that cannot now be adhered to in a world economy that has changed directions.

In Southeast Asia, the crisis at present is complicated by the fact that Indonesia also faced a domestic political crisis leading up to the resignation of President Suharto and to widespread civil unrest. The internal violence and continued political uncertainty caused a massive flight of foreign and, more seriously, ethnic Chinese capital. Only time will tell when some of this investment capital will begin to return to Indonesia. Elsewhere in Southeast Asia, the economies are starting to rebuild. As some predictability returns to global industries, firms throughout Southeast Asia will return to the things that they do best and for which they can find buyers. The lessons learned in the financial crisis will put Asian entrepreneurs on a new footing. Manufacturing processes will be streamlined, debt diminished, and economic relationships tested for reliability and trustworthiness.

Conclusion

I will conclude by returning to Alan Greenspan's analysis in order briefly to contrast his argument with mine. Did cronyism and the lack of transparency cause the Asian business crisis? And as a result of the crisis, will the Asian economies converge toward the Western form of free market capitalism?

I hope my analysis shows that these are the wrong questions to ask. When we examine Asian economies, we should not look for what is not there, but for what *is* there and for how it works. When economic analysts look at Asian economies, they often see what is not there. Treating Asian economies as negative cases, they try to explain the crisis in terms of how Asian economies differ from the way Western economies are supposed to function (but actually do not). This is not a logical approach.

But if we look at how these economies actually work, we see something else. My own analysis suggests that the chief factors underlying the crisis involve a historical shift in the organization of the global economy from producer-driven manufacturing systems to demand-responsive reflexive manufacturing. The earlier successes of Japanese and Korean business groups rested exactly on their ability to create giant producer-driven manu-facturing systems. To accomplish this, they created negotiated alliances between the state and the business groups and among firms in business groups. It is a mistake to think of these alliances as cronyism and of Japanese and Korean economies as being examples of "crony capitalism". They are, in fact, a type of modern capitalism that does not rest on culture alone, but rather on the creation of distinctive and very advanced manufac-turing systems. Different from the American system of capitalism, these manufacturing systems were globally extremely competitive with the same generation of American and European corporations; so efficient, in fact, that they forced Western firms into a global restructuring.

Good relationships are important in business and will remain so, but transparency is not all that it is cracked up to be. If anything, the strong linkages within the Japanese and Korean business groups have helped them survive thus far, largely through being able to resist restructuring. More transparency and less mutual commitment might have caused some of the business groups and perhaps the Japanese economy to collapse entirely, and would have made the collapse in Korea much worse. In Southeast Asia, institutionalized currency and equity markets were sufficiently open to allow institutional investors to get their money out quickly enough to collapse the economy effectively. Just think what a little more openness would have done in China.

More importantly, Greenspan's prediction of a global convergence is based on an inadequate understanding, not only of how these Asian economies work, but also of how the U.S. economy works. An analysis of global capitalism must look beyond the ways in which formal institutional-ized markets operate and must put capitalist activities in the foreground of our understanding. This will not give us a model or an image, but rather an account of how capitalism has changed and continues to change.

Finally, if my analysis is correct, then we should also understand that there is, strictly speaking, no Western model of capitalism to converge upon.

The organization of American firms differs from the organization of German firms, which is different again from the organization of British or Italian firms, and, of course, there are plenty of differences within each country. To lump them all together for the purpose of arguing that Asian firms should become more like Western firms is to misunderstand the way capitalist economies build on top of social and political institutions to create organized firms and groups of firms that are effective in the global arena.

I believe that both Japanese and Korean business groups will have to reorganize, but I do not believe that either will end up resembling an American corporation or a Chinese family-owned enterprise. Instead, these groups will have to reinvent themselves, will have to find within their organizational repertoires new ways to become economically viable again. But rest assured, whatever the future brings, the relational foundation of Asian economies will continue.

Notes

1 A more complete list of these articles is found on Nouriel Roubini's website, RGE Monitor. The address is http://www.rgemonitor.com (accessed 24 January 2006).

2 Prices for products and services are assumed to be set through an equilibrating process between all buyers and all sellers, in which selling price would include: (1) inputs whose prices are set by foreground institutions (e.g., markets in credit and in commodities); (2) labor whose wages are set competitively; and (3) value added in manufacturing.

3 These are my terms for what other observers have also seen. I take no credit for discovering these changes. The reason that I have attached new labels is because I want to emphasize the large-scale organizational qualities of these changes (Feenstra and Hamilton 2006).

4 The following argument is developed more fully in Gereffi and Hamilton 1994.

5 Gary Gereffi has pioneered the global commodity chain approach. For good descriptions of the approach see Gereffi (1994a; also see Gereffi and Korzeniewicz 1994 and Bonacich *et al.* 1994; and Gereffi and Hamilton 1996).

6 This discussion of "reflexive manufacturing systems" is based on my own research, first in Taiwan (Hamilton 1997), and later in the United States. Some discussion of this research is found in Gereffi and Hamilton 1996.

7 The best of this literature (e.g., Lim and Pang 1994; Lim 1995; Stallings 1995; Chen and Drysdale 1995; Naughton 1997) traces shifting patterns of export development to changing factors of political economy (e.g., government policy) and technology, including foreign direct investments. Although subtle in many ways, this highly descriptive literature is, generally speaking, not sensitive to substantial organizational differences existing between economies having very similar political economies and the same access to advanced technology. For an analysis that emphasizes crucial differences in economic organization among countries, see Whitley 1992; Lazonick *et al.* 1997; Hollingsworth and Boyer 1997; Orrù *et al.* 1997.

8 I should note that an artifact of this mode of analysis is to place the explanations of development on a continuum between the strong state, at one end, and the free market, at the other end. For a preliminary exploration of this bias, and its perniciousness, see Hamilton 1994.

9 Economist Robert Feenstra and I (Feenstra and Hamilton 2006) have developed a simulated model of industrial structure that produces multiple equilibria and

that clearly shows both the importance of embedded structures for economic outcomes and the sensitivity of these structures to price structures. We have corroborated these models with empirical data from Taiwan and South Korea.

10 For a first-rate comparative analysis of the level of debt leverage between South Korean manufacturing firms and those found in a selected sample of other countries, see Zeile 1993.

11 The process towards merchandising in the U.S. was directly enhanced by Japanese and Korean successes. More than a few former manufacturers began to subcontract, on an OEM basis, with Korean and Japanese firms. Ford and Chrysler both had models of their cars built in Korea. Once an industrial strength of the U.S., television production moved almost entirely to Asian production sites, even though the brand names of the former producers, such as RCA and Magnovox, persisted for a while.

12 The accelerating success of East Asian countries in global export trade and the expanding trade deficit in the United States prompted the Plaza Accord meeting, where U.S. negotiators successfully argued that Asia's currencies had been kept artificially low and ought be allowed to float to find their "true" level.

13 The effects of these currency adjustments increased even further in 1991 when China devalued its currency, thereby making China Asia's low-cost producer for many labor intensive manufactured goods. China's revaluation had the effect of undermining Southeast Asia's competitive advantage, as currencies there were rising or were stable in value against the U.S. currency.

9 Reciprocity and control

The organization of Chinese family-owned conglomerates

Applying the generally accepted
Aerodynamic principles it
Became clear to them that
Bees could not
Fly.
Wing-loading too high,
Power-loading too high:
No way.
And since bees could not fly
It followed obviously that they
Could not collect pollen and nectar and
Thus couldn't transmit
Pollen from this flower to that.
Therefore in a majority of instances
Flowers couldn't exist.
And just as obviously a bee that couldn't fly
Couldn't exist.[1]

To poke fun at themselves and at their own branch of science, aeronautical engineers once proved that bees could not fly. With considerably more seriousness, organization specialists, applying sound principles of management, have demonstrated that Chinese family-owned firms cannot grow large and cannot undertake sizeable and complex projects. This reasoned conclusion leads to a second one: because Chinese firms cannot succeed in enterprises requiring scope or scale, those economies in which large Chinese family firms are found in some numbers must, therefore, be examples of "ersatz capitalism" (Yoshihara 1988), speculative economies that are hollow at the core. This conclusion implies that an economy organized by Chinese firms cannot flower and bear the fruits of a capitalist way of life.

Both conclusions, however, ignore the simple reality that Chinese family-owned firms do grow very large, that they do undertake sizeable and serious projects, and that the economies in which they exist have flourished in the last quarter of the twentieth century and will continue to flourish in the twenty-first. Like the allusion in Peyton Houston's wonderful poem, the impossibility of the existence of large Chinese family firms belies their success throughout much of the capitalist world. Clearly, there is a gap between theory and fact.

The financial crisis that humbled Asian economies throughout 1997 and 1998 made this gap even more obvious. The economies seemingly the most deeply affected by the crisis in East and Southeast Asian turn out, however, not to be the Chinese-dominated economies at all, such as those in China, Hong Kong, Taiwan, or Singapore. Although these economies were certainly shaken, most of the firms and, more importantly, the basic economic institutions remained sound. Instead, the big-firm economies of South Korea and Japan, the very epitome of capitalism in Asia, suffered the most, to their very core, and sparing nothing – not even the banks, the biggest firms, or the integrity of the most prized economic institutions. The other set of hard-hit economies were those of Thailand, Indonesia, and Malaysia, all economies that experienced huge inflows of foreign direct investment which created speculative property and manufacturing bubbles and encouraged firms to incur high debt levels. If ethnic-Chinese-dominated economies were really "ersatz" economies, then this financial crisis should have revealed the fragility of large Chinese firms and/or Chinese-dominated economies. Instead, the very firms most susceptible to the currency fluctuations were those closest to the corporate ideal – the *chaebol* of South Korea and the bank-centered *keiretsu* of Japan, both consisting of large, state-of-the-art manufacturing and service-oriented firms.

The Asian crisis also reveals something else. It forces us to see that we cannot understand economies by looking solely at the nature of individual firms. We cannot understand the nature of individual firms unless we obtain a more encompassing view of how those firms fit into the organization of the national, regional, and global economies. The *chaebol* of South Korea suffered greatly in the ongoing currency and credit crisis, not because their firms are large, but rather because the *chaebol* networks of firms are so heavily in debt to local and international banks and, through cross-shareholding, to other firms in the same network. The state has not only condoned this debt structure, it has actively encouraged it through its sponsorship of loan initiatives that guided the *chaebol* into larger and ever more complex, capital-intensive manufacturing projects. Before the financial crisis, high levels of business group indebtedness and the state's control of the financial system were one of the means by which the state officials controlled the *chaebol*. With the crisis, however, this indebtedness, coupled with the bank's inability to extend credit any further because of a lack of liquidity, forced many *chaebol* firms into bankruptcy.

In contrast, large Chinese-owned firms largely escaped bankruptcy because their economic strategies were relatively uninfluenced by state directives and their levels of debt were lighter and spread over a variety of financial sources, including substantial networks of co-owners. There is a good chance that most of the largest Chinese-owned firms will emerge from the Asian crisis on a sounder footing than they had before it occurred, but the same cannot be said of many of the largest firms in Japan and South Korea.

In this chapter, I want to rethink the conventional interpretation of the Chinese family firm and offer a new way to theorize it. I will argue that, when many management theorists think of the family firm, they think of the nature of families in general, and of Western families in particular. What they do not see is that familism in the Chinese context represents a way of organizing – a model of group formation – that can be quite flexible and may be applied to many different kinds of economic organization in many different contexts. In this chapter, I shall discuss the analytical dimensions of the Chinese family firm that make it an important, effective and highly resilient way of organizing spatially dispersed economic activities.

The Chinese family firm as an object of comparative analysis

In the 1980s, journalists as well as academics raised the visibility of Chinese entrepreneurs by popularizing their achievements, calling them, among other things, the "Lords of the Rim" (Seagrave 1995; see also Abegglen 1994; East Asia Analytical Unit 1995; Fallows 1995; Fukuyama 1995; Pan 1990). Nearly every major news and business magazine (e.g., *Time*, *The Economist*, *Far Eastern Economic Review*), and many U.S. newspapers (e.g., *LA Times*, *San Jose Mercury*, *New York Times*) ran feature stories on Chinese entrepreneurs, valorizing the *guanxi* ties (personal connections) among them and the business networks founded on these ties. With the Asian business crisis in 1997, however, the tone of the articles about Chinese businesses changed almost overnight. The *guanxi* relationships that commentators had only a short time earlier praised so highly were now vilified. *Guanxi* suddenly became cronyism, and the economies where these relationships occurred were now used as examples of "crony capitalism". Amazingly, in the rush to criticise, all Asian firms were considered to be of the same hue. In regard to cronyism, Chinese networks from every location were tossed into the same conceptual morass as the Japanese and Korean networks.

The quickness to glorify (and the equal speed of the denouncement of) the interpersonal foundations of Chinese business suggests that most commentators have only a superficial understanding of Chinese business practices. One could criticise these analysts for failing to do their homework, but in truth there has been relatively little solid research on Chinese businesses. The relative absence of detailed empirical analyses of Chinese firms has encouraged analysts to adopt a general theoretical approach that often relies on making Eurocentric comparisons. As I alluded in the Introduction, there is a substantial literature arguing that Chinese family firms are unsuitable organizations for advanced capitalist economies (e.g. Yoshihara 1988;

Hwang 1984; Redding 1990; Fukuyama 1995). This literature rests on assumptions about the intrinsic nature of capitalist enterprises that have been drawn from writings about the golden age of corporate capitalism in the U.S. (e.g. Chandler 1977, 1990). Held up against these models of Western capitalism, Chinese firms are found wanting. Family ownership, patriarchal authority, problems with succession, lack of professional management, weak employee loyalty, relative lack of research and development – these and other imputed traits convince many observers (e.g. Redding 1990, 1991; Fukuyama 1995) that Chinese firms will remain small and temporary and will be incapable of generating a genuinely capitalist economy. Most specialists argue that, in the next generation, most Chinese businesses will either have to adopt Western corporate forms of organization and management (at which time, the theory goes, they will lose any distinctively Chinese quality) or be increasingly marginalized in a world of global corporations.

Although the conclusion reached from this comparison is widely held, the comparison itself is flawed at both ends. The Western side of the comparison is based on a now outdated conception of capitalist economies. The assumption is that what we call industrial capitalism is a relatively stable economic phenomenon, is global in its reach, and is compatible with only a few types of economic organization that are supposedly most efficient and capable of surviving in a competitive environment: namely, Western-style corporations. Recent scholarship regarding the modern world economy, however, questions these assumptions. This research (e.g. Hollingsworth and Boyer 1997; Orrù *et al.* 1997) demonstrates that there are organizational differences among even geographically adjacent economies, such as the British, German, and French forms of economic organization (at the level of both the firm and the economy as a whole), not to mention the differences between the more geographically dispersed Asian and Western forms of capitalism. This research (Saxenian 1994; Gereffi 1994a) also shows that organizational diversity exists in the same advanced capitalist locations – for example, in California's Silicon Valley, where large and small, local and foreign multinationals rub shoulders with recent startups. Finally, and most significantly, this research (Gereffi *et al.* 2005; Gereffi 1994a; Harrison 1994) shows that a worldwide transformation in the global economy is under way, a transformation that is pushing firms toward the development of inter-firm networks and away from establishing vertically integrated production systems. If the vertically integrated corporation was ever the organizational ideal that Chandler makes it out to be – and there are now plenty of studies questioning his conclusions (Fligstein 1990; Roy 1997) – then that time has surely passed and new forms of organization, including inter-firm networks, have emerged. To compare the way Chinese firms operate in the late 1990s to a now defunct model of capitalist organization is surely a fallacious approach.

The Chinese side of the comparison is also flawed. Here, analysts assume greater coherence and more uniform qualities to Chineseness, the Chinese family, and the Chinese family firm than are in fact the case. In an interesting essay, Susan Greenhalgh (1994) argues that much of the literature about the Chinese family firm builds on an Orientalist view of the Chinese family. Citing her indebtedness to Said (1978), she writes (1994: 749) that an Orientalist discourse is "a stereotype-filled discourse that constructs the Orient in terms of timeless essences and stresses the Orient's separation from and opposition to the West". An Orientalist view of the Chinese family essentializes the traditional, collectivist, and mutually beneficial nature of the Chinese family. Such a view, borne of what Greenhalgh (1994: 749) calls "armchair Sinology", obfuscates the fact that at the core of the Chinese family are considerable inequalities in power between the genders and between generations. Even though specialists often represent the Chinese family firm as the embodiment of an enduring, traditional, and harmonious culture, the Chinese family firm is in fact as Greenhalgh argues (1994: 750) a "political infrastructure" in which "power differentials . . . lie behind the disparities in economic roles and rewards in the family business". To the extent that Greenhalgh is correct, and I believe she is, then Chinese family firms are not remnants of the past, but rather are active social constructions in the present, constructions having economic as well as social purposes. Viewed this way, Chinese entrepreneurs knowingly draw on those institutional resources available to them, such as the organizing principles for the Chinese family, to create economically active groups that they can control on the basis of familial authority. In this sense, families and family firms are not concrete phenomena to be analysed as objects, but rather are processes to be understood dynamically.

Although Greenhalgh's essay helps to de-objectify the Chinese family and situate any consideration of Chinese families in specific times and places, it begs the question about interpreting the family as political infrastructure. There may be "no place beyond power" (Greenhalgh 1994: 768, cited in Kondo 1990: 305), but we should ask, "What is this system of power that creates and legitimizes such power differences between the genders and the generations?" This question is important because these inequalities, by Greenhalgh's own admission (1994: 769), constitute some of the most overlooked "features of contemporary life" in Chinese society, widespread in their occurrence and pervasive in their effects. These inequalities obviously do not result from the naked use of force, with elders and males exacting compliance in each and every instance of activity. Instead, this is a system of power in which such inequalities are normatively (but not necessarily personally) accepted as legitimate and are inter-subjectively understood, regardless of whether specific people consider the inequalities to be morally right or wrong. Moreover, as a mode of organizing the economy, this system of power is not restricted to family members alone, but cognitively situates, in an organized matrix of activity, those within and outside family-owned firms.

If indeed both sides of the comparison are flawed, then research on the Chinese family firm should not be based on a Western ideal of business organization, however implicitly such a comparison might be made. The negative question about how and why Chinese firms depart from a Western ideal simply will not lead to a genuine understanding of how Chinese-owned firms do, in fact, operated in the late-twentieth-century world economy or how they will come to operate in the twenty-first century.[2] Instead, we should try to understand Chinese firms in their own right, including diversity among them – and then (and only then) begin to make contrasts with non-Chinese firms. This procedure is the only way to specify whatever, if any, distinctive features Chinese firms may have *vis-à-vis* other possible categories of firm.

The inner and outer manifestations of Chinese patriarchal control

If we conceive of Chinese firms as being organized through a system of power based on family organizational principles, then we should recognize from the outset that they are not in some way mirror images of Western firms. Instead, they rest on socially accepted organizational principles that have no necessary correspondence to the organizational principles found in the Western societies (Hamilton 1994).

Fei Xiaotong (1992), one of the founders of a non-Eurocentric social science, described the principles of Chinese social organization earlier and more insightfully than anyone else has done. His theory is not deduced from a general theory of society, but rather is drawn from a deep and specific understanding of Chinese society gained from many years of fieldwork and study. In order to theorize his understanding of Chinese society, he contrasts Chinese and Western patterns of social organization heuristically. This technique allows him to accent certain features of Chinese social organization that would be obscured were there no comparisons at all, or were the comparisons mainly to establish a universally applicable, variable-based theory of social organization (Fei 1992: 7–8).

According to Fei, as well as to many subsequent researchers whose work supports Fei's theory (Chen 1994; King 1991), the organizational principles[3] of Chinese society are social and relational rather than personal and jurisdictional, as they are in the West. Recognizing that both Chinese and Western societies share all four characteristics, Fei argues that the basic building blocks of Chinese society consist of differentially categorized social relationships. Individuals in Chinese society evaluate who they are and how they maneuver in relation to others by cognitively juxtaposing their ongoing social interactions with a grid of predefined categories of social relationships that normatively define the identities and the social responsibilities of those with whom are interacting. Fei calls this consensually validated framework of action "*chaxugeju*", which I translate as "differential mode of association" (Fei 1992). The characteristic feature of the differential mode of association is that every dyadic relationship between ego and another person is constrained by a distinctive set of normative expectations. Those relationships closest to ego, such as one's relationship to a father or mother, are the most precisely defined, the most demanding, and the most hierarchical. Those relationships less immediate, but yet still familiar, such as with a classmate or a person from one's hometown, are framed by qualitatively different sets of expectations. Those relationships still more remote from ego, such as the impersonal relationships between a storeowner and a customer, are constrained by still different sets of expectations. Fei uses an analogy to characterize this pattern of social organization, that of ripples resulting from throwing a rock into a pond of water. In this analogy, ego stands at the point where the rock hits the water. The resulting rings of ripples closest to where the rock hits the water are the strongest, signifying the sets of relationships that require the most attention. As the rings move further out they grow weaker, signifying sets of relationship that are less demanding. And the point where the rings disappear altogether signifies the end of moral demands on the ego.

Kwang-kuo Hwang (1987), in theorizing the framework of action in Chinese society, has divided these sets of relationships into three categories. Those closest to ego are defined as "expressive ties", indicating those relationships that are emotionally as well as normatively binding. Those relationships furthest from ego are defined as "instrumental ties" and are governed by a utilitarian calculus. Between the two extremes, according to Hwang, is a large and extremely significant category of diverse relationships that he identifies as "mixed ties". Hwang, following colloquial Chinese, identifies an activated mixed-tie relationship by the term *guanxi*, literally meaning relationship or connection. Examples of such possible *guanxi* include relations between distant relatives, classmates, neighbors, colleagues, teachers and students, people coming from the same hometown, or any other particularistic trait of similarity. When activated, these relationships combine elements of both extremes, of a certain amount of expressiveness and a clear-eyed means–end orientation. If one or both of the parties to a mixed tie chooses not to engage in a relationship, the mixed tie is dormant, requiring few to nil demands on either person.

Should the two parties agree, a mixed-tie relationship can be activated so that the tie between the two individuals is mutually constrained by what Hwang calls "the rule of *renqing*" (1987: 953). *Renqing* literally means human emotion. As Hwang (1987: 953–4) describes it, however, *renqing* has three different meanings that make it, when applied to a mixed-tie relationship, into a very complex principle of interaction. First, it means an empathic understanding of the "emotional responses of an individual confronting the various situations of daily life". Second, it means a gift that one gives in recognition of the emotionally-defined situation of the other.[4] Hwang (1987: 954) writes that "in Chinese society, when one has either happy occasions or difficulties, all one's acquaintances are supposed to offer a gift or render some substantial assistance. In such cases, it is said that they send their renqing". Third, *renqing* identifies a "set of social norms by which one has to abide to in order to get along well with other people in Chinese society." These norms are the rules of reciprocity. "A good person", writes Yunxiang Yan (1996b: 123; also see 1996a) in her extensive study of *guanxi* and *renqing* in a Chinese village, "always interacts with others (with whom you have a mixed tie) in a reciprocal way. This reciprocity is characterized by the obligation of giving, receiving, and returning gifts in the long run." So significant are these norms of reciprocity and the social relationships they spawn that they form the organizational medium through which Chinese society is constituted (Fei 1992; King 1985, 1991; Kipnis 1997; Hamilton 1991b; Yan 1996a and 1996b; Chen 1994; Lui 1998). In the words of Douglas North (1990), this organizational medium provides the "rules to the game" for Chinese society.

For the purposes of this chapter, the important point is that family relationships (defined as those within a household or *jia*) are defined in terms of *xiao* (filial piety or obedience) and not *renqing*. Close relationships with people outside the family are defined through rules of *renqing* and not *xiao*. Both *xiao* and *renqing* define sets of obligations, and hence both represent forms of authority, but the two sets of obligations are quite different. Whereas relationships defined in terms of *xiao* are hierarchical, the relationships defined in terms of *renqing* are, in principle, horizontal in nature. Applying this very brief discussion of the sociology of Chinese society to our analysis of the Chinese family, we can now define analytically the principal axis of power and authority. The head of the Chinese household, normally the eldest male, has a position of patriarchal authority *vis-à-vis* others within the household, but his patriarchal power does not normatively extend beyond the members of the household. Instead, the patriarch's connection to others outside the household is defined in terms of the norms of reciprocation. With this distinction between the inner and outer aspects of patriarchal control in mind, we can now examine the intra- and inter-firm organization of Chinese family businesses.

The three-way distinction between ownership, management, and control

The organization of Chinese businesses is shaped by the three-way distinction between ownership, management, and control. In most small Chinese-run businesses, especially those with modest capital requirements, ownership, management, and control are usually concentrated within a single family, even though some informal division of labor would probably exist between husband, wife, and children. As Chinese-run firms grow larger and the business requirements become more complex, the three-way distinction between ownership, management, and control becomes more formalized and is institutionalized in work routines and organizational design. Although it does not always work this way in practice, in principle, as firms grow larger and more complex, ownership is shared, management is segmented, and control is centralized.

Ownership networks

During the course of the nineteenth century, the practice of forming limited companies based on British corporate law was adopted in and diffused throughout China.[5] Since that time, most Chinese entrepreneurs have raised the capital required to start their business by splitting the ownership of firms between family and non-family members. The founder of the business might claim a founder's share, often 51 percent, based on his willingness to use his own and his family's labor to run the business. The actual investment capital, however, might be raised from a network of people, including family members, more distant kinsmen, and usually friends (and friends of friends) who are linked to the founder through a series of connections. This practice allows the ownership of firms to be spread across the social landscape, to be an aspect of *renqing*, and to be based on the norms of reciprocity (Chen 1995). Accordingly, at some later time, when another person in the interconnected networks needs investment capital, the founder of the first business would feel obligated, according to the norms of reciprocity, to invest money in that firm. This is so much the case that some analysts have viewed Chinese business networks as being founded on mutual indebtedness (Wickberg 1965; Tien 1953; Geertz 1963; Mark 1972; Limlingan 1986: 86–93; DeGlopper 1995: 204–14; Numazaki 1991a, 1991b, 1997; Chen 1994: 75–106; Chen 1995). The pool of shared capital is circulated within the interconnected networks, raising the capacity of everyone in the networks to succeed. Because each person's success depends on the trustworthiness of everyone else, the network rests on mutual reputation in the past, mutual trust and mutual surveillance in the present, and the possibility of mutual sanctions in the future. Although such ownership networks are personal, they are also strictly instrumental.

Studies of Taiwanese businesses provide some good examples of the structure of shared ownership. In Chen Chieh-hsuan's extensive research (1994, 1995; also see Winn 1994) of small and medium-sized firms in Taiwan, he shows that most small businesses rely on capital raised from borrowing from one's network of family and friends. Sometimes local business people use rotating credit associations to raise money; and sometimes they ask for personal loans from distant family members and from their networks of friends and colleagues. Entrepreneurs will engage in this practice even if they have sufficient money to start a firm, simply in order to establish a network of alliances built on reciprocity, which is cemented through building credit relationships. The same basic ownership structure also exists for the largest Taiwan business groups (Hamilton 1997; Semkow 1994). Every firm in a population of the nearly 800 firms that make up Taiwan's 100 largest business groups is owned by a discrete set of owners.[6] Within individual business groups, there is considerable overlap among principal shareholders, but a remarkably little overlap among shareholders between business groups. This finding demonstrates, as Numazaki (1991a, 1991b) and others (Mark 1972; Greenhalgh 1988) also observed, the importance of personal networks in the growth of Taiwan's capitalist economy.

This manner of raising investment capital begs the question of whether the capital raised through family, friends, and colleagues represents "ownership" in the Western sense of the term. In the West, ownership connotes "property rights" which confer the right of control. In the case of Chinese firms, control is distinguished from ownership. In fact, most owners in a limited partnership usually regard themselves as "silent partners" who have a claim only on the money loaned (and on the relationship signified by the loan) and not on the actual control of the business.[7] The exceptions to this prove the rule. In recent times, this shareholder–entrepreneur relationship has been altered by the development of equity markets institutionalized on the basis of Western laws, which specify the rights of the shareholders to control management. In such cases, founding entrepreneurs are very aware of the necessity to maintain 50 percent ownership, and, though lacking the necessary capital, have developed a number of shareholding schemes to maintain control. The most common of such strategies is to pool borrowed capital in one or more privately held, limited-partnership firms that in turn own enough publicly offered shares that, when added to the founder's and the founder's family's shares, will give the entrepreneur undisputed control.

In this setting, therefore, ownership of shares does not confer property rights. What this system of shared ownership does confer, however, is a relational foundation for creating very complex networks that are themselves useful for other business purposes (Chen 1994, 1995; Limlingan 1986; Numazaki 1991a, 1991b; Shieh 1992; Jamann 1994; Yeung 1997). Often, the principal investors will also be associated with the founder through other types of business relationships – for example, through sub-contracting or distribution linkages. Equally important, a system of shared ownership based on reciprocity facilitates the flow of information about entrepreneurial opportunities, which helps to explain the speed at which Chinese production and distribution networks can shift the location of operations or product lines (Landa 1994; Hsing 1997; Pack 1992).

The separation between management and control

Making ownership a function of reciprocal networks separates ownership from the internal organization of family-owned enterprises. In family enterprises, where the boundaries between households and firms are ambiguous, hierarchical obedience based on the norms of filial piety (*xiao*) is the normative expectation. These expectations are most evident when the firms are small and use mostly the labor of household members. In such cases, enterprise management and control overlap with the principles of household management and control.

Within families, wives often manage the households and track the accounts. Similarly, Kao Cheng-shu and his colleagues (Kao 1999) show that in small and medium-sized firms in Taiwan, the wife of the owner typically manages the laborers or keeps the firm's books, often doing both. The husband controls the allocation of resources; he decides where and how to invest, and he maintains his *guanxi* connections with his network of friends and colleagues, which is often a time-consuming and very expensive activity.

Several studies on the corporate kinship units in South China show that a similar split between management and control occurs within lineage corporations too (Cohen 1976; Faure 1989b). The eldest male members of the lineage control lineage resources and make long-term allocation of resources. Day-to-day management of lineage lands and enterprises is in the hands of junior members of the lineage.

The same distinction between day-to-day management and long-term control over resources also applies to large firms (Lasserre 1988). In fact, the distinction goes to the core of how very large family enterprises are typically run. Management and control are institutionalized as two different sets of tasks. On the one hand, day-to-day management requires a close relationship between employers and employees that duplicates the pattern of authority within households. Typically, this situation is best achieved in small groups, where the persons in charge (*laoban*) or their representatives forms fictive kinship ties with non-family members for purposes of control. To create such ties, the husband or wife may utilize generation and gender inequality as a way to increase the obedience of employees. Entrepreneurs may hire non-household kinsmen and the sons and daughters of friends and neighbors to enhance their management of work. Employment in such small firms can be very oppressive and exploitative to everyone concerned, particularly the family members of the owner, as Greenhalgh (1994) rightly notes (see also Gates 1987; Shieh 1992).

As firms grow larger or more complex, however, patriarchy becomes particularly onerous to those who have no relationship to the owner. In Taiwan, for example, the high rate of employee turnover and the clear preference to own one's own firm is an indication of the tension between owners and non-family employees (Shieh 1992). This problem of how to create a management structure in larger firms is typically solved in either of two ways. First, heads of the family businesses may segment their holdings by creating a number of small and medium-sized firms instead of one large firm. The entrepreneurs then create a management hierarchy that best suits each of the firms they own. This duplication of management hierarchy (Hamilton 1997) means that entrepreneurs would have distinct administrative positions in each firm. Second, should the firms be large enough (or the tasks complex enough), the entrepreneurs would possibly also hire trained managers to be in charge of day-to-day management. The segmentation of family holdings into several independent firms, and the lack of any unified command structure, make it very difficult for professional managers to assume a higher level of control than that of the management of labor and the work process.

While management is segmented, control over family resources is centralized. Owners typically take control of their firms by centralizing personnel and accounting functions, especially the allocation of money (Lasserre 1988; Semkow 1994; Yeung 1997). One businessman, quoted by Tong Chee Kiong, nicely illustrates this form of centralization.

> My father made all the decisions when he was alive. He formed a board to help run the business; this board made the decisions. But this was only in name. In actuality my father made all the decisions himself still, especially in non-technical matters like investment, getting loans, negotiations with banks, finance companies, suppliers and so on. But he consulted the rest in very technical things. Anyway, he had the last say. After all, the business was his. Even when we, his children, had any suggestions, we had to go through our father's friends first because my father felt that as head of the family, he was to be obeyed at all times.
>
> (Tong 1991: 181)

The centralization of major decisions and the control of budgets allow owners to assume personal, and perhaps patriarchal, control over family assets. This form of centralization gives heads of family businesses the deal-making capabilities for which the Chinese are so well known. It also helps explain the flexibility and speed with which Chinese businesses can transfer assets and start new operations. Because the family head is also the person who has the responsibility for extending horizontal ties beyond the family, many of these transactions involve opportunities generated through networks of friends and friends of friends.

Although an owner may assume personal control, these assets are not his alone. They are the long-term possession of families and not of individuals, and, if the patriarchal principle of inheritance is followed, the assets will be split equally among the entrepreneur's sons after his death (*fenjia*) (Wong 1985). This principle of partible inheritance pushes heads of family businesses toward starting multiple firms, which can later be divided among the family, instead of expanding the size of existing firms. However, as I explain elsewhere (Hamilton 1997), partible inheritance is only one of many pressures in Chinese-dominated economies that favor segmentation rather than concentration of assets. Ironically, the business strategy of "not putting all your eggs in one basket" reinforces the importance of centralized decision-making, which in turn supports the personal and the patriarchal characteristics of Chinese business organization.

The tension between inner and outer aspects of family-owned businesses

As the preceding discussion makes clear, entrepreneurs face an ongoing tension between managing labor and resources inside the firm and obtaining the resources and opportunities necessary for the family assets to grow outside the firm. On the one hand, Chinese entrepreneurs use the principle of *xiao* (best conceptualized in this context as "obedience to patriarchy") to organize the inner (*nei*) realm of their business. Using the principles embodied in *xiao*, Chinese entrepreneurs want to manage and control their own businesses and the long-term fate of those businesses on an authoritative basis that is apart from the demands of both family members and business colleagues. If businesses grow large, entrepreneurs often elect to subdivide their firms, through creating internal divisions and hiring professional managers, or through starting independent firms that re-concentrate the entrepreneur's authority and create a new profit center.

On the other hand, using their family-centered resources, Chinese entrepreneurs attempt to organize the outer (*wai*) realm based on the norms of reciprocity (*renqing*) in order to create, and maintain themselves within, wider structures of opportunity. In Chinese-dominated economies, this outer realm of interpersonal and interfirm relationship is as important, if not more so, as an inner system of control, because it is in this outer realm that businesspeople establish the business networks that make Chinese enterprises so dynamic. The success of large Chinese family-owned enterprises comes from their ability to solve these basic problems of the internal and external organization of the firm: that is, to make this tension between inner and outer business activities into a source of entrepreneurship. In the concluding section of this chapter, I want to illustrate how this tension manifest in the Chinese entrepreneurship has become more global in recent decades.

Conclusion: the globalization of Chinese family enterprises

Bees do fly, and Chinese businesses do grow large and complex, and do function well in the modern world. The size and complexity of Chinese businesses, however, are deceptive phenomena, largely because Western concepts of vertical and horizontal integration do not apply very well to the expansion of Chinese business. Conglomeration is a more appropriate concept, but that, too, does not clarify Chinese business strategy. The important dimensions of Chinese businesses involve the personal nature of the relationships both inside and outside the firm. Networks inside the firm embody the hierarchical patriarchal principle requiring personal obedience to the *laoban*. Outside the firm, collegiality and reciprocity define networks. These linkages, too, are highly personal. Therefore, when Chinese entrepreneurs want to expand their assets locally, they do not necessarily expand the size or geographical boundaries of their existing firms, but rather they diversify by starting new firms and creating new alliances. The form of expansion is perhaps best called "opportunistic diversification" (Hamilton and Kao 1990; Hamilton 1997).

This same general strategy of investment is followed when Chinese expand their business interests across national boundaries. In recent decades, Chinese entrepreneurs, considered as a group, have been major foreign investors in many Asian economies. For example, the Chinese outside of China (including Hong Kong Chinese) invested considerably more than any other group in China (Naughton 1997). Before the 1997–8 business crisis, ethnic Chinese foreign direct investment (primarily from Taiwan and Hong Kong) equaled or exceeded Japanese investment in many Southeast Asian countries, and was considerably beyond the level of investment of the United States and the countries of Europe (Chung 1997).

The Chinese patterns of globalization, however, differ considerably from the patterns of Japanese and Western foreign direct investments. There are, of course, many variations within all these patterns, but there are also recurring themes. In this conclusion, I will list five of these recurring themes of Chinese global investments that have been observed in the last decade. The sociology of the Chinese firm, which I have outlined above, explains these recurring patterns better than alternative explanations.

First, the general pattern of foreign direct investment for Japanese and Western corporations is for the largest firms to globalize first. Smaller firms may expand later, if at all. The general pattern of foreign direct investment for Chinese firms is for the *small and medium-sized firms* to globalize first, to be followed later, if at all, by the largest business groups. This pattern of expansion for Chinese firms is particularly pronounced for Taiwan- and Hong Kong-based firms (Naughton 1997; Dobson and Chia 1997; Chen *et al.* 1995; Hsing 1998).[8] This pattern of globalization is largely explained by the fact that networks of small and medium-sized firms in Hong Kong and Taiwan can mobilize resources more quickly and respond faster to consumer demand than large firms. As a consequence, they gradually became the primary export manufacturers, and the large firms gradually became the suppliers of intermediate parts and services for the export production to the smaller firms (Hamilton 1997; Liu *et al.* 1993). When currency inflation after 1985 began to undermine the export competitiveness of Taiwan- and Hong Kong-based firms, the small firms quickly relocated to Southeast Asia, and in particular to the People's Republic of China, where they could employ less expensive labor (Hsing 1998). The success of the small and medium-sized firms and the rapidity of their response are largely explained by the sociology of Chinese family firms. The success of the small and medium-size firm sector arises from the Chinese capability to mobilize entrepreneurial resources through horizontal networks. The rapidity of response is largely explained by the entrepreneur's centralized deal-making ability, which is a characteristic of an economy organized through patriarchally controlled family firms.

Second, when Western and Japanese corporations expand overseas, they expand existing firms geographically and organizationally by creating branches, subdivisions, or joint ventures. When Chinese entrepreneurs globalize, they start *new and independent firms*. This pattern of expansion for Chinese firms seems to be true regardless of whether these independent firms extend or relocate an existing business originally started elsewhere or represent a completely new business venture. In the new location, the firms typically constitute new sets of owners and often establish new sets of business alliances that will be useful in the future. While certainly not universally true, this generalization seems to hold for all sizes of firms. For example, the global expansion of the Charoen Pokphand Group (CP Group) is typical of most Chinese large enterprise groups (Brown 1998; Hamilton and Waters 1997; Yeung 1999). Owned by ethnic Chinese, the CP Group is the largest multinational business group in Thailand and one of the largest single investors in China. Before the group consolidated somewhat during the Asian business crisis, it consisted of 250 companies worldwide, 130 of which were located in China (*Far Eastern Economic Review*, 23 January 1997, p. 38). The CP pattern of global expansion is to start new, independently owned companies for each business venture in each location. The network of owners differs for each company, even though there remains a similar core set of owners across all companies, centering on the personal holdings of CP's Chairman, Dhanin Chearavanont. A number of researchers (Chen *et al.* 1995; Dobson and Chia 1997; Hsing 1998; Liu *et al.* 1993) have observed similar patterns for smaller firms as well, but without noting its significance from a comparative point of view. This pattern arises as a consequence of the internal and external organization of Chinese firms. New companies represent distinctive sets of external (*wai*) alliances (and thus a distinctive network of owners) that the entrepreneurs put together from their social and economic community. Once established, however, companies also manifest the entrepreneurs' desire to establish their personal authority inside (*nei*) the company by creating clear relationships linking workers and managers to the entrepreneurs.

Third, most overseas investments take the form of personal rather than corporate investment. Therefore, very large family holdings are possible, even though the sizes of the constituent firms may be modest. The personal nature of deal-making and overseas investment has been noted by many observers of Chinese family enterprises (Lasserre 1988; Redding 1990; Numazaki 1997; East Asia Analytical Unit 1995; Sender 1991; Tong and Yong 1991; Kao 1993). As explained above, the personal quality of many investments reflects the combination of centralized patriarchal control (*nei*) and of the entrepreneurial importance of external *guanxi* networks (*wai*) for creating economic opportunity. This pattern of investment tends to de-emphasize the importance of firms, and stresses the significance of family assets. The goal of the entrepreneur is to increase family assets and make them continue and increase across generations. The continuity and importance of firms is secondary to the continuity of family assets.

Fourth, because most overseas ventures represent distinct alliances, with capital or with labor, in the long run most overseas ventures will probably become *grounded in the local economy*. Several analysts (Chen *et al.* 1995; Dobson and Chai 1997) have observed that, when Chinese entrepreneurs invest in enterprises outside their home society, the new firms tend to be "assimilated" quickly into the local economy. In the case of Taiwanese entrepreneurs investing in Southeast Asia and China, researchers have found that before moving the entrepreneurs were involved in Taiwan-based networks of production. Once these entrepreneurs invested in a factory overseas they could not fully duplicate the old network in the new location. Therefore, the owners tended to develop larger and more vertically integrated firms in the new location (Chen *et al.* 1995; Hsing 1997). Even so, the entrepreneurs have to draw heavily on local labor, local capital, and local connections to facilitate their control of the new economic environment, and this local embeddedness quickly leads to lessening ties back to Taiwan and deepening relationships in the new locale.

Fifth, most Chinese entrepreneurs with extensive overseas direct foreign investments develop *diversified investment strategies*, by investing in different kinds of projects in different locations. This strategy resembles the careful management of a portfolio of distinct investments rather than a strategy of creating a large corporate presence, which is characteristic of most Western and Japanese entrepreneurship. Many journalists and scholars have noted the global diversity achieved by all of the heads of the largest Chinese-owned conglomerates (Lasserre 1988; East Asian Analytic Unit 1995; Seagrave 1995; Sender 1991; Kao 1993; Yeung 1999). For instance, Y.K. Pao, Li Ka-Shing, Robert Kuok, Chin Sophonpanich, Dhanin Chearavanont, Wang Yung-chi, Tsai Wan-lin, and Liem Sioe Liong, to name just a few of the best-known Chinese entrepreneurs, all have global investments in many firms and are listed among the world's richest men. Their assets, however, are not concentrated in any one firm, but rather spread across many firms in different businesses in many different global locations. This same pattern is not the exception, but rather the rule for Chinese entrepreneurs who invest globally.

A sociology of Chinese business also helps to explain this pattern. In Chinese-dominated societies, the medium for organizing the economy is a family-centered system of social relationships. In such an economy, the measures of economic success are the size and composition of family assets and their ability to be passed across generations. Diversified assets are typically less risky than assets concentrated in one location. Long-term diversification is particularly advantageous, because partible inheritance practices undermine the short-term advantages of enlarging the firm to achieve economies of scope and scale. One key to successful diversification is to gain access to information, material, and fiscal resources through establishing and maintaining reciprocal relationships with a wide circle of friends and colleagues. These reciprocal relationships, in turn, facilitate the development of many different kinds of business opportunities.

In this chapter, I have argued that the modal form of organizing Chinese family enterprises combines centralized internal controls within firms based on patriarchy and external controls of the economic environment through establishing resource-rich networks based on reciprocity. This form of enterprise is not a type of organization, but rather a mode of organizing. It is a process as much as a configuration. As a mode of organizing, it is highly flexible, suitable for both large and small firms. This family mode of organizing business is temporally dynamic; it adapts to changing business conditions and to changing times. Economically and geographically, it is expansive, capable of generating complex networks. As a rule, these economic networks are more attuned to commercial and light industrial endeavors than to heavy industry. But this type of networking has also proven itself to be highly competitive in such globalized sectors as high technology, including the capital-intensive semiconductor industry (Zhou 1996; Saxenian 1998). It is clear, therefore, that Chinese family firms are not temporary phenomena that will fade away with modernization and with the spread of Western science and technology, but rather embody flexible techniques to establish what are, in the final analysis, essentially non-bureaucratic business organizations.

Notes

1 "Impossibility of the Bee", by Petyon Houston 1985; quoted by permission.
2 For a discussion of the appropriate uses of negative questions in comparative, historical sociology, see Hamilton 1985b.
3 I define "organizational principles" in a very simple way, as the institutional means or medium by which groups of people are put together.
4 "In Chinese society, when one has either happy occasions or difficulties, all one's acquaintances are supposed to offer a gift or render some substantial assistance. In such cases, it is said that they send their *renqing*" (Hwang 1987: 954).
5 This conclusion comes from the dissertation research of Wei-Keung Chung (2004). Also see Kirby 1995.
6 The ownership data examined in Hamilton (1997) was for 1983, but the same held true in Taiwan fifteen years later (China Credit Information Service 1998).
7 This is a very old practice (see Anonymous 1887) that continues today.
8 By contrast, in Southeast Asia, the largest Chinese-owned enterprise groups are the most likely to globalize, mainly because the largest groups form the linkage between local business and foreign ventures.

10 Competition and organization

A re-examination of Chinese business practices[1]

China's purchasing power is a topic that has captured the imagination of businesspeople around the world. An article in the *Financial Times* (7 November 1994: IV) illustrates the typical line of reasoning. Right now in China, says the article, the "ownership of ball-point pens averages only 0.5 per person. In the U.S. the figure is nine. If Chinese consumption were to reach U.S. levels, more the 10 billion additional pens would be sold." Similar thinking has led to calculations about the number of phones the Chinese will use in the year 2010, the number of televisions they will watch, the number of cars they will drive, the number of oranges they will eat. If only the Chinese would consume standard products at levels comparable to the consumption of those products elsewhere, so the reasoning goes, then the factories and farms producing those products, whether in the United States or Europe or Japan or Taiwan or Southeast Asia, could go on producing those products forever. China's 1.1 billion people, one fifth of the world's total population, represent to non-Chinese businesses everywhere an untapped body of consumers with unlimited demands for the products that they make and the services that they offer.

This image, captured in the minds of many businesspeople, makes some sense. In 1994, the International Monetary Fund changed the way it calculates the size and growth of national economies around the world. The IMF previously measured the size and growth of economies by converting their GDP to dollars at the prevailing market exchange rates. In 1993, however, the IMF decided to measure economies based on what they call "purchasing-power parities". This measure puts purchasing power, that is, price of purchasing goods and services in local currencies, at the center of the equation for calculating the relative size and growth rates of the world's economies. Using the new measures, the IMF now computes that China is the third-biggest economy in the world, behind only the United States and Japan. It is only a matter of time, a short time, they conclude, before China will be the largest economy in the world.

These recalculations surprised many people. Here is China, an economy with one of the world's lowest per capita incomes outside of the African continent, that is also, ironically, actually one of the world's largest economies. Of course, the point that no one missed in this irony is that the Chinese economy is growing at a breakneck speed, indeed is one of the fastest-growing economies in the world; and that the Chinese with the most money are consuming products voraciously. The rate of increase in per capita income has exceeded that of its Asian neighbors, with per capita income doubling twice in the 1990s alone. To the world's businesses, this increase in per capita income means additional purchasing power, and if businesses want to tap the rising China market, they had better be there now, on the ground floor, so that they can go up with the market, up with the rising demand.

The vision of the Chinese consumer, this dream of the untapped one billion, has produced the equivalent of a gold rush. Nearly every sizeable American and European business with products or services to sell is exploring the China market. An entire industry of consultants and writers now offers advice on how to enter the market. Americans and Europeans are not the only ones trying to discover a market there. Over the past five years there has been a huge increase in direct foreign investments in China by firms who want to get there first. Hong Kong and Taiwan investors lead the way. In Hong Kong, for example, investors who began with the idea that the Guangdong hinterland could provide cheap labor for Hong Kong's industrial economy now realize that, if they do not start selling products to China, everything from clothes to condominiums, then someone else will. Never slow to understand business, Taiwanese investors are also now in the hunt for the Chinese consumer, and so, too, are the Japanese and the Singaporeans.

The items that foreign investors are pushing include large infrastructure projects, such as entire phone systems and power plants, but also consumer products. According to the *Financial Times* (7 November 1994: IV), "Consumer products companies are . . . in the vanguard of foreign investors. Unilever, Proctor and Gamble, General Electric, and Electrolux have all recently announced ambitious plans to target the household products and appliance markets." Even larger consumer targets are underway. The Japanese are building department stores, WalMart, together with the Charoen Pokphand Group from Thailand, is opening superdiscount houses all across China, and various groups of investors are building shopping malls and row after row of houses.

Indeed, the gold rush is on, but the dream of finding riches in the China market is like a recurring nightmare. It has been repeated, again and again, at regular intervals, ever since China was opened to foreign trade in the 1840s. But history shows that it is a dream that rarely comes true. I will not predict here how the current rush to China will pan out, but I will report on some of the earlier attempts by foreigners to find the China market and give some explanations for their general lack of success.

Competing for the Chinese consumer

The history of foreign trade with China has been a history of trying to find what the Chinese will buy and will keep on buying over time. Let us start from the beginning. During the last dynasty, the household of the Qing emperors supervised foreign trade. Throughout much of the era, trade with foreigners was confined to the Canton area. For a portion of the year, foreign traders would live on Shamien Island, a site nestled in the Pearl River across from the heart of Canton city. There the traders, mostly British, along with a few other Europeans and Americans, bought from the emperor's official merchants the teas, the silks, and the porcelains for which Western consumers had developed an insatiable appetite.

The problem these Western traders initially faced was that they could not readily find any products that they could sell to the Chinese in sufficient quantity to offset the cost of these Chinese goods. The Chinese would buy a few clocks, which they called "sing-songs", and some other luxury goods, but the Westerners always had to make the bulk of their payment in silver bullion, which they had to ship all the way from Europe and the Americas. The Western traders felt that, if only the China market were opened to free trade, then there would be no problem finding products the Chinese would buy in great quantity.

This system of closed and controlled exchanges, the so-called factory system, was destroyed when the Western traders found a product that the Chinese would buy, and they forcibly opened China so that the Chinese could buy it. The product was, of course, opium. Western traders initially purchased the opium in India and then smuggled it into China. When the Chinese protested about all this smuggling, and began to forbid trade altogether, gunboat diplomacy ensued. The opium wars broke out, and soon China was forced under the so-called treaty port system to open many coastal and river ports to Western trade.

Under the new regime of free trade, Western opium traders flourished, but only for a relatively short time. By the 1870s, British opium traders had begun to complain bitterly about Chinese competition, and by 1879, in a number of treaty ports, Chinese opium traders had completely vanquished their Western counterparts (Hamilton 1977a). The demand for opium among Chinese consumers had not dipped, but in fact had risen greatly. In fact, the Westerners had been beaten at their own game, and a group of Westerners were so angered by the success of Chinese traders that they did what Westerners often do in these circumstances. Claiming unfair trade practices, they sued. The court case that resulted, featuring the British against the Swatow Opium Guild, was quite a famous one; the top Chinese official in Shanghai, the Taotai, himself presided over the case in the Mixed Court, and the proceedings were transcribed and published in the *North China Herald*. I will discuss the case in more detail later in the chapter, but suffice it to say at this point that the trial did not help the Westerners at all.

They never successfully traded opium again, never on the scale and never with the profits, that they had traded in that short interval after China opened up.

What happened to Western opium traders also happened to almost every other group of Western merchants. One of the most significant failures that the Westerners experienced was in the very symbol of England's industrial revolution: cotton cloth (Hamilton 1977b). British exports of cotton cloth to Latin America, Southeast Asia, and Japan had been and remained for a time quite substantial, but in China, after an initial jump, British cotton exports had leveled off and even started to decline. By the 1890s, the Manchester cotton manufacturers, who had dreamed in their day of the China market, became worried enough to commission a team of British investigators to go off to China to find out what happened to the trade in cotton textiles. This was the Blackburn Commission, which toured the interior of China for the better part of a year, from August 1896 to June 1897, to discover why the Chinese were not buying British cottons.

Their answer was a little surprising then, but would not surprise us now: along with government interference in free trade, the commission found that there was too much competition from Chinese handicraft producers – not the old traditional producers in central China, but rather the new handicraft producers who were popping up all over China. These new handicraft producers were buying imported Indian cotton yarn in great quantities, were making cloth from it, and selling it in the marketplace at prices cheaper than the British could produce their own cloth. The British manufacturers never determined how to compete with those handicraft producers, so British textiles took an upmarket position to these handicraft textiles, as a quasi-luxury, as it were, but this niche was also wiped out a little later with production from the Shanghai cotton mills that sprang up after World War One.

The first decades of the twentieth century were not good ones for Western traders in China either. Two historians, Kerrie MacPherson and Clifton Yearley (1987), made a fine analysis of Western traders in Shanghai during this era. They found that Western traders, merchants, and financiers, with a few notable exceptions such as the Hong Kong and Shanghai Bank, fared very badly. At every turn, their Chinese counterparts beat them out. This outcome was true for import/export trade, for industrial manufacturing, for banking, and even in department store retailing. MacPherson and Yearley reached the following conclusion:

> Whether the British are depicted as free traders or as free trade imperialists, in Shanghai they came face to face with a China that was not only different, but also not far "behind" them. They entertained contact with the highly organized world of Chinese trade – a dense, cellular world that was competitive in most realms of commerce and finance, if not in manufacturing. Accordingly, the British watched the nature of their

enterprise shift, and then, for the most part, atrophy or fail. They were not absorbed; rather, after the halcyon days of the *taipans*, . . . they were discouraged and generally beaten at their own game.

(Macpherson and Yearley 1987: 203)

MacPherson and Yearley's study shows in considerable detail that the Western traders could not survive on the level of profits, what they call "the 2½ percent margin", that the Chinese were able to survive on. Gradually, business-minded Westerners, frustrated at not finding the China market, returned home.

In this era, between the two world wars, no one tells the story of Western frustrations in China better than Carl Crow. The owner of an advertising agency in Shanghai, Crow wrote a book that every Western businessman and businesswoman trying to sell something in China should read. The book is entitled *Four Hundred Million Customers*. That was supposedly the population of China in the late 1920s. The book is full of stories, some very funny, of trying to find Western products that the Chinese would buy. Western manufacturers would come to China, positive that their products would sell, because they sold well elsewhere. But seldom would the Chinese buy them, and often for the strangest reasons. Occasionally, however, they would find a product that did sell, but, says Crow (1937: 271), "as soon as some foreign product which is easily manufactured builds up a good business in China, one or more Chinese manufacturers produce a product with packages and brand names which are similar." Crow illustrated this tendency with a story about selling haircream. His agency had found a "sticky pomade" that developed a good sale, but as soon as the product was established on the market, an imitation brand appeared, "and an average of one or more new imitations appeared every month. We finally", he said, "began collecting them, like new issues of postage stamps. At one time we had twenty-one varieties."

The Chinese not only eliminated their Western competitors all along the China coast, but also they did the same wherever the Chinese migrated in any sizeable numbers. This was especially true for Southeast Asia, where Western merchants and industrialists began in the nineteenth century with considerable technological advantages, as well as political ones due to colonialism, but gradually Chinese competition eased them out of the domestic economy in Southeast Asia. G. William Skinner's account (1957: 103–4) of the rice-cleaning mills in Thailand is characteristic of what happened all through Southeast Asia. In 1877, only about twenty years after Thailand was opened to "free trade", Westerners owned all the steam-driven rice-cleaning mills in Thailand. Westerners initially had an advantage in using this technology, but the Chinese, who had been driven out of the rice-cleaning business, began to buy the new technology, and by 1879, the Chinese owned as many steam mills as the Westerners. Then the numbers of Chinese mills "mushroomed – 17 in 1889, 23 in 1895, and over 50 in 1912.

Meanwhile several Western mills sold out to Chinese millers or burned down and were not replaced, and few new ones were built. By 1912, only three Western-owned mills were still in operation." In import/export trade, it had been no contest; the Chinese merchants firms had driven the Westerners out much earlier.

Conspiracy or combination

Many more examples could be given, but by now the main thesis is clear. In head-to-head competition, Chinese merchants and industrialists usually won against their Western counterparts. Why did they win? What advantage did they have?

First of all, Western failures were not due to low demand from Chinese consumers. With no demand, there would naturally be no sale. But the sources seem quite clear. "The Chinese everywhere emphatically has [a taste for luxury]", concluded the Blackburn Commission (Bourne 1898: 115). "He (sic) may be trusted to buy luxuries to the full extent of his means." "No one", said Carl Crow (1937: 15), "gets more enjoyment out of a bargain than the Chinese, or will search further or haggle more ardently to get one, but on the other hand, no one will more stubbornly and successfully resist attempts to sell him something that he does not want, no matter what the price may be." There is plenty of evidence to suggest that the Chinese were then and continue to be consummate consumers, and thus the failure of Westerners in China was not due to the lack of Chinese purchasing power or Chinese interest in buying, but rather was due to the success of Chinese business-people.

Therefore, the question to focus on is, why were the Chinese in these cases able to compete so successfully? In answer to such questions, writers usually round up the usual list of suspects. This list consists largely of what is known as "cultural traits". Chinese traders worked hard, for long hours, and they denied themselves what others regarded as the basic necessities of life, such as some leisure time or a decent place to live. They would also work for less and save more than their competitors, the 2½ percent margin that MacPherson and Yearley talked about, and they would educate their children to the full extent of their abilities, so that the next generation would do even better.

Although I can certainly agree that these traits are important, I also know that many very successful Chinese do not possess all of them. And many other people who are not Chinese do possess these traits or many of them, even though, as a group, these people are not as successful as the Chinese. I do not think, therefore, that these very general traits are the decisive factors for explaining these specific occurrences.

Neither did the British opium merchants who sued the Swatow Opium Guild in the Mixed Court case that I mentioned earlier. These British merchants had a theory about why they lost out, and, based on that theory, they took their Chinese competitors to court for settlement. The case is long and complicated, and I have written about it elsewhere (Hamilton 1977a), so I will just summarize it here.

The gist of the case is this. Western merchants charged the Swatow Opium Guild with conspiracy. "The Swatow men", claimed T. W. Duff, one of the plaintiffs, "hold the whole opium trade of Chinkiang in their own hands . . . ; in fact the treaty port of Chinkiang is entirely closed to us, and it is through the great influence of the Swatow Guild" (*North China Herald*, 9 September 1879: 255). The plaintiffs presented evidence that the Guild employed terrorist tactics against those who were not Swatow men, forcing even Westerners to fall in line with the designs of the Guild. "What injures one foreigner injures another", warned Duff, for what was afoot would drive all Westerners from the China trade. He went on (*North China Herald*, 23 September 1879: 255), "[There] is something working, a system, a kind of underground current, beneath each foreign hong that is astonishing. Not a single one of us can trade independently, and the treaty is no good at all as long as this underground system exists." The *North China Herald*, which not only recorded much of the trial verbatim but also devoted front page columns to comment on its significance, placed the case in a broader perspective. Here for the first time, said an editorial (*North China Herald*, 23 September 1879: 290), the trial was exposing the "inner workings of the Chinese guilds". Few Westerners "had any idea of the extent to which foreign commerce was being tampered with by combinations striking at the root of all wholesome trade" (*North China Herald*, 23 September 1879: 289). In the vocabulary of trade talks today, the British complained that there were "no level playing fields".

The Westerners alleged conspiracy, but the Chinese defendants, seven named men in all, speaking through their English lawyers, claimed that the Westerners were completely in error. They did not understand how the Chinese did business. Chinese merchants were not conspiring, they were combining – a crucial difference. The Chinese case rested on two points. First, they claimed that the mere existence of a group of merchants did not constitute a treaty violation, and hence could not be subject to a suit. After all, they said, various types of capitalist monopolies, craft unions, consumer associations, and even labor unions were "well established in England", and they should be allowed in China as well (*North China Herald*, 17 October 1879: 385). Certainly the treaty did not forbid such combinations.

The second point was the more important one. The lawyer for the defense declared:

> And now must be mentioned a most important fact, and one which to a great extent alters the whole complexion of the case . . . namely, that the so-called "Swatow Guild" is no Guild at all . . . It seemed to be assumed on all sides, apparently, at least so far as the plaintiffs' case had gone, that there was a Swatow Opium Guild in Shanghai; that it was a closed combination

of opium traders, formed for the purpose of grasping a monopoly of trade. That . . . was a totally erroneous and an unfounded assumption.

The crux of the defendants' case was that the Westerners totally misunderstood how the Chinese organized their commercial activities. There was no Swatow Opium Guild, but rather a *Chao-hui Hui-kuan*, a place in Shanghai and another unconnected place in Chinkiang where people who came from two districts in the hinterland of Swatow, Chao-yang, and Hui-lai, could freely associate with their fellow regionals. Their association was informal, and such business as was done in the *hui-kuan* was unorganized and was not a function of the *hui-kuan* itself.

The Chinese Taotai sided with the Chinese defendants, and the British stomped out the court room, vowing to appeal. Whether the Chinese opium traders constituted a combination or a conspiracy is, of course, a matter of interpretation, but both sides recognized that the crucial reason the British could not compete with the Chinese was that they could not penetrate the organization of the Chinese traders.

If we go back over other cases of Chinese success and Western failure, we would find that in each case the organizational dimension is, in fact, the crucial factor. Chinese businesses organize in a way that places outsiders with whom they compete at a disadvantage.

The organizational dimension

What is this organizational dimension? In the Swatow opium case, the organization was a *hui-kuan*, an association of people coming from the same place. As the defendants in the Swatow opium case claimed, *hui-kuan* are loose-knit organizations, places where people make friends and build fellow-regional ties with like-minded people from the same general location in China. In this regard, *hui-kuan* are like a lot of other associations in China: trade associations, surname associations, lineage associations, secret societies, temple associations, alumni associations, literary associations – the list goes on. All these associations are identity- and relationship-building groups. Their avowed purpose is, typically, to celebrate the kind of person represented by the group – for instance, the kind of person from a certain district or province or the graduate from a certain university, or the holder of a certain surname.

These associations differ from what we think of in the West as voluntary associations. Voluntary associations are clubs with members, with precise organizational boundaries, with some kind of governing body and specified purpose, and with written duties and responsibilities for the members. Chinese associations, however, are not so clear-cut as these, and are not so well defined and neatly bounded. Rather, these Chinese groups focus on the relationships that bind the members into a common identity and that form a moral community out of which a sense of duty and obligation arises.

What do these relationships have to do with business? We normally think of Chinese business as centered on small family firms, each firm representing a household enterprise. Numerous accounts of Chinese business practices focus on these household enterprises. Anthropological ethnographies of village life in China and Taiwan also encourage us to think of the commercial world as a world dominated by these family firms. Wong Siu-lun's theory (1985) of the four-generational cycle of the Chinese family firm also leads our thinking in this direction of focusing just on the family firm.

While the family is indeed important, it is, in reality, only one side of Chinese business. The other side is the network in which the Chinese firms exists. Both sides work in tandem, each being dependent on the other for economic success. The household enterprise is the node in the network. These networks can be production networks, distribution networks, or ownership and financial networks. The firms, or more likely their owners, are linked together so that in combination they achieve more than they could on an individual basis. Consider ownership, for example. From many sources, including my own research, we know that heads of households normally control the assets of family businesses, but the actual ownership of the businesses is very often shared among limited partners.

We should distinguish between these two types of ownership. On the one hand, the family that runs the business normally controls the majority share of the ownership, and has the final decision on how the business operates. This control of assets and planning is the prerogative of the head of house-hold in a family firm and is normally tightly held even if the firm grows quite large. On the other hand, in most cases that I know of or have read about, there is a category of owners, which I term *guanxi* owners, who contribute money and expect returns on that money, but who have little or no say in how the business is run. Every *family* firm that I have looked at in Taiwan and Hong Kong have these two types of ownership (while not all firms are necessarily family firms, most are.) In the U.S. the family owns the firm, along with the bank or, if large enough to be listed on the stock market, the shareholders. But in China, whether or not it is listed, firms usually have the two types of owners in addition to the contribution of banks and equity share holders.

Financial networks and commercial or production networks normally overlap. People who work in the same networks, such as toymaking or even distributing opium, will often share financial resources on a reciprocal basis. This reciprocation creates economically functioning networks that also operate on debt, both financial debt and, just as importantly, moral debt – a trust based on solid relationships, ties that one can count on. As one Chinese trader in Southeast Asia put in:

> . . . we Chinese are always financially tight. We depend a lot on giving credit. For example, rubber from Thailand may be sent here first and

then we pay later, or my buyer will give me money first to buy the rubber. Either way, with this sort of credit giving, you can basically take and run. So *xinyong* (trust) is important. With *xinyong*, I can do business up to a few hundred thousand dollars, even though I have, maybe, only ten thousand dollars.

(Yong 1992: 94)

These *guanxi* networks, therefore, add scope and depth to the family firm. By being part of such networks, family firms are tied to other family firms so that, in combination, they reach beyond the limitation imposed by their size, both geographically and economically. These networks rest on trust and reciprocation. They are not normally vertically arranged in terms of command, as are the Japanese *kereitsu* and the Korean *chaebol*. Instead they are horizontal, based on risk, information, and profit-sharing. One way to understand these networks is to consider the example of the *qianhui*, the money club, the rotating credit association. These groups form among people who trust each other; everyone pools the same amount of money, at the appointed intervals; one person gets full use of the money, and then the next person, and then the next after that, until everyone has had an opportunity. Westerners would rather put their money in the bank or in the stock market, and they might worry about someone taking off with the money, or gambling it away, for that does happen among the Chinese from time to time. But, besides being a way to get or to save some money, these rotating credit associations are also a place where one can "collateralize one's social relationships", turn them into money and opportunity (Biggart 2001).

Reciprocal social relationships, therefore, become a way to do business, a way to make deals. Clifford Geertz's account of Chinese peddlers in Indonesia is really a description of the way a lot of Chinese do business. The peddler, he said, typically wants

. . . to spread [himself] thin over a very wide range of deals rather than to plunge deeply in any one. Putting all one's eggs in a single basket is not a favored mode of procedure . . . As a result, large, or even moderately large, single deals with only two people involved are very rare, even in cases where the traders are large enough to handle such deals alone. Both large and small transactions usually involve a multiplicity of people, each making a small contribution and each taking out a small return. A trader contracting even a fairly petty agreement will look for others to go in with him; and, in fact, there is widely felt normative obligation on the part of traders to allow other people to cut into a good thing. . . . The individual trader, unless he is very small indeed, is the center of a series of rapidly forming and dissolving one-deal, compositely organized trading coalitions.

(Geertz 1963)

As Geertz describes, each investment is split into many parts and distributed to others in the network. The profits are also split, so that everyone gets just a little bit. This is the 2½ percent margin that MacPherson and Yearley talked about (1987). What is crucial is not the low rate of return, but rather the well-being and continuity of the network. When the network succeeds, everyone in the network succeeds, and the margins continue and may even go up for everyone. But when one person bolts, violating the trust of the others, then everyone stands to lose, because the network may actually fall apart. For this reason, relationship-building is a fundamental feature of Chinese business. Relationships bearing trust (*xinyong*) and human heartedness (*ganjing*) are what hold the networks together and give everyone the flexibility to make deals and to profit from them as partners in business.

If there were no competition in the marketplace and no deals to be made, then Chinese business people would have no incentive to combine. It is the competition, the hot competition, that pushes Chinese businesspeople towards strategies of shared risk. Without the risk, there is no need to share the profit. Competition, in other words, creates the conditions for cooperative organization. Among Chinese businesspeople, competition and *guanxi* organization go hand in hand, and I believe this is the reason that Westerners, with their corporate forms of organization that separate one firm from another, one entrepreneur from another, have historically been unable to compete head-to-head with the Chinese.

Conclusion

How will Western firms fare in the China market in the next two or three decades? Will they end the same way as they have done over the past two centuries, dashed on the rocks of Chinese sociability? Or has the world changed with greater industrialization and globalization? Many Westerners honestly believe that they have a real chance to sell to the one billion plus Chinese consumers, but I do not believe it will work out this way.

As I said, I cannot predict the future, but I can report on several trends that make some sense in light of what I have talked about so far. One of my colleagues, Gary Gereffi, a professor at Duke University, has done a great deal of research on what he calls commodity chains, the links or steps that go into the production and distribution of specific commodities. He has examined, in particular, footwear and textiles commodity chains, and he has shown over the last decade, that the structures of both commodity chains in Asia have changed substantially (Gereffi and Korzeniewicz 1990, 1994). In the 1970s, U.S.-based merchandisers subcontracted much of their manufacturing directly to manufacturers in one of the Asian NICs. By the 1980s, with rising labor costs in the original NICs, the U.S. merchandisers encouraged their Asian partners to shift their production to other locations in Asia to take advantage of cheaper labor. This relocation allowed the development of what Gereffi calls "triangle manufacturing systems" where the original Asian manufacturer now becomes the intermediary between Western merchandisers and the Asian manufacturers. This shift has encouraged a number of Asian apparel manufacturers to move up the commodity chain to establish their own retail houses, their own design shops, and their own brand names, like the Fang brothers' Episode, and Jimmy Lai's Giordano. Gradually, the Westerners are being eased out of the trade in Asian textiles.

Another example is the Charoen Pokphand Group, a Thailand-based, Chinese-owned conglomerate that started as an agri-business – breeding, feeding, and marketing chickens. Before the Asian financial crisis the firm was the largest foreign investor in China, with no less than 57 different joint ventures in China alone. Different firms in the group were listed on the stock markets in at least seven countries. Ownership of firms was parceled out, shared among key investors, even though the control of the group was centralized in the Bangkok headquarters of the CP Group. For the past fifteen years, the group has been slowly moving into the retail end of commodity chains and had recently signed agreements with Wal-Mart to open super-discount stores in Hong Kong and China. The CP Group was somewhat like Wal-Mart's compradore, a broker between the West and China that allows the Western firm to maintain a distance from the messiness and intricacies of dealing with the Chinese, a distance that may increase as time goes on, as competition increases, and as Chinese horizontal organizations coalesce.

These are just a few examples that could be given. They suggest that, for Westerners, but maybe also for the Japanese, and Southeast-Asian Chinese, the gold rush in China will be like a lot of gold rushes everywhere. A few will strike it rich, but most will just struggle on, dreaming the dream of the one billion plus Chinese consumers. "None of us", said Carl Crow (1937: 315) at the close of his book, "ever prosper to the extent we think our work justifies, but we have compensations. The work [of selling to the Chinese] is always interesting and, in spite of our years of disillusionment, all of us secretly cherish the thought that a reasonable number of the 400 million may buy our goods next year." We will see.

Notes

1   This chapter was first prepared and delivered as a lecture for the Royal Asiatic Society, Hong Kong Branch, December 16 1994. I wish to thank Elizabeth Sinn for the encouragement to prepare this chapter.

11 Ethnicity and capitalist development

The changing role of the Chinese in Thailand

(with Tony Waters)

Why are the Chinese so successful in business? This question has been asked again and again in reference to the Chinese in virtually every location outside of China where they have settled in any substantial numbers in the past 150 years. Many anthropological and historical accounts of the Chinese in this or that location suggest answers to the question, but the answers often end up being either too broad or too narrow. The broad answers are usually sociological, and the narrow answers are either historical or cultural. In this chapter, we steer a middle course between the two extremes. Rather than asking *why* the Chinese are economically successful, we will examine the organizational contexts of their success.

In order to frame our organizational approach, it is important to distinguish it from conventional sociological interpretations. Many sociologists argue that some ethnic minorities, the Chinese being one, naturally excel in commerce and trade. The reasons for minority success, they contend, are to be found in five advantages conferred by the conditions of ethnicity and minority status.

Three of these advantages come from the nature of minority status itself. The first is market objectivity. In his famous essay, "The Stranger", Georg Simmel (1950) maintained that minority status makes persons into ever-present strangers, people "who are here today and stay tomorrow" but who do not quite fit into an established social framework. Because they are socially marginal, minorities are able to maneuver in the marketplace with an objectivity unavailable to people who are more deeply entangled in the social order and have more invested in the status quo.

A second advantage comes from the experience of being sojourners, temporary migrants whose journeys may extend across generations (Siu 1952). Sojourners, defining their migration as temporary, choose not to, and perhaps cannot, socially integrate into a host society. Their mobility blocked, migrants look inward. As a group of long-term temporary settlers, they create sets of institutionalized motivations and practices that favor hard work, maximum savings, and reluctance to invest in social status activities in the host society (Waldinger, Aldrich and Ward 1990).

The third advantage is that ethnicity nurtures the ability of people in relatively small, well-bounded groups to create close-knit networks. Scholars (Granovetter 1985; Light 1972; Light and Bonacich 1988; Waldinger, Aldrich and Ward 1990) have examined such networks in some detail and find that they increase trust and predictability among economic actors, a condition that reduces economic risk and enhances economic success.

The two other sources of economic advantage arise, as an interaction effect, from the minority group's relation to the host society. This host–minority relationship sometimes creates an "opportunity structure" (Waldinger, Aldrich and Ward 1990: 21) that provides two sources of minority economic advantage. First, advantage ensues from the fact that the economic system in the host society has a differentiated occupational structure that allows members of minority groups to monopolize selected economic roles and niches that are important for the overall economy, but that are otherwise difficult to fill. In occupying such niches, minority entrepreneurs become dependent on an economic order in which minority status and host hostility combine to create a stable "middleman minority" (Bonacich 1973). The second and related source of advantage arises when a dominant political group actively bestows economic privileges on minority groups. In effect, political elites ethnicize key economic roles while simultaneously denying ethnic groups access to political power. In this context, such groups as the Jews in medieval Spain or the Chinese in colonial Southeast Asia become "pariah capitalists" (Hamilton 1978a).

These five interrelated explanations for minority economic success are so often mentioned in the sociological literature that they would appear to be propositions to all ethnic groups and not just a few. In fact, the sociological literature on minority capitalism concentrates more or less exclusively on only a handful of groups, with the Jews, the overseas Chinese, the overseas Indians, and more recently the Koreans in the United States being the most prominently mentioned groups. Other groups are cited only rarely, and then in special social and historical circumstances.

So commonly mentioned are these few groups that the question may not be simply why minorities succeed in business, but rather why some minorities succeed so widely and not others. This latter question has some importance in both Southeast Asia and Central Europe because only a few groups are really prominent in either location. Other groups in a particular locale or in a particular niche have, on occasion, achieved economic success, but overwhelmingly the Chinese and the Indians are *the* economic minorities of Southeast Asia and the Jews were *the* economic minority of East–Central Europe until World War Two. Why not other groups? Why primarily only these few? The sociological literature does not address these questions very well.

If the sociological interpretations are too broad and overgeneralized, then the historical and cultural explanations go to the opposite extreme. They focus on the extraordinary qualities of particular groups or particular people within a group. To explain Chinese success in Southeast Asia, for instance, some writers select cultural traits that the Chinese traditionally have, such as a high regard for education, hard work, and obedience (e.g. Kahn 1979; Tai 1989), a precocious ability to handle money (Freedman 1959), and a Confucian emphasis on self-discipline and family welfare (Berger and Hsiao 1988). Other writers prefer more specific explanations that border on mere historical particularism. Chinese success in a particular location is explained through a succession of events and the accomplishments of key entrepreneurs. The inference drawn from cultural and historical explanations is that Chinese success is to be explained in terms of either endogenous predetermined traits or idiosyncratic events and personalities. Such explanations single out the Chinese and, by implication, suggest that other groups simply do not possess the same cultural traits or produce such extraordinary individuals.

Without a doubt, the sociology, history, and cultural traditions of the overseas Chinese have significant bearing on their economic success, but explanations for their success going to either extreme do not tap the institutional and organizational variations that the Chinese have encountered historically and cross-culturally in the many societies to which they have migrated. Moreover, when such variations are examined closely, one must question and qualify the extensiveness and historical continuity of Chinese entrepreneurship. Most Chinese migrants were unsuccessful, and many died penniless in places distant from their homeland. More importantly, even the most successful Chinese did not succeed in just one way but rather in many ways, ways as numerous as the institutional and organizational contexts of the societies in which they lived and worked. It is this ability to be flexible, to adapt their businesses to strikingly different contexts, that the Chinese have demonstrated repeatedly.

In this chapter we examine the institutional and organizational variations that Chinese have encountered historically in a single society, and the adaptations they have made to these variable conditions. Specifically, we analyse three distinct institutional "situations" confronted by the Chinese in recent Thai history and to which they have responded by reconstructing the nature of Chinese ethnicity *vis-à-vis* the Thai majority. For each situation, we examine, first, the institutional context and, second, the entrepreneurial strategies used by those Chinese who successfully adapted to change. We illustrate these situations by looking closely at one leading, highly successful Chinese family in each period.

Configurations of Chinese capitalism in Thailand[1]

The Chinese have been the prominent economic minority in Thailand for hundreds of years. Many chroniclers of this fact have stressed the continuity of Chinese entrepreneurship, without also noting the changing nature of their entrepreneurial involvements. Although it is true that the Chinese have been successfully engaged in the Thai economy for a long while, that economy has changed drastically several times. In the twentieth century alone, the Thai economy went through two substantial organizational transformations, the first concomitant with a change in government in the 1930s, and the second with rapid globalization of the economy in the 1970s and 1980s. Throughout all periods, the Chinese have occupied crucial economic roles, but there has been little continuity in their involvement over time. Different sets of Chinese, operating in organizationally distinct ways, have dominated the economy in each period. Moreover, in each period, the Chinese in Thailand have reconstructed themselves as an ethnic group.

The first period dates from the eighteenth century and ended abruptly in 1932. It was the period of strong patrimonial rulership by the Thai kings, centralized control over portions of the economy, and an economically privileged and politically powerful Chinese minority. Its transformation began in the middle of the nineteenth century, when Thailand opened to Western traders and Western influence, and culminated in 1932 with the creation of a Western-style state.

The second period began with a coup d'état. In 1932, junior military officials and civil servants forced the Thai king to accept comprehensive reforms that created a constitutional state. The king became a figurehead in an authoritarian regime led by military and bureaucratic arms of the government. The factionalized government created an economy that looked like a patchwork quilt; every agency had its economic preserve and every top official his connections for gaining wealth. During this period, a combination of political harassment and Thai xenophobia created a cohesive, embattled, but yet economically significant Chinese minority.

The transformation to the third period began gradually in the late 1950s and early 1960s, when the pace of global economic development quickened and gradually transformed the Thai domestic economy into an export-oriented, trade-based economy closely linked with global capitalism. The new period, however, became fully engaged only in 1973, when the military elites relinquished their hold on the government and civilian-led governments took over. During this third period, which is still very much in the process of formation, the People's Republic of China returned to global prominence, some Japanese business groups moved significant portions of their manufacturing capabilities to Thailand and elsewhere in Southeast Asia, and Chinese overseas capitalism, centered in Hong Kong, Singapore, and Taiwan, became a major economic force throughout East and Southeast Asia.

The Chinese in Thailand linked themselves to these economic movements, and in the process they have significantly refocused themselves. No longer members of a harassed, inward-looking minority group, the Chinese in Thailand have embraced the outside world and reaffirmed their Chinese identity, as well as maintaining their Thai identity. Some Thai Chinese have become highly successful global economic actors and members of a world community of "Chinese overseas", loyal both to China as a civilization and to the political state in which they live.

Patrimonial rulership and dependent capitalism

Before the middle of the nineteenth century, the kings of Siam ruled the territory of what is now Thailand as a patrimonial regime. Like rulers of patrimonial regimes elsewhere (Weber 1978), the Thai kings had to establish an independent base for their own personal power in order to offset the authority of decentralized traditional elites. They centrally administered their regimes through agencies of the royal household that were staffed by dependent subjects, often Chinese. This independent power base provided leverage against the Thai hereditary aristocracy, which controlled much of rural society through a complex system of patron–client relationships (Hong 1984: 9–37; Akin 1969, 1975; Hewison 1989: pp. 33–50). The royal household did not tax the lands of the aristocracy directly, but rather maintained its hegemony *vis-à-vis* the aristocracy by creating reliable streams of revenue coming from royal monopolies, in-kind tax farming, and tributes of local produce, ranging from tropical lumbers, tin, rice, and spices to luxury goods such as birds' nests (for bird's-nest soup) and ivory. The royal household then exported these products in the monopolized tributary trade with China (Hong 1984: 38–74).

The Thai kings were able to maintain their hegemony only with the help of the Chinese, who ran the tributary trade and staffed key positions in the royal household. The use of aliens to enhance one's own political power is common in most patrimonial regimes (Weber 1978; Eisenstadt 1963; Coser 1972), but the rulers of Siam went considerably beyond this strategy. Chinese privileges began in the early eighteenth century when the rulers of Siam at the time cultivated a small Chinese minority in Bangkok to run the tributary trade with China (Skinner 1957; Sarasin 1977; Hong 1984). At this time, imperial China, the celestial empire, had high status in Southeast Asia, as did the Chinese traders who travelled to Siam. Living at court and largely serving the kings, a few Chinese became trusted allies in the kings' struggle for power with the aristocracy and with neighboring kingdoms.

The position of the Chinese, however, changed greatly in the last half of the eighteenth century, when Taksin, a descendant of a Chinese trader and a Thai mother, became king. Taksin came to the throne during a period of intense warfare in 1766–7, when the Burmese captured the imperial city of Ayutthaya. A trusted aide to the king at the time, Taksin fled the capital city, regrouped the Thai forces, and led them to victory. He recaptured Ayutthaya and defeated the Burmese decisively. Then he took the throne, and held it for fourteen years until 1782. During his reign, he transferred the capital city to the site of present-day Bangkok and encouraged migration from the Teochiu dialect area in Southeastern China, his father's native home. Taksin was later deposed, but his successor, whose reign title was Rama I and who started the present Chakkri dynasty, was also half Chinese, and was married to Taksin's daughter. He was "invested under an authentic Chinese name, Cheng Hua" (Skinner 1957: 24, 26).

The Bangkok period that began with the reign of Rama I marked the high point in the tributary trade with China (Sarasin 1977). A large portion of the royal revenues derived from the royal trading monopolies. Wanting to increase their wealth and political position, the Chakkri kings encouraged Chinese migration, so much so that Bangkok became a predominantly Chinese city (Skinner 1957: 80–90). Initially, the Chinese migrants were not embedded in local society. Being distant from the Thai aristocracy, the Chinese were more loyal to the king and the royal household than to anyone else. Moreover, as relationships with particular families deepened, the kings granted to those Chinese with whom they had the closest ties licenses for tax farming and for trading monopolies. Favored Chinese became court household officials with administrative duties. Chinese elites and members of the Thai royal household regularly intermarried.

The inward-directedness of this patrimonial kingdom ended with the Bowring Treaty in 1855. In the middle of the nineteenth century, the Thai rulers realized that Western powers were going to conquer and colonize every possible location in Southeast Asia in the name of free trade. Unlike other Southeast Asian states, Siam escaped colonialism and maintained its independence by allowing Westerners and Western modernizing practices into Thailand (Wyatt 1969). In the 1850s, tributary relations with China ended, as did the royal monopolies on overseas trade. Western merchants established trading houses in Bangkok and opened the Thai economy to international influences. With the increased economic opportunities offered by Western commerce, the Chinese began to migrate to Thailand in still greater numbers and to transfer their loyalties (Skinner 1957). A few prominent Chinese families continued their linkage with the royal household, serving primarily as tax farmers, but many Chinese merchants also developed connections with Western traders and increasingly became the compradores for Western trading houses. These compradores focused initially on the export of teak and rice, but soon began to organize extractive industries such as tin mining as well.

By the 1890s, income for the royal household, primarily from tax farming and overseas trading, had fallen. The fiscal basis of the state was in jeopardy and in need of reform (Hong 1984: 111–33). The king and his household officials began to search for new ways to create the wealth needed to preserve the political and economic privileges of the royal family. In the 1890s, the Chakkri kings began to modernize the state structure and, as earlier kings had done, relied on Chinese dependents to make the new strategy work. Using Chinese capital, expertise, and labor, the royal household began to create and establish monopoly ownership over a group of capitalist enterprises. Through these enterprises, the state began the construction of Thailand's infrastructure and systematically extracted its primary resources.

The core of these patrimonially rooted enterprises was the Privy Purse Bureau, which later became The Crown Property Bureau, the largest landowner and infrastructure conglomerate in Thailand today (Suehiro 1989).

In the late nineteenth century, under direct control of the king, the Privy Purse Bureau began to invest heavily in railways, tramways, shipping, mining, banking, and construction, starting one or more firms for each endeavor (Suehiro 1989: 93). In each such venture, the royal household pooled its investments with money raised from those Chinese who had been previously associated with the royal household, as well as from foreign sources. Among the most important enterprises to begin this way were the Siam Commercial Bank and Siam Cement, founded, respectively, in 1906 and 1913. By the time of the 1932 revolution, the royal household had effective control over, and partial ownership of, most of Thailand's significant infrastructure.

At the same time that the royal household was using Chinese capital and expertise to create modern enterprises, the structural situation of the Chinese in Thailand began to shift decisively. No longer a small, privileged minority, they were becoming far more numerous, and their influence was spreading. Not only were the Chinese no longer the kings' dependents, but by the early twentieth century they were becoming his competitors. They worked for Westerners, for the aristocracy, and especially for themselves.

This was the period when the Thai kings first began to Westernize their political practices and to justify their rule by using the political vocabulary of the Western nation-state. Siam, the kingdom, became Thailand, the nation-state, which encompassed all of the Thai people. In this redefinition of political legitimacy, the Chinese rather suddenly became ethnic strangers instead of privileged insiders. By 1914, King Rama VI saw Chinese economic power as being unearned and undeserved, and using a European analogy he accused the Chinese of being the "Jews of the East" (cited in Landon 1941: 34–43). This change in attitude among the Thais regarding the Chinese soon became widespread as a consequence of the 1932 coup.

Royal patronage and the Khaw family

Exercising their patrimonial position at the top of the aristocratic hierarchy, the Chakkri kings claimed large portions of the Thai economy that were not strictly controlled by local elites. Throughout the period, the kings and the officials in the royal household controlled access to the key routes by which wealth could be generated, especially tax-farming and licensed trading. The kings and the kings' officials, some of whom were Chinese themselves, favored appointing Chinese for these economically privileged roles. Accordingly, from the Chinese point of view, one of the primary routes to enrichment was to court the royal prerogative. The strategies to accomplish this goal were many, but generally included demonstrations of loyalty and economic prowess. To Illustrate these strategies, we will look at one of the best-known Chinese families in this period, the Khaw family, whose success illustrates concretely the structure of opportunities and the constraints that the Chinese faced in the nineteenth and early twentieth centuries.

The Khaw family, according to Jennifer Cushman (1986: 58; 1991), achieved a position of preeminence "equalled by few others in the kingdom" of Siam. The founder of the family, Khaw Soo Cheang (1799–1882), an immigrant from the Hokkien region of Southeastern China, arrived penniless in Penang in 1822. Shortly afterward, he moved to Ranong in southern Siam, where he found a job trading tin between the Muslim principalities of the Malay peninsula, in what were then vassal territories of the Siamese king in Bangkok. His early success earned him sufficient wealth to bid successfully in the royal household for the tin mining concession for Ranong. This role permitted him to organize tin mining in the region and to collect in-kind taxes from tin miners. He then sold the tin on the international market for cash and used the cash to make his tax payments to the royal household in Bangkok. In order to expand his own profits, as well as that of the king, he recruited a large number of immigrant Chinese laborers for tin mining. This effort was so successful that, in 1854, he was appointed Governor of Ranong, and, in 1862, he was awarded the title of *phraya*, the second-highest rank in royal service (Cushman 1986: 64).

Serving the king loyally and well, Khaw Soo Cheang was able to obtain similar privileges for his sons. One son, Khaw Sim Kong, succeeded him in 1877 and remained in charge of the administration of Ranong province until 1895. Other sons obtained Thai appointments in other provinces of the South, including Krabi, Trang, and Phuket (Suehiro 1989: 64–5). At the same time that he sought high positions for his sons, Khaw Soo Cheang was actively involved in establishing shipping and mining businesses based in Penang. Under the direction of his surviving sons, the family developed an extensive set of firms, known as the Khaw Group.

The control that the family had over both the politics and the economy in southern Siam was fairly typical of how the Siamese empire was administered during the nineteenth century (Cushman 1991). Such a system demanded a great deal of trust between the royal household, centered in Bangkok, and the administrators and tax farmers in the peripheral regions. Failure to remit tax payments could threaten the fiscal stability of the crown, and for this reason the alien Chinese proved somewhat more reliable than locally-based aristocrats, who had their own followers to support.

The Chinese position, however, had always been rather precarious, for they served at the whim of the kings. To consolidate their position in the new economic climate that was emerging in the second half of the nineteenth century, the Khaw family, like other Chinese families, began to establish alliances with aristocratic families located in their region in southern Thailand and began to engage in economic endeavors on both sides of the emerging Thai–Malay border. In Siam, the Khaws married into families of the minor Thai nobility, including the Nanakhon family which controlled the area immediately north of Ranong, as well into the Bunnag family, members of which controlled the Thai crown during the minority of King Rama V and the Ministry of the South during his majority. At the same time in Malaysia, where the Malay rajahs were in the process of severing tributary relationships with the Thai crown in exchange for British protection, the Khaw family began to arrange marriage alliances with the elite Chinese trading houses of Penang.

These connections, arranged through marriage, business, and political patronage, gave the Khaw family a great deal of leverage when European interests began to focus on the tin mines of the isthmus at the turn of the century. Western industrialists had developed dredging equipment that could be used to exploit the areas' alluvial tin deposits more completely than Chinese mining techniques had been able to accomplish. This equipment, however, required more capital and different expertise than the Khaw family possessed. Accordingly, during the period that British interests were opening the closed trading system throughout the Malay peninsula, the Khaw family began to enter into agreements with British and Australian adventurers who could provide the capital to purchase the dredging equipment and ships to transport the tin ore to smelters. They established the Tongkah Mining and Dredging Company and the Far Eastern Shipping Lines, both under the leadership of Khaw Sim Bee, youngest son of Khaw Soo Cheang (Cushman 1986, 1991).

In 1913, when he was the head of the family in its period of greatest influence and wealth, Khaw Sim Bee was assassinated. Thereafter, the family began to go into a decline. After a few years of having only modest success in Western-oriented commerce, the Khaw family began to sell off its key businesses and tried to revive its alliances with the Thai king. In an effort to maintain the family's economic interests, Khaw Sim Bee's nephew, Khaw Joo Tek, was able to re-establish a link to the royal household through building a special relationship with Prince Damrong, minister of the interior. For a short time this linkage stabilized the family's influence in Thailand's southern periphery, but when the military revolted in 1932, the patron–client relationships on which the family's influence was based disappeared. The family's distance from the center of influence in Bangkok, as well as its inability at a crucial moment to maintain its commercial position and wealth, originally obtained through political patronage, led to its decline. As a consequence, what was in the early days one of the most influential Sino–Thai families in terms of both economic power and political authority waned in the transition to a new era.

The strategy of obtaining an official position in the patrimonially organized economy was also used by many other Chinese families. It worked only so long as the kings and the royal household actually organized the economy. Once their prerogatives ended with governmental reforms in 1932, the strategy no longer worked. Although some Thai–Chinese families continued to serve the royal household, notably the Sarasin family (Suehiro

1989: 89–90), their roles shrank and their numbers dwindled. Only a few Chinese were able to continue as managers in the kings' Western-style companies and as political brokers. Moreover, such previously privileged families who were able to make successful transitions into more recent economic climates did so primarily as Thais rather than as Chinese, and as politicians rather than as entrepreneurs. These families were ethnically assimilated into Thai society and no longer played a role in the entrepreneurial elite that became the driving force in the industrialization of the Thai economy.

Military regimes, factional politics, and ethnic oppression

Southeast Asia in the late nineteenth century had come to serve as an important source of primary products for industrialized Western countries. Metal ores such as tin, tropical lumbers, tropical oils, tea, and rice were the area's key primary exports. But even though the trade-based economies in the late nineteenth and early twentieth centuries had been directed largely by Western colonial interests and core Western merchant houses, large portions of that economy had actually been controlled by the Chinese (Skinner 1957: 102–9).

In the middle of the nineteenth century, a mass migration of Chinese from south China, mostly from the area of Teochiu (Ch'ao Chou), arrived in Bangkok. Connected through various types of trading associations, fellow-regional clubs, secret societies, and surname associations, Chinese merchants and petty traders quickly became prominent players in the new trade-based domestic economy. This situation was similar to what was going on elsewhere in Southeast Asia, because, even though Thailand was not colonized, it underwent an economic transformation much like that which took place in the colonial parts of the region (Crissman 1967; Wickberg 1994).

Following lines of existing economic opportunity, these Chinese quickly established themselves in small, commercially-oriented businesses such as selling sundry goods, rice trading and milling, native banking, and simple manufacturing (alcoholic beverages, soft drinks, bottling plants, etc.). These small businesses were not dependent on royal concessions or other favors from the patrimonial state. This wave of migration created a substantial concentration of Chinese in Bangkok. In 1954, the Chinese constituted about half of the total population of the greater Bangkok area (Skinner 1957: 203–7). As William Skinner (1958) describes so nicely, the Chinese community focused inward upon itself, being controlled through dialect associations, secret societies, and such umbrella community associations as the Chinese Chamber of Commerce. It was from the ranks of this new kind of Chinese–Thai that the next, and quite different wave of successful Chinese entrepreneurs was to emerge.

Relations between the new Chinese migrants and the Thai community became strained in the first decades of the twentieth century as a result of these new developments, but it was not until 1932 that Thai xenophobia against the Chinese was fully awakened by a nationalist military regime that came to power at that time through a bloodless coup (Landon 1941).

This coup was led by a group of Thai military officers who toppled the patrimonial state and established a constitutional monarchy. The king was removed from the exercise of day-to-day power, though the royal household retained much of its wealth and prestige. The military installed a government led by a dominant political party, the People's party, that was administratively centered on key bureaucratic ministries. As in many intensely nationalistic developing countries in the 1930s, the model for the regime was authoritarian fascism. And as in many of the countries that turned authoritarian during this period, political rule was precarious. (Since 1932 there have been twenty-one attempted coups, of which ten have been successful (Fry 1992: 83–105).)

During the forty-year period from 1930s to the 1970s, and especially after World War Two when revolving coalitions of military officials and police gained control of the government, political elites attempted to create a national economy by employing import-substitution strategies (Hewison 1989: 76–91). They were following the accepted development theories of the day, but the enactment of these strategies resulted in competing cliques within the government and gradually turned whole sectors of the economy into political benefices (Riggs 1967: 242–310). Government ministries, each staffed with a segment of the elite, took pieces of the economy, allocating different sectors to different bureaucratic units, each of which developed its set of state-owned enterprises.

The Chinese minority, accordingly, developed a fundamentally different, far narrower and more strained relationship with the Thai elite after the 1932 revolution than had obtained before. Chinese intermarriages with the Thai elites became rare. Instead, as Skinner (1958) has shown, marriage alliances took place primarily within the Chinese community. This practice helped build a degree of ethnic solidarity that had been unknown in the earlier period and which is becoming rare once again today. Interethnic arm-twisting replaced the patrimonial embrace that had been experienced before the 1932 revolution. The Chinese became a national minority that had to be cut off from external alliances. Chinese resources could be squeezed in service of the state and those who represented the state – the military and civil service elites.

Coupled with the political shift and the change in relations between the Chinese and the Thai elites, there were also significant changes in the economy of Thailand, and in the rest of Southeast Asia (Baker 1981). The decline of international trade and the deliberate promotion of greater self-sufficiency created a propitious environment for local industrial growth.

The key Chinese entrepreneurs to arise in this period differed from those of the earlier era. Most of the economically privileged Chinese of the patrimonial state had been losing their patronage even before 1932, and few were able to make the transition into economic prominence in the second period. "Indeed," notes Suehiro Akira (1989: 110), "it is very rare when one finds the names of the descendants of the prominent tax farmer families in the major industries after the 1932 Revolution." Instead, most of the Chinese who became economically important during the nationalist period achieved success at first in small businesses. Their prominence within the Chinese community then made them brokers between the Chinese minority and the Thai elites (Skinner 1957, 1958, 1968). Such people became representatives of a new type of Sino–Thai relationship that arose as part of the government's attempt to isolate the "Chinese problem". It was this deliberate government policy and the new isolation of the Chinese that created what was essentially a new kind of pariah entrepreneurial class.

After 1950, the Thai elites began to nationalize the economy. Thai leaders continued to believe that local economies were in fact "national economies" and that, to be progressive, they needed to be more or less autonomous and self-sufficient. This belief coincided not only with the previously right-wing developmentalism of pre-war fascist regimes but with the emergent anti-colonialist leftist vision of how formerly colonial economies could best escape backwardness (Gereffi and Wyman 1990). They further believed that, in order to build such an economy, there needed to be state-sponsored and party-sponsored development. Accordingly, through government and party channels, the military elites proceeded to claim those infrastructure and resource-based areas of the economy not already claimed by the Crown Property Bureau, and to set up import-substitution industries (Riggs 1967; Suehiro 1989: 122–34). The Ministry of Communications developed the airlines, the Ministry of the Industry built petroleum refineries and electricity generators, the Ministry of Finance controlled the tobacco monopoly, and the Ministry of Defense and the Ministry of Finance opened banks. So critical were the areas developed by the government during this era that, in 1986, eleven of the nineteen largest companies in Thailand were still owned by government ministries.

What role did the Chinese entrepreneurs have in this new economy? The military governments after World War Two were short of capital, so to establish their enterprises they turned toward the previously stigmatized Chinese, who could provide it. Leading Chinese businessmen were able to mobilize resources within the Chinese community by using their connections, and they began to forge a whole new set of alliances with the military elite. This action not only generated finance for nationalistic projects but also allowed them to make more money for themselves, as well to enrich select Thai officials.

Pariah entrepreneurship and the Sophonpanich family

After the 1932 coup, Thailand's military governments created a highly factionalized government that helped generate but then preyed on Chinese wealth. The competing elite factions had political positions but only limited access to wealth, and the Chinese had some wealth but only limited access to political protection. These complementary interests created a structural situation in which ethnic oppression and economic privilege worked hand in hand to achieve a more or less stable symbiosis between Thai elites and Chinese businessmen. Those Chinese who wished to enrich themselves during this period had to develop interethnic alliances with a winning faction and to lay themselves open to systematic extractions. In exchange, they gained economic privileges. Perhaps the best illustration of this kind of pariah entrepreneurship is the Sophonpanich family.

The family's wealth was first established by Chin Sophonpanich (1910–88). He was born to a Teochiu father, a commercial clerk, and his Thai wife, in Thonburi, near Bangkok. Though he received his primary education in Swatow in China, Chin Sophonpanich returned to Bangkok at seventeen. He worked as a clerk, a laborer, and a noodle seller, before establishing his own business selling construction materials. Later, he opened a hardware and canned goods store and began trading with Hong Kong and Singapore.

In 1944, using resources from a number of his own businesses and in cooperation with other close business associates, Chin helped found and became a director of the Bangkok Bank (Hewison 1989: 192–205). Immediately after World War Two, he established several independent firms in gold trading, currency exchange, and insurance. Together these firms became the base for Chin's Asia Trust group, the assets of which he used to increase his holdings in Bangkok Bank. He became president of the bank in 1952.

Also in 1952, the military government of Thailand issued a directive through the police director-general that required the Chinese to establish three centralized associations, one for organizing gold trading, one for jewelry trading, and one for banking. This was done the better to tap Chinese wealth. Chin became the head of the association of commercial bankers. Using connections with some high military figures that he developed through this position, he obtained substantial financial backing for the Bangkok Bank from the Ministry of Economic Affairs. In exchange for its support, several generals were appointed to key positions on the bank's board of directors. The Ministry of Economic Affairs initially owned 60 percent of the total shares of the Bangkok Bank.

Chin was then able to play a central role in Bangkok's Chinese community in the early 1950s. Skinner (1958) ranked him as the sixth-most influential figure in that community in 1952. In large part, this influence was owing to his role as banker and agent for Police General Phao, for whom he often spoke in Chinese councils (Skinner 1958: 99). Like other Thai Chinese of his era, Chin took a Thai name, Sophonpanich, and adopted Thai citizenship. At the same time, he maintained his identity as an overseas Chinese. Indeed, so close was his attachment to his native region that he built a school named after his father in his home village in China. On one occasion,

he even disavowed his Thai citizenship during a trip to China in order to
avoid the Thai military draft. He also went to the trouble of reinstating it,
however (Skinner 1958: 99–100). He was a fervent anti-communist and a
strong supporter of the Kuomintang regime in Taiwan.

The years between 1957 and 1973 was a crucial one for all Thai banks. In
1957, the military faction that served as Chin's political patron was ousted
from power by another military group. As a consequence, he had to flee
Thailand. He lived in exile in Hong Kong for five years. Leaving his son
Chatri in charge of his Thailand-based business, Chin made aggressive
investments in the Hong Kong financial markets and established an overseas
arm of the Bangkok Bank. He returned to Thailand in 1963 and soon began
consolidating his control of the bank.

By 1963, the Thai economy had begun to expand, and the government
had relaxed the anti-Chinese laws and changed its naturalization laws to
allow Chinese to obtain Thai citizenship more easily. Less subject to threats
of arrest and deportation in the new political climate, Chin gradually began
to increase his ownership share of the Bangkok Bank. By 1968, the
Sophonpanich family's shares exceed those of the government for the first
time. The family holdings were further augmented when Chin was able to
take control of the shares of the military leaders who were forced into exile
in the coup of 1973. Suehiro's analysis (1989: 247) shows that the family
controlled 32 percent of the Bank in 1982, while the government held only
8.1 percent. The government, however, maintained some control of the bank
through a succession of powerful political officials it placed on the board of
directors.

In the 1970s and 1980s, the Bangkok Bank group was able to benefit from
Thailand's transition to an open global economy, and it became one of
Thailand's biggest financial institutions. Although the group now engages in
diverse businesses and has continued to expand in recent years to become
more international in scope, like other groups formed in the 1930s and 1940s
it still bears the imprint of its origins. Its major branches, managed by Chin's
sons, remain centered in the financial sector and embedded in the local Thai
economy.

Internationalization of capitalism in Thailand, and the overseas Chinese connection

From the 1932 coup to the Vietnam War era, the Thai economy was largely a
domestic one, with the international component confined mainly to rice and
lumber exports. At first, the economy expanded slowly, but in the late 1950s
there began a sustained increase in gross national product (Falkus 1991).
During this period the financial sector and large enterprises within the
country were largely state owned or state sponsored. On the one side, there
were the quasi-private, quasi-state-owned Crown Properties Bureau, and on
the other, the various government agencies. Both the royal household and the

government elites, however, continued to use Chinese capital and expertise to achieve their own interests.

In the late 1960s, the industrial structure of Thailand began to change decisively. A new round of military coups beginning in 1957 kept the elites circulating at the top, making patronage a sometimes risky blessing. Now with sizeable capital resources behind them, Chinese entrepreneurs became less willing to court political favors. Moreover, a coup in 1972 resulted in the seizure of the financial assets of many major military figures, which in turn began the process of disentangling capital formation from political privilege.

These uncertainties in the political climate were matched by changes in East Asian economies. Rather quickly in the late 1960s and 1970s, first Japan and then the Asian newly industrializing countries – South Korea, Taiwan, Hong Kong, and Singapore – became aggressively export-oriented and created an economic change that would soon engulf the entire region. In 1960, only 1.2 percent of Thailand's exports were manufactured goods, but by the early 1970s, investments from Japanese as well as Western multinational corporations began to alter the structure of economic opportunities in the Thai economy (Somsak and Chirathivat 1990; Narongchai *et al.* 1993). By 1980, with 32.3 percent of its total exports consisting of manufactured goods, Thailand had become a cheap labor platform for firms operating out of Japan, Hong Kong, and Singapore. This trend accelerated in the 1980s, so that by 1988 67.5 percent of Thailand's total exports were manufactured goods. By the 1990s, Thailand's economy had been totally restructured, moving from a politically-bounded domestic economy to an open, export-oriented segment of the global economy.

The internationalization and industrialization of the Thai economy quickly changed the ownership networks linking firms. The largest change was the emergence of export-oriented sectors, particularly in large-scale manufacturing and agriculture. Firms in the manufacturing sector, including companies in automobile assembly (Siam Motors), textiles (Saha Union), and consumer goods (Sahapathanapibul), often grew from joint ventures with producers in Japan or the United States, or out of contract buying by Western merchandisers. Many of these firms were part of large industrial conglomerates active in a number of areas. Capitalization of these enterprises typically required large amounts of money, as well as technical know-how, and big banks established in the previous economic period, such as Bangkok Bank and Thai Farmers Bank, quickly became leading lenders to the new industrialists. These banks also added industrial firms to their own holdings, but by and large they did not provide the entrepreneurial leadership for the internationalization of the Thai economy. This leadership, instead, was supplied by yet another new group of Chinese entrepreneurs.

Suehiro Akira's excellent study of the enterprise structure of the modern Thai economy provides the context in which to understand the new group of Chinese entrepreneurs. He shows that, by the middle of the 1980s, virtually all of the largest firms in the most advanced sectors of the economy were "members of 'groups of companies' rather than large independent firms" (Suehiro 1989: 218–19). These business groups, which dominated all sectors of the economy, were, according to Suehiro, predominantly owned and controlled by the Chinese minority. In his examination of "over seventy leading 'Thai' business groups in the early 1980s", he found that "non-ethnic Chinese groups numbered only three". One of the three was the group of firms owned by the Crown Property Bureau, another was the group owned by the Military Bank, and the third, the Siam Vidhaya group, was owned by a Thai–Indian family. All the other business groups "belonged to naturalized or local-born Chinese, all of whom held Thai citizenship" (Suehiro 1989: 9). Chinese-owned big businesses were divided into two main types – finance and banking, and the new industrial groups. The bank-centered groups had all originated in the second period, in the 1940s and 1950s, but the industrial groups largely dated from the late 1960s and early 1970s.

The newest Chinese business groups to emerge in Thailand, those of the industrialists, are groups that have taken advantage of Thailand's increasingly large pool of cheap, skilled labor to establish a wide range of export-related industries. As relative newcomers, the industrialists are not part of the traditional leadership of the old Thai–Chinese community. They have maintained closer contacts with the Chinese communities of Hong Kong, Singapore, the People's Republic of China, and Taiwan than have the previous generations of Thai–Chinese. If they had any ties at all with the Thai governmental elite and the royalty, the connections tended, initially at least, to be weak. For those able to transform what were originally successful small businesses into large ones, the initial capital appears to have come from joint ventures and bank loans, but their rapid expansion was funded through their development of a web of alliances among internationally oriented capitalists, usually from overseas Chinese communities. Among the most successful examples are the Charoen Pokphand group and the Sahapathanapibul group. Other examples include the automobile manufacturing enterprises of the Pornprapha family (Siam Motors) and the textile conglomerate Saha Union, as well as Japanese- and Singaporean-financed steel processing concerns. These operations are still dominated by their original rags-to-riches founders.

The new Chinese industrialists became a leading segment of a thoroughly reconstructed Chinese minority in Thailand. As late as the 1960s, Fred Riggs (1967) could refer to the Chinese as being "pariah entrepreneurs", but by the 1990s it was clear to Kevin Hewison (1993: 177) that this concept "increasingly appears as an unrealistic description of actuality". As Kasian Tejapira (1997) points out, the status of the Chinese has risen greatly in Thailand in recent years. Chinese–Thais are no longer a stigmatized minority group. By the 1990s they had reclaimed their ethnicity and were reconstructing it to fit it to regional and global, instead of merely local, definitions (Ong and Nonini 1997). By the 1990s, the Chinese in Thailand had joined the middle class, had grown powerful again in politics (Hewison 1993), and had become one of several new forces, including the Thai Buddhist establishment (Keyes 1993), participating in the bourgeoisification of Thai society.

Global capitalism and the Charoen Pokphand family

In 1994, one of the largest foreign investors in the People's Republic of China was the Charoen Pokphand (CP) Group, Thailand's largest transnational business group.[2] Although the younger of the two founding brothers (Chia Ek Chor, the elder, and Chia Seow Nooy) first migrated from Shantou (Swatow) in Guangdong province to Bangkok in 1917, the core firms of the Group did not begin to grow rapidly until the early 1970s.[3] During the intervening years, the brothers ran a struggling seed business that in the 1950s began to specialize in supplying animal feed, especially for chickens. In the 1960s, the two developed a formula for combining chicken breeding with feed milling. To put their method into operation, they reached an agreement with Arbor Acres, a firm in the Rockefeller group. This formula proved so successful that by 1969 the company had an annual turnover of about $1.5 million U.S.

In about 1970, the entire business began to change rapidly as the big banks finally grasped the potential for capitalist agriculture and food processing (Sompop and Suwanjindar 1992). One of the turning points came when an American, fleeing from the Vietnam war, started a chicken farm but left Thailand owing the Bangkok Bank a large amount of money. The bank asked the Charoen Pokphand feed mill to take over the farm. The formula evolved whereby the CP Group would loan Thai farmers money, teach them how to raise chickens, and even help them erect buildings. They supplied chicks and feed to the farmers, who in turn sold the grown chickens back to the feed mill for marketing. The entire operation depended on the marketing end to sell the processed chickens to high-volume buyers – grocery stores, restaurants, and fast-food franchises. In the early days, the CP Group allocated each farmer 10,000 chickens, but in recent years the figure has been raised to 50,000.

The company grew quickly during the 1970s because the Central Bank of Thailand had a policy that a certain percentage of its loan portfolio had to go to the agricultural sector. The CP Group was one of the safest players. Government banks would channel money into the agricultural sector by loaning money to farmers, who agreed to engage in contract farming with the CP Group (Sompop and Suwanjindar 1992). CP would co-sign the loan. What was safe for the banks and good for Thai farmers proved to be greatly advantageous for CP as well.

The CP Group then began to grow rapidly by expanding the same business to other countries – first to Indonesia, then to Taiwan, the PRC, Turkey, Portugal, and the Philippines. In each case, the same scenario was repeated: integrated feed mills, chicken breeding, contract farming, and then processing and marketing the poultry. The marketing end of the commodity chain drove the production end.

By the 1980s, because of its spectacular growth, CP began to receive a lot of attention, and many firms wanted to enter into joint ventures with it. The Group then began to diversify from its original agricultural base. In 1982–3, in central Thailand, it began raising shrimp, using the same formula that had worked with chickens. In 1987, drawing on the founders' close connections in the PRC, the CP Group started manufacturing businesses in Shanghai, making motorcycles with a license from Honda and brewing beer with a license from Heineken. Also in 1987, CP received the 7–11 and Kentucky Fried Chicken franchises for Thailand and started the Makro retail stores (originally, Price Club). In 1989, it entered the petrochemical business in a joint venture with Solvay, the giant Belgian firm. And in August 1992, CP signed a contract to build one of the world's largest privately owned public works projects – at the time second only to the tunnel being built under the English Channel – the telecommunication infrastructure for Thailand, a project worth $3 billion U.S. And in 1994, it signed a joint-venture agreement with Wal-Mart to establish super-retail stores throughout East and Southeast Asia.[4]

Despite great diversity of businesses, all of the firms in the CP Group are run similarly. Each relies on networks among independent producers, independent investors, or both. Most of the manufacturing firms are based on joint ventures and subcontracting. Throughout most of the 1980s the CP Group was decentralized by country, but in the late 1980s the family members in charge reorganized the Group into nine functional units, all run from headquarters in Bangkok. The nine are the Seed, Agro Chemical, and Fertilizer Unit (which was started in 1921), the Agro Business (integrated feed and animal production begun in 1951), the International Trading Unit (1980), the Aqua Business (shrimp farming, 1982–3), the Retail and Wholesale Businesses (1987), the Automotive Division (motorcycles, 1987), the Real Estate Unit (1989), Petrochemicals (1989), and finally, Telecommunications (1992).

The Group now relies heavily on professional managers. Family members maintain ardently that the Group is not run as a family business, although most of the founders' thirteen sons and many other close relatives are or have been among its leading employees. The sons all have seats on the board of directors, and Dhanin and Sument Chiaravanont (sons of the elder brother, Ek Chor) make most of the major decisions. The other sons all own shares in the Group, none of which is traded. Family business or not, the CP Group is a creation of deal-making, the quintessential characteristic of the overseas Chinese entrepreneur, of which Dhanin Chiaravanont is one of the best-known examples.

Conclusions

The Chinese in Thailand have been economically successful for hundreds of years, through many political and economic transformations. Their success, however, cannot be explained strictly in terms of either local conditions or local historical situations. Nor can it be explained through a sociology of minority capitalism. Explanations of this kind must match the generality of the phenomena they attempt to explain (Sewell 1967). The Chinese are economically successful throughout Southeast Asia, as well as in other locations around the world. Local histories, even a succession of local histories, cannot explain what is, after all, a general occurrence.

Moreover, Chinese business practices in situations where the Chinese are in the minority are remarkably similar to those in situations in which Chinese are in the majority. A sociology of minority capitalism cannot explain Chinese economic success when their entrepreneurial strategies in locations such as Hong Kong (Wong 1985, 1988a, 1988b) and Taiwan (Greenhalgh 1988) are similar, if not identical, to those they use in Southeast Asia (Redding 1990; Kuo 1991; Tong 1991) and other locations where they are in the minority. And if the accounts given of the entrepreneurial efforts of the Chinese in the Peoples Republic of China are correct (Vogel 1989; Nee 1992; Nee and Young 1991; Lin 1995; Wank 1999), it appears that the organizational strategies of Chinese entrepreneurs in China are the same as those elsewhere.

Therefore, the explanations for Chinese success in Thailand cannot simply be adduced from the details of Thai history, from the biographies of successful Chinese in Thailand, or from a sociology of Chinese minority status. Instead the explanation requires a careful investigation of the phenomenon generally, and thus even a reasonable hypothesis lies beyond the scope of this chapter.

Analysis of the Chinese in Thailand does, however, offer some theoretical insights into the economic transformations that have occurred in Thailand and into the roles the Chinese played in them. Analytically, and hence somewhat artificially, we can conceptualize the two as, first, an institutionalized context in which economic action occurs, and, second, the entrepreneurial strategies themselves. We recognize, of course, that entrepreneurial strategies also influence the institutionalized structure, but it makes sense theoretically to distinguish the two in order to understand better how context and action fit together.

In this chapter we have argued that the structure of political authority interacts with historically developed configurations of economic activities to create an institutional context for economic action and organization. Royal patrimonialism, military factionalism, and regional and international politics have established the structured contexts that shape Chinese entrepreneurship. The Chinese developed entrepreneurial strategies that took advantage of the opportunities they discovered or created in a particular time and place. Tax farming, banking, and global manufacturing – these and other strategies reflect the context of Chinese involvement.

We suggest, however, that successful entrepreneurship in one context does not automatically transfer to another. Entrepreneurship is situational and is, therefore, "path dependent". Successful entrepreneurship is always tied to actual situations of economic involvement. When the Chinese of one era seized upon a course of action, they tried to routinize it to make it more predictable and less risky. By creating a routinized approach to obtaining wealth, Chinese entrepreneurs embedded themselves in a set of political alliances, interdependent economic networks, and habitual economic practices. When the context altered, through either political or economic changes, the previous alliances, embedded networks, and economic practices made it difficult to adapt to new conditions. Old alliances often precluded new ones, established network ties undermined or at least channeled the ability to create new connections, and the economic practices successful in one era became woefully out of date in the next. As a consequence, the Chinese who were the leading entrepreneurs at one time did not automatically carry that role forward in the next period.

The story of the Chinese in Thailand, then, is not one of economic or even ethnic continuity. Instead, it is a story of changes, of sudden transformations, of ethnic reconstructions, and of a succession of distinct groups of Chinese entrepreneurs. To tell the story of the Chinese in Thailand accurately is to tell the story of these discontinuities. The only constants have been the disproportionately high level of Chinese success and the extraordinary ability of new groups of immigrant Chinese to adapt to whatever situation they found. What it is about the Chinese that accounts for this success remains poorly explained.

Notes

1   The following discussion on the Chinese in Thailand draws freely on our companion paper (Hamilton and Waters 1995), "Chinese Capitalism in Thailand: Embedded Networks and Industrial Structure". In this chapter we emphasize the structural situation facing the Chinese, and their response; in the companion paper we emphasize the economic consequences of Chinese entrepreneurship on the trajectory of economic development in Thailand.
2   The history of the CP group is based on interviews with several sons of Chia Seow Nooy.
3   Around 1965, the family took Thai names. Chiaravanont is a Thai version of the Chinese family name. The reason for the name change was because of prejudice among Thai officials at the time, and they judged it safer to take Thai names.
4   The joint venture with Wal-Mart ended a little over a year after it began.

Bibliography

Abegglen, J. C. (1994) *Sea Change: Pacific Asia as the New World Industrial Center*. New York: The Free Press.

Abernathy, F. H., Dunlop, J.T., Hammond, J. H. and Weil, D. (1999) *A Stitch in Time: Lean Retailing and the Transformation of Manufacturing – Lessons from the Apparel and Textile Industries*. New York: Oxford University Press.

Abolafia, M. Y. (1997) *Making Markets: Opportunism and Restraint on Wall Street*. Cambridge, Mass.: Harvard University Press.

Abstract of Information on Currency and Measures in China (1889–90) *Journal of the China Branch of the Royal Asiatic Society*, New Series 24:48–135.

Adams, M. J. (1969) *System and Meaning in East Sumba Textile Design: A Study in Traditional Indonesian Art*, Cultural Report Series No. 16. New Haven: Yale University Southeast Asia Studies.

Akin, R. (1969) *The Organization of Thai Society in the Early Bangkok Period, 1782–1873*, Data Paper no. 74. Ithaca, N.Y.: Cornell University, Department of Asian Studies, Southeast Asia Program.

Akin, R. (1975) "Clientship and Class Structure in the Early Bangkok Period", in G. W. Skinner and A. T. Kirsch (eds), *Change and Persistence in Thai Society*. Ithaca, N.Y.: Cornell University Press.

Almond, G. A. (1966) *Comparative Politics: A Developmental Approach*. Boston: Little Brown.

Almond, G. A. and Coleman, J. S. (eds) (1960) *The Politics of Developing Areas*. Princeton, New Jersey: Princeton University Press.

Amin, S. (1974) *Modern migrations in Western Africa*. Oxford: Oxford University Press.

Amsden, A. H. (1985) "The State and Taiwan's Economic Development", in P. B. Evans, D. Rueschemeyer, and T. Skocpol (eds), *Bringing the State Back In*. Cambridge: Cambridge University Press.

Amsden, A. H. (1989) *Asia's Next Giant: South Korea and Late Industrialization*. New York: Oxford University Press.

Amsden, A. H. (2001) *The Rise of the "the Rest": Challenges to the West from Late-Industrializing Economies*. New York: Oxford University Press.

Anderson, P. (1974a) *Passages from Antiquity to Feudalism*. London: New Left Books.

Anderson, P. (1974b) *Lineages of the Absolutist State*. London: New Left Books.

Anonymous (1887) "Chinese Partnerships: Liability of the Individual Members", *Journal of the China Branch of the Royal Asiatic Society*, New Series, Vol. 22, p. 41.

Anonymous (1932) "Native Banks in Canton", *Chinese Economic Journal* 11(3): 187–90.

Aoki, M. (1988) *Information, Incentive, and Bargaining in the Japanese Economy*. Cambridge: Cambridge University Press.

Aoki, M. (1990) "Toward an Economic Model of the Japanese Firm", *Journal of Economic Literature* 28 (March): 1–27.

Aoki, M. (1992) "Decentralization–Centralization in Japanese Organization: A Duality Principle", in S. Kumon and H. Rosovsky (eds), *The Political Economy of Japan. Volume Three: Cultural and Social Dynamics*. Stanford: Stanford University Press.

Aoki, M. and Dore, R. (eds) (1994) *The Japanese Firm: The Sources of Competitive Strength*. London: Oxford University Press.

Appelbaum, R. P. and Smith, D. (2001) "Governance and Flexibility: The East Asian Garment Industry", in Frederic C. Deyo, Richard F. Doner, and Eric Hershberg (eds), *Economic Governance and the Challenge of Flexibility in East Asia*. Lanham, MD: Rowman and Littlefield.

Apter, D. (1965) *The Politics of Modernization*. Chicago: University of Chicago Press.

Asher, D. and Smithers, A. (1998) "Japan's Key Challenges for the 21st Century: Debt, Deflation, Default, Demography, and Deregulation", *SAIS* Policy Forum Series.

Baker, C. (1981) "Economic Reorganizaiton and the Slump in South and Southeast Asia", *Comparative Studies in Society and History* 23, 325–49.

Balazs, E. (1964) *Chinese Civilization and Bureaucracy*. New Haven: Yale University Press.

Becherucci, L. (1969) "Raphael and Painting", in *The Complete Works of Raphael*. New York: Harrison House.

Becker, G. S. (1996) *Accounting for Tastes*. Cambridge, Mass.: Harvard University Press.

Becker, H. (1986) *Doing Things Together: Selected Papers*. Evanston, Ill.: Northwestern University Press.

Bellah, R. (1957) *Tokugawa Religion: The Cultural Roots of Modern Japan*. New York: The Free Press.

Bellah, R. (1970) "Father and Son in Christianity and Confucianism", in R. Bellah (ed.), *Beyond Belief*. New York: Harper and Row.

Bendix, R. (1964) *Nation-Building and Citizenship: Studies of Our Changing Social Order*. New York: Wiley.

Bendix, R. (1974) "Inequality and social structure", *American Sociological Review* 39: 149–61.

Bendix, R. (1977) *Max Weber: An Intellectual Portrait*. Berkeley: University of California Press.

Bendix, R. (1978) *Kings or People and the Mandate to Rule*. Berkeley: University of California Press.

Berger, P. L. (1984) "An East Asian Development Model", *The Economic News* 3079: 6–8.

Berger, P. L. and Hsiao, H.-H. M. (eds) (1988) *In Search of an East Asian Development Model*. New Brunswick, NJ: Transaction Books.

Berger, R. M. (1980) "The Development of Retail Trade in Provincial England, ca. 1550–1700", *The Journal of Economic History* 40, 123–8.

Bergere, M. (1968) "The Role of the Bourgeoisie", in M. C. Wright (ed.), *China in Revolution*. New Haven: Yale University Press.

Biddick, K. (1985) "Medieval English Peasants and Market Involvement", *The Journal of Economic History* 45: 823–31.

Biggart, N. W. (1990) "Institutionalized Patrimonialism in Korean Business", *Comparative Social Research* 12: 113–33.

Biggart, N. W. (2001) "Banking on Each Other: The Situational Logic of Rotating Savings and Credit Associations", *Advances in Qualitative Organization Research*, 3:129–153.

Biggart, N. W. and Guillén, M. F. (1999) "Developing Difference: Social Organization and the Rise of the Auto Industries of South Korea, Taiwan, Spain and Argentina", *American Sociological Review,* 64, October, 722–47.

Biggart, N. W. and Hamilton, G. G. (1992) "On the Limits of a Firm-based Theory to Explain Business Networks: The Western Bias of Neoclassical Economics", in N. Nohria and R. G. Eccles (eds), *Networks and Organizations: Structure, Form, and Action.* Boston: Harvard Business School Press.

Biggs, T. S. (1988a) "Financing the emergence of small and medium enterprise in Taiwan: Heterogeneous firm size and efficient intermediation. Employment and Enterprise Policy Analysis Project", EEPA Discussion Paper 16.

Biggs, T. S. (1988b) "Financing the emergence of small and medium enterprise in Taiwan: Financial mobilization and the flow of domestic credit to the private sector. Employment and Enterprise Policy Analysis Project", EEPA Discussion Paper 15.

Blackburn Commission (1898) *Report of the Mission to China of the Blackburn Chamber of Commerce, 1896–7.* Blackburn: The North-east Lancashire Press.

Block, F. (1987) *Revising State Theory.* Philadelphia: Temple University Press.

Blok, A. (1974) *The Mafia of a Sicilian village, 1860–1960.* New York: Harper.

Bluestone, B., Hanna, P., Kuhn, S., and Moore, L. (1981) *The Retail Revolution: Market Transformation, Investment, and Labor in the Modern Department Store.* Boston: Auburn House.

Bluestone, B. and Harrison, B. (1982) *The Deindustrialization of America.* New York: Basic Books.

Bonacich, E. (1973) "A theory of middleman minorities", *American Sociological Review* 38: 583–94.

Bonacich, E., Cheng, L., Chinchilla, N., Hamilton, N., and Ong, Paul (1994) *Global Production: The Apparel Industry in the Pacific Rim.* Philadelphia: Temple University Press.

Bonacich, E. and Waller, D. V. (1994) "The Role of U.S. Apparel Manufacturers in the Globalization of the Industry in the Pacific Rim", in E. Bonacich, L. Cheng, N. Chinchilla, N. Hamilton, and P. Ong (eds), *Global Production: The Apparel Industry in the Pacific Rim.* Philadelphia: Temple University Press.

Borden, N. H. (1947) *The Economic Effects of Advertising.* Chicago: Richard D. Irwin.

Bourne, F. S. A. (1989) *Report of the Mission to China of the Blackburn Chamber of Commerce, 1986–7.* Blackburn: The North-East Lancashire Press.

Brandt, L. (1989) *Commercialization and Agricultural Development in East-Central China, 1870–1937.* Cambridge: Cambridge University Press.

Braudel, F. (1972) *The Mediterranean and the Mediterranean World in the Age of Philip II.* New York: Harper Colophon Books.

Braudel, F. (1976 [1966]) *The Mediterranean and the Mediterranean World in the Age of Philip II,* trans. Sean Reynolds, 2 vols. New York: Harper and Row.

Braudel, F. (1981 [1979]) *The Structure of Everyday Life.* New York: Harper and Row.

Braudel, F. (1982 [1979]) *The Wheels of Commerce.* New York: Harper and Row.

Braudel, F. (1984 [1979]) *The Perspective of the World.* New York: Harper and Row.

Bray, F. (1999) "Towards a critical history of non-Western technology", in Timothy Brook and Gregory Blue (eds), *China and Historical Capitalism: Genealogies of Sinological Knowledge.* Cambridge: Cambridge University Press.

Brenner, F. (1977) "The Origins of Capitalist Development: A Critique of Neo-Smithian Marxism", *New Left Review* 104: 25–92.

Brenner, R. (1976) "Agrarian Class Structure and Economic Development in Pre-Industrial Europe", *Past and Present* 70: 30–75.

Brewer, J and Porter, R. (1993) *Consumption and the World of Goods.* London: Routledge.

Brinton, M. C. and Kariya, T. (1998) "Institutional Embeddedness in Japanese Labor Market", in M. C. Brinton and V. Nee (eds), *The New Institutionalism in Sociology*. New York: Russell Sage Foundation.

British Parliamentary Papers (1880) "Commercial Reports from Her Majesty's Consuls in China: 1879", (c. 2718) LXXV.

Brook, T. (ed.) (1989) *The Asiatic Mode of Production in China*. Armonk, N.Y.: M. E. Sharpe.

Brook, T. and Blue, G. (1999) *China and Historical Capitalism: Genealogies of Sinological Knowledge*. Cambridge: Cambridge University Press.

Brown, I. G. (1987) "The Siamese Administrative Elite in the Early Twentieth Century and the Historical Origins of Underdevelopment in Siam", in *Essays in Honour of E. H. S. Simmonds*, Lai Su Thai, School of Oriental and African Studies, London.

Brown, I. G. (1988) *The Elite and the Economy in Siam, c. 1890–1920*. Singapore: Oxford University Press.

Brown, R. A. (ed.) (1998) "Overseas Chinese Investments in China – Patterns of Growth Diversification and Finance: The Case of Chareoen Pokphand", *The China Quarterly*, no. 155, 610–36.

Brown, S. A. (1997) *Revolution at the Checkout Counter*. Cambridge, Mass.: Harvard University Press.

Bruner, E. M. (1961) "Urbanization and ethnic identity in North Sumatra", *American Anthropologist* 63:508–21.

Bruner, E. M. (1974) "The expression of ethnicity in Indonesia", in A. Cohen (ed.), *Urban Ethnicity*. London: Tavistock.

Bryan, R. R. (1979) "Migration, the industrial economy, and collective consumption", *International Social Science Journal*, 31: 282–303.

Bucklin, L. P. (1972) *Competition and Evolution in the Distributive Trades*. Englewood Cliffs, NJ.: Prentice Hall.

Bunbongkarn, S. (1987) *The Military in Thai Politics, 1981–86*. Singapore: Institute of Southeast Asian Studies.

Burawoy, M. (1985) *The Politics of Production: Factory Regimes under Capitalism and Socialism*. London: Verso.

Burger, T. (1987) *Max Weber's Theory of Concept Formation: History, Laws, and Ideal Types*. Durham, N.C.: Duke University Press.

Burgess, J. S. (1928) *The Guilds of Peking*. New York: Columbia University Press.

Business in Thailand (1988a) "Arsa Says Goodbye to Washington and Hello (Again) to Bangkok", July: 28–31.

Business in Thailand (1988b) "Profiles of Chatri Sophonpanich", November: 85–90.

Business in Thailand (1988c) "Dr. Amnuay Viravan", November: 107–111.

Business in Thailand (1992a) "Thai Pure Drink Co. Ltd.", February: 84–6

Business in Thailand (1992b) "Pattee Sarasin", May: 8.

Business in Thailand (1992c) "Bangkok Bank Ltd.", June: 66.

Business Review (1987a) "The Night Chari Shines Among the Stars", September 15: 38–42.

Business Review (1987b) "Thailand's Kennedy Clan", November: 13–26.

Business Review (1987c) "Businessman: After 29 Years in the Foreign Service, Arsa Sarasin", December 15: 15.

Buss, A. E. (1985) *Max Weber and Asia*. Munich: Weltforum Verlag.

Campbell, C. (1987) *The Romantic Ethic and the Spirit of Modern Consumerism*. Oxford: Basil Blackwell.

Cardoso, R. H. and Faletto, E. (1979) *Dependency and Development in Latin America*, Trans. Marjory Mattingly Urquidi. Berkeley: University of California Press.

Castells, M. (1996) *The Rise of the Network Society*. Oxford: Blackwell Publishers.

Cellini, B. (1948) *The Autobiography of Benvenuto Cellini*, trans. J. A. Symonds. New York: Doubleday and Company.

Chamberlin, E. H. (1950) *The Theory of Monopolistic Competition*. Cambridge, Mass.: Harvard University Press.

Chan, K. B. and Chiang, C. S. N. (1994) *Stepping Out: The Making of Chinese Entrepreneurs*. Singapore: Prentice Hall.

Chan, K. B. and Tong C. K. (1993) "Rethinking Assimilation and Ethnicity: The Chinese in Thailand", *International Migration Review* 27: 140–68.

Chan, W. K. K. (1982) "The Organizational Structure of the Traditional Chinese Firm and its Modern Reform", *Business History Review* 56,2 (Summer): 218–35.

Chandler, A. D. Jr. (1977) *The Visible Hand: The Managerial Revolution in American Business*. Cambridge, Mass: Harvard University Press.

Chandler, A. D. Jr. (1990) *Scale and Scope: The Dynamics of Industrial Capitalism*. Cambridge, Mass: Harvard University Press.

Chandler, A. D. Jr. and Daems, H. (eds) (1980) *Managerial Hierarchies: Comparative Perspective on the Rise of the Modern Industrial Enterprise*. Cambridge, Mass.: Harvard University Press.

Chandra. B. (1968) "Reinterpretation of nineteenth-century Indian economic history", *The Indian Economic and Social History Review* 5: 35–75.

Chang, C.-L. (1962) *The Income of the Chinese Gentry*. Seattle: University of Washington Press.

Chang, P. (1957) "The Distribution and Relative Strength of the Provincial Merchant Groups in China, 1842–1911". Unpublished dissertation. Seattle: University of Washington.

Chao, K. (1975) "The growth of a modern cotton textile industry and the competition with handicrafts", in D. H. Perkins (ed.), *China's Modern Economy in Historical Perspective*. Stanford: Stanford University Press.

Chao, K. (1977) *The Development of Cotton Textile Production in China*. Cambridge, Mass.: Harvard University Press.

Chao, K. (1986) *Zhongguo Jingji Zhidu Shilun* (History of Chinese economic institution). Taipei: Lianjing.

Chen, C. H. (1994) *Xieli wangluo yu shenhuo jiegou: Taiwan zhongxiao qiye de shehui jiji fenxi* (Mutual aid networks and the structure of daily life. A social economic analysis of Taiwan's small- and medium-sized enterprises). Taipei: Lianjing.

Chen, C. H. (1995) *Huobi wangluo yu shenhuo jiegou: Difang jinrong, zhongxiao qiye Taiwan shisu shehui zhi zhuanhua* (Monetary networks and the structure of daily life: Local finances, small and medium-sized enterprises, and the transformation of folk society in Taiwan). Taipei: Lianjing.

Chen, C. H. (1998) *Taiwan chanye de shehuixueyanjiu* (Sociological research on Taiwan's industries). Taipei: Lianjing.

Chen, C. N. (1985) "Kinship Ethic and Economic Rationality: A Preliminary Study on Max Weber and His Study on Chinese Society". Unpublished paper presented at the Chinese University of Hong Kong.

Chen, C. Y. (1997) *Gongyehua chongde chuantonghua – Hemei fangzhiye zhi yanzhou* (The traditionalism of industrialization – Research on the cotton industy in Hemei). *Difang shehui* (Local society) 1, 1: 211–54.

Chen, E. K. Y. and Drysdale, P. (1995) *Corporate Links and Foreign Direct Investment in Asia and the Pacific*. Pymble, Australia: Harper Educational.

Chen, T. (1940) *Emigrant Communities in South China. A Study of Overseas Migration and Its Influence on Standards of living and Social Change*. New York: Institute of Pacific Relations.

Chen, Tain-jy *et al.* (1995) *Taiwan's Small- and Medium-sized Firms' Direct Investment in Southeast Asia*. Taipei: Chung-Hua Institution for Economic Research.

Chen, Y. (1984) *Chaye tongshi* (The general history of tea). Beijing: Nongye Chubanshe.

Cheng, L.-L. and Sato, Y. (1998) "The Bicycle Industries in Taiwan and Japan: A Preliminary Study Toward Comparison between Taiwanese and Japanese Industrial Development", *Joint Research Program Series* No. 124. Tokyo: Institute of Developing Economies.

Cheng, T. Y. (1985) *The Economy of Hong Kong*. Hong Kong: Far East Publications.

China Credit Information Service (Zhonghua Zhengxinso) (comp.) (1983) *Taiwan diqu jitua qiye yanjiu, 1983–1984* (Business groups in Taiwan, 1983–1984), Taipei: China Credit Information Service.

China Credit Information Service (Zhonghua Zhengxinso) (comp.) (1985) *Taiwan diqu jitua qiye yanjiu, 1985–1986* (Business groups in Taiwan, 1985–1986), Taipei: China Credit Information Service.

China Credit Information Service (Zhonghua Zhengxinso) (comp.) (1998) *Taiwan diqu jitua qiye yanjiu, 1998–1999* (Business groups in Taiwan, 1998–1999). Taipei: China Credit Information Service.

Chirot, D. (1977) *Social Change in the Twentieth Century*. New York: Harcourt Brace Jovanovich.

Chiu, S. W. K., Ho, K. C., and Lui, T. L. (1997) *City-States in the Global Economy, Industrial Restructuring in Hong Kong and Singapore*. Boulder, Col.: Westview Press.

Choi, C. Y. (1978) *Chinese migration and settlement in Australia*. Sydney: Sydney University Press.

Choonhavan, K. (1984) "The Growth of Domestic Capital and Thai industrialization", *Journal of Contemporary Asia* 14, 2: 135–46.

Chou, T. C. (1985) *Industrial Organization in the Process of Economic Development: The Case of Taiwan, 1950–1980*. Louvain-la-Neuve: Universite Catholique de Louvain, Faculte des Science Economiques, Sociales et Politiques.

Chow, P. C. Y. and Kellman, M. H. (1993) *Trade – the Engine of Growth in East Asia*. Oxford: Oxford University Press.

Ch'u, T.-T. (1969) *Local Government in China under the Ch'ing*. Stanford: Stanford University Press.

Chuan, H.-S. (1979) *"Qing Kangxi nianjian Jiangnan ji fujin diqu demi jia* (The prices of rice in Jiangnan and neighboring areas during the Kangxi period (1662–1722))", *The Journal of the Institute of Chinese Studies of the Chinese University of Hong Kong*, X, no.l: 63–103.

Chuan, H.-S. and Kraus, R. A. (1975) *Mid-Ch'ing Rice Markets and Trade: An Essay in Price History*. Cambridge, Mass.: Harvard University Press.

Chung, C. (1997) "Division of Labor across the Taiwan Strait: Macro Overview and Analysis of the Electronics Industry", in Barry Naughton (ed.), *The China Circle: Economics and Technology in the PRC, Taiwan, and Hong Kong*. Washington D.C.: Brookings Institution Press.

Chung, K. H. and Lee, H. C. (eds) (1989) *Korean Managerial Dynamics*. New York: Praeger.

Chung, W. K. (2004) *The Emergence of Corporate Forms in China, 1872–1949: An Analysis on Institutional Transformation*. Unpublished dissertation. Seattle: University of Washington.

Chung, W. K. and Hamilton, G. G. (2001) "Social Logic as Business Logic: Guanxi, Trustworthiness, and the Embeddedness of Chinese Business Practices", in R. P. Appelbaum, W. L. F. Felstiner, and V. Gessner (eds), *Rules and Networks: The Legal Culture of Global Business Transactions*. Oxford: Hart Publishing.

Clad, J. (1989) *Behind the Myth: Business Money and Power in Southeast Asia*. London: Hyman.

Clark, R. (1979) *The Japanese Company*. New Haven: Yale University Press,

Clarkson, L. A. (1985) *Proto-lndustrialization: The First Phase of Industrialization*. London: Macmillan.

Cochran, S. (1980) *Big Business in China: Sino-Foreign Rivalry in the Cigarette Industry, 1890–1930*. Cambridge, Mass.: Harvard University Press.

Cochran, S. (2000) *Encountering Chinese Networks: Western, Japanese, and Chinese Corporations in China, 1880–1937*. Berkeley: University of California Press.

Cohen, A. (1969) *Custom and Politic in Urban Africa*. London: Routledge and Kegan Paul.

Cohen, A. (1971) "Cultural strategies in the organization of trading diasporas", in C. Meillassoux (ed.), *The Development of Indigenous Trade and Markets in West Africa*. Oxford: Oxford University Press.

Cohen, M. (1976) *House United, House Divided, The Chinese Family in Taiwan*. New York: Columbia University Press.

Cohen, N. E. (2002) *America's Marketplace: The History of Shopping Centers*. Lyme, CT.: Greenwich.

Coles, J. (1949) *Standards and Labels for Consumer Goods*. New York: Ronald Press.

Collins, R. (1980) "Weber's Last Theory of Capitalism: A Systematization", *American Sociological Review* 45: 925–42.

Collins, R. (1997) "An Asian Route to Capitalism: Religious Economy and the Origins of Self-Transforming Growth in Japan", *American Sociological Review* 62 (December): 843–65.

Collins, R. (1999) *Macrohistory: Essays in Sociology of the Long Run*. Stanford: Stanford University Press.

Cooke, C. W. (1858) *China: Being The Times Special Correspondence from China in the Years 1857–58*. London: Routledge.

Coser, L. (1972) "The Alien as a Servant of Power: Court Jews and Christian Renegades", *American Journal of Sociology* 37: 574–80.

Crissman, L. (1967) "The Segmentary Structure of Urban Overseas Chinese Communities", *Man* 2: 185–204.

Crow, C. (1937) *Four Hundred Million Customers: The Experiences – Some Happy, Some Sad – of An American in China, and What They Taught Him*. New York: Harper and Brothers.

Cumings, B. (1984) "The Origins and Development of the Northeast Asian Political Economy: Industrial Sectors, Product Cycles, and Political Consequences", *International Organizations* 38:1–40.

Cushman, J. (1986) "The Khaw Group: Chinese Business in Early Twentieth-century Penang", *Journal of Southeast Asian Studies* 17, 1 (March): 58–79.

Cushman, J. (1991) *Family and State: the Formation of a Sino–Thai Tin-Mining Dynasty, 1797–1932*. Oxford: Oxford Univeristy Press.

Cushman, J. and Wang G. (eds) (1988) *Changing Identities of the Southeast Asian Chinese since World War II*. Hong Kong: Hong Kong University Press.

Daily Economic News (1986) *Firm Directory of Korea for 1985*. Seoul.

Dalton, G. (1969) "Theoretical issues in economic anthropology", *Current Anthropology* 10: 63–80.

Davis, A. (1967) *Package and Print, The Development of Container and Label Design*. New York: C. N. Potter.

Davis, W. (1973) *Social Relations in a Philippine Market*. Berkeley: University of California Press.

Dawson, R. (1967) *The Chinese Chameleon*. London: Oxford University Press.

Decennial Reports (1882–1891 and 1892–1901) Imperial Maritime Customs, Shanghai.

DeGlopper, D. R. (1995) *Lukang, Commerce and Community in a Chinese City*. Albany, N.Y.: State University of New York Press.

Desan, P. (1984) "Nationalism and History in France during the Renaissance", *Rinascimento* 24: 261–88.

de Tocqueville, A. (1955) *The Old Regime and the French Revolution*. Garden City, N.Y.: Anchor Books.

de Tocqueville, A. (1969) *Democracy in America*, trans. J. P. Mayer. New York. Doubleday.

Deuchler, M. (1992) *The Confucian transformation of Korea: A Study of society and ideology*. Cambridge, Mass.: Council on East Asian Studies, Harvard University.

Deyo, F. C. (ed.) (1987) *The Political Economy of the New Asian Industrialism*. Ithaca, N.Y.: Cornell University Press.

Dicken, P. (1998) *Global Shift: Tranforming the World Economy*, 3rd edn. New York: Guilford Press.

Dietrich, C. (1972) "Cotton Culture and Manufacture in Early Ch'ing China", in W. E. Willmott (ed.), *Economic Organization in Chinese Society*. Stanford: Stanford University Press.

DiMaggio, P. and Powell W. W. (1983) "The Iron Cage Revisited: Institutional Isomorphism and Collective Rationality in Organizational Fields", *American Sociological Review* 48: 147–60.

Dobson, W. and Chia S. Y., (eds) (1997) *Multinationals and East Asian Integration*. Ottawa: International Development Research Centre.

Doner, R. F. (1990) *Driving a Bargain: Automobile Industrialization and Japanese Firms in Southeast Asia*. Berkeley: University of California Press.

Dore, R. P. (1983) "Goodwill and the Spirit of Capitalism", *British Journal of Sociology* 34: 459–82.

Dore, R. P. (1986) *Flexible Rigidities: Industrial Policy and Structural Adjustment in the Japanese Economy, 1970–80*. Stanford: Stanford University Press.

Dore, R. P. (1987) *Taking Japan Seriously*. Stanford: Stanford University Press.

Douglas, M. and Isherwood, B. (1979) *The World of Goods*. New York: W. W. Norton.

Drezner, D. (2004) "The Outsourcing Bogeymen", *Foreign Affairs* 83:3 (May/June).

Duara, P. (1988) *Culture, Power, and the State*. Stanford: Stanford University Press.

Dunlop, J. T. and Rivkin, J. W. (1997) "Introduction" in Stephen A. Brown, *Revolution at the Checkout Counter*. Cambridge, Mass.: Harvard University Press.

Dutton, H. I. (1984) *The Patent System and Inventive Activity During the Industrial Revolution, 1750–1852*. Manchester: Manchester University Press.

Dyer, W. G. Jr. (1986) *Cultural Change in Family Firms*. San Fransisco: Jossey-Bass.

East Asia Analytical Unit (1995) *Overseas Chinese Business Networks in Asia*. Australia: Department of Foreign Affairs and Trade.

Economic Planning Board, Republic of Korea (1985) *Report on Industrial Census for 1983*. Seoul: Economic Planning Board.

Eisenstadt, S. N. (1963) *The Political Systems of Empires*. New York: Free Press.

Eisenstadt, S. N. (1973) *Tradition, Change, and Modernity*. New York: Wiley.

Eisenstadt, S. N. (1981) "Cultural Traditions and Political Dynamics: The Origins and Modes of Ideological Politics", *British Journal of Sociology* 32, 2: 155–81.

Eisenstadt, S. N. (1982) "The Axial Age: The Emergence of Transcendental Visions and the Rise of Clerics", *European Journal of Sociology* 23, 2: 294–314.

Eisenstadt, S. N. (1987) *European Civilization in a Comparative Perspective*. Oslo: Norwegian University Press.

Eisenstadt, S. N. (1996) *Japanese Civilization: A Comparative View*. Chicago: University of Chicago Press.

Elias, N. (1978) *The Civilizing Process*, trans. Edmund Jephcott. New York: Urizen Books.

Elvin, M. (1963) "The Mixed Court of the International Settlement of Shanghai (until 1911)", *Papers on China* 17: 138.

Elvin, M. (1972) "The High-Level Equilibrium Trap: The Causes of the Decline of Invention in the Traditional Chinese Textile Industries", in W. E. Willmott (ed.), *Economic Organization in Chinese Society*. Stanford: Stanford University Press.

Elvin, M. (1973) *The Pattern of the Chinese Past*. Stanford: Stanford University Press.

Elvin, M. (1974) "The Administration of Shanghai, 1905–1914", in M. Elvin and G. W. Skinner (eds), *The Chinese City between Two Worlds*. Stanford: Stanford University Press.

Elvin, M. and Skinner, G. W. (1974) *The Chinese City Between Two Worlds*. Stanford: Stanford University Press.

Evans, P. B. (1979) *Dependent Development: The Alliance of Multinational, State, and Local Capital in Brazil*. Princeton, N.J.: Princeton University Press.

Evans, P. B. (1985) "Transnational Linkages and the Economic Role of the State: An Analysis of Developing and Industrialized Nations in the Post World War II Period", in P. B. Evans, D. Rueschemeyer, and T. Skocpol (eds), *Bringing the State Back In*. Cambridge: Cambridge University Press.

Evans, P. B. (1987) "Class, State, and Dependence in East Asia: Lessons for Latin Americanists", in F. C. Deyo (ed.), *The Political Economy of the New Asian Industrialism*. Ithaca, N.Y.: Cornell University Press.

Evans, P. B. (1995) *Embedded Autonomy: States and Industrial Transformation*. Princeton, N.J.: Princeton University Press.

Evans, P. B. (1997) "State Structures, Government-Business Relations, and Economic Transformation", in Sylvia Maxfield and Ben Ross Schneider, *Business and The State in Developing Countries*. Ithaca, N.Y.: Cornell University Press.

Evans, P. B. and Rauch J. E. (1999) "Bureaucracy and Growth: A Cross-National Analysis of the Effects of 'Weberian' State Structures on Economic Growth", *American Sociological Review* 64 (October): 748–65.

Evans, P. B., Rueschemeyer, D. and Skocpol, T. (1985) *Bringing the State Back In*. Cambridge: Cambridge University Press.

Evans, P. B. and Stephens, J. D. (1988) "Development and the World Economy", in N. J. Smelser (ed.), *Handbook of Sociology*. Newbury Park, CA: Sage.

Ewen, S. (1976) *Captains of Consciousness*. New York: McGraw-Hill.

Fairbank, J. K. (1968) *New Views of China's Tradition and Modernization*. Washington, D.C.: American Historical Society.

Fairbank, J. K., Eckstein, A. and Yang, L.-S. (1960) "Economic Change in Early Modern China: An Analytic Framework", *Economic Development and Cultural Change* 9:1–26.

Fairbank, J. K., Reischauer, E. O., and Craig, A. M. (1964) *East Asia: The Modern Transformation*. Boston: Houghton Mifflin.

Falkus, M. (1991) "The Economic History of Thailand", *Australian Economic History* Review XXXI: 53–71.

Fallers, L. A. (1966) "A note on the 'trickle effect' ", in R. Bendix and S. M. Lipset (eds), *Class, Status and Power*. New York: Free Press.

Fallows, J. (1995) *Looking at the Sun: The Rise of the New East Asian Economic and Political System*. New York: Vintage Books.

Faure, D. (1989a) *The Rural Economy of Pre-liberation China*. Hong Kong: Oxford University Press.

Faure, D. (1989b) "The Lineage as Business Company: Patronage versus Law in the Development of Chinese Business", *Proceeding of the Second Conference on Chinese Economic History (January 5–7, 1989)*. Taipei: Institute of Economics, Academia Sinica.

Faure, D. (1994) *China and Capitalism: Business Enterprise in Modern China*. Hong Kong: Hong Kong University of Science and Technology.

Feenstra, R. C. (1996) *U.S, Imports, 1972–1994: Data and concordances*. NBER Working Paper no. 5515, March, with accompanying CD-ROM.

Feenstra, R. C. and Hamilton, G. G. (2006) *Emergent Economies, Divergent Paths: Economic Organization and International Trade in South Korea and Taiwan*. Cambridge: Cambridge University Press.

Feenstra, R. C., Yang, T. H., and Hamilton, G. G. (1993) "Market structure and international trade: Business groups in East Asia", *Working Paper Series*, National Bureau of Economic Research, No. 4536.

Feenstra, R. C., Yang, T. H., and Hamilton. G. G. (1999) "Business Groups and Product Variety in Trade: Evidence from South Korea, Taiwan and Japan", *Journal of International Economics*, 48, June: 71–100.

Feeny, D. (1982) *The Political Economy of Productivity: Thai Agricultural Development, 1880–1975*, Vancouver: University of British Columbia Press.

Fei, X. T. (1992 [1947]) *From the Soil: The Foundations of Chinese Society*. Trans., Introduction, and Epilogue by G. G. Hamilton and Z. Wang. Berkeley: University of California Press.

Feuer, L. S. (ed.) (1954) *Karl Marx and Friedrich Engels*, Garden City, N.Y.: Anchor Books.

Feuerwerker, A. (1958) *China's Early Industrialization: Shen Hsuan-huai (1844–1916) and Mandarin Enterprise*. Cambridge, Mass.: Harvard University Press.

Feuerwerker, A. (1969) *The Chinese Economy ca. 1870–1911*, Michigan Papers in Chinese Studies, No 5, Ann Arbor: Center for Chinese Studies.

Feuerwerker, A. (1970) "Handicraft and Manufactured Cotton Textiles in China. 1871–1910" *Journal of Economic History* 30: 338–78.

Feuerwerker, A. (1984) "The State and the Economy in Late Imperial China", *Theory and Society* 13, 3: 297–326.

Feuerwerker, A. (1985) "Qing Economic History and World Economic History", prepared for the Symposium on the occasion of the Sixteenth Anniversary of the founding of the First Historical Archives of China, Beijing.

Feuerwerker, A. (1992) "Questions about China's Early Modern Economy History that I Wish I Could Answer", *Journal of Asian Studies* 51, 4: 757–69.

Fewsmith, J. (1983) "From Guild to Interest Group: The Transformation of Public and Private in Late Qing China", *Comparative Studies in Society and History* 25: 617–740.

Fields, K. J. (1995) *Enterprise and the State in Korea and Taiwan*. Ithaca, N.Y.: Cornell University Press.

Financial Times (1994) "Survey on China", 7 November, pp. I–X.

Fine, B. and Leopold, E. (1993) *The World of Consumption*. London: Routledge.

Fligstein N. (1990) *The Transformation of Corporate Control*. Cambridge, Mass.: Harvard University Press.

Fligstein, N. (2001) *The Architecture of Markets: An Economic Sociology of Twenty-First-Century Capitalist Societies*. Princeton, N.J.: Princeton University Press.

Folsom, K. (1968) *Friends, Guests, and Colleagues: The Mu-Fu System in the Late Ch'ing period*. Berkeley: University of California Press.

Foucault, M. (1979) *Discipline and Punish*, trans. Alan Sheridan. New York: Vintage Books.

Fox, R. W. and Lears, T. J. J. (eds) (1983) *The Culture of Consumption: Critical Essays in American History 1880–1980*. New York: Pantheon.

Frank, A. G. (1967) *Capitalism and Underdevelopment in Latin America*. New York: Monthly Review Press.

Frank, A. G. (1970) "The development of underdevelopment", in R. I. Rhodes (ed.), *Imperialism and Underdevelopment*. New York: Monthly Review Press.

Free China Review, November (1988) 38, 11: 10.

Freedman, M. (1959) "The Handling of Money", *Man* 59: 64–5.

Freedman, M. (1965) *Lineage Organization in Southeastern China*. New York: Humanities Press.

Friedland, J. (1989) "A Finger in Every Pie: Saha Group Dominates Thailand's Consumer Markets", *Far Eastern Economic Review* 28.

Fruin, W. M. (1992) *The Japanese Enterprise System: Competitive Strategies and Cooperative Structures*. Oxford: Clarendon Press.

Fry, G. (1992) "Thailand's Political Economy: Change and Persistence", in C. Clark and S. Chan (eds), *The Evolving Pacific Basin in the Global Political Economy, Domestic and International Linkages*. Boulder, Col.: Lynne Rienner.

Fu, Y. L. (1957) *Mingdai Jiangnan shimin jingji shitan* (Exploratory essay on the urban economy of the Kiangnan area during the Ming dynasty). Shanghai: Shanghai Renmin Chubanshe.

Fu, Y. L. (1980) *Ming Qing shidai shangren ji shangye ziben* (Merchants and commercial capital in Ming Qing China). Beijing: Renmin Chubanshe.

Fujita, M., Krugman, P., and Venables, A. J. (1999) *The Spatial Economy: Cities, Regions, and International Trade*. Cambridge, Mass.: The MIT Press.

Fukuyama, F. (1995) *Trust: The Social Virtues and the Creation of Prosperity*. New York: Free Press.

Futatsugi, Y. (1986) *Japanese Enterprise Groups*. Kobe: School of Business, Kobe University.

Galenson, W. (1979) *Economic Growth and Structural Change in Taiwan*. Ithaca, N.Y.: Cornell University Press.

Gallagher, J. and Robinson, R. (1953) "The imperialism of free trade", *Economic History Review* 6: 1–15.

Gandhi. M. P. (1931) *How to Compete with Foreign Cloth*. Calcutta: Book Company.

Garbett, G. K., and Kapferer, B. (1970) "Theoretical orientations in the study of labour migration", *The New Atlantis* 2: 179–97.

Garon, S. (1987) *The State and Labor in Modern Japan*. Berkeley: University of California Press.

Gates, H. (1987) *Chinese Working-Class Lives: Getting by in Taiwan*. Ithaca, N.Y.: Cornell University Press.

Geertz, C. (1962) "The rotating credit association: A 'middle rung' in development", *Economic Development and Cultural Change* 10: 241–63.

Geertz, C. (1963) *Peddlers and Princes: Social Development and Economic Change in Two Indonesian Towns*. Chicago: University of Chicago Press.

Geertz, C. (1980) *Negara*. Princeton, N.J.: Princeton University Press.

General Agreement on Tariffs and Trade (1988) *International Trade*, Geneva: GATT Secretariat.

Gereffi, G. (1994a) "The International Economy and Economic Development", in Neil Smelser and Richard Swedberg (eds), *The Handbook of Economic Sociology*. Princeton, N.J.: Princeton University Press.

Gereffi, G. (1994b) "The Organization of Buyer-Driven Global Commodity Chains: How U.S. Retail Networks Shape Overseas Production Networks", in G. Gereffi and M. Korzeniewicz (eds), *Commodity Chains and Global Capitalism*. Westport, Conn.: Greenwood Press.

Gereffi, G. (1999) "International Trade and Industrial Upgrading in the Apparel Commodity Chain", *Journal of International Economics* 48, 1 (June): 37–70.

Gereffi, G. and Hamilton, G. G. (1996) "Commodity Chains and Embedded Networks", paper presented at the Annual Meeting of the American Sociological Association.

Gereffi, G., Humphrey, J. and Sturgeon, T. (2005) "The Governance of Global Value Chains", *Review of International Political Economy* 12 (1), 78–104.

Gereffi, G. and Korzeniewicz, M, (1990) "Commodity Chains and Footwear Exports in the Semiperiphery", in W. Martin (ed.), *Semiperipheral States in the World-Economy*. Westport, Conn.: Greenwood Press.

Gereffi, G. and Korzeniewicz, M. (1994) *Commodity Chains and Global Capitalism*. Westport, Conn.: Praeger.

Gereffi, G. and Pan, M. L. (1994) "The Globalization of Taiwan's Garment Industry", in E. Bonacich, L. Cheng, N. Chinchilla, N. Hamilton, and P. Ong (eds), *Global Production: The Apparel Industry in the Pacific Rim*. Philadelphia: Temple University Press.

Gereffi, G., Spener, D. and Bair, J. (2002) *Free Trade and Uneven Development: The North American Apparel Industry after NAFTA*. Philadelphia: Temple University Press.

Gereffi, G. and Wyman, D. (eds) (1990) *Manufacturing Miracles: Paths of Industrialization in Latin America and East Asia*. Princeton, NJ: Princeton University Press.

Gerlach, M. (1992) *Alliance Capitalism: The Strategic Organization of Japanese Business*. Berkeley: University of California Press.

Gernet. J. (1962) *Daily Life in China on the Eve of the Mongol Invasion 1250–1276*. New York: Macmillan.

Gerschenkron, A. (1962) *Economic Backwardness in Historical Perspective*. Cambridge, Mass.: Harvard University Press.

Giddens, A. (1979) *Central Problems in Social Theory: Action, Structure, and Contradiction in Social Analysis*. Berkeley: University of California Press.

Giddens, A. (1984) *The Constitution of Society*. Berkeley: University of California Press.

Gilkey, G. R. (1967) "The United States and Italy: Migration and repatriation", *Journal of Developing Areas* 2: 23–37.

Girling, F. A. (1964) *English Merchants' Marks: A Field Survey of Marks Made by Merchants and Tradesmen in England between 1400 and 1700*. Oxford: Oxford University Press.

Girling, J. (1981) *Thailand, Society and Politics*. Ithaca, N.Y.: Cornell University Press.

Gladwell, M. (2004) "The Terrazzo Jungle", *The New Yorker*, March 15.

Golas, P. J. (1977) "Early Ch'ing Guilds", in G. W. Skinner (ed.), *The City in Late Imperial China*, Stanford: Stanford University Press.

Gold, T. B. (1986) *State and Society in the Taiwan Miracle*. Armonk, N.Y.: M. E. Sharpe.

Goldscheider, C. (1971) *Population Modernization and Social Structure*. Boston: Little, Brown.

Goldstone, J. (1996) "Gender, Work and Culture: Why the Industrial Revolution Came Early to England and Late to China", *Sociological Perspectives* 39,1: 1–21.

Granovetter, M. (1985) "Economic action and social structure: The problem of embeddedness", *American Journal of Sociology* 91: 481–510.

Granovetter, M. (1994) "Business groups", in N. Smelser and R. Swedberg (eds), *Handbook of Economic Sociology,* Princeton, NJ: Princeton University Press.

Graves, N. B. and Graves, T. D. (1974) "Adaptive strategies in urban migration", in B. J. Siegel *et al.* (eds), *Annual Review of Anthropology*, Vol. 3. Palo Alto: Annual Reviews Inc.

Gray, C. E. (1991) "Hegemonic Images: Language and Silence in the Royal Thai Polity", *Man* (N.S.) 26: 43–65.

Greenhalgh, S. (1988) "Families and Networks in Taiwan's Economic Development", in E. Winckler and S. Greenhalgh (eds), *Contending Approaches to the Political Economy of Taiwan*. Armonk, N.Y.: M. E. Sharpe.

Greenhalgh, S. (1994) "De-Orientalizing the Chinese Family Firm", *American Ethnologist* 21, 4: 746–75.

Greenspan, A. (1998a) "Testimony of Chairman Alan Greenspan before the Committee on Banking and Financial Services, U.S. House of Representatives", 30 January 1998.

Greenspan, A. (1998b) "Testimony of Chairman Alan Greenspan before the Committee on Foreign Relations, US Senate", 12 February 1998.

Greenspan, A. (1998c) "Monetary Policy Testimony and Report to the Congress", 24 February 1998.

Gugong bowuyuan Ming Qing danganbu (comp.) (1978) *Qingdai dangan shiliu congbian* (The source materials on Qing history), Beijing: Zhonghua Shuju.

Hadley, E. (1970) *Anti-trust in Japan.* Princeton, N.J.: Princeton University Press.

Haggard, S., Maxfield, S., and Schneider, B. R. (1997) "Theories of Business and Business-State Relations", in S. Maxfield and B. R. Schneider (eds), *Business and the State in Developing Countries.* Ithaca, N.Y.: Cornell University Press.

Hall, P. A. and Sockice, D. (2001) *Varieties of Capitalism: The Institutional Foundations of Comparative Advantage.* New York: Oxford University Press.

Halperin-Donghi, R. (1973) *The Aftermath of Revolution in Latin America,* New York: Harper and Row.

Halperin-Donghi, R. (1975) *Politics, Economy and Society in Argentina in the Revolutionary Period.* Cambridge: Cambridge University Press.

Hamashita, T. (2003) "Tribute and Treaties: Maritime Asia and Treaty Port Networks in the Era of Negotiation, 1800–1900", in G. Arrighi, T. Hamashita, and M. Selden (eds), *The Resurgence of East Asia: 500, 150, and 50 Year Perspectives.* London: Routledge.

Hamilton, G. G. (1977a) "Chinese Merchant Associations: Conspiracy or Combination", *Ch'ing-shih wen-ti* 3: 50–71.

Hamilton, G. G. (1977b) "Ethnicity and Regionalism: Some Factors Influencing Chinese Identities in Southeast Asia", *Ethnicity* 4: 337–51.

Hamilton, G. G. (1977c) "Chinese Consumption of Foreign Commodities: A Comparative Perspective", *American Sociological Review* 42: 877–891.

Hamilton, G. G. (1978a) "Pariah Capitalism: A Paradox of Power and Dependence", *Ethnic Groups: An International Periodical of Ethnic Studies* 2: 1–15.

Hamilton, G. G. (1978b) "The structural sources of adventurism", *American Journal of Sociology* 83: 1466–80.

Hamilton, G. G. (1979) "Regional Associations and the Chinese City: A Comparative Perspective", *Comparative Studies in Society and History* 21: 346–61.

Hamilton, G. G. (1984a) "Configurations in History: The Historical Sociology of S.N. Eisenstadt", in T. Skocpol (ed.), *Vision and Method in Historical Sociology.* Cambridge: Cambridge University Press.

Hamilton, G. G. (1984b) "Patriarchalism in Imperial China and Western Europe: A Revision of Weber's Sociology of Domination", *Theory and Society* 13, 3: 393–426.

Hamilton, G. G. (1985a) "Why No Capitalism in China: Negative Questions in Comparative Historical Sociology", in A. E. Buss (ed.), *Max Weber in Asian Studies,* Leiden: E. J. Brill.

Hamilton, G. G. (1985b) "Temporary Migration and the Institutionalization of Strategy", *International Journal of Intercultural Relations* 9: 405–25.

Hamilton, G. G. (1989) "Heaven is High and the Emperor is Far Away", *Revue europeenne des sciences sociales* 27: 141–67.

Hamilton, G. G. (1990b) "Patriarchy, patrimonialism and filial piety: A comparison of China and Western Europe", *British Journal of Sociology* 41, 1: 77–104.

Hamilton, G. G. (ed.) (1991a) *Business networks and economic development in East and Southeast Asia.* Hong Kong: Centre of Asian Studies, University of Hong Kong.

Hamilton, G. G. (1991b) "The Organizational Foundations of Western and Chinese Commerce: A Historical and Comparative Analysis", in G. G. Hamilton (ed.),

Business Networks and Economic Development in East and Southeast Asia. Hong Kong: Centre of Asian Studies, University of Hong Kong

Hamilton, G. G. (ed.) (1994) *Asian Business Networks*. Berlin: de Gruyter.

Hamilton, G. G. (1996a) "Overseas Chinese Capitalism", in Tu W.-M. (ed.), *The Confucian Dimensions of Industrial East Asia,* Cambridge, Mass.: Harvard University Press.

Hamilton, G. G. (1996b) "The Quest for a Unified Economics", *Industrial and Corporate Change* 5, 3: 907–16.

Hamilton, G. G. (1997) "Organization and Market Processes in Taiwan's Capitalist Economy", in M. Orrù, N. W. Biggart, and G. G. Hamilton (eds), *The Economic Organization of East Asian Capitalism*. Thousand Oaks, CA: Sage Publications.

Hamilton, G. G. (2000) "Reciprocity and Control: The Organization of Chinese Family-owned Conglomerates", in H. W.-C. Yeung and K. Olds (eds), *Globalization of Chinese Business Firms*. New York: St Martins Press.

Hamilton, G. G. and Biggart, N. W. (1988) "Market, culture, and authority: A comparative analysis of management and organization in the Far East", *American Journal of Sociology* 94 (Supplement): S52–S94.

Hamilton, G. G., and Feenstra R. (1995) "Varieties of hierarchies and markets", *Industrial and Corporate Change* 4, 1.

Hamilton, G. G., Feenstra, R., Choe, W. G., Kim C. K., and Lim, E. M. (2000) "Neither States Nor Markets: The Role of Economic Organization in Asian Development", *International Sociology* 15 (2, June): 291–308.

Hamilton, G. G. and Kao, C.-S. (1987) "Max Weber and the Analysis of East Asian Industrialization", *International Sociology* 2: 289–300.

Hamilton, G. G. and Kao, C.-S. (1990) "The Institutional Foundations of Chinese Business: The Family Firm in Taiwan", *Comparative Social Research* 12: 95–112.

Hamilton, G. G. and Lai, C. K. (1988) "Consumerism without Capitalism: Consumption and Brand Names in Late Imperial China", in B. Orlove and H. Rutz (eds), *The Social Economy of Consumption*. New York: University Press of America.

Hamilton, G. G. and Waters, T. (1995) "Economic Organization and Chinese Business Networks in Thailand", in E. K. Y. Chen and P. Drysdale (eds), *Corporate Links and Direct Foreign Investment in Asia and the Pacific,* Pymble, Australia: HarperEducational.

Hamilton, G. G. and Waters, T. (1997) "Ethnicity and Capitalist Development: The Changing Role of the Chinese in Thailand", in D. Chirot and A. Reid (eds), *Essential Outsiders: Chinese and Jews in the Modern Transformation of Southeast Asia and Central Europe*. Seattle: University of Washington Press.

Hamilton, G. G., Zeile, W., and Kim, W.-J. (1990) "The Network Structures of East Asian Economies", in S. R. Clegg and S. G. Redding (eds), *Capitalism in Contrasting Cultures*. Berlin: de Gruyter.

Hanchett, T. W. (1996) "U.S. Tax Policy and the Shopping-Center Boom of the 1950s and 1960s", *American Historical Review* 101 (October).

Hanley, S. B. (1997) *Everyday Things in Premodern Japan: The Hidden Legacy of Material Culture*. Berkeley: University of California Press.

Hanley, S. B. and Yamamura. K. (1977) *Economic and Demographic Change in Preindustrial Japan, 1600–1868*. Princeton, N.J.: Princeton University Press.

Hao, Y.-P. (1986) *The Commercial Revolution in Nineteenth-Century China. The Rise of Sino–Western Mercantile Capitalism*. Berkeley: University of California Press.

Hao, Y.-P. (1970) *The Comprador in Nineteenth Century China*. Cambridge, Mass.: Harvard University Press.

Harrison, B. (1994) *Lean and Mean: The Changing Landscape of Corporate Power in an Age of Flexibility*. New York: Basic Books.

Harrison, B. and Bluestone, B. (1988) *The Great U-turn: Corporate Restructuring and the Polarizing of America*. New York: Basic Books.

Hartwell, R. (1967) "A Cycle of Economic Change in Imperial China: Coal and Iron in Northeast China, 750–1350", *Journal of the Economic and Social History of the Orient* 10: 102–59.

Hartz, L. (1955) *The Liberal Tradition in America*. New York: Harcourt Brace.

Harvey, D. (1990) *The Condition of Postmodernity*. Oxford: Basil Blackwell.

Hatch, W. and Yamamura, K. (1996) *Asia in Japan's Embrace*. Cambridge: Cambridge University Press.

Hayes, J. (1963) "Cheng Chau, 1850–1898", *Journal of the Hong Kong Branch of the Royal Asiatic Society* 3: 88–106.

He, B. (1966) *Zhongguo huiguan shilun* (An historical survey of landsmannschaften in China). Taipei: Xuesheng Shuju.

Heath, A. (1976) *Rational choice and social exchange*. Cambridge: Cambridge University Press.

Hechter, M. (1975) *Internal Colonialism: The Celtic Fringe in British National Development, 1536–1966*. London: Routledge and Kegan Paul.

Hechter, M. (1978) "Group formation and cultural division of labor", *American Journal of Sociology,* 84: 293–318.

Hegel, G. (1900) *The Philosophy of History*. New York: The Colonial Press.

Henderson, J. J. (1879) *An International Court for China*. Shanghai: American Presbyterian Mission Press.

Herman, T. (1956) "Cultural Factors in the Location of Swatow Lace and Needlework Industry", *Annals of the Association of American Geographers* 46: 123.

Hershatter, G., Honig, E., Lipman, J., and Stross, R. (1996) *Remapping China: Fissures in Historical Terrain*. Stanford: Stanford University Press.

Heuser, R. (1975) "The Chinese Trademark Law of 1904: A Preliminary Study in Exterritoriality, Competition, and Late Ch'ing Law Reform", *Oriens Extremus* 22, 1: 183–210.

Hewison, K. (1981) "The Financial Bourgeois in Thailand", *Journal of Contemporary Asia* 11, 4: 395–412

Hewison, K. (1989) *Bankers and Bureaucrats: Capital and the Role of the State in Thailand*. New Haven: Monograph Series 34, Yale Center for International and Area Studies.

Hewison, K. (1993) "Of Regines, State and Pluralities: Thai Politics Enters the 1990s", in K. Hewison, R. Robison, and G. Rodan (eds), *Southeast Asia in the 1990s. Authoritarianism, Democracy, and Capitalism*. St. Leonards, Australia: Allen and Unwin.

Hicks, G. L. (ed.) (1993) *Overseas Chinese Remittances from Southeast Asia, 1910–1940*. Singapore: Select Books.

Higgott, R. and Robison, R. (eds) (1985) *Southeast Asia: Essays in the Political Economy of Structural Change*. London: Routledge and Kegan Paul.

Hilton, R. H. (1985) "Medieval Market Towns and Simple Commodity Production", *Past and Present* 109: 3–23.

Hirschman, A. (1977) *Passion and the Interests: Political Arguments for Capitalism before Its Triumph*. Princeton, N.J.: Princeton University Press.

Hirth, F. and Rockhill, W. W. (1970) *Chau Ju-kua*. Taipei: Ch'eng-wen.

Ho, P. T. (1954) "The Salt Merchants of Yang-chou: A Study of Commercial Capitalism in Eighteenth Century China", *Harvard Journal of Asiatic Studies* 17: 130–68.

Ho, P. T. (1964) *The Ladder of Success in Imperial China*. New York: John Wiley and Sons.

Ho, P. T. (1966) *Zhonghuo huiguan shilun* (A Historical Survey of Landsmannschaften in China). Taipei.

Ho, P. T. (1967) "The significance of the Ch'ing period in Chinese history", *Journal of Asian Studies* 26: 189–95.

Ho, S. P. S. (1978) *Economic Development of Taiwan, 1860–1970*. New Haven: Yale University Press.

Hohenberg, P. M. and Lees, L. H. (1985) *The Making of Urban Europe 1000–1950*. Cambridge, Mass.: Harvard University Press.

Hollingsworth, J. R. and Boyer, R. (1997) *Contemporary Capitalism: The Embeddedness of Institutions*. Cambridge: Cambridge University Press.

Hong, L. (1984) *Thailand in the Nineteenth Century, Evolution of the Economy and Society*. Singapore: Institute of Southeast Asian Studies.

Hopkins, T. K. and Wallerstein. I. (1986) "Commodity Chains in the World-Economy Prior to 1800", *Review* 10, 1:157–70.

Hornblower, S. (2005) "Wal-Mart and China: A Joint Venture", available online (15 Jan 2006) at http://www.pbs.org/wgbh/pages/frontline/shows/walmart/secrets/wmchina.html

Hou, C. M. (1963) "Economic Dualism: The Case of China, 1840–1937", *The Journal of Economic History* 23: 277–97.

Hou, C. M. (1965) *Foreign Investment and Economic Development in China, 1840–1937*. Cambridge, Mass.: Harvard University Press.

Hourwich, I. (1912) *Immigration and Labor*. New York: G. P. Putnam's Sons.

Houston, P. (1985) "Impossibility of the Bee", *Open Places* 38/39 (Spring): 209.

Hsi, A. (1972) "Social and economic status of the merchant class of the Ming dynasty: 1368–1644". Unpublished dissertation, Urbana-Champaign: University of Illinois.

Hsing, Y. T. (1997) "Building *Guanxi* across the Straits: Taiwanese Capital and Local Chinese Bureaucrats", in A. Ong and D. Nonini (eds), *Ungrounded Empires. The Cultural Politics of Modern Chinese Transnationalism*. New York: Routledge.

Hsing, Y. T. (1998) *Making Capitalism in China: The Taiwan Connection*. New York: Oxford University Press.

Hsing, Y.-T. (1999) "Trading Companies in Taiwan's Fashion Shoe Networks", *Journal of International Economics* 48 (1, June): 101–20.

Hu, T.-L. (1984) *My Mother-in-Law's Village: Rural Industrializaiton and Change in Taiwan*. Taipei: Institute of Ethnology, Academia Sinica.

Huang, P. C. C. (1980) *The Development of Underdevelopment in China*. Armonk, N.Y.: M. E. Sharpe.

Huang, P. C. C. (1985) *The Peasant Economy and Social Change in North China*. Stanford: Stanford University Press.

Huang, P. C. C. (1990) *The Peasant Family and Rural Development in the Yangzi Delta, 1350–1988*. Stanford: Stanford University Press.

Huang, P. C. C. (1991) "A Reply to Ramon Myers", *Journal of Asian Studies* 50, 3: 629–33.

Huang, R. (1974) *Taxation and Government Finance in Sixteenth-Century Ming China*. Cambridge: Cambridge University Press.

Huang, W. and Xia, L. (comp.) (1984) *Jindai Shanghai diqu fangzhi jingji shiliao xuanji* (The source materials on economic history from the Modern Shanghai gazetteer). Shanghai: Shanghai Renmin Chubanshe.

Huntington, S. P. (1968) *Political Order in Changing Societies*. New Haven: Yale University Press.

Hwang, K. K. (1984) "*Rujia lunli yu qiye zuzhi xingtai* (Confucian theory and types of enterprise organization)", in *Zhongguo shi guanli* (Chinese-style management). Taipei: Gongshang Shibao.

Hwang, K. K. (1987) "Face and favor: The Chinese power game", *American Journal of Sociology,* 92: 944–74.

Ilbo Hankook (1985) *Pal Ship O nyndo hankook ui 50 dae jae bul* (The 50 top chaebol in Korea). Seoul, Korea.

Imai, K.-I. (1988) "The Corporate Network of Japan", *Japanese Economic Studies* 16: 3–37.

Imperial Maritime Customs Reports (1875) *Annual Trade Reports.*

Imperial Maritime Customs Reports (1882–92, 1892–1901) *Decennial reports*, China.

Ingram, J. C. (1955) *Economic Change in Thailand since 1950.* Stanford: Stanford University Press.

Ingram, J. C. (1971) *Economic Change in Thailand, 1850–1970.* Stanford: Stanford University Press.

Isaacs, H. (1951) *The Tragedy of the Chinese Revolution.* Stanford: Stanford University Press.

Jackall, R. (1988) *Moral Mazes, The World of Corporate Managers.* New York: Oxford University Press.

Jackson C. J. (1970) *Readings in the sociology of migration.* London: Pergamon.

Jacobs, J. B. (1979) "A Preliminary Model of Particularistic Ties in Chinese Political Alliance: Kanch'ing and Kuan-hsi in a Rural Taiwanese Township", *China Quarterly* 78: 237–73.

Jacobs, N. (1958) *The Origins of Modern Capitalism and Eastern Asia.* Hong Kong: Hong Kong University Press.

Jai, B. (1986) "*Quanli shishi* (Some Reflections on Power)", *Legein Monthly* 133: 23–32.

Jamann, W. (1994) *Chinese Traders in Singapore: Business Practices and Organizational Dynamics.* Bielefeld Studies on the Sociology of Development. Saarbrucken, Germany: Verlag fur Entwicklungspolitik Breitenbach GmbH.

James, W. (1907) *Pragmatism: A New Name for Some Old Ways of Thinking.* New York: Longmans, Green.

Jamieson, G. (1921) *Chinese Family and Commercial Law.* Shanghai: Kelly and Walsh.

Jansen, K. (1990) *Finance, Growth and Stability: Financing Economic Development in Thailand, 1960–86.* Brookfield, VT: Avebury.

Jernigan, T. (1905) *China in Law and Commerce.* New York: Macmillan.

Jiangsu sheng bowuguan (Jiangsu provincial museum) (1959) *Jiangsu sheng Ming-Qing yilai beike ziliao xuanji* (Selected Ming-Qing epigraphic materials from Jiangsu province). Beijing: Sanlian Shudian.

Johnson, C. (1982) *MITI and the Japanese Miracle.* Stanford: Stanford University Press.

Jones, E. L. (1968) "Agricultural Origins of Industry", *Past and Present* 40: 58–71.

Jones, E. L. (1973) "The Fashion Manipulators: Consumer Tastes and British Industries, 1660–1800", in L. P. Cain and P. J. Uselding (eds), *Business Enterprise and Economic Change.* Ohio: The Kent University Press.

Jones, E. L. (1974) *Agriculture and the Industrial Revolution.* Oxford, Basil Blackwell.

Jones, E. L. (1981) *The European Miracle: Environments, Economies, and Geopolitics in the History of Europe and Asia.* Cambridge: Cambridge University Press.

Jones, E. L. (1988) *Growth Recurring: Economic Change in World History.* Oxford: The Clarendon Press.

Jones, E., Frost, L., and White, C. (1993) *Coming Full Circle: An Economic History of the Pacific Rim.* Boulder, Col.: Westview Press.

Jones, S. M. – see Mann, S.

Jorgensen, J. J., Hafsi, T., and Kiggundu, M. N. (1986) "Towards a Market Imperfections Theory of Organizational Structure in Developing Countries", *Journal of Management Studies* 24, 4: 419–42.

Jung, K. H. (1984) "Trade Channel Evolution between Korea and the United States", in K. Moskowitz (ed.), *From Patron to Partner: The Development of U.S.– Korean Business and Trade Relations.* Lexington, Mass.: Lexington Books.

Ka, C.-M. and Selden, M. (1986) "Original Accumulation, Equity and Late Industrialization: The cases of Socialist China and Capitalist Taiwan", *World Development* 14, 10/11: 1293–1310.

Kahn, H. (1979) *World Economic Development. 1979 and Beyond*. London: Croom Helm.

Kalberg, S. (1980) "Max Weber's Types of Rationality: Cornerstones for the Analysis of Rationalization Processes in His History", *American Journal of Sociology* 85: 1145–79.

Kang, T. W. (1989) *Is Korea the Next Japan? Understanding the Structure, Strategy, and Tactics of American's next Competitor*. New York: The Free Press.

Kantorowicz, E. H. (1957) *The King's Two Bodies: A Study of Mediaeval Political Theology*. Princeton, N.J.: Princeton University Press.

Kao, C. S. (1986) *Rationalization and the Development of Western Capitalism – Max Weber and Beyond,* (in Chinese). Taipei: Lien-Ching.

Kao, C. S. (1999) *Toujia Niang* (The boss's wife). Taipei: Lien Ching.

Kao, C. S. and Hamilton, G. G. (2000) "Reflexive Manufacturing: Taiwan's Integration in the Global Economy", *International Studies Review* 3, 1 (June): 1–19.

Kao, C. S. and Hamilton, G. G. (2006) "The Round Table: A Reconsideration of Chinese Business Networks", in S. L. Wong (ed.), *Paradigms and Perspectives on Hong Kong Studies*. Hong Kong: University of Hong Kong Press.

Kao, C.-S. and Hamilton, G. G. (forthcoming) "Making Money: The Integration of Taiwan's Businesspeople in the Global Economy".

Kao, J. (1993) "The Worldwide Web of Chinese Business", *Harvard Business Review* 93 (March–April): 24–36.

Kenney, M. and Florida, R. (1993) *Beyond Mass Production: The Japanese System and Its Transfer to the U.S.* New York: Oxford University Press.

Kerri, J. N. (1976) "Studying voluntary associations as adaptive mechanisms: A review of anthropological perspectives", *Current Anthropology* 17: 23–47.

Keyes, C. F. (1993) "Buddhist Economics and Buddhist Fundamentalism in Burma and Thailand", in M. E. Marty and R. S. Appleby (eds), *Fundamentalism and the State: Remaking Polities, Economies, and Militance.* Chicago: The University of Chicago Press.

Kim, E. M. (1991) "The Industrial Organization and Growth of the Korean Chaebol: Integrating Development and Organizational Theories", in G. G. Hamilton (ed.), *Business Networks and Economic Development in East and Southeast Asia*. Hong Kong: Centre of Asian Studies, University of Hong Kong.

Kim, E. M. (1997) *Big Business, Strong State: Collusion and Conflict in Korean Development*. Albany, N.Y.: State University of New York Press.

Kim, E. M. (ed.) (1998) *Four Asian Tigers: Economic Development and the Global Political Economy*. New York: Academic Press.

Kim, H. R. (1993) "Divergent Organizational Paths of Industrialization in East Asia", *Asian Perspective* 17: 105–35.

Kim, H. R. (1994) "The State and Economic Organization in a Comparative Perspective. The Organizing Model of the East Asian Political Economy", *Korean Social Science Journal* 20: 91–120.

Kim, H. R. (1998) "Family Capitalism and Corporate Structure in South Korea", *Korea Focus* 6: 55–67.

King, A. Y. C. (1985) "The Individual and Group in Confucianism: A Relational Perspective", in D. Munroe (ed.), *Individual and Holism*. Ann Arbor: Center for Asian Studies, University of Michigan.

King, A. Y. C. (1991) "Kuan-hsi and network building: A sociological interpretation", *Daedalus* 120, 2: 63–84.

King, F. (1965) *Money and Monetary Policy in China, 1845–1895*. Cambridge, Mass.: Harvard University Press.

Kipnis, A. B. (1997) *Producing Guanxi: Sentiment, Self, and Subculture in a North China Village*. Durham, N.C.: Duke University Press.

Kirby, W. C. (1995) "China Unincorporated: Company Law and Business Enterprise in Twentieth-Century China", *The Journal of Asian Studies* 54, 1 (February): 43–63.

Kojima, K. and Ozawa, T. (1984) *Japan's General Trading Companies: Merchants of Economic Development.* Paris: Development Centre of the Organisation for Economic Cooperation and Development.

Kondo, D. K. (1990) *Crafting Selves: Power, Gender, and Discourses of Identity in a Japanese Workplace.* Chicago: Chicago University Press.

Kotenev, A. M. (1925) *Shanghai: Its Mixed Court and Council,* Shanghai: North China Daily News and Herald.

Krugman, P. R. (1991) *Geography and Trade.* Cambridge, Mass.: The MIT Press.

Krugman, P. R. (1994) *Rethinking International Trade.* Cambridge, Mass.: The MIT Press.

Krugman, P. R. (1996) *The Self-Organizing Economy.* Oxford: Blackwell.

Kuo, E. C. Y. (1991) "Ethnicity, Polity, and Economy: A Case Study of the Mandarin Trade and the Chinese Connection", in G. G. Hamilton (ed.), *Business Networks and Economic Development in East and Southeast Asia.* Hong Kong: Centre of Asian Studies, University of Hong Kong.

Kuo, S. W. Y., Ranis, G., and Fei. J. C. H. (1981) *The Taiwan Success Story: Rapid Growth with Improved Distribution in the Republic of China, 1952–1979.* Boulder, Col.: Westview Press.

Kuo, T. Y. and Liu, K. C. (1978) "Self-strengthening: the Pursuit of Western Technology", in *The Cambridge History of China, Late Ch'ing 1800–1911,* Part 1, Volume 10, edited by John K. Fairbank. Cambridge: Cambridge University Press.

Kuwayanna, Y. (1973) *Trade Marks and Symbols.* New York: Van Nostrand Reinhold Company.

Lai, C.-K. and Hamilton, G. G. (1986) "*Jinshi Zhongguo shangbiao yu quanguo dushi shichang* (Trademark and national-urban market in late imperial China)", Proceedings of the Conference on Regional Studies of Modern China. Taipei: Institute of Modern History, Academia Sinica.

Lai, X. (1984) *Jiawanglu* (Selected works of Lai Xinxia). Tianjin: Nankai Daxue Chubanshe.

Lamley, H. J. (1990) "Lineage and Surname Feuds in Southern Fukien and Eastern Kwangtung under the Ch'ing", in K.-C. Liu (ed.), *Orthodoxy in Late Imperial China.* Berkeley: University of California Press.

Landa, J. T. (1994) *Trust, Ethnicity, and Identity: Beyond the New Institutional Economics of Ethnic Trading Networks, Contract Law, and Gift-Exchange.* Ann Arbor: The University of Michigan Press.

Landon, K. P. (1941) *The Chinese in Thailand.* New York: Russell and Russell.

Langlois, R. (2003) "The Vanishing Hand: The Changing Dynamics of Industrial Capitalism", *Industrial and Corporate Change,* 12, 2: 351–85.

Laothamatas, A. (1992) *Business Associations and the New Political Economy of Thailand.* Boulder, Col.: Westview Press.

Lardy, N. R. (2003) "United States–China Ties: Reassessing the Economic Relationship". Testimony before the House Committee on International Relations, U.S. House of Representatives, Washington D.C., 21 October 2003.

Lasek, E. (1983) "Imperialism in China: A Methodological Critique", *Bulletin of Concerned Asian Scholars* 15: 50–64.

Lasserre, P. (1988) "Corporate Strategic Management and the Overseas Chinese Groups", *Asia Pacific Journal of Management* 5, 2: 115–31.

Lauwerier, O. L. J. and Schermer, A. D. (eds) (1987) *The Oriental Challenge: Investigations on Business Opportunities in Thailand.* Singapore: Eburon Delft.

Lazerson, M. H. and Lorenzoni, G. (1999) "The Firms that Feed Industrial Districts: A Return to the Italian Source", *Industrial and Corporate Change* 8, 2: 235–66.

Lazonick, W. (1991) *Business Organization and the Myth of the Market Economy.* Cambridge: Cambridge University Press.

Lazonick, W., Dore, R., De Jong, H. W., and Admiral, P. H. (1997) *The Corporate Triangle: The Structure and Performance of Corporate Systems in a Global Economy.* Oxford: Blackwell.

Lee, S. H. and Song, H. K. (1994) "The Korean Garment Industry: From Authoritarian Patriarchism to Industrial Paternalism", in E. Bonacich, L. Cheng, N. Chinchilla, N. Hamilton, and P. Ong (eds), *Global Production: The Apparel Industry in the Pacific Rim.* Philadelphia: Temple University Press.

Lee, S. Y. (1990) *Money and Finance in the Economic Development of Taiwan.* London: Macmillan.

Lee, Y. K. (1985) "Conglomeration and Business Concentration, The Korean Case", in *Industrial Policies of the Republic of Korea and the Republic of China.* Seoul: Korea Development Institute.

Leeds, A. (1964) "Brazilian Careers and Social Structures", *American Anthropologist* 66: 1321.

Leff, N. (1977) "Capital Markets in the Less Developed Countries: The Group Principle", in R. I. McKinnon (ed.), *Money and Finance in Economic Growth and Development: Essays in Honor of Edward S. Shaw.* New York: Dekker.

Leff, N. (1978) "Industrial Organization and Entrepreneurship in the Developing Countries: The Economic Groups", *Economic Development and Cultural Change* 26, 4: 661–75.

Lei, C. (1984) "Lei Yunshang he ciushenwan", *Gongshang jingji shiliao congkan* 4: 230–4.

Lethbridge, H. J. (1971) "The District Watch Committee: The Chinese Executive Council of Hong Kong", *Journal of the Hong Kong Branch of the Royal Asiatic Society* 11: 116–41.

Levy, B. (1988) "Korean and Taiwanese Firms as International Competitors: The Challenges Ahead", *Columbia Journal of World Business* (Spring): 43–51.

Levy, B. (1991) "Transactions Costs, the Size of Firms, and Industrial Policy: Lessons from a Comparative Case Study of the Footwear Industry in Korea and Taiwan", *Journal of Development Economics* 34: 151–78.

Levy, H. S. (1967) *Chinese Footbinding.* New York: Bell Publishing Co.

Levy, M. (1949) *The Rise of the Modern Chinese Business Class.* New York: Institute of Pacific Relations.

Levy, M. (1953/4) "Contrasting Factors in the Modernization of China and Japan", *Economic Development and Cultural Change* 2: 161–97.

Levy, M. (1972) *Modernization: Latecomers and Survivors.* New York: Basic Books.

Lew, S.-C. and Park, B.-Y. (2000) "Commodity Chains in East Asia and the Development of the Electronics Industry in South Korea", *International Studies Review* 3, 1 (June): 43–58.

Li, C. N. (1967) *The Political History of China, 1840–1928.* Stanford: Stanford University Press.

Li, H. (1980) *Ming Qing yilai Beijing gongshang huiguan beike xuanbian* (Selected Ming-Qing epigraphic materials on Trade Guilds from Beijing). Beijing: Wenwu Chubanshe.

Li, R. P. (1983) *Zhongguo gudai fangzhi shigao* (A draft history of the premodern Chinese textile industry). Hunan: Yuelu Shushe.

Liao, C. H. and Huang, C. C. (1994) "Attitudinal Changes of Farmers in Taiwan", in J. D. Aberbach, D. D., and K. L. Sokoloff (eds), *The Role of the State in Taiwan's Development.* Armonk, N.Y.: M. E. Sharpe.

Light, I. (1972) *Ethnic Enterprise in America,* Berkeley: University of California.

Light, I. and Bonacich, E. (1988) *Immigrant Entrepreneurs: Koreans in Los Angeles, 1965–1982.* Berkeley: University of California Press.

Lim, E. M. (2002) *Big Horses Don't Die: The Chaebol Dominance in the Course of Korean Industrializaiton*. Unpublished dissertation, Department of Sociology, University of Washington.

Lim, H. R.(1998) *Korea's Growth and Industrial Transformation*. New York: St Martin's Press.

Lim, L. Y. C. (1995) "Southeast Asia: Success through International Openness", in Barbara Stallings (ed.), *Global Change, Regional Response: The New International Context of Development*. Cambridge: Cambridge University Press.

Lim, L. Y. C. and Fong, P. E. (1991) *Foreign Direct Investment and Industrialization in Malaysia, Singapore, Taiwan, and Thailand*. Paris: OECD Development Centre.

Lim, L. Y. C. and Gosling, P. (eds) (1983) *The Chinese in Southeast Asia*. Singapore: Maruzen Asia.

Lim, L. and Pang, E. F. (1994) "The Southeast Asian Economies: Resilient Growth and Expanding Linkages", *Southeast Asian Affairs 1994*, Singapore: Institute of South East Asian Studies, 1994, 20–33.

Limlingan, V. S. (1986) *The Overseas Chinese in ASEAN: Business Strategies and Management Practices*. Manila: Vita Development Corporation.

Lin, M. (1985) *Qingmo shehui liuxing xishi yapian yanjiu: gongjimian zhi fenxi* (The study on the fashion of opium consumption in late Qing society: the supply side analysis (1773–1906)). Unpublished PhD dissertation. Taipei: Guoli Taiwan Shifan Daxue (National Taiwan Normal University).

Lin, N. (1995) "Market Socialism and Local Corporatism in Action in Rural China", *Theory and Society* 24: 301–54.

Lin, P. A. (1991) "The Social Sources of Capital Investment in Taiwan's Industrialization", in Gary G. Hamilton (ed.), *Business Networks and Economic Development in East and Southeast Asia*. Hong Kong: Centre of Asian Studies, University of Hong Kong.

Lippit, V. (1980) "The Development of Underdevelopment in China", *Modern China* 4, 3: 251–328.

Little, I. M. D. (1979) "An Economic Reconnaissance", in W. Galenson (ed.), *Economic Growth and Structural Change in Taiwan*. Ithaca, N.Y.: Cornell University Press.

Liu, G. (1982) "*Woguo shangpin guanggao shihua* (History of Chinese commercial advertisement)", *Qiusuo* (Hunan) 2: 64.

Liu, K. C. (1962) *Anglo-American Steamship Rivalry in China, 1862–1874*. Cambridge, Mass.: Harvard University Press.

Liu, K. C. (ed.) (1990) *Orthodoxy in Late Imperial China*. Berkeley: University of California Press.

Liu, P. C., Liu, Y. C., and Wu, H. L. (1993) *The Manufacturing Enterprise and Management in Taiwan*. Discussion Paper No. 9304. Taipei: Institute of Economics, Academia Sinica.

Liu, Y. C. (1979) "*Lun Zhongguo zibenzhuyi mengya de lishi qianti* (On the historical preconditions for the sprouts of capitalism in China)", *Zhongguo shi yanjiu* 2: 32–46.

Liu, Y. C. (1982) *Qingdai qianqi nongye zibenzhuyi mengya chutan* (A preliminary study of the sprouts of capitalism in agriculture in the early Qing period). Fuzhou: Fujian Renmin.

Liu, Z. Q. (1984) "*Wanming chengshi fengshang chuta* (A preliminary study of fashion in late Ming cities)", *Zhongguo wenhua*, Shanghai, Fudan Daxue Chubanshu, 1: 190–208.

Lockridge, K. A. (1985) *A New England Town*. New York: W. W. Norton.

Lofland, J. (1976) *Doing Social Life*. New York: John Wiley.

Lopez, R. S. and Raymond, I. W. (eds) (1955) *Medieval Trade in the Mediterranean World*. New York: Columbia University Press.

Lui, T. L..(1998) "Trust and Chinese Business Behaviour", *Competition and Change: The Journal of Global Business and Political Economy* 3, 3: 335–57.

Ma, L. J. C. (1971) *Commercial Development and Urban Change in Sung China, 960–1279*. Ann Arbor: Department of Geography, University of Michigan.

MacGowan, D. J. (1886) "Chinese Guilds, or Chambers of Commerce and Trade Unions", *Journal of North-China Branch of the Royal Asiatic Society* 21: 133–92.

McKendrick, N., Brewer, J., and Plumb, J. H. (1982) *The Birth of a Consumer Society: The Commercialization of Eighteenth Century England*. Bloomington: Indiana University Press.

Mackie, J. (1992) "Changing Patterns of Chinese Big Business in Southeast Asia", in R. McVey (ed.), *Southeast Asian Capitalists*. Ithaca, N.Y.: Cornell University, Cornell Southeast Asian Program.

McNeil, W. H. (1982) *The Pursuit of Power: Technology, Armed Force, and Society since A.D. 1000*. Chicago: University of Chicago Press.

MacPherson, K. L. and Yearley, C. K. (1987) "The 2½% Margin: Britain's Shanghai Traders and China's Resilience in the Face of Commercial Penetration", *Journal of Oriental Studies* 25, 2: 202–34.

McVey, R. (ed.) (1992) *Southeast Asian Capitalists*. Ithaca: Cornell University Southeast Asia Program.

Maingalam, J. J. and Schwarzweller, H. K. (1970) "Some theoretical guidelines toward a sociology of migration", *International Migration Review* 4: 4–21.

Management Efficiency Research Institute (1985) *Korea's fifty major groups for 1983 and 1984* (in Korean). Seoul: Management Efficiency Research Institute.

Management Efficiency Research Institute (1986) *Financial Analysis of Korea's Fifty Major Groups for 1986* (in Korean). Seoul: Management Efficiency Research Institute.

Mangin, W. (1959) "The role of regional association in the adaptation of rural population in Peru", *Sociologus* 9: 23–55.

Mangin, W. (ed.) (1970) *Peasants in Cities*. Boston: Houghton Mifflin.

Mann, M. (1986) *The Sources of Social Power: A History of Power from the Beginning to A.D. 1760*, vol. 1. Cambridge: Cambridge University Press.

Mann, S. (1972) "Finance in Ningpo: The 'Ch'ien Chuang', 1750–1880", in W. E. Willmott (ed.), *Economic Organization in Chinese Society*. Stanford: Stanford University Press.

Mann, S. (1974) "The Ningpo Pang and Financial Power at Shanghai", in M. Elvin and G. W. Skinner (eds), *The Chinese City Between Two Worlds*. Stanford: Stanford University Press.

Mann, S. (1976) "A Note on Stone Rubbings", *Ch'ing-shih wen-t'i* 3: 76–89.

Mann, S. (1981) "Misunderstanding the Chinese Economy – A Review Article", *The Journal of Asian Studies* 40: 539–57.

Mann, S. (1987) *Local Merchants and the Chinese Bureaucracy, 1750–1950*. Stanford: Stanford University Press.

Marchand, R. (1985) *Advertising the American Dream: Making Way for Modernity, 1920–1940*. Berkeley: University of California Press.

Mark, L. L. (1972) *Taiwanese Lineage Enterprises: A Study of Familial Entrepreneurship*. Unpublished dissertation, University of California, Berkeley.

Marsh, F. (1983) *Japanese Overseas Investment: The New Challenge*. Special Report, No. 142. London: The Economist Intelligence Unit.

Marshall, G. (1982) *In Search of the Spirit of Capitalism*. New York: Columbia University Press.

Marx, K. (1959) *Basic Writings on Politics and Philosophy*. New York: Anchor Books.

Marx, K. (1965 [1857–58]) *Pre-Capitalist Economic Formations*. London: Lawrence and Wishart.

Marx, K. (1967 [1876]) *Capital: A Critique of Political Economy*. New York: International Publishers.

Marx, K. (1968) *Karl Marx on Colonialism and Modernization*, S. Avineri (ed.). Garden City, N.Y.: Doubleday.

Mason, M. G. (1939) *Western Concepts of China and the Chinese, 1840–1876*. New York: Hyperion.

Mazumdar, S. (1998) *Sugar and Society in China: Peasants, Technology, and the World Market*. Cambridge, Mass.: Harvard University Press.

Mead, G. H. (1932) *The Philosophy of the Present*. Chicago: Chicago University Press.

Meinhardt, P. (1971) *Inventions Patents and Trade Marks*. London: Gower Press.

Mennell, S. (1989) *Norbert Elias: Civilization and the Human Self-Image*. Oxford: Basil Blackwell.

Meyer, J. and Hannan, M. (1979) *National Development and the World System*. Chicago: University of Chicago Press.

Meyer, J. and Rowan, B. (1977) "Institutionalized Organizations: Formal Structure as a Myth and Ceremony", *American Journal of Sociology* 83: 340–62.

Meyer, R. D. (1986) "Cigarette Artistry: Packaging Images", *The Free China Review* 36, 2: 13–19; 36, 3: 22–9.

Ming Qing Suzhou gongshangji beike ji (Selected Ming-Qing industrial and commercial epigraphic materials from Suzhou) (1981), Nanjing: Jiangsu Renmin Chubanshe.

Mitchell, J. C. (1969) "The concept and use of social networks", in J. C. Mitchell (ed.), *Social Networks in urban situations*. Manchester: Manchester University Press.

Mitchell, J. C. (1974) "Social networks", in B. J. Siegel *et al.* (eds), *Annual Review of Anthropology*, vol. 3. Palo Alto: Annual Reviews Inc.

Mitchell, K. (1995) "Flexible Circulation in the Pacific Rim: Capitalisms in Cultural Context", *Economic Geography* 71, 4: 364–82.

Mokyr, J. (1977) "Demand vs. Supply in the Industrial Revolution", *Journal of Economic History* 37: 981–1008.

Molloy, S. (1980) "Max Weber and the Religions of China: Any Way out of the Maze?", *The British Journal of Sociology* 31: 377–400.

Moore, B. Jr. (1966) *Social Origins of Dictatorship and Democracy*. Boston: Beacon Press.

Morikawa, H. (1992) *Zaibatsu, The Rise and Fall of Family Enterprise Groups in Japan*. Tokyo: University of Tokyo Press.

Morris, M. D. (1968) "Towards a reinterpretation of nineteenth-century Indian economic history", *The Indian Economic and Social History Review* 5: 1–15.

Morse, H. B. (1908) *The Trade and Administration of the Chinese Empire*. Shanghai: Kelly and Walsh.

Morse, H. B. (1909) *The Gilds of China*. London: Longmans, Green and Co.

Moulder, F. V. (1977) *Japan, China, and the Modern World Economy*. Cambridge: Cambridge University Press.

Murphey. R. (1969) "Traditionalism and colonialism: changing urban roles in Asia", *Journal of Asian Studies* 9: 67–84.

Murphey, R. (1970) *The Treaty Ports and China's Modernization: What Went Wrong?*, Michigan Papers in Chinese Studies. No. 7. Ann Arbor: University of Michigan Center for Chinese Studies.

Murphey, R. (1974) "The Treaty Ports and China's Modernization", in M. Elvin and G. W. Skinner (eds), *The Chinese City between Two Worlds*. Stanford: Stanford University Press.

Myers, R. H. (1970) *The Chinese peasant economy. Agricultural development in Hopei and Shantung, 1890–1949*. Cambridge, Mass.: Harvard University Press.

Myers, R. H. (1974) "Some Issues on Economic Organization during the Ming and Ch'ing Periods: A Review Article", *Ch'ing-shih wen-t'i* 3: 77–97.

Myers, R. H. (1980) *The Chinese Economy, Past and Present*. Belmont, Cal.: Wadsworth.

Myers, R. H. (1984) "The Economic Transformation of the Republic of China on Taiwan", *The China Quarterly* 99: 500–28.

Myers, R. H. (1991) "How Did the Modern Chinese Economy Develop? – A Review Article", *Journal of Asian Studies* 50, 3: 604–28.

Nanjing daxue lishixi Ming-Qingshi hanjiushi (ed.) (1980) *Ming-Qing zibenzhuyimengya yanjiulunwenji* (A collection of essays on the sprout of capitalism in Ming-Qing). Shanghai: Shanghai Renmin Chubanshe.

Nanjing daxue lishixi Zhongguo gudaishi jiaoyanjiushi (Nanjing university history department, Chinese history teaching and research Group) (1960) *Zhongguo zibenzhuyi mengya wenti taolunji, xubian* (Essays on the sprouts of capitalism in China). Beijing: Sanlian Shudian 2.

Narongchai, A., Jansen, K., and Pongpisanupichit, J. (1993) *International Capital Flows and Economic Adjustment in Thailand*. Bangkok: Thailand Development Research Institute, Research Monograph No. 10.

Nathan, A. (1972) "Imperialism's Effects on China", *Bulletin of Concerned Asian Scholars* 4: 3–8.

National Council of Applied Economic Research, New Delhi (1959) *Survey of the Handloom Industry in Karnataka and Sholapur*. Bombay: Asia Publishing House.

Naughton, B. (1996) *Growing Out Of the Plan: Chinese Economic Reform, 1978–1993*. Cambridge: Cambridge University Press.

Naughton, B. (ed.) (1997) *The China Circle: Economics and Technology in the PRC, Taiwan, and Hong Kong*. Washington, D.C.: Brookings Institution Press.

Neale, E. (1862) "Commercial report on British trade at the nine new ports opened to commerce by the treaty of Tientsin", *British Parliamentary Papers*, 1862 (2960) LV111: 374–400.

Nee, V. (1992) "Organizational Dynamics of Market Transition: Hybrid Forms, Property Rights, and Mixed Economy in China", *Administrative Science Quarterly* 37: 1–27.

Nee, V. and Young, F. W. (1991) "Peasant Entrepreneurs in China's 'Second Economy': An Institutional Analysis", *Economic Development and Cultural Change* 39: 293–310.

Needham, J. (1956) *Science and Civilisation in China*, vol. 2. Cambridge: Cambridge University Press.

Needham, J. (1969a) *The Grand Titration*. Toronto: University of Toronto Press.

Needham, J. (1969b) *Within the Four Seas*. London: George Allen & Unwin.

Needham, J. (1970) *Clerks and Craftsmen in China and the West*. Cambridge: Cambridge University Press.

Nelli, H. (1964) "The Italian padrone system in the United States", *Labor History* 5: 153–68.

Nelson, B. (1949) *The Idea of Usury*. Princeton, N.J.: Princeton University Press.

Nelson, B. (1974) "Sciences and Civilizations, East and West", in R. J. Seeger and R. S. Cohen (eds), *Philosophical Foundations of Science*. Boston: D. Reidel.

Nelson, B. (1975) "The Quest for Certitude and the Books of Scripture, Nature, and Conscience", in O. Gingerich (ed.), *The Nature of Scientific Discovery*. Washington, D.C.: Smithsonian Institution Press.

Neville, N. and Bell, H. (1898) *Report of the Mission to China of the Blackburn Chamber of Commerce, 1896–7*. Blackburn: The North-East Lancashire Press.

Niida, N. (1950) "Religious and Regional Bands in Merchant and Craft Guilds in Peking", *Folklore Studies* 9: 179–206.

Nishijima, S. (1984) "The Formation of the Early Chinese Cotton Industry", in L. Grove and C. Daniels (eds), *State and Society in China: Japanese Perspectives on Ming-Qing Social and Economic History*. Tokyo: University of Tokyo Press.

Noble, G. (1987) "Contending Forces in Taiwan's Economic Policymaking", *Asian Survey* 27, 6 (June, 1987), pp 683–704.

North China Herald and Supreme Court and Consular Gazette (Various years), Shanghai.

North, D. C. (1990) *Institutions, Institutional Change and Economic Performance*. Cambridge: Cambridge University Press.

North, D. C. and Thomas, R. P. (1973) *The Rise of the Western World: A New Economic History*. Cambridge: Cambridge University Press.

Numazaki, I. (1986) "Networks of Taiwanese Big Business", *Modern China* 12: 487–534.

Numazaki, I. (1991a) *Networks and Partnerships: The Social Organization of The Chinese Business Elite in Taiwan*. Unpublished dissertation, Michigan State University.

Numazaki, I. (1991b) "The Role of Personal Networks in the Making of Taiwan's Guanxiqiye (Related Enterprises)", in G. G. Hamilton (ed.), *Business Networks and Economic Development in East and Southeast Asia*. Hong Kong: Centre of Asian Studies, University of Hong Kong.

Numazaki, I. (1993) "The Tainanbang: The Rise and Growth of a Banana-Bunch-Shaped Business Group in Taiwan", *The Developing Economies* 31, 4: 485–510.

Numazaki, I. (1997) "The Laoban-led Development of Business Enterprises in Taiwan: An Analysis of the Chinese Entrepreneurship", *The Developing Economies* 35, 4 (December): 440–57.

Oakes, G. (1977) "The Verstehen Thesis and the Foundations of Max Weber's Methodology", *History and Theory* 16: 11–29.

Oakes, G. (1988) *Weber and Rickert: Concept Formation in the Cultural Sciences*. Cambridge, Mass.: The MIT Press.

Office of the Prime Minister (1990) *National Income of Thailand*, 1990 edn. Bangkok: Office of the Prime Minister.

Okumura, H. (1982) "Interfirm Relations in an Enterprise Group", *Japanese Economic Studies* 10: 53–82.

Okumura, H. (1991) "Intercorporate Relations in Japan", in G. G. Hamilton (ed.), *Business Networks and Economic Development in East and Southeast Asia*. Hong Kong: Centre of Asian Studies, University of Hong Kong.

Omohundro, J. T. (1973) "Chinese merchant society in the Philippines", *Philippine Sociological Review* 21: 169–85.

Omohundro, J. T. (1981) *Chinese Merchant Families in Illoilo*. Athens, OH: The Ohio University Press.

Omohundro, J. T. (1983) "Social Networks and Business Success for the Philippine Chinese", in L. Lim and P. Gosling (eds), *The Chinese in Southeast Asia*. Singapore: Maruzen Asia.

O'Neil, J. (1986) "The Disciplinary Society: From Weber to Foucault", *British Journal of Sociology* 37, 1: 42–60.

Ong, A. and Nonini, D. (1997) *The Cultural Politics of Modern Chinese Transnationalism*. London: Routledge.

Orlove, B. S. (1974) "Reciprocidad, desigualdld y dominacion", in G. Alberti and E. Mayer (eds), *Reciprocidad e Intercambio en los Andes Pemanos*. Lima: IEP Edicions.

Orlove, B. S. (1986) "Barter and Cash Sale on Lake Titicaca: A Test of Competing Approaches", *Current Anthropology* 27, 2.

Orrù, M. (1991) "Practical and Theoretical Aspects of Japanese Business Networks", in G. G. Hamilton (ed.), *Business Networks and Economic Develop-*

ment in East and Southeast Asia. Hong Kong: Centre of Asian Studies, University of Hong Kong.

Orrù, M., Biggart, N. W., and Hamilton, G. G. (1991) "Organizational Isomorphism in East Asia", in W. Powell and P. DiMaggio (eds), *The New Institutionalism in Organizational Analysis*. Chicago: Chicago University Press.

Orrù, M., Biggart, N. W., and Hamilton, G. G. (1997) *The Economic Organization of East Asian Capitalism*. Thousand Oaks, Cal.: Sage.

Orrù, M., Hamilton, G. G., and Suzuki, M. (1989) "Patterns of Inter-Firm Control in Japanese Business", *Organization Studies* 10, 4: 549–74.

Otte, F. (1928) "The Evolution of Bookkeeping and Accounting in China", *Annalen der Betriebswirtschaft* 2: 166–80.

Owens, R. and Nandy, A. (1975) "Organizational growth and organizational participation: Voluntary associations in a West Bengal city", *Contributions to Indian Sociology* 9: 19–53.

Pack, Howard. (1992) "New Perspectives on Industrial Growth in Taiwan", in G. Ranis (ed.), *Taiwan, From Developing to Mature Economy*. Boulder, Col.: Westview Press.

Paige, J. (1974) "Kinship and polity in stateless societies", *American Journal of Sociology* 80: 301–20.

Pan, L. (1990) *Sons of the Yellow Emperor: A History of the Chinese Diaspora*. Boston: Little Brown.

Pan, R. (1758) *Dijing suishi jisheng*, (reprint). Beijing: Beijing Guji Chubanshe.

Parsons, T. (1949) *The Structure of Social Action*. Glencoe, Ill.: The Free Press.

Parsons, T. (1977) *The Evolution of Societies*. Englewood Cliffs, N.J.: Prentice-Hall.

Parsons, T. and Smelser, N. (1956) *Economy and Society: A study in the Integration of Economics and Social Theory*. London: Routledge and Kegan Paul.

Pempel, T. J. (1999) "The Developmental Regime in a Changing World Economy", in M. W. Cummings (ed.), *The Developmental State*. Ithaca, N.Y.: Cornell University Press.

Peng, H. J. (1989) *Taiwan qiye yezhu de "guanxi" jiqi zhuanbian, yige shehuixue de fenxi* (Relationships among Taiwan business owners and their changes: A sociological analysis). Unpublished dissertation, Tunghai University.

Peng, Z. (1983) *"Qingdai qianqi shougongyi de fazhan* (The development of handicraft industry in early Qing period)", in Nanjing daxue lishixi Ming-Qingshi hanjiushi (ed.), *Ming-Qing zibenzhuyimengya yanjiu lunwen ji* (A collection of essays on the sprout of capitalism in Ming-Qing). Nanjing: Jiangsu Renmin.

Perkins, D. H. (1969) *Agricultural Development in China, 1368–1968*. Chicago: Aldine.

Perkins, D. H. (ed.) (1975) *China's Modern Economy in Historical Perspective*. Stanford: Stanford University Press.

Perrow, C. (2002) *Organizing America: Wealth, Power, and the Origins of Corporate Capitalism*. Princeton, N.J.: Princeton University Press.

Perry, E. J. and Wong, C. (1985) *The Political Economy of Reform in Post-Mao China*. Cambridge, Mass.: Harvard University, Council on East Asian Studies.

Petrovic, M. and Hamilton, G. G. (2006) "Making Global Markets: Wal-Mart and Its Suppliers", in N. Lichtenstein (ed.), *Wal-Mart: Template for 21st Century Capitalism*. New York: The New Press.

Pilditch, J. (1970) *Communication by Design: A Study in Corporate Identity*. London: McGraw-Hill.

Piore, M. J., and Sabel, C. F. (1984) *The Second Industrial Divide: Possibilities for Prosperity*. New York: Basic Books.

Pirenne, H. (1937) *Economic and Social History of Medieval Europe*. New York: Harcourt, Brace and World.

Platt, D. C. M. (1973) "Further objections to an 'Imperialism of free trade', 1830–60", *The Economic History Review* 26: 77–91.

Plumer, C. (1971) *Africa Textiles, an Outline of Handcrafted Sub-Saharan Fabrics*. East Lansing: Michigan State University, African Studies Center.

Poggi, G. (1978) *The Development of the Modern State*. Stanford: Stanford University Press.

Poggi, G. (1983) *Calvinism and the Capitalist Spirit, Max Weber's Protestant Ethic*. Amherst: The University of Massachusetts Press.

Polanyi, K. (1957 [1944]) *The Great Transformation*. Boston: Beacon Press.

Polanyi, K., Arensberg, C. M., and Pearson, H. W. (eds) (1957) *Trade and Market in the Early Empire*. Chicago: Henry Regnery.

Pomeranz, K. (2000) *The Great Divergence: Europe, China, and the Making of the Modern World Economy*. Princeton, N.J.: Princeton University Press.

Popper, K. (1964) *The Poverty of Historicism*. New York: Harper Torchbooks.

Porter, M. E. (1990) *The Competitive Advantage of Nations*. New York: The Free Press.

Portes, A. and Walton, J. (1981) *Labor, Class, and the International System*. New York: Academic Press.

Powell, W. W. and DiMaggio, P. (eds) (1991) *The New Institutional in Organizational Analysis*. Chicago: Chicago University Press.

Pratt, E. E. (1999) *Japan's Protoindustrial Elite: The Economic Foundations of the Gono*. Cambridge, Mass.: Harvard University Press.

Prechel, H. (2000) *Big Business and the State: Historical Transitions and Corporate Transformation, 1880s–1990s*. Albany: State University of New York Press.

Prestowitz, C. (1988) *Trading Places: How We Allowed Japan to Take the Lead*. New York: Basic Books.

Primov, G. (1974) "Aymara-Quechua relations in Puno", *International Journal of Comparative Sociology* 15: 167–81.

Purcell, V. (1965) *The Chinese in Southeast Asia*, 2nd edn. London: Oxford University Press.

Qian, Y. (1979) *Luyuan conghua* (reprint). Beijing: Zhonghua Shuju.

Quanguo Mingte chanpin (Famous native products in China) (1982) Shanxi: Shanxi Renmin Chubanshe.

Rauch, J. E. (1999) "Networks versus Markets in International Trade", *Journal of International Economics* 48, 1 (June): 7–36.

Rauch, J. E. (2001a) "Business and Social Networks in International Trade", *Journal of Economic Literature,* 39, December, 1177–203.

Rauch, J. E. (2001b) "Black Ties Only? Ethnic Business Networks, Intermediaries, and African American Retail Entrepreneurship", in Alessandra Casella and James E. Rauch (eds), *Networks and Markets*. New York: Russell Sage.

Rawski, E. S. (1972) *Agricultural Change and the Peasant Economy of South China*. Cambridge, Mass.: Harvard University Press.

Rawski, E. S. (1991) "Research Themes in Ming-Qing Socioeconomic History – The State of the Field", *Journal of Asian Studies* 50, 1 (February): 84–111.

Rawski, T. G. (1989) *Economic Growth in Prewar China*. Berkeley: University of California Press.

Raychaudhuri, T. (1968) "A re-interpretation of nineteenth-century Indian economic history?", *The Indian Economic and Social History Review* 5: 77–100.

Reardon, T. C., Timmer, P., Barrett, C. B., and Berdeguc. J. (2003) "The Rise of Supermarkets in Africa, Asia, and Latin America", *American Journal of Agricultural Economics* 85 (5).

Redding, G. (1990) *The Spirit of Chinese Capitalism*. Berlin: Walter de Gruyter.

Redding, G. (1991) "Weak Organizations and Strong Linkages: Managerial Ideology and Chinese Family Business Networks", in G. G. Hamilton (ed.), *Business Networks and Economic Development in East and Southeast Asia*. Hong Kong: Centre of Asian Studies, University of Hong Kong.

Redding, S. C. (1980) "Cognition As an Aspect of Culture and Its Relation to Management Processes: An Exploratory View of the Chinese Case", *Journal of Management Studies* 17: 127–48.

Redding, S. G. and Pugh, D. S. (1986) "The Formal and the Informal: Japanese and Chinese Organizational Structures", in S. R. Clegg, D. C. Dunphy, and S. G. Redding (eds), *The Enterprise and Management in East Asia*. Hong Kong: Centre of Asian Studies, University of Hong Kong.

Redding, S. G. and Simon, T. (1986) "Network and Molecular Organizations: An Exploratory View of Chinese Firms in Hong Kong", in K. C. Mun and T. S. Chan (eds), *Proceedings of the Inaugural Meeting of the Southeast Asia Region Academy of International Business*. Hong Kong: The Chinese University of Hong Kong Press.

Redding, S. G. and Wong, G. (1986) "The Psychology of Chinese Organizational Behaviour", in M. Bond (ed.), *The Psychology of Chinese People*. Hong Kong: Oxford University Press.

Regan, K. (1999) "The Retail Industry – Trends in the Next Century", in D. DiNapoli (ed.), *Workouts and Turnarounds II: Global Restructuring Strategies for the Next Century.* New York: Wiley.

Reich, R. B. (1992) *The Work of Nations*. New York: Vintage Books.

Remer, C. F. (1933) *Foreign Investments in China*. New York: Macmillan.

Republic of China (1983) *Report on Industrial and Commerical Surveys, Taiwan Area*. Taipei: Directorate-General of Budget, Accounting and Statistics.

Republic of China (1985) *Input–Output Tables, Taiwan Area*. Taipei: Directorate-General of Budget, Accounting and Statistics.

Republic of China (1986) *Yearbook of Labor Statistics*. Taipei: Directorate-General of Budget, Accounting and Statistics.

Republic of China (1987) *Taiwan Statistical Data Book, 1987*. Taipei: Council of Economic Planning and Development.

Reynolds, B. L. (1974) "Weft: the technological sanctuary of Chinese handspun yarn", *Ch'ing-shih wen t'i* 3:1–19.

Rhee, Y. W, Ross-Larson, B., and Pursell, G. (1984) *Korea's Competitive Edge: Managing the Entry into World Markets*. Baltimore: The Johns Hopkins University Press.

Rhoads, E. J. (1974) "Merchant Associations in Canton, 1895–1911", in M. Elvin and G. W. Skinner (eds), *The Chinese City between Two Worlds*. Stanford: Stanford University Press.

Riggs, F. (1967) *Thailand, The Modernization of a Bureaucratic Polity*. Honolulu: East-West Centre Press.

Ringer, F. (1997) *Max Weber's Methodology: The Unification of the Cultural and Social Sciences*. Cambridge, Mass.: Harvard University Press.

Robinson, D., Byeon, Y., and Teja, R., with Tseng, W. (1991) *Thailand: Adjusting to Success, Current Policy Issues*. Washington D.C.: International Monetary Fund.

Rosenbaum, A. L. (ed.) (1992) *State and Society in China: The Consequences of Reform*. Boulder, Col.: Westview Press.

Roth, G. (1978) "Introduction", in Max Weber, *Economy and Society*. Berkeley: University of California Press.

Roth, G. and Schluchter, W. (1979) *Max Weber's Vision of History*. Berkeley: University of California Press.

Rowe, W. T. (1984) *Hankow: Commerce and Society in a Chinese City: 1796–1889*. Stanford: Stanford University Press.

Rowe, W. T. (1985) "Approaches to Modern Chinese Social History", in O. Zunz (ed.), *Reliving the Past: The Worlds of Social History*. Chapel Hill: The University of North Carolina Press.

Rowe, W. T. (1989) *Hankow: Conflict and Community in a Chinese City, 1796–1895*. Stanford: Stanford University Press.

Roxman, G. (ed.) (1981) *The Modernization of China*. London: The Free Press.

Roy, W. G. (1997) *Socializing Capital: The Rise of the Large Industrial Corporation in America*. Princeton, N.J.: Princeton University Press.

Rozman, G. (1973) *Urban netuorks in Ch'ing China and Tokugaua Japan*. Princeton, N.J.: Princeton University Press.

Sabel, C. and Zeitlin, J. (1985) "Historical Alternatives to Mass Production: Politics, Markets and Technology in Nineteenth Century Industrialization", *Past and Present* 108: 133–76.

Sabloff, J. A. and Lamberg-Karlovsky, C. C. (eds) (1975) *Ancient Civilization and Trade*. Albuquerque: University of New Mexico Press.

Said, E. S. (1978) *Orientalism*. New York: Random House.

Samuels, R. J. (1987) *The Business of the Japanese State*. Ithaca, N.Y.: Cornell University Press.

Sarasin, V. (1977) *Tribute and Profit: Sino–Siamese Trade 1652–1853*. Cambridge, Mass.: Council on East Asian Studies, Harvard University.

Saxenian, A. (1994) *Regional Advantage: Culture and Competition in Silicon Valley and Route 128*. Cambridge, Mass.: Harvard University Press.

Saxenian, A. (1998) "Silicon Valley's New Immigrant Entrepreneurs and their Asian Networks". Paper presented at the International Conference on Business Transformation and Social Change in East Asia, 22–23 May, Tunghai University, Taiwan.

Saxenian, A. (1999) *Silicon Valley's New Immigrant Entrepreneurs*. San Francisco: Public Policy Institute of California.

Schafer, E. H. (1963) *The Golden Peaches of Samarkand*. Berkeley: University of California Press.

Schechter, F. I. (1925) *The Historical Foundations of the Law Relating to Trademarks*. New York: Columbia University Press.

Scherer, F. M. (1970) *Industrial Market Structure and Economic Performance*. Chicago, Rand McNally.

Scherer, R. M. and Ross, D. (1990) *Industrial market structure and economic performance*, 3rd edn. Boston: Houghton Mifflin.

Schluchter, W. (1981) *The Rise of Western Rationalism: Max Weber's Developmental History*. Berkeley: University of California Press.

Schluchter, W. (1983) *Max Webers Studie über Konfuzianismus und Taoismus: Interpretation und Kritik*. Frankfurt: Suhrkamp.

Schluchter, W. (1989) *Rationalism, Religion, and Domination*, trans. Neil Solomon. Berkeley: University of California Press.

Schmalensee, R. and Willig, R. D. (eds) (1989) *Handbook of industrial organization*, 2 vols. Amsterdam: North-Holland.

Schram, S. R. (ed.) (1985) *The Scope of State Power in China*. Hong Kong: Chinese University of Hong Kong Press.

Schwartz, B. I. (1985) *The World of Thought in Ancient China*. Cambridge, Mass.: Harvard University Press.

Scitovsky, A. T. (1985) "Economic Development in Taiwan and South Korea: 1965–1981", *Food Research Institute Studies* 19, 3: 215–64.

Scott, J. C. (1972) "The erosion of patron–client bonds and social change in rural Southeast Asia", *Journal of Asian Studies* 32: 5–37.

Scott, J. (1991) "Networks of corporate power: A comparative assessment", *Annual Review of Sociology* 17: 181–203.

Scott, W. R. and Meyer, J. (1994) *Institutional Environments and Organizations: Sturctural Complexity and Individualism*. Thousand Oaks, CA: Sage.

Seagrave, S. (1995) *Lords of the Rim: The Invisible Empire of the Overseas Chinese.* New York: G. P. Putnam's Sons.

Semkow, B. W. (1994) *Taiwan's Capital Market Reform: The Financial and Legal Issues.* Oxford: Oxford University Press.

Sender, H. (1991) "Inside the Overseas Chinese Network", *Institutional Investor,* August: 30: 29–43.

Sewell, W. H. Jr. (1967) "Marc Bloch and the Logic of Comparative History", *History and Theory* 6: 208–18.

Shafer, M. (1997) "The Political Economy of Sectors and Sectoral Change: Korea Then and Now", in S. Maxfield and B. R. Schneider (eds), *Business and the State in Developing Countries.* Ithaca, N.Y.: Cornell University Press.

Shanghai beike ziliao xuanji (Selected epigraphic materials from Shanghai) (1980) Shanghai: Shanghai Renmin Chubanshe.

Sharlene, J. (1981) *The Sociology of Georg Simmel.* New York: Free Press.

Sheard, P. (1986) "Main Banks and Internal Capital Markets in Japan", *Shoken Keizai* 157: 255–85.

Sheldon, C. D. (1958) *The Rise of the Merchant Class in Tokugawa Japan, 1600–1868.* Locust Valley, N.Y.: J. J. Augustin.

Shen, G. (1983) *Shangbiaofa qiantan* (The introduction of the trademark law). Falu Chubanshe.

Shiba, Y. (1970) *Commerce and Society in Sung China.* Ann Arbor: University of Michigan, Center for Chinese Studies.

Shibusawa, K. (ed.) (1958) *Japanese Life and Culture in the Meiji Era*, vol. 5. Tokyo: Toyo Bunko.

Shieh, G. S. (1992) *"Boss" Island: The Subcontracting Network and Micro-Entrepreneurship in Taiwan's Development.* New York: Peter Lang.

Shigeshi, K. (1953) *Shina keizaioshi kosho* (Studies in Chinese Economic History). Tokyo: Toyo Bunko.

Simmel, G. (1950) *The Sociology of Georg Simmel.* Glencoe, Ill.: The Free Press.

Siu, P. (1952) "The Sojourner", *American Journal of Sociology* 56 (July), 34–44.

Skeldon, R. (1977) "Regional associations: A note on opposed interpretations", *Comparative Studies in Society and History* 19: 506–10.

Skinner, G. W. (1957) *Chinese Society in Thailand.* Ithaca, N.Y.: Cornell University Press.

Skinner, G. W. (1958) *Leadership and Community in the Chinese Community of Thailand.* Ithaca, N.Y.: Cornell University Press.

Skinner, G. W. (1964–5) "Marketing and Social Structure in Rural China", *Journal of Asian Studies* 24: 3–43, 195–228, 363–99.

Skinner, G. W. (1968) "Overseas Chinese Leadership: Paradigm for a Paradox", in G. Wijeyewardene (ed.), *Leadership and Authority: A Symposium.* Singapore: University of Malaya Press.

Skinner, G. W. (1971) "Chinese peasants and the closed community: An open and shut case", *Comparative Studies in Society and History* 13: 270–81.

Skinner, G. W. (1976) "Mobility Strategies in Late Imperial China: A Regional Systems Analysis", in C. A. Smith (ed.), *Regional Analysis,* vol. 1. New York: Academic Press.

Skinner, G. W. (ed.) (1977) *The City in Late Imperial China.* Stanford: Stanford University Press.

Skinner, G. W. (1985) "Presidential Address: The Structure of Chinese History", *Journal of Asian Studies* 462: 271–92.

Sklair, L. (ed.) (1994) *Capitalism and Development.* London: Routledge.

Skocpol, T. (1979) *States and Social Revolutions.* Cambridge: Cambridge University Press.

Skocpol, T. (1985) "Bringing the State Back In: Strategies of Analysis in Current Research", in P. B. Evans, D. Rueschemeyer, and T. Skocpol (eds), *Bringing the State Back In*. Cambridge: Cambridge University Press.

Smelser, N. (1959) *Social Change in the Industrial Revolution*. Chicago: The University of Chicago Press.

Smelser, N. (1963) "Mechanism of Change and Adjustment of Changes", in W. E. Moore and B. F. Hoselitz (eds), *Industrialization and Society*. UNESCO: Mouton.

Smelser, N. (1976) *The Sociology of Economic Life*. Englewood Cliffs, N.J.: Prentice-Hall.

Smith, A. (1991 [1776]) *The Wealth of Nations*. New York: Knopf.

Smith, C. T. (1971) "The Emergence of a Chinese Elite in Hong Kong", *Journal of the Hong Kong Branch of the Royal Asiatic Society* 11: 74–115.

Smith, T. (1959) *The Agrarian Origins of Modern Japan*. Stanford: Stanford University Press.

Solinger, D. J. (1984) *Chinese Business under Socialism*. Berkeley: University of California Press.

Sompop, M. and Suwanjindar, S. (1992) "Contract Farming and Outgrower Schemes in Thailand", in D. Glover and L. T. Ghee (eds), *Contract Farming in Southeast Asia*. Kuala Lumpur: Institute for Advanced Studies, University of Malaya.

Somsak, T. and Chirathivat, S. (1990) "Mangement of Thailand's International Economic and Trade Relations", in S. Prasith-rathsint (ed.), *Thailand on the Move: Stumbling Blocks and Breakthroughs*. Bangkok: Thai University Research Association.

Song, R. (comp.) (1817) *Songjiangfuzhi* (reprint). Taiwan: Chengwen Chubanshe.

Soulard, F. (1997) *The Restructuring of Hong Kong Industries and the Urbanization of Zhujian Delta, 1979–1989*. Hong Kong: Chinese University of Hong Kong.

Speare, A. Jr. (1992) "Taiwan's Rural Populace: Brought in or Left out of the Economic Miracle?", in D. F. Simon and M. Y. M. Kau (eds), *Taiwan: Beyond the Economic Miracle*. Armonk, N.Y.: M. E. Sharpe.

Spence, J. (1975) "Opium Smoking in Qing China", in F. Wakeman Jr. and C. Grant (eds), *Conflict and Control in Late Imperial China*. Berkeley: University of California Press.

Spulber, D. F. (1996) "Market Microstructure and Intermediation", *Journal of Economic Perspectives* 10, 3 (Summer): 135–52.

Spulber, D. F. (1998) *Market Microstructure: Intermediaries and the Theory of the Firm*. Cambridge: Cambridge University Press.

Sricharatchanya, P. (1988) "Not Just Chicken Feed: Thai Agribusiness Multinational Grows by Leaps and Bounds", *Far Eastern Economic Review* 3 March.

Stallings, B. (ed.) (1995) *Global Change, Regional Response: The New International Context of Development*. Cambridge: Cambridge University Press.

Stephenson, G. M. (1964) *A History of American Immigration, 1820–1924*. New York: Russell and Russell.

Stiglitz, J. E. and Yusuf, S. (eds) (2001) *Rethinking the East Asian Miracle*. New York: Oxford University Press.

Storper, M. and Salais, R. (1997) *Worlds of Production: The Action Frameworks of the Economy*. Cambridge, Mass.: Harvard University Press.

Strauss, A. (1991) "Mead's Multiple Conceptions of Time and Evolution: Their Contexts and Their Consequences for Theory", *International Sociology* 6, 4 (December): 411–26.

Strayer, J. R. (1970) *On the Medieval Origins of the Modern State*. Princeton, N.J.: Princeton University Press.

Sudarkasa, N. (1974–75) "Commercial migration in West Africa", *African Urban Notes* 1: 61–103.

Suehiro, A. (1989) *Capital Accumulation in Thailand, 1855–1985*. Tokyo: Centre for East Asian Cultural Studies.

Swedberg, R, (1998) *Max Weber's Economic Sociology*. Princeton, N.J.: Princeton University Press.

Swedberg, R. (2003) *Principles of Economic Sociology*. Princeton, N.J.: Princeton University Press.

Tai, H.-C. (1989) *Confucianism and Economic Development: An Oriental Alternative?* Washington, D.C.: Washington Institute Press.

Tanaka, Y., Mori, M., and Mori, Y. (1992) "Overseas Chinese Business Community in Asia: Present Conditions and Future Prospects", *Pacific Rim Business and Industries* 2: 2–24.

Taub, R. P. (1974) *American Society in Tocqueville's Time and Today*. Chicago: Rand McNally.

Taylor, R. (1989) "Chinese Hierarchy in Comparative Perspective", *Journal of Asian Studies* 48, 3: 490–511.

Tejapira, K. (1997) "Imagined Uncommunity: The *Lookjin* Middle Class and Thai Official Nationalism", in D. Chirot and A. Reid (eds), *Essential Outsiders: Chinese and Jews in the Modern Transformation of Southeast Asia and Central Europe*. Seattle: University of Washington Press.

The Chinese Economic Monthly (1925) "Unwritten Code of Chinese Commercial Law", 2, 9(June): 1–3.

Thomas, G., Meyer, J., Ramirez, F., and Boli, J. (eds) (1987) *Institutional Structure: Constituting State, Society, and the Individual*. Newbury Park, CA: Sage.

Thompson, E. P. (1963) *The Making of the English Working Class*. New York: Vintage Books.

Tien, J.-K. (1953) *The Chinese of Sarawak: A Study of Social Structure*. London: London School of Economics Monographs on Social Anthropology, 12.

Tilly, C. (ed.) (1975) *The Formation of National States in Western Europe*. Princeton, N.J.: Princeton University Press.

Tilly, C. (1992) *Coercion, Capital, and European States, AD 990–1992*. Cambridge, Mass.: Blackwell Publishers.

Tomasi, S. (1975) *Piety and power*. New York: Center for Migration Studies.

Tong, C. K. (1991) "Centripetal Authority, Differentiated Networks: The Social Organization of Chinese Firms in Singapore", in G. G. Hamilton (ed.), *Business Networks and Economic Development in East and Southeast Asia*. Hong Kong: Centre of Asian Studies, University of Hong Kong.

Tou, J. L. (1942) *Tongxiang zuzhi zhi yanjiu* (Research on Native Place Association). Chongqing: Zhengzhong Shuchu.

Truzzi, M. (ed.) (1974) *Verstehen*. Reading, Mass.: Addison-Wesley.

Tsurumi, Y. (1984) *Sogoshosha: Engines of Export-Based Growth*. Montreal: The Institute for Research on Public Policy.

Tu, W. M. (1984) "*Gongye dongya yu rujia jingshen* (Industrial East Asia and the spirit of capitalism)", *Tianxia zazhi* 41: 124–37.

Tu, W. M., Hejtmanek, M., and Wachman, A. (eds) (1991) *The Confucian World Observed, A Contemporary Disucssion of Confucian Humanism in East Asia*. Hawaii: The East-West Center.

Turner, B. S. (1981) *Weber and Islam: A Critical Study*. London: Routledge and Kegan Paul.

Turner, M. (1996) "Hong Kong Design and the Roots of Sino-American Trade Disputes", *The Annals of the American Academy* 547 (September): 37–53.

Twitchett, D. S. (1963) *Financial Administration under the T'ang Dynasty*. Cambridge: Cambridge University Press.

Twitchett, D. S. (1966) "The T'ang Market System", *Asia Major* (n.s.) 12: 202–48.

Twitchett, D. S. (1968) "Merchant, Trade, and Government in Late T'ang", *Asia Major* 14: 63–95.

United States Department of State (1879) *Despatches from the United States Consul in Shanghai*. Copy No. 706.

Vallas, S. P. (1999) "Rethinking Post Fordism: The Meaning of Workplace Flexibility", *Sociological Theory* 17, 1 (March): 68–101.

van der Sprenkel, O. (1963) "Max Weber on China", *History and Theory* 3: 348–70.

van der Sprenkel, S. (1962) *Legal Institutions in Manshu China*. London: The Athlone Press.

van der Sprenkel, S. (1977) "Urban Social Control", in G. W. Skinner (ed.), *The City in Late Imperial China*. Stanford: Stanford University Press.

Veblen, T. (1953) *The Theory of the Leisure Class*. New York: Mentor Books.

Vogel, E. F. (1989) *One Step Ahead in China: Guangdong under Reform*. Cambridge, Mass.: Harvard University Press.

Von Laue, T. H. (1961) "Imperial Russia at the turn of the century: the cultural slope and the revolution from without", *Comparative Studies in Society and History* 3: 353–67.

Wade, R. (1990) *Governing the Market: Economic Theory and the Role of Government in East Asian Industrialization*. Princeton, N.J.: Princeton University Press.

Wakeman, F. Jr. (1975) *The Fall of Imperial China*. New York: The Free Press.

Walder, A. G. (1986) *Communist Neo-Traditionalism: Work and Authority in Chinese Industry*. Berkeley: University of California Press.

Walder, A. G. (1995) "Local Governments as Industrial Firms: An Organizational Analysis of China's Transitional Economy", *American Journal of Sociology* 101: 263–301.

Waldinger, R., Aldrich, H., and Ward, R. (1990) *Ethnic Entrepreneurs: Immigrant Business in Industrial Societies*. Newbury Park, CA: Sage Publications.

Wallerstein, I. (1974) *The Modern World-System. Capitalist Agriculture and the Origins of the European World Economy in the Sixteenth Century*. New York: Academic Press.

Wallerstein, I. (1984) *The Politics of the World-Economy*. Cambridge: Cambridge University Press.

Wallerstein, I. (1991a) *Unthinking Social Science*. Cambridge: Polity Press.

Wallerstein, I. (1991b) *Geopolitics and Geoculture*. Cambridge: Cambridge University Press.

Wang, G. (1991) *China and the Chinese Overseas*. Singapore: Times Academic Press.

Wang, G. (1999) "Chineseness: The Dilemmas of Place and Practice", in G. G. Hamilton (ed.), *Cosmopolitan Capitalists: Hong Kong and the Chinese Diaspora at the End of the Twentieth Century*. Seattle: University of Washington Press.

Wank, D. L. (1999) *Commoditizing Communism: Markets, Power, and Ideology in Southeast China*. Cambridge: Cambridge University Press.

Ward, B. (1972) "A Small Factory in Hong Kong: Some Aspects of Its Internal Organization", in W. E. Willmott (ed.), *Economic Organization in Chinese Society*. Stanford, CA: Stanford University Press.

Watson, J. L. (1975) *Emigration and the Chinese Lineage*. Berkeley: University of California Press.

Weber, M. (1946) *From Max Weber: Essays in Sociology*, trans., ed., and with an introduction by H. H. Gerth and C. W. Mills. New York: Oxford University Press.

Weber, M. (1949 [1905]) *The Methodology of the Social Science*, trans. and ed. E. Shils and H. Finch. Glencoe, Ill.: Free Press.

Weber, M. (1951 [1915]) *The Religion of China*, trans. and ed. H. Gerth. Glencoe, Ill.: Free Press.

Weber, M. ([1904–5] 1958) *The Protestant Ethic and the Spirit of Capitalism*, trans. T. Parsons. New York: Charles Scribner's Sons.

Weber, M. (1958 [1921]) *The Rational and Social Foundations of Music*, trans. D. Martindale, J. Riedel, and G. Neuwirth. Carbondale, Ill.: Southern Illinois University Press.

Weber, M. (1961 [1923]) *General Economic History*, trans. F. Knight. New York: Collier.

Weber, M. (1978 [1922]) *Economy and Society*, trans. and ed. G. Roth and C. Wittich. 3 vols. Berkeley: University of California Press.

Weber, M. (1988 [1909]) *The Agrarian Sociology of Ancient Civilizations*, trans. R. I. Frank. London: Verso.

Weinstein, J. (1968) *The Corporate Ideal in the Liberal State, 1900–1918*. Boston: Beacon Press.

Westney, D. E. (1987) *Imitation and Innovation: The Transfer of Western Organizational Patterns to Meiji Japan*. Cambridge, Mass.: Harvard University Press.

Westney, D. E. (1996) "The Japanese Business System: Key Features and Prospects for Change", *Journal of Asian Business* 12, 1: 21–50.

Whimster, S. and Lash, S. (eds) (1987) *Max Weber: Rationality and Modernity*. London: Allen and Unwin.

White, G. (1984) "Developmental States and Socialist Industrialisation in the Third World", *Journal of Development Studies* 20: 97–120.

White, H. C. (2002) *Markets from Networks: Socioeconomic Models of Production*. Princeton, N.J.: Princeton University Press.

White, L. Jr. (1964) *Medieval Technology and Social Change*. New York: Oxford University Press.

Whitley, R. (1992) *Business Systems in East Asia*. London: Sage.

Whitley, R. (1999) *Divergent Capitalisms: The Social Structuring and Change of Business Systems*. New York: Oxford University Press.

Wickberg, E. (1965) *The Chinese in Philippine Life, 1850–1898*. New Haven: Yale University Press.

Wickberg, E. (1994) "Overseas Chinese Adaptive Organizations, Past and Present", forthcoming in R. Skeldon (ed.) *Reluctant Exiles,* Armonk, N.Y.: M. E. Sharpe.

Wiens, M. C. (1976) "Cotton Textile Production and Rural Social Transformation in Early Modern China", *The Journal of the Institute of Chinese Studies of the Chinese University of Hong Kong* 7, 2: 515–34.

Wiens, M. C. (1980) "Lord and Peasant, The Sixteenth to the Eighteenth Century", *Modern China* 6: 3–39.

Will, P. and Wong, R. B. (1991) *Nourish the People: The State Civilian Granary System in China, 1650–1850*. Ann Arbor: Center for Chinese Studies.

Williams, E. T. (1927) *China, Yesterday and Today*. New York: Harrap.

Williams, F. W. (1892) "Chinese and Medieval Guilds", *The Yale Review* l: 200–17, 275–90.

Williams, R. (1976) *Keywords, A Vocabulary of Culture and Society*. New York: Oxford University Press.

Williamson, O. E. (1975) *Markets and Hierarchies: Analysis and Antitrust Implications*. New York: Free Press.

Williamson, O. E. (1985) *The Economic Institutions of Capitalism*. New York: Free Press.

Williamson, O. E. (1991) "Comparative economic organization: The analysis of discrete structural alternatives", *Administrative Science Quarterly* 36: 269–96.

Willmott, W. E. (1972) *Economic Organization in Chinese Society*. Stanford: Stanford University

Winckler, E. A. and Greenhalgh, S. (eds) (1988) *Contending Approaches to the Political Economy of Taiwan*. Armonk, N.Y.: M. E. Sharpe.

Winn, J. K. (1994) "Relational Practices and the Marginalization of Law: Informal Financial Practices of Small Businesses in Taiwan", *Law and Society Review* 28, 2: 193–232.

Wittfogel, K. (1957) *Oriental Despotism*. New Haven: Yale University Press.

Wolf, E. R. (1982) *Europe and the People without History*. Berkeley: University of California Press.

Womack, J. P., Jones, D. T., and Roos, D. (1990) *The Machine that Changed the World*. New York: Harper Perennial.

Wong, R. B. (1992) "Chinese Economic History and Development: A Note on the Myers-Huang Exchange", *Journal of Asian Studies* 51, 3: 600–11.

Wong, R. B. (1997) *China Transformed: Historical Change and the Limits of European Experience*. Ithaca, N.Y.: Cornell University Press.

Wong, S. L. (1985) "The Chinese Family Firm: A Model", *British Journal of Sociology* 36: 58–72.

Wong, S. L. (1988a) "The Applicability of Asian Family Values to Other Sociocultural Settings", in P. Berger and M. Hsiao (eds), *In Search of an East Asian Development Model*. New Brunswick, N.J.: Transaction Books.

Wong, S. L. (1988b) *Emigrant Entrepreneurs: Shanghai Industrialists in Hong Kong*, *Sociology* 36. Hong Kong: Oxford University Press.

Woo, J. E. (also known as Woo-Cumings, J. E.) (1991) *Race to the Swift: State and Finance in Korean Industrialization*. New York: Columbia University Press.

Woo, W. T. (1990) "The Art of Economic Development: Markets, Politics, and Externalities", *International Organization* 44, 3: 403–29.

Woo, W. T., Sachs, J. D., and Schwab, K. (eds) (2000) *The Asian Financial Crisis: Lessons for a Resilient Asia*. Cambridge, Mass.: The MIT Press.

Woo-Cumings, M. (1999) *The Developmental State*. Ithaca, N.Y.: Cornell University Press.

Woo-Cumings, M. (2001) "Miracle as Prologue: The State and the Reform of the Corporate Sector in Korea", in J. E. Stiglitz and S. Yusuf (eds), *Rethinking the East Asian Miracle*. New York: Oxford University Press.

World Bank (1993) *The East Asian Miracle: Economic Growth and Public Policy*. Washington, D.C.

Wright, M. C. (1962) "Revolution from without?", *Comparative Studies in Society and History* 4: 247–52.

Wu, C. M. (1985) *Zhongguo Zibenzhuyi Yu Guonei Chichang* (Chinese Capitalism and Internal Market). Beijing: Zhongguo Shehui Kexue Chubanshe.

Wyatt, D. (1969) *The Politics of Reform in Thailand: Education in the Reign of King Chulalongkorn*. New Haven: Yale Univesity Press.

Xiao, S.-T. and Zheng, B.-X. (1982) *Zhongguo tutechan chuanshuo* (The story of Chinese native products). Shanghai: Shanghai wenyi Chubanshe.

Xu, X. (1981) *Yapian zhanzheng qian Zhongguo mianfangzhi shougongye de shangpin shengchan yu zhibenzhuyi mengya wenti* (Commodity production and the sprouts of capitalism in China's handicraft weaving industry before the Opium War). Nanjing: Jiangsu renmin chubanshe.

Xu, X. (1988) "The Struggle of the Handicraft Cotton Industry against Machine Textiles in China", *Modern China* 14, 1 (January): 31–49.

Xu, X. (ed.) (1992) *Jiangnan tubushi* (The history of native cloth in Jiangnan). Shanghai: Shanghai shehui kexueyuan.

Xu, Z. Y. (1827) *Sanyi bitan in Biji xiaoshuo daguan* (Collected works of notebooks and novels), reprint. Nanjing: Jiangsu Guangning guji.

Yan, Y. X. (1996a) "The Culture of *Guanxi* in a North China Village", *The China Journal* 35 (January): 1–25.

Yan, Y. X. (1996b) *The Flow of Gifts. Reciprocity and Social Networks and a Chinese Village*. Stanford: Stanford University Press.

Yanagida, K. (1957) *Japanese Manners and Customs in the Meiji Era,* vol. 4. Tokyo: Toyo Bunko.

Yang, H.-Y. and Zhao, J.-Q. (1984) *Beijing Jingji Shihua* (The stories of Beijing economic history). Beijing: Beijing Chubanshe.

Yang, L.-S. (1952) *Money and Credit in China.* Cambridge, Mass.: Harvard University Press.

Yang, L.-S. (1961) *Studies in Chinese Institutional History.* Cambridge, Mass.: Harvard University Press.

Yang, L.-S. (1970) "Government Control of Urban Merchants in Traditional China", *Tsing Hua Journal of Chinese Studies* 8: 186–206.

Yang, M. M. H. (1989) "The gift economy and state power in China", *Comparative Studies in Society and History* 31, 1: 40–1.

Yang, N.-Y. (1937) "The Rise and Decline of the Shansi: Native Banks", *Central Bank of China Bulletin* 3: 301–16.

Yao, S. (1987) "The Fetish of Relationships: Chinese Business Transactions in Singapore", *Sojourn* 2: 89–111.

Ye, M-Z. (1981) *Yueshibian,* reprint. Shanghai: Shanghai Guji Chubashe.

Yen, Z.-P. (1963) *Zhongguo mianfangzhi shikao* (Draft history of China's cotton textile industry). Beijing.

Yeung, H. W. C. (1997) "Business Networks and Transnational Corporations: A Study of Hong Kong Firms in the ASEAN Region", *Economic Geograpy* 73, 1 (January): 1–25.

Yeung, H. W. C. (1999) "The Internationalization of Ethnic Chinese Business Firms from Southeast Asia: Strategies, Processes, and Competitive Advantage", *International Journal of Urban and Regional Research* 23: 103.

Yeung, H. W. C. and Olds, K. (eds) (1999) *The Globalisation of Chinese Business Firms.* London: Macmillan.

Yong, P. K. (1992) *The Social Foundation of Chinese Rubber Businesses in Singapore.* Unpublished thesis, Department of Sociology, National University of Singapore.

Yoshihara, K. (1988) *The Rise of Ersatz Capitalism in South-east Asia.* Oxford: Oxford University Press.

Yoshino, M. Y. and Lifson, T. B. (1986) *The Invisible Link: Japan's Sogo Shosha and the Organization of Trade.* Cambridge, Mass.: The MIT Press.

Young, A. (1992) "A Tale of Two Cities: Factor Accumulation and Technical Change in Hong Kong and Singapore", in O. Blanchard and S. Fischer (eds), *NBER Macroeconomics Annual, 1992.* Cambridge, Mass.: The MIT Press.

Young, A. (1993) "Lessons from the East Asian NICs: A Contrarian View", *European Economic Review* 38, 964–73.

Young, A. (1995) "The Tyranny of Numbers: Confronting the Statistical Realities of the East Asian Growth Experience", *Quarterly Journal of Economics* 60, 3 (August), 641–80.

Yu, Y. S. (1985) "Confucian Thought and Economic Development: Early Modern Chinese Religious Ethics and the Spirit of the Merchant Class" (in Chinese), *The Chinese Intellectual* 6: 3–46.

Yu, Z. (1996) "Inter-firm Linkages, Ethnic Networks, and Territorial Agglomeration: Chinese Computer Firms in Los Angeles", *Papers in Regional Science* 75, 3: 265–91.

Yue, S. S. (1980) "*Beijing Tongrentang de huigu yu zhanwang* (The history and the future of Beijing Tongrentang)", Gongshang shiliao (Wenshi Ziliao Chubanshe) 1: 152–74.

Yule, H. (ed.) (1914) *Cathay and the Way Thither.* London: Hakluyt Society.

Zeile, W. J. (1993) *Industrial targeting, business organization, and industry productivity growth in the Republic of Korea, 1972–1985.* Unpublished dissertation, Department of Economics, University of California, Davis.

Zeng, Z.-Y. (1980) *Zhongguo jiuzhi* (The history of the Chinese wine). Beijing: Zhongguo Luyou Chubanshe.

Zhao, L. (1980) *Xiaoting zalu*, reprint. Beijing: Zhonghua Shuju.

Zheng, L. (1979) "*Qingdai de jingji dangan shiliu* (Sources on Qing economic history)", *Gugong bowuyuan yuankan* (Beijing) 3: 59–64.

Zhongguo renmin daxue Zhongguo lishi jiaoyanshi (Chinese Peoples University, Chinese history teaching and research group) (1957) *Zhongguo zibenzhuyi mengya wenti taolunji* (Essays on the sprouts of the capitalism in China). Beijing: Sanlian Shudian.

Zhonghua, Z. (comp.) (1985) *Taiwan jiqu jitua qiye yanjiu* (Business Groups in Taiwan). Taipei: China Credit Information Service.

Zhou, M. (1980) *Wulin Jiushi*. Zhejiang Renmin Chubanshe.

Zhou, Y. (1996) "Inter-Firm Linkages, Ethnic Networks and Territorial Agglomeration: Chinese Computer Firms in Los Angeles", *Papers in Regional Science*, 75, 3, 265–91.

Zhou, Z.-H. (1971) Zhongguo zhongyao shangpin (The important commodities in China). Taipei: Xuesheng Shuju.

Zhu, G.-C. (1983) *Zhejiang Mingchan Qutan* (The famous native products in Zhejiang), Beijing: Zhongguo Luyou Chubanshe.

Zhuang, Z.-X. and Chen, X.-X. (1941) "*Zhongguo tongxiang tuanti di yanjiu* (Research on Chinese native place associations)", *Lingnan xuebao* 6: 50–73.

Index